THE MYSTICAL EVOLUTION
IN THE
DEVELOPMENT AND VITALITY
OF THE CHURCH

BY

THE VERY REVEREND JOHN G. ARINTERO, O.P., S.T.M.

Translated by

FR. JORDAN AUMANN, O.P.

Dominican House of Studies
River Forest, Illinois

NIHIL OBSTAT

        Fr. Leonardus Callahan, O.P.
        Fr. Guillelmus Curran, O.P.

IMPRIMI POTEST

        Fr. Petrus O'Brien, O.P.
        Prior Provincialis

Chicago, Ill., 12 Junii, 1948

NIHIL OBSTAT

        G. H. Guyot, C.M.
        Censor Librorum

IMPRIMATUR

        ✠ Joseph E. Ritter
        Archiepiscopus

St. Ludovici, die 18 Martii, 1949

OMNIA PER MARIAM

TRANSLATOR'S PREFACE

THIS translation of *La Evolución Mística* introduces Father John G. Arintero, O.P., to the English-reading public. Although comparatively unknown in the United States, except for passing references to his writings which are found in a few theological works, Father Arintero attained great renown in his native Spain for his profound learning and his personal sanctity. Because of his success as the champion of the true traditional doctrine in mystical theology, he is acclaimed the precursor of the current movement toward the realization of mystical ideals.

To forestall any criticism of Father Arintero's style and method of procedure, let it be remembered that he looked upon the sublime truths of the supernatural life as one would gaze upon a precious stone, turning it this way and that to catch its full brilliance and luster. There may be some persons who will question the wisdom of including excerpts from the writings of modern mystics that as yet are unknown to most readers. Many of these souls were under the guidance of Father Arintero, and he saw in their experiences the perpetual vitality of the mystical power of the Church. He uses them, then, to show that the heights of the mystical life are by no means a relic of the past, but that there are souls even today who have scaled and are scaling the mount of perfection.

I here express my deep gratitude to the Very Reverend Father Provincial of the Province of Spain, who gave permission for this English translation of *La Evolución Mística;* to the Very Reverend Father Peter O'Brien, O.P., Provincial of the Province of St. Albert the Great, for his kindly interest and unfailing encouragement; to Father Vitalis Fueyo, O.P., of Avila, Spain, for his careful reading and checking of the entire translation; and to the Very Reverend Father Sabino Lozano, O.P., of Salamanca, Spain, for his helpful advice.

TRANSLATOR'S PREFACE

Thanks are due also to Sister M. Timothea, O.P., of Rosary College, who first acquainted the translator with the works of Father Arintero and gave many practical suggestions; to Father Mark Barron, O.P., of Madison, Wisconsin, for reading the entire manuscript; and to the Dominican Sisters of St. Catherine Convent, Racine, Wisconsin, and Miss Elinor Martin, Chicago, Illinois, for typing the manuscript. I am grateful also to countless others who, in one way or another, have helped me in the task of preparing this book for publication.

Finally, acknowledgment and gratitude must be voiced to the following publishers and individuals for permission to quote from their works: Mr. Allison Peers, London, and Sheed and Ward, New York and London, for quotations from the *Complete Works of Saint Teresa;* Benziger Brothers, New York, and Burns Oates and Washbourne, London: the English version of the *Summa theologica* and the *Summa contra Gentiles;* Newman Bookshop, Westminster, Maryland: Lallemant's *Spiritual Doctrine;* Mr. Allison Peers, Burns Oates and Washbourne, Newman Bookshop: *Complete Works of St. John of the Cross;* Mr. Louis Bernicken, Mt. Vernon, Ohio: the Ven. Mary Agreda's *The City of God;* Rev. Father Anselm Townsend, O.P., Oak Park, Illinois, translator of Gardeil's *The Gifts of the Holy Ghost in the Dominican Saints;* Routledge and Kegan Paul, London: Poulain's *The Graces of Interior Prayer;* B. Herder Book Co., St. Louis, Missouri: Tixeront's *History of Dogmas* and Caussade's *Abandonment to Divine Providence.* The quotations from Froget's *The Indwelling of the Holy Spirit* are reprinted with permission of the copyright owners, the Missionary Society of St. Paul the Apostle in the State of New York.

May this book serve as an impetus to those who are still timid about venturing into the realms of the supernatural life. May it clarify the problems and difficulties which beset those who are well along the way and those whose task it is to direct such souls.

JORDAN AUMANN, O.P.

Dominican House of Studies
River Forest, Illinois

Foreword

I KNEW Father Arintero in the famous Convent of St. Stephen in Salamanca, the centuries-old seat of saints and scholars, when his mystical activity had reached its full flowering both in his life and in his works. When I arrived at Salamanca to pursue a course in theology, Father Arintero had just retired from teaching. This he did because his hearing was becoming more and more defective and also because he wished, with the consent of his superiors, to devote the rest of his life to the publication of the many books and articles that he had conceived in his mind. Yet it was my good fortune to hear him lecture now and then as a substitute when, for some reason or other, the regular professor could not conduct class.

Father Arintero was always a model religious in his work and activity. I never saw him waste a moment. Whenever he came down to walk in the garden, he invariably carried a book in his hand or a sheaf of galley proofs in one hand and a pencil in the other. On one occasion I was fortunate enough to receive a small assignment from him and thus contribute my little grain of sand to the great mystical edifice which was erected by that master.

In addition to his intense literary activity, he maintained a vast spiritual correspondence, especially with nuns. In his own religious life, he lived what he taught. He scrupulously observed silence and was most punctual for all community exercises. When the community entered choir, it always found Father Arintero in his place. In the refectory he ate whatever was set before him, without the slightest affectation, but he never overlooked any small detail that might give him an opportunity to mortify his taste.

He was very observant of poverty. Any piece of paper no longer useful for anything else, he used for his notes. I never saw him in a new habit. During the winter, which is severe in Salamanca, he used to wear a pair of home-made fleece-lined slippers. These slippers were already old when I knew him, but each winter they would reappear with more patches. I never saw him wear any others.

I noticed that Father Arintero limped slightly. This limp was caused by the penitential band of netted wire which he wore around one of his legs. Notwithstanding, he always had a smile on his face, but without any affectation at all. His simplicity was natural, not studied.

He possessed a wonderful perspicacity for the discernment of spirits. I recall that on one occasion there was proposed to us students a certain written account in which a priest gave ample and stirring testimony of the visions and revelations of a soul whom he was directing. Later on we learned that this same account had been shown to Father Arintero in order to obtain his impression and that, after reading it carefully, he had answered in these words: "I do not see the spirit of God in this." Actually it was learned a little later that the spirit of God had not been at work in that particular case.

In his younger days Father Arintero, who had been assigned by his superiors to teach at the College at Vergara, dedicated himself zealously to the natural sciences. I heard from one of his fellow professors that on one occasion Father Arintero was sent to Paris by his superiors to buy some equipment for the College laboratory. In his journey by train, he traveled in the lowest class and ate only bread and cheese during the entire trip in order to be able to purchase more articles. His life was already tending to the heights of mysticism at that time.

Through the multitude of his books and articles, the foundation and direction of the magazine, *La Vida Sobrenatural*, which still flourishes with the same energy and vigor which he imparted to it, the intense direction of souls which occupied him during the second phase of his life, Father Arintero has left a trail, a trend, a mystical school that is well defined. His teachings have been accepted by many writers and, what is more important, they have been and are being lived by many souls who have traveled and are traveling along that same mystical path. It is undeniable that to Father Arintero belongs a place of honor in the present intense movement toward mystical theology and the present-day living of the mystical life by

FOREWORD

many souls who, amid the tumult of this century, are continually elevated to God.

For that reason I take special satisfaction in seeing this work of Father Arintero translated into English. Thus many persons who are unable to read this book in the language in which it was originally written, will gain profit from his wise doctrines.

Father Arintero did not concern himself with literary style. He placed all his attention on the idea, the substance of the thing. Frequently his paragraphs, his sentences, even his words, possess a multiple significance.

Therefore, dear reader, do not read this book rapidly. Do not let your eyes quickly scan its pages as if you were reading a novel. Do not even read it as you would any book of piety. Try to read it with care and, if possible, to meditate upon it. In this way you will enrich your understanding and you will more and more arouse the desire to climb the mystical ladder which leads to the Supreme Good.

> Fr. Emmanuel Suarez, O.P.
> Master General

Dominican House of Studies
River Forest, Illinois

Biographical Note

FATHER Arintero was born at Lugueros in the province of León, Spain, in 1860. From childhood he felt a vocation to the religious life and he realized this calling by receiving the Dominican habit at Corias in 1875. There he made his novitiate and pursued his studies in philosophy and theology. Before the end of his theological course, he was sent to the University of Salamanca to study the natural sciences. It was at that renowned University that he received his degree of Licentiate in Philosophy and at the same time he received from his Order the degree of Lector of Sacred Theology.

During the five years spent at Salamanca (1881–86), Father Arintero came into contact with a number of French Dominicans who had been expelled from their own country and had taken refuge with their brethren in the convent of St. Stephen at Salamanca. Among the refugees was Father Hyacinth-Marie Cormier, later to become Master General of the Dominican Order, whose cause for beatification is now being promoted in Rome.

From 1886 to 1898 Father Arintero was a professor in the field of science and this work carried him into many colleges and universities of the Order at Vergara, Corias, Valladolid, Rome, and, finally, Salamanca. The burdens of lecturing and teaching during this period of his life did not prevent Father Arintero from devoting a great deal of time and effort to writing. As one of his associates remarked, it was astonishing that one man could read so much and retain so much of what he read. This was evidenced from the ease with which he could locate citations which he needed for his books and articles.

During this first period of his life, Father Arintero's works were principally apologetic. Indeed, he showed a tendency to consider

BIOGRAPHICAL NOTE

scientific studies as the very foundation of any defense of the Church and the only bulwark against the attacks of modern rationalist scientists. Therefore he placed his own vast knowledge of science at the service of religion and Christian philosophy.

Among the books which came from the pen of Father Arintero at this time were: *La Evolución y la Filosofía Christiana, El Diluvio Universal, La Evolución y la Mutabilidad, El Hexámeron y la Ciencia Moderna, La Providencia y la Evolución.*

At this period of Father Arintero's life a remarkable change took place, for he then abandoned the natural sciences in order to embark on a higher course. This change, however, was not a sudden one, for he had been during many years the spiritual director of several communities of nuns. As a director he had come into contact with certain souls advanced in the spiritual life and, by a mutual interaction, he influenced and guided these souls with sound doctrine while they, in turn, inspired and directed him by the holy example of their lives. By the time Father Arintero returned to Salamanca in 1903, his soul was a teeming caldron of things mystical. He had come to realize that here in mystical theology he possessed all in one piece what in the natural sciences he had possessed only in part. It was laudable that he should have defended the faith against the attacks of modern scientists, but it was much more praiseworthy, he thought, to make known to the world the marvels which God works in souls that give themselves to His loving direction.

From 1903 until 1928, the year he died, Father Arintero gave himself to the things of God, both in doctrine and in practice. His labors in magazines, books, pamphlets, and especially in the direction of souls, were truly amazing. It would be difficult to find any man who used his time more profitably for the greater glory of God and the good of souls. His spiritual correspondence alone, most of which has been gathered together since his death, would fill volumes. In a short time he became an authority in the discernment of spirits and the direction of souls, so that it was common to hear the question: "What does Father Arintero think of this point?"

To him belongs the honor of being the leader of the modern trend back to the traditional teaching of mystical theology. The works written during this second phase of his life give evidence of his whole-hearted devotion to mystical matters: *La Evolución*

BIOGRAPHICAL NOTE

Orgánica, La Evolución Doctrinal, La Evolución Mística, El Mecanismo Divino, Grados de Oración, Cuestiones Místicas, La Verdadero Mística Tradicional, Escala de Amor, and *La Perfección Cristiana.*

In addition to the publication of so many books, Father Arintero was responsible for the inauguration of the famous magazine, *La Vida Sobrenatural*, which has gained world-wide renown. As a reward for his labors and a recognition of his profound learning, the Dominican Order conferred on him its highest degree, Master of Sacred Theology.

The position of authority which this saintly Dominican has attained in Europe as a master of the spiritual life and a staunch defender of the traditional teaching on mystical theology is owing in no small measure to the personal sanctity which accompanied his erudition. His fellow religious have frequently testified to his strict observance of the Dominican life; his extreme aversion to waste of time; his dauntless courage in the face of the attacks and accusations which were brought against him when he first began to write in defense of the faith and the traditional mystical doctrine.

His life as a Dominican was characterized above all by his spirit of poverty, his humility, and his zeal to aid souls by imparting sound doctrine to them. During his last illness, Father Arintero assured one of his brethren, "I promise you that if the Lord, in His infinite mercy, deigns to take me to Himself, I shall be of more use to these works from heaven than I was here on earth." Shortly before his death, the holy friar made this statement about his teaching and writing: "Within a few hours I shall be brought before the tribunal of God, and I assure you that our teachings concerning contemplation are the true doctrines and that they represent the traditional Christian teaching; but the contrary doctrines are deviations which serve only to mislead souls."

Since Father Arintero's death in 1928, a great devotion has arisen in his honor and many persons are working assiduously for his ultimate beatification. May all those who reap benefits from this translation assist by their prayers in this cause.

Contents

	PAGE
TRANSLATOR'S PREFACE	
FOREWORD	
BIOGRAPHICAL NOTE	
INTRODUCTION	

PART I

THE SUPERNATURAL LIFE, ITS OPERATIONS AND GROWTH

CHAPTER
I. GENERAL IDEA OF THE MYSTICAL LIFE ... 16
   A. Mysticism and Asceticism ... 17
      1. So-called Ordinary and Extraordinary Ways ... 19
      2. Spiritual Infancy, Adolescence, and Maturity ... 20
      3. Renewal and Transformation ... 22
   B. Justification by the Holy Ghost and Deification ... 23
      1. Infinite Value of Grace ... 24
      2. Reality of Divine Adoption and Filiation ... 26
      3. Dignity of the Christian ... 28
   C. Sublime Notions of the Fathers Concerning Deification ... 29
      1. The Role of the Holy Ghost ... 30
      2. Abasement of the Word; Elevation of Man ... 33
      3. Summary ... 34
      4. Status of this Doctrine Today ... 38

II. THE DIVINE LIFE OF GRACE ... 41

ARTICLE I

CONCEPT OF THE SUPERNATURAL LIFE ... 42
   A. The Supernatural Order a Participation in the Divine Life ... 43
      1. Ineffable Realities ... 45

CONTENTS

		PAGE
	2. Incorporation in Christ	48
B.	Deification and Union with God	54
	1. Harmony of the Natural and Supernatural	54
	2. The Divine Life in Itself and in Us	58
	3. The Image and Likeness of God	60
	4. Restoration and Elevation	62
	5. The Path of Calvary and Transfiguration	64
	6. Words of Life and Their Incomprehensibility	65

ARTICLE II

The Grace of God and the Communication of the Holy Ghost — 67

- A. Sanctifying Grace — 67
  1. Effects of Sanctifying Grace — 68
  2. Grace and Nature — 71
  3. Our Creation in Jesus Christ — 75
- B. Communication of the Holy Ghost — 79
  1. Life of the Head and the Members — 80
  2. Dignity of the Sons of God — 83
  3. Natural and Adoptive Filiation — 84
  4. Participation in the Spirit of Jesus Christ — 85

ARTICLE III

Adoption and Justification — 86

- A. Characteristics of Divine Adoption — 86
- B. Sanctification and Justification — 90
  1. The Power of Grace and Its Manifestations — 90
  2. Falsity of Imputed Justice — 93
  3. Justification a Renewal and Continual Growth — 94
  4. Catholic Dogmas and True Progress — 98
- Appendix — 102

ARTICLE IV

Indwelling of the Holy Ghost — 106

- A. Grace and the Divine Indwelling — 107
  1. Presence of God in the Just Soul — 108
  2. Vivifying Action of the Holy Ghost — 109
  3. Mission, Giving, and Indwelling of the Holy Ghost — 111
- B. The Loving Presence of the Trinity — 113
  1. Ignorance of This Doctrine — 114
  2. The Beauty of the House of God — 115
- Appendix — 117

CONTENTS

ARTICLE V

CHAPTER	PAGE
GRACE AND GLORY	119

- A. Eternal Life, Inchoate and Perfect . . . 120
  1. Happiness of the Saints on Earth and the Blessed in Heaven . . 121
  2. Vision of God in the Word through the Holy Ghost . 124
  3. Union of Beatific Love . 128
- B. Identity of the Life of Glory and the Life of Grace . 130
  1. Union of Faith, Hope, and Charity Augmented by the Gifts . 130
  2. Present Glory of the Sons of God . 131
  3. The Delights of Divine Friendship . 132
- C. The Supernatural Life, the Kingdom of God on Earth . 135
  1. Manifestation of the Divine Life . 136
  2. Longings for Dissolution and Union with God . 139

ARTICLE VI

FAMILIAR RELATIONS WITH THE DIVINE PERSONS . 140

- A. Fellowship with God and Participation in His Life . 140
  1. Proper Attribution and Appropriation . 141
  2. Role of Each Person in Adoption and Deification . 144
  3. Divine Indwelling . 148
  4. Divine Paternity . 150
- B. Relations with the Word . 152
  1. Christ as Our Brother . 152
  2. Christ, the Good Shepherd and Cornerstone . 155
  3. Christ as Spouse of our Souls . 156
  4. Christ, the Head of the Mystical Body . 157
- C. The Divine Spouse . 160
  1. Espousal of the Word with Just Souls . 162
  2. Characteristics, Intimacy, and Fruits of This Union . 164
  3. Singular Dignity of Consecrated Virgins . 169
- Appendix . 171
- D. Relations with the Holy Ghost . . 173
  1. The Holy Ghost as the Spirit of Love . 173
  2. Gift of God and Fount of Living Water . 175
  3. Source of All Sanctity . 177
  4. Spirit of Adoption and Mystical Unction . 180
  5. Influence of the Holy Ghost on Christ and the Faithful . 181
- Appendix . 187

CONTENTS

CHAPTER		PAGE
III.	PARTICIPATION IN THE DIVINE ACTIVITY	195
	A. The Operation of Grace	195
	1. Necessity of Infused Powers	197
	2. Natural and Supernatural Potencies	199
	3. The Two Supernatural Principles of Operation	201
	B. The Supernatural Virtues	204
	1. Division and Number of Supernatural Virtues	205
	2. The Theological Virtues	206
	3. The Moral Virtues	209
	4. Necessity of Acquired and Infused Moral Virtues	209
	C. The Gifts of the Holy Ghost	216
	1. Comparison of the Gifts and the Virtues	216
	2. The Gifts and the Mystical Life	220
	3. Necessity of the Motion and Promptings of the Holy Ghost	224
	D. Existence of the Gifts in All the Just	228
	1. Importance and Nature of the Gifts	229
	2. Mode of Operation of the Gifts	232
	3. Rare Discretion of the Saints	236
	E. Pneumatic Psychology	238
	1. Life-giving Action and Inspiration of the Holy Ghost; Diabolical Possession and Suggestion	239
	2. Awareness of the Divine Indwelling	241
	3. Laborious Activity of Meditation; Fruitful Passivity of Contemplation	243
	Appendix	246
	F. Special Work of Each of the Gifts	257
	1. Manifestation of the Gifts	261
	2. Excellence of the Gifts	263
	3. Pneumatic Psychology and the Organism of the Church	267
	G. Fruits of the Holy Ghost and the Beatitudes	273
	1. Comparison of the Gifts with the Fruits and Beatitudes	276
	2. The Working of the Holy Ghost in Souls	281
	Appendix	284
IV.	SPIRITUAL GROWTH	289
	A. Necessity of Growth in God as Individuals and as Members of the Church	289
	1. Growth and Merit	290
	2. Spiritual Growth of the Individual	294

CONTENTS

CHAPTER	PAGE
3. Growth of Members of the Mystical Body	295
B. Individual Growth and Particular Functions	298
1. Recollection in God	299
2. Prayer	300
3. Exterior Works	303
4. Mortification and Humility	306
5. General and Particular Examination	307
6. Need for Moderation and Direction	307
7. Qualifications of a Spiritual Director	309
8. The Religious Vows	312
9. Pious Conversations and Spiritual Reading	313
Appendix	314
C. Collective Growth and the Sacramental Functions	318
1. The Role of Each Sacrament	319
2. Importance of the Eucharist and Penance	321
3. The Sacramentals	325
4. Devotion to the Blessed Virgin	326
D. Singular Importance of the Eucharist	328
1. Eucharistic Union and the Mystical Marriage	329
2. More Intimate Union with the Father, Holy Ghost, and Blessed Virgin	335
3. Fruits of the Eucharist	338
Appendix	343
V. SUMMARY AND CONCLUSIONS	347
A. Concept of the Life of Grace	347
B. Nature, Function, and Growth of the Supernatural Life	353

Introduction

WE must here examine and consider attentively the hidden and mysterious development of the inner life of the Church. This consideration is fundamental and the most important of all, because that inner life and the exigencies of the vital process are the source of the Church's development in doctrine and organization.

The organization of the Church is a necessary condition for the visible manifestation of her internal efficacy; her doctrine is an expression of the law of her organic and vital relationships. Thus, the external progress of the Church, be it organic or doctrinal, disciplinary or liturgical, bespeaks an internal progress, an increase of life. This latter, indeed, is the essential and fundamental progress on which the others depend and to which they are ordained and subordinated. Without it they would be meaningless, for the inner life of the Church is the final cause and motivation of all her external growth.

Without the ardor of charity, which is the characteristic property and the certain indication of that interior life, all things else profit nothing.[1] The mere increase of organs without a corresponding vital energy would do nothing more than multiply needs and afflictions. "Thou hast multiplied the nation, and hast not increased the joy." [2] But if "the flesh profits nothing," the spirit of Jesus Christ "gives life" and the words of our Savior are all "spirit and life." [3]

The Son of God came into the world to incorporate us into Himself and to make us live by Him as He Himself lives by the Father. He came that men might possess life eternal and that this life might

---

[1] Cf. I Cor. 13.
[2] Isa. 9:3.
[3] John 6:64.

be manifested in them more and more fully, "that they may have life and may have it more abundantly." [4] That mysterious life is the life of His grace, true eternal life, in which St. Peter commands us to grow when he says: "But grow in grace and in the knowledge of our Lord and Savior Jesus Christ." [5] This progress or growth in the life of grace is what constitutes the *mystical evolution*.

This mysterious evolution by which Christ Himself is formed in us [6] is the principal purpose of divine revelation and the basis for all growth and development. To this evolution is ordained the divine light of faith, to it the entire gospel, to it the institution of the Church and even the incarnation of the divine Word. For faith is ordained to charity, which is the bond of perfection; and the dogmas of our faith, as a modern apologist puts it, are not so much for finding intellectual satisfaction as for motivating us to seek the gift of God, the living water of the Holy Ghost, and the power of His vivifying grace. The Gospel was written "that believing, you may have life in His name," [7] and the purpose of the Church is the sanctification of souls.

The Word came into this world and became the Son of Man to make men sons of God and to fill them with His life, restoring and gathering together all things to draw them to Himself.[8] For that reason He told us: "I am come to cast fire on the earth; and what will I, but that it be kindled?" [9] This fire is that of the Holy Ghost which must animate us, inflame us, purify us, renew and perfect us, transforming us even to the point of deifying us.

From this truth can be concluded the tremendous importance of these studies in which is treated the search for the precious pearl and the digging of the hidden treasure of the Gospel. To some degree these studies draw aside the veil of the great mysteries of the kingdom of God in souls and disclose the adequate cause for the manifold and resplendent manifestations of the life and infinite powers of the holy Catholic Church. By means of these studies is discovered that ineffable supernatural life which animates and sus-

---

[4] John 10:10. Cf. 6:55-58.
[5] Cf. II Pet. 3:18.
[6] Gal. 4:19.
[7] John 20:31.
[8] John 1:12; 3:16; 12:32.
[9] Luke 12:49.

INTRODUCTION

tains the Church and which, in spite of the malice and sloth of men, the hostility from without and the indolence, inertia, and sluggishness within, gives the Church an imperishable and autonomous existence and fills it with indescribable charm. This supernatural life conducts the Church with infallible security along the divine paths of truth and goodness while merely human societies obstinately move in the same cycle of error and vice.

If any study is edifying and instructive to the highest degree, and at the same time apologetic, it is certainly the study of the mystical evolution; of that prodigious expansion of grace as the vital principle of a divine order, and of its multiple manifestations and glorious effects in the Church as a bio-social organism and in each of the faithful as members of that mystical body.[10] In this study even the most humble Christian will learn how to appreciate worthily his immeasurable dignity as a son of God and to act in all things in conformity with that dignity, despising the grandeurs of the world.[11] He will learn to cherish the divine gift, to love it with all his heart and to cultivate it with all possible solicitude. As a result, he will wholeheartedly detest sin, not only serious sin, which despoils him of that dignity and makes him fall miserably into the power of darkness, but even light sins which place an obstacle to the friendship of God and the uninterrupted flow of His grace, thereby conditioning him for an irreparable fall. He will be inspired to undertake sacrifice in order to root out the very last seed of evil and to acquire the divine virtues. He will, as a consequence, be permeated and transformed by the mystical evangelical ferment. Moreover, he will generously resolve to pass through fire and water to purge himself completely of all earthly dross and to abandon himself fully to the hands of God so that he may be converted, as St. Gregory Nazianzen so beautifully says, into a finely tuned instrument whence the Holy Ghost draws divine melodies.[12]

The priest, who ought to indoctrinate and direct souls both from the pulpit and in the sacred tribunal of penance, will learn how to

---

[10] See the interesting article, *Deificación*, (in *Ideales*, July and August, 1907) by Father Joseph Cuervo, O.P., to whom I must express my gratitude for the great help he gave me in this work.
[11] St. Jerome, *Ep. 9*: "Learn holy pride; know that it is greater than those others."
[12] St. Gregory Nazianzen, *Orat. ad popul.*, 43, no. 67: "A musical instrument vibrated by the Spirit, proclaiming in melody, the divine power and glory."

inculcate in them the true spirit of Jesus Christ, to preserve them from the misguidance of an individualistic spirit and from the countless snares which the world, the flesh, and the devil hold for them. He will learn how to direct, encourage, and stimulate souls, when, under the impulse of the divine Guest, they begin the way which is at once the sorrowful and glorious way of configuration with the Savior. The minister of God will then be able to comfort and direct them, instead of paralyzing them through his ignorance or disconcerting them or exposing them to ruin, as unfortunately often happens.

It is certain that ignorance and the lack of ardor in directors are the cause of the ruin of many souls. Some of these souls remain stationary, others are misguided and never find the path of the mystical life. Even the more generous souls needlessly suffer indescribable hardships and interior trials. They are unable to walk because God wishes to lead them by a different path, and yet they do not dare to fly, under the inspiration of the Holy Ghost, because their wings are fettered by the imprudence of blind directors. How often it happens that the little ones ask for the bread of the divine word and there is no one to impart it to them! [13] From the lips of the priest they seek knowledge of the ways of God and find only the false lights of worldly prudence. Believing themselves to be in the hands of an experienced guide, they let themselves be directed by a blind man who leads them to the precipice.[14] So it is that piety is cooled and faith itself is lost because of the lack of masters who know how to speak with grace [15] and to exhort with sound doctrine.[16]

Why is it that our holy religion has less and less hold on the people? Why, instead of the spirit and life that it is, is it so often reduced to empty externals, routine practices, and a dead symbolism? Why that cold indifference with which the generality of those who call themselves Christians look upon sacred things?

Undoubtedly one of the most weighty reasons is that today few persons feel keenly and understand deeply and attempt to make known in a fitting manner the great mysteries of the kingdom of

[13] Lam. 4:4.
[14] Matt. 15:14.
[15] Col. 4:6.
[16] Titus 1:9.

INTRODUCTION

God in souls and the marvels which the vivifying Spirit works in them.[17] Studies of the Christian life are looked upon with disdain. Few speak to the people in language that is frank and simple, vital and not artificial, and that comes from an inflamed and illuminated heart. Seldom do we hear that energetic, animated, and throbbing language which is associated with the apostles and the Fathers. It is not to be wondered at, then, that many of the faithful, like the disciples at Ephesus, have not even heard, nor do they know, that there is a Holy Ghost who sanctifies souls (Acts 19:2).[18]

Such Christians will be unable to give a reason for their faith to those who ask it, as St. Peter commands, and yet this is necessary for all of us today. They will not be able to fulfill the wish of St. Paul:

---

[17] *Ascent of Mount Carmel*, Bk. III, chap. 45: "Wherefore, however lofty be the doctrine that is preached, and however choice the rhetoric and sublime the style wherein it is clothed, it brings as a rule no more benefit than is present in the spirit of the preacher."

[18] "If those who are noble according to worldly standards are so much interested in verifying the lineage of their illustrious ancestry, how is it possible," asks Father Terrien (*La grâce et la gloire*, Introd.), "that we Christians, who, through baptism belong to the lineage of God Himself and are His sons by adoption and the brothers of Jesus Christ, ignore or understand so poorly the grandeur and glory which are contained in these titles? Do not ask those who are Christians in name only; ask even the great number of those who glory in professing their faith, and, what is more, in practicing it. Ask them how much they value their divine filiation and their state of grace, which is the most highly esteemed after that of glory. On hearing their answers you will see with what reason Christ could say to them: 'If you but knew the gift of God!' The very most that they can imagine is that they live in peace with Him, that their sins have been forgiven, and that if they do not commit new sins they will one day enjoy eternal bliss. But few understand and meditate upon that wonderful divine renewal which takes place in their hearts, that regeneration which transforms the innermost nature and faculties of the adopted sons of God, that deification which makes man God. As a consequence they value but little what they understand so poorly and they make no effort to acquire, preserve, and increase this unknown treasure. . . .

"If the faithful live in such ignorance of the treasures with which they have been so liberally endowed by the Father of mercy, the blame falls in great part on those who, by vocation, are charged to instruct them. . . . Seldom do they speak of these mysteries; and when they do, it is done in a manner so vague and with words so ambiguous that their hearers are enchanted by the language but do not comprehend the thought. Nor let it be said, as sometimes happens, that these matters are too lofty to be grasped by the simple faithful. . . . The apostles did not proceed in this way. What are the Epistles of St. Paul (not to mention the other Epistles), but a continual preaching of the mysteries of grace and divine filiation? Yet they were addressed to all Christians. . . . To say that Christians today lack the culture necessary to understand these things is to forget the activity of the divine Spirit who interiorly enlightens the intellect of the faithful that they may understand the truths which are announced to them. 'That we may know the things that are given us from God' (I Cor. 2:12)."

"Walk with wisdom towards them that are without, redeeming the time." [19] Not knowing how to give an answer, they will repel outsiders instead of attracting them, and they will even place themselves in great danger. If they do not walk with that wisdom which is not conquered by evil, they will easily be led along the path to perdition.

In other times the generality of the faithful keenly appreciated the divine mysteries. When asked about them, they could reply divinely for it was not they who spoke, but the Spirit of the Father who spoke in them.[20] We are not surprised that they captivated the enemy by their sublime speech.

Today, unfortunately, the situation has been reversed, and many Christians, instead of converting others, are themselves misled "by philosophy and vain deceit, according to the tradition of men, according to the elements of the world." [21] In their hearts is not the true light of life; nor on their lips, the word of salutary wisdom.[22] "The heart of a wise man understandeth the time and answer," [23] but those who are ignorant of the things of God devote themselves uselessly to the study of the mentality of their adversaries in order to adapt themselves to it. Since they do not sacrifice themselves to become all things to all men to gain them for Jesus Christ, they themselves are lost through lack of divine discretion and learned zeal.

The growing prestige of the natural sciences, which have made such rapid progress; the deep-seated prejudice in favor of the sufficiency and complete autonomy of human reason; and the havoc which rationalist criticism has caused: all of these explain the loss by the supernatural order of its divine enchantment and its growing repulsion for many people. On the one hand they look upon the supernatural as the destroyer and disturber of reason itself, an alien and violent invasion that would paralyze all human activities. On the other hand the supernatural order is regarded as something impossible of verification by such extrinsic arguments as are currently in

---

[19] Col. 4:5; cf. Eph. 5:15 f.
[20] Matt. 10:20.
[21] Col. 2:8.
[22] St. Mary Magdalen of Pazzi exclaims: "O divine Word, Thou givest to him who follows Thee a vivifying light, glorifying and eternal, which gives life to the soul and controls and vivifies all its thoughts, words, and actions. So a word from such a soul is as a fiery dart which pierces the hearts of creatures" (*Œuvres*, Part III, chap. 5).
[23] Eccles. 8:5.

INTRODUCTION

vogue. So it is that many sincere and learned men look upon the supernatural order with aversion or disdain because of the false idea they have formed about it. Unfortunately a number of ignorant apologists have contributed to this condition by speaking of what they do not understand.

How can we make a breach in these and many other souls, who, from ignorance or malice, close their ears to the word of God and their hearts to the influxes of His grace? How can they be made to see that in the supernatural order they will not encounter death, but rather that mode of life which they need? What method can we use to lead the learned ones, haughty in their "inalienable autonomy" and pompous science, to the humble service of Christ and the holy folly of the Cross?

The apologetic method most universal, most efficacious, most facile, and most in harmony with the systems of present-day thought is a positive exposition, vital and pulsating with the mysteries of the Christian life and the whole process of the deification of souls. Such a method will demonstrate in a practical way that the supernatural does not come to us as an exterior and violent imposition, oppressing us and depriving us of our nature, but as an increase of life, freely accepted, liberating and ennobling us. It does not destroy our humanity; it makes us superhuman, sons of God, gods by participation. "For God so loved the world as to give His only-begotten Son; that whosoever believeth in Him may not perish, but may have life everlasting." [24]

The living and true God, the God of infinite goodness, does not come to us to kill or paralyze but to deify us, to make us participants in His own life, virtue, dignity, happiness, and absolute power and sovereignty. By communicating His Spirit to us He gives us the only true autonomy and liberty, the glorious liberty of sons of God. "Where the Spirit of the Lord is, there is liberty." [25]

If we could but make these sublime truths better understood, how many souls would be captivated! To how many could be said what the Savior said to the Samaritan woman: "If thou didst know the gift of God!" [26] If they but knew the indescribable enchantments

---
[24] John 3:16.
[25] Cf. II Cor. 3:17.
[26] John 4:10.

and ineffable delights which lie hidden beneath the external sorrows and tribulations, it is certain that many of those who show so great an aversion to the spiritual life would then desire it with all their hearts and would strive in very truth to dedicate themselves entirely to it, cooperating with that grace by which God stimulates them. "All you that thirst, come to the waters." [27] Taste, and you will see how delicious they are. Heed the divine invitation, and your souls will live. "You shall draw waters with joy out of the savior's fountains." [28]

If what cannot be assimilated and vivified seems violent and odious or at least useless to us, then what gives an increase of true life is profitable, desirable, and loved by all. If, in accordance with modern taste, our holy religion were explained positively as the origin of infinite light and an inexhaustible fountain of life, many of its enemies would then esteem it and be interested in it, instead of not even wishing to hear it mentioned. Many learned men today remain obdurate before the arguments of extrinsic apologetics, although composed with the most commendable logic. How enthusiastically would they open their hungry hearts to the supernatural if they were to see it presented as it is in itself, as an irradiation of the life and infinite love of a God enamored of our souls! Many learned and distinguished men, loving what is good and noble, sacrifice themselves in the search for truth and virtue. But they are too much concerned with scientific criticism and exasperated, perhaps, by the assaults of thoughtless apologists who move on planes far removed from contemporary thought. Consequently these noble men obstinately resist the terminology which today is rarely understood or considered.

These same men would give an attentive ear if only they recog-

---

[27] Isa. 55:1. But "if you do not believe, you shall not understand" (Isa. 7:9), and if you do not experience truth, you will never see it. St. Thomas says: "Spiritual things must be tasted before they are seen, for no one knows them unless first he tastes them. For that reason it is said: 'Taste and see!' " (*In Ps.* 33.)

"Seek the life of God which is filled with true life, sure delights, and permanent joy.... Taste and you will see the sweetness of interior recollection in God, those secret promptings, those gentle inspirations, those sweet impulses, those admirable lights, that patience in suffering in God, that guiding love, that liberality in assisting, that largess in rewarding. See how tenderly He loves, how gently He woos, how fiercely He defends, how delicately He constrains. Outside of God you will not find joy nor perfect friendship.... All other friendships are bonds which give only the appearance of security and they are artifices of affection." Cf. Ven. Palafox, *Varón de deseos*, Introd.

[28] Isa. 12:3.

INTRODUCTION

nized that such terminology speaks to them frankly in accents of love and sincerity, like that of the apostles and Fathers. For theirs was a vital and pulsating language in which they said what they experienced and which came from the depths of their hearts. They seemed to infuse into the hearts of others the very spirit which they themselves possessed. If used today, that divine language, those words of life confirmed by example and such works of light as glorify the heavenly Father, would make us realize that we cannot be perfect men without being perfect Christians. St. Augustine expresses it thus: "There are as many perfect men as there are true sons of God."

So, when men come to understand to some extent the divine gift and to discover the hidden treasure, then will they exchange for it all that they possess. They will reproach us for being so slow in making known to them such an incomparable good. With ineffable joy mixed with sweet tears, they will exclaim in the words of the great convert: "O thou Beauty ever ancient yet ever new, too late have I known Thee; too late have I loved Thee." [29] They will lament having been so vain in their own conceits, ashamed now of ever having doubted the objective truth of our sacrosanct dogmas.

If this could happen to those who are enemies, with still greater reason will it be so in the case of the many Christians who live in complete ignorance of these truths. Many sinners would be converted and many lukewarm Christians would be inflamed and would resolve to follow valiantly the paths of virtue if they but knew the incomparable dignity of a Christian as a son of God, brother of Jesus Christ, and living temple of the Trinity, who dwells in so many hearts without their realizing it or doing anything about it. Surely many of those who seek frantically the fleeting goods of this world would be able to live holy lives if they realized how important it is that they preserve and cultivate the divine treasure, and how great is their obligation to nurture the mystical seed of eternal life, a treasure which they keep buried in their hearts without letting it increase. Unfortunately, few know the rich and glorious heritage which Jesus Christ has conferred upon His saints [30] and the rigorous obligation which all of us have, by the mere fact of having been baptized to Him, to be vested in Him and to conform ourselves to His

---

[29] St. Augustine, *Confessions*, Bk. X, chap. 27.
[30] Eph. 1:18.

THE MYSTICAL EVOLUTION

likeness, truly aspiring to our sanctification in Truth as our only goal.[81]

"Jesus Christ," observes Weiss,[82] "founded His Church only that it might be holy (Eph. 5:26). The true society of the faithful ought to be a holy people (I Pet. 2:9). All who receive the Christian faith are called to sanctity (Rom. 1:7; I Cor. 1:2). Either a person must aspire to it, or he must renounce the name of Christian, the title of saint. What God wills is our sanctification (cf. I Thess. 4:3)."

Spiritual souls should find in these studies much information which should supply, in part, for the scarcity of directors which they so frequently lament. They should here discover the solution of many of their difficulties and most potent inducements to undergo their Calvary. Inexplicable joy and tranquillity will be theirs at the verification of their timid suspicions of the ineffable work of deification as it is realized in themselves; of the deeply intimate activity of the sanctifying Spirit; of the adorable presence of the entire Trinity; and of that sweet and loving relationship by which they are bound to each one of the three divine Persons. Finally, how animated they will become upon closer examination of the successive phases through which they must pass in order to arrive at intimate union and transformation, perfect configuration with Christ, and the solemn moment when, impressed with His divine image, they will be able to say with the Apostle: "For me, to live is Christ"! [33]

Therefore these humble pages are directed to all. Through these pages we desire to serve all, saying with the Psalmist: "Who is the man that desireth life: who loveth to see good days?" [84] Such a man will find here, if not all that he desires on the subject or all that could be said about it (for there are no limits), at least some indications of the path which he must take to satisfy his hunger and thirst for justice, life, truth, and love. On the other hand, this is the best de-

---

[81] Cf. Rom. 8:29; Eph. 1:4; John 3:3; 17:17-26.
[82] *Apologie*, art. 4.
[83] "Contemplative souls," says Alverez de Paz (*De inquisitione pacis*, Bk. V, Part III, Introd.), "need to be made aware of this wisdom, for fear of the illusion that they have been deceived—when as a matter of fact, they have not. Nor should they weep, for they have not been victimized. The danger is that, when actually ensnared by some wile of the devil, they should rejoice in vain confidence. Furthermore, they need this precious wisdom to recognize and acknowledge the gifts they receive, give thanks for them, and correspond with them by the purity of their lives."
[84] Ps. 33:13.

INTRODUCTION

fense of the Church that we can make; the best means of guarding against all aberrations and of avoiding and repairing the damage of those exaggerated tendencies of speculative thought, sentimentality, traditionalism, and modernism which cause so much agitation, confusion, and lamentable desertions in our day.

Without an exposition, however brief, of the basis of the spiritual life and the growth in Christian perfection, the defense of our religion would always be incomplete and defective.[85] To make God's Church loved, no better way can be found than to show the ineffable attractions of its inner life. To present only its inflexible exterior aspect is almost to disfigure it and make it disagreeable; it is, in a sense, to despoil it of its glory and its principal enchantments. All its glory is from within. Today more than ever, as Blondel notes, to attract men to the Church, it is essential to make known to them the heavenly splendors of its divine spirit.

Presented as it is in itself, without disguise or mitigation, and without weakening and disfigurement through the abject and narrow standards of human evaluation, the Church, full of grace and truth in imitation of its Spouse, gives perpetual testimony of its divine mission and is its own best defense. Actually, divine truth needs no defense; it needs only to be presented in its innate splendor and irresistible force.

According to one type of symbol the Church appears as the house and city of God, the gate of heaven, and the living temple of the Holy Ghost. According to another type, it is a divine family, "a chosen generation, a kingly priesthood, a holy nation, a purchased people," [86] a people ruled by God Himself, who converses familiarly with His subjects, who are but so many sons. At other times the Church is represented as a garden of divine delights where all virtue and holiness bloom. Or it is a field where the divine word grows and fructifies, a flock of sheep who know their Shepherd and follow Him while He calls them by name and gives them eternal life.

Apart from these three types of symbols, which are called *archi-*

[85] "In a defense of Christianity, so far as it is spirit and life," says Weiss (*Apologie*, Introd.), "the doctrine of perfection must be treated at any cost." In another place (*ibid.*, nos. 6–9) he says: "The principal causes of spiritual frigidity and paralysis in these days are the lack of an understanding of this salutary doctrine and the indifference to sanctity. What our age needs more than anything else is true saints, new and perfect men, true Christians who are spiritual and perfect."

[86] Cf. I Pet. 2:9.

THE MYSTICAL EVOLUTION

tectonic, sociological, and *agricultural,* there are two other types, even more appropriate, which enable us to penetrate more deeply and to soar more loftily in the consideration of the divine mysteries. These are the *sacramental* and *organo-anthropological* symbols. According to them the Church is represented, respectively, as the spouse of the Lamb of God, who takes away the sins of the world, and as the mystical body of Jesus Christ. We shall devote ourselves preferably to these two types of symbols without, however, excluding the others when they are to the point.

These symbols are so varied and so numerous in order that we may see that no single one of them nor all of them together is an adequate representation of a reality so exalted that it surpasses the limits of our poor language and all the categories of our limited thought, transcending the most lofty knowledge and intuition of our weak and vacillating reason. Each symbol portrays but one aspect of that ineffable reality which is in some way conjectured but never fully grasped; nor can it be explained by an adequate definition. All the symbols taken together succeed in giving us a more exact idea, obliging us at the same time to prescind in great measure from the forms which seem mutually to exclude each other. Such terms enable us to rise far above our weak sophisms and evaluations, to know with the knowledge of Christ and to admire in silence and to contemplate by the light and grace of the Holy Ghost. Only thus can we appreciate divinely what cannot be uttered in human words or conceived by human thought.

If no symbol can exhaust the manifold vital aspects of the Church, if no system can contain so striking a reality, then any attempt to define it technically is to debase and destroy it, as if of set purpose. Because it transcends all systems and human concepts, it cannot be explained in terms peculiar to any epoch of history or school of philosophy. More profitable if we should let the concepts pass before the mind and admire their flexibility and richness than chain them to the narrowness of our views. To contemplate in silence the treasures of life and divine science contained in the mystical body of Jesus Christ, and to ponder them in the daring and inspired phrases of Sacred Scripture and the great saints who felt these things keenly: surely this is better than to systematize them, in the

INTRODUCTION

vain hope of forcing them into the limited categories of our thought. Even if such systematization could enable us to comprehend these concepts, it would by that very fact disfigure what in itself is incomprehensible. If it is foolish to measure the water of the ocean with a shell, it is much more foolish to measure with the human mind the inexhaustible treasures of divine wisdom.

The prestige of the supernatural order cannot be re-established by presenting it in the manner of those who defame it nor even as we ourselves consider it humanly. It must be seen as it is in itself and as it pleased God to embody it in His Church. Knowing well what the Church is, we shall understand what her members ought to be. Those members, in turn, will learn to appreciate the gift of God and to correspond with His divine grace, striving to live ever as sons of the light, nurturing the seed of divine life and imperishable glory which they possess in themselves. To what a notable degree would the level of Christian life be raised, and what an excellent defense of religion the works of the generality of the faithful would provide, if we would all truly strive to know and appreciate the "new and living way which He hath dedicated for us through the veil, that is to say, His flesh"! [87] For we are members of the divine mystical body and from its Head we are continually receiving wonderful influxes.

We cannot fully explain the things we shall now treat. Their beauty, sublimity, and heavenly savor surpass the limits of human speech. The inner nature of the supernatural life; its excellence, which surpasses all created things; the way it is lived; the phases through which souls successively pass, suffering and enjoying the incredible until they are completely divested of the old man and clothed with the new: all this is truly ineffable. "Of whom we have much to say, and hard to be intelligibly uttered." [88]

This task is not only difficult, it seems almost temerarious. If the great mystics, who were filled with the Holy Ghost and had died to the world and were living a life hidden with Christ in God, rarely succeeded in speaking of these things, what can we say who are so unfamiliar with them? These are matters so sublime and so indescribable, so incomprehensible and so inexplicable, that even when

---
[87] Heb. 10:20.
[88] Heb. 5:11.

they are experienced, one is scarcely able to understand them, much less comprehend them. Even if they be comprehended ever so little, yet it is impossible to speak of them.

But we must not for that reason remain silent, since mystical growth is the principal purpose of divine revelation and the source of every kind of progress in holy Church. Hence we must foster this mystical growth at all costs.[39] It is necessary, then, to recall some of the things taught by the great mystical theologians who had the good fortune to know and experience the mysteries of that marvelous life and to be able to observe and describe in some measure its wonderful growth.[40] Therefore, to the best of our ability we must summarize, coordinate, and translate into human language whatever the mystical authors, especially such as are inspired, have told us in their own language, which is truly divine.

To substantiate our particular conclusions we shall cite, in appendixes and notes, certain conclusive excerpts from the great spiritual masters and from souls who better understood or were better

---

[39] "The desire of the indivisible Trinity, which is the source of life," says St. Dionysius (*Hier. eccles.*, chap. 1, no. 3), "is the salvation of all rational creatures. And salvation is found in deification, that is, in the most perfect assimilation and union with God."

St. Teresa, *The Interior Castle*, sixth mansions, chap. 4: "I cannot help feeling the pity of it when I see how much we are losing, and all through our own fault. For, true though it is that these are things which the Lord gives to whom He will, He would give them to us all if we loved Him as He loves us. For He desires nothing else but to have those to whom He may give them, and His riches are not diminished by His readiness to give." Our Lord once said to her (*Life*, chap. 40): "Ah, daughter, how few are they who love Me in truth! If people loved Me, I should not hide My secrets from them." Again, in her *Way of Perfection*, chap. 16, she says: "Therefore, daughters, if you want me to tell you the way to attain to contemplation, do allow me to speak at some length about these things. . . . If you have no wish either to hear about them or to practice them, . . . I assure you, and all persons who desire this blessing, that *in my opinion* you will not attain true contemplation." *Ibid.*, chap. 17: "Let such a one make herself ready for God to lead her by this road if He so wills; if He does not, the whole point of *true* humility is that she should consider herself happy in serving the servants of the Lord and in praising Him." In another place, she adds (*Life*, chap. 18): "My chief aim is to cause souls to covet so sublime a blessing."

[40] St. Catherine of Genoa, *Dialogues*, Part III, chap. 11: "Without some manifestation, however imperfect it might be, of the ineffable mysteries of the divine life in souls, there would be in the world nothing but lying and confusion. Therefore the soul illumined by the light from on high cannot be silent. Love inflames it to the point of making it overcome all obstacles in order to diffuse the fruits of ineffable peace which the God of all consolation produces in it (II Cor. 1). This will happen all the more when the soul sees men foolishly lost in the search for worldly pleasures which are incompatible with their future immortal glorification."

INTRODUCTION

able to reveal the ineffable impressions of the infinite reality. Since the breathings of the Spirit are so varied and since each soul experiences and describes them in his own way and from some particular aspect, we shall take care that these texts are likewise varied. In this way one can form a comparatively accurate idea of that inexpressible treasure, and any soul which begins to experience these things will be able to know and understand something of what is taking place within itself.

Even if only one soul receives spiritual benefit, we shall consider our efforts and labors well spent. If, then, anyone, in spite of our incompetence, finds light and food here, thanks be to the Father of Light who knows how to make use of unprofitable instruments. Let such a soul offer a prayer that the author, who up to this time was nothing more than a mere channel, be changed into a shell, to use the phrase of St. Bernard (*Serm. 18 in Cant.*).

With divine help we shall treat, first, of the supernatural life and its principal elements; secondly, of the development of this life in particular souls or of individual mystical growth; and thirdly, of the mystical growth of the Church as a whole.

CHAPTER I

General Idea of the Mystical Life

"MYSTICAL" means the same as "hidden." The mystical life is the mysterious life of the grace of Jesus Christ in faithful souls who, dead to themselves, live hidden with Him in God.[1] More properly it is that interior life which just souls experience when, animated and possessed by the Spirit of Jesus Christ, they receive more and more perfectly, and sometimes clearly perceive, His divine impulses, delightful or painful, whereby they grow in union and conformity with Him who is their Head until they become transformed in Him.

By mystical evolution we understand the entire process of the formation, growth, and expansion of that prodigious life until Christ is formed in us,[2] and we are transformed in His divine image.[3]

This life can be lived unconsciously, as an infant lives its rational or specifically human life. It is in this way that beginners live and, in general, all those who are called simple ascetics. They journey to perfection by the "ordinary paths" of laborious meditation on the divine mysteries, mortification of the passions, and the methodical exercise of the virtues and pious practices. This life can also be lived consciously, with a certain intimate experience of the mysterious touches, divine influxes, and vivifying presence of the Holy Ghost. This is the way the generality of more advanced souls are accustomed to live, those who have arrived at the perfect practice of the virtues, and also those other privileged souls whom God freely

[1] Col. 3:3.
[2] Gal. 4:19.
[3] See II Cor. 3:18.

GENERAL IDEA OF THE MYSTICAL LIFE

selects at a very early stage to carry them more quickly—in His arms, as it were—through the extraordinary ways of infused contemplation.

Souls living thus, more or less conscious of the divine life, are usually called mystics or contemplatives: mystics, by reason of the innermost experience which they have of the hidden mysteries of God; contemplatives, because their habitual mode of prayer is that contemplation which God Himself lovingly infuses in whom He wishes, when He wishes, and as He wishes, without its being due in any way to human industry in acquiring, perfecting, or even prolonging it.

On the other hand, the habitual mode of prayer of ascetics is discursive meditation. With that ordinary grace which is denied to no one, all of us can attain and even perfect this form of prayer, until it is changed imperceptibly into what is called the prayer of simplicity. This latter is a sort of contemplation, partly infused and partly acquired and usually accompanied by a loving presence of God. Caused by a singular impulse from the consoling Spirit, this presence of God effects the gradual transition from the ascetical to the mystical state.

Mysticism and Asceticism

Ascetics (from ἀσχητής, meaning "to exercise") is the name given to that science which teaches the "ordinary" ways or, rather, the rudiments or first stages of Christian perfection. More particularly, it reveals the manner of meditating well in order to acquire virtues and root out vices. Furthermore, it teaches how all the practices of the purgative way and some of the practices of the illuminative and unitive ways are to be performed.

The term "mysticism" is properly reserved for "the experimental knowledge of the divine life in souls elevated to contemplation"[4]

---

[4] Says Gerson: "Mystical theology has for its object the experimental knowledge of the things of God produced by the intimate union of love." This knowledge is acquired chiefly through the gift of wisdom which, as Sauvé remarks (*Etats mystiques*, p. 120), "has as its characteristic to enable one to taste the things of faith. Then the soul actually seems to taste, feel, touch, and experience these things instead of seeing them imperfectly from a distance or knowing them by hearing alone." This is in conformity with what St. Thomas teaches (*In I Sent.*, dist. 14, q.2, a.2, ad 3): "through the gift [of wisdom] there is effected in us a union with

THE MYSTICAL EVOLUTION

although in general it embraces the whole spiritual life. This science is essentially esoteric, as is the science of optics to the blind, and no one can well understand or appreciate it without having been initiated into it by his own experience. The efforts of the mystics to translate such experience into intelligible language seems as enigmatic to us who are ignorant as do colors to the blind. Yet such efforts are of greater value and give us a better understanding of the ineffable mysteries of the spiritual life than what could be taught by speculative theology, which views these mysteries externally and only through the investigations of reason.[5] "The things also that are of God no man knoweth, but the Spirit of God"[6] and him to whom the Son chooses to reveal them.[7]

Those mysterious concepts which can be acquired without any personal experience constitute the external aspect of mysticism. However imperfect they may be, they are of the greatest interest since they make possible the recognition of the sublime mysteries of the spiritual life and of that marvelous growth in grace which terminates in glory.[8] Moreover, they are indispensable to every spiritual director who wishes to fulfill his obligation of guiding and not misleading souls. He who possesses a true spirit of piety and something of a Christian sense—although through lack of ex-

---

God according to the mode proper to that Person; i.e., through love, when the Holy Ghost is given. Hence this knowledge is quasi-experimental." So it becomes a prelude of glory. "The interior savor of divine wisdom is like a certain foretaste of future happiness" (*Opusc.* 60, chap. 24).

[5] Ven. Bartholomew of the Martyrs, O.P., writes: "Mystical theology consists in lofty contemplation, ardent affection, and transcendent raptures by means of which we are more easily able to arrive at a knowledge of God than by human studies. This mysterious theology treats of the experimental knowledge of God, which the saints call by various names because they are distinct aspects of this same knowledge: contemplation, ecstasy, rapture, dissolution, transformation, union, exultation, jubilation, entrance into the divine obscurity, taste of God, embrace or kiss of the Spouse, etc. These things cannot be comprehended by those who have never experienced them, just as one can never make a blind man have a true concept of color. . . . Concerning these things the Lord has said (Matt. 11): 'Thou hast hid these things from the wise and prudent, and hast revealed them to little ones.'" Cf. *Compendium mysticae doctrinae*, chap. 26.

[6] See I Cor. 2:11.

[7] Matt. 11:27.

[8] "What the mystics say of our transformation in God applies to the whole supernatural life. The mystical life is nothing other than the life of grace made conscious and known experimentally, as the life in heaven is that of grace developed, perfected, and brought to the completion of its slow and hidden growth" (Bainvel, *Nature et surnaturel*, p. 76).

perience he may not understand these concepts very well—will surely not consider them incredible. Nor will he be shocked by them, as is the case of those of little spirituality, who imitate the unbelievers. "But the sensual man perceiveth not these things that are of the Spirit of God. . . . But the spiritual man judgeth all things; and he himself is judged of no man." [9]

1. SO-CALLED ORDINARY AND EXTRAORDINARY WAYS

Simple ascetics, although they sometimes feel or to some extent perceive supernatural manifestations, are not yet able to note clearly what those manifestations are since they are still infants in virtue. Neither are such souls sufficiently conscious of these spiritual manifestations so as to know how to distinguish them from purely natural phenomena. The ordinary principles of operation by which the spiritual life is exercised and manifested in simple ascetics are the infused virtues. Although these are supernatural, they work in a connatural or human manner. The gifts of the Holy Ghost, by which one works *supra modum humanum* and exercises the mysterious spiritual senses, as yet influence these souls but rarely, and even then very weakly. Therefore it is seldom possible at this stage to distinguish and recognize the supernatural except in those effects which are called "miracles of grace," those sudden conversions a soul sometimes experiences when it finds itself fervent, strong, and filled with courage and holy desires, where formerly it was lukewarm, fragile, inclined to evil, and reluctant to do good.

Working as they do, in a human manner, such souls must be encouraged to proceed, as it were, on foot, and to arouse their own initiative to practice virtue and overcome difficulties under the guidance of the obscure light of faith and in accordance with the norms of Christian prudence. Seldom will they note the continual impulses of the divine Consoler, who secretly moves, sustains, and comforts them. But when, confirmed in virtue and having conquered themselves, they conform their wills more and more to that of God, they begin to feel and perceive certain desires, impulses, and instincts which are entirely new and truly divine. These movements do not proceed, nor could they proceed, from the souls themselves, for they carry the soul on to something hitherto unknown, to a new type of

[9] See I Cor. 2:14 f.

life and a much higher perfection. These souls now cannot rest until they have faithfully set these desires and impulses to work, and in so doing they enkindle other and even more lofty and ardent desires.

As these souls continue to follow the impulses of the Holy Ghost with docility, they gradually perceive His touches more and more clearly, taking note of His loving presence and recognizing the life and virtues which He infuses in them. In this way they begin, little by little, to work principally through the gifts, which are manifested now to a high degree and as something superhuman. So they come to possess an innermost experience of the supernatural within themselves and they enter fully into the mystical state.

In this happy state habitual prayer is manifestly produced in the soul by the divine Consoler, who "pleads for us with inexpressible groanings" and makes us pray as we ought. Now with greater frequency and ever more clearly all His gifts guide the soul. Especially is this true of the gift of wisdom, by which divine things are tasted and experienced; and of the gift of understanding, by which the profound secrets of God are penetrated. Also, at times, the gifts of fear, of piety, of fortitude, of knowledge, or of prudence may predominate.

"The Spirit breatheth where He will; and thou hearest His voice, but thou knowest not whence He cometh and whither He goeth. So is everyone that is born of the Spirit." [10] So it is that certain privileged souls begin to feel His delicate touches at a very early stage. Ordinarily, however, the soul does not perceive these things clearly as supernatural until it is far advanced on the path of virtue and so united to the divine will that it neither softens nor stifles the voice of the Spirit. At this stage it does not resist His impulses but follows Him with docility, permitting Him to work freely in it.

2. SPIRITUAL INFANCY, ADOLESCENCE, AND MATURITY

In the beginning, then, we usually live this divine life unconsciously and after the manner of infants, without recognizing the new vital principle, the Holy Ghost Himself, who vivifies our souls, renews our hearts, and enables us to be truly spiritual and to live as worthy sons of God. Great numbers of Christians and even religious, although these latter have vowed to follow diligently the path of

[10] John 3:8.

GENERAL IDEA OF THE MYSTICAL LIFE

evangelical perfection, never leave this phase of spiritual infancy, which is proper to ascetics and beginners. Yet would that many Christians might at least be converted and become like unto little children that they might be admitted into the kingdom of heaven.

Those "children" who do not yet realize that they are sons of God and who, although they live by Him, work according to their own designs and caprices and keep the spirit confined, must be considered carnal and not spiritual men.[11] They usually follow the prudence of the flesh and are guided by the judgments of human prudence rather than by those of Christian prudence, which, in conjunction with the gift of counsel, constitutes the prudence of the spirit.

But if, perfected in virtue, they enter into the maturity of perfect men, then the light and prudence of the Spirit of Jesus Christ will begin to shine on their foreheads, according to the statement of the Apostle: "Rise, thou that sleepest, and arise from the dead; and Christ shall enlighten thee." [12] Once they have truly subjected the prudence of the flesh, which is death, to that of the spirit, which is life and peace, they will begin to live as spiritual men, as inspired ones, moved by the impulses of the divine Consoler. They will feel more or less keenly His vivifying influxes. Then, when they see themselves moved by the Spirit of Christ, they will realize that they are sons of God; for that same Spirit of adoption who animates them, gives them evident testimony of the fact, as when He prompts them to call the omnipotent God "Father." [13] That action is an immediate effect of the gift of piety. They call God by the loving name of Father without ever realizing that it is the Spirit who prompts them to do so.

All those who are unconsciously moved by the Spirit, though they are sons of God by that very fact, are, nevertheless, no more than simple ascetics; for as yet they lack that vivid innermost experience of divine things. That experience or awareness is given by the gifts of knowledge, counsel, and understanding, which bring them to the spiritual age of discretion and make them conscious of what they are. It is given in a special way by the gift of wisdom, which, with the help of the diverse spiritual senses, enables them to recognize the

[11] Cf. I Cor. 3:1.
[12] Eph. 5:14.
[13] Rom. 8:6–16.

touches of the Spirit and to feel, to taste, to see how sweet is the Lord.[14] Then it is that the soul enters fully into the mystical life without fear of having to return to the ordinary practices of the ascetical life each time the impulse and sweet inspiration of the Spirit cease.

He breathes where He wills and when He wills, and the soul does not usually know whither He goes; in spite of this fact, by His gentle breathing He carries it under full sail to safe port. When that breathing ceases, the soul must navigate by means of oars at the risk of being held back by the waves. But as the soul begins to enter upon the high sea, the perpetual and tranquil currents of the ocean of living water are observed and the impulses and inspirations are more and more ceaseless. Then the "current of the river of grace gladdens the city of God" and the breath of the Holy Ghost now shows whence He comes and whither He is leading the soul.

3. RENEWAL AND TRANSFORMATION

Then follows the prodigious working of grace, which is realized in great part during the night of the senses. During this period, grace subjects the senses to right reason illumined by Christian prudence. It likewise ensures the practice of the supernatural virtues, uniting the soul to God in perfect conformity of will and disposing it to follow His promptings, which gradually become more and more constant. Yet the operation of grace is realized still better in the night of the spirit, wherein the supernaturalized reason is subjected to the supreme and uniquely infallible norm of almost total direction by the divine Consoler. It is then that the soul "in darkness and secure, by the secret ladder, disguised" experiences a renewal or metamorphosis which enables it to pass from the simple conforming union in which there yet remained, to some extent, its own proper initiative and direction, to the transforming union in which God becomes "all things in all," the sole director and ordinary guide of its life.

In that former state the soul was like a silkworm buried in its cocoon, inert, imprisoned, hidden. It comes forth now as something entirely different: a butterfly, possessing organs suitable for life in a more rarefied atmosphere, and able to feed on the nectar of flowers. It is no longer a creeping thing as formerly, nor does it now feed on

---

[14] See St. Augustine, *Confessions*, Bk. X, chap. 27.

base things. Such is the beautiful simile used by St. Teresa [15] to explain what takes place in the soul that comes forth entirely transformed and renewed and, as it were, possessed of new spiritual organs, so that it lives now only according to the Spirit.

Thus the soul appears as something entirely different, with desires, impulses, sentiments, and thoughts having nothing of the earth about them nor anything human. They are absolutely divine, since it is the very Spirit of God who excites and regulates them. Then the soul perceives and understands that not only does it work with the power of Christ; but that it has become entirely like to Jesus Christ—having died and risen with Him and received the perfect impress of His living Seal—and that He Himself works and lives in it and through it and with it. Now in all truth the soul can say: "I live, now not I, but Christ liveth in me," for the life of the soul is Christ Himself, whose Spirit animates it completely and reigns therein with absolute sovereignty.

Justification by the Holy Ghost and Deification

From what has been said, one can understand the supreme importance of this mystical evolution which carries us, virtue by virtue, to mystical union with God and the deifying transformation. Christ said that He came to cast fire on the earth and He desired that the earth be set on fire. This fire is the Holy Ghost, who must animate, inflame, purify, and perfect us, transforming us to the point of deification.

This deification, so well known to the Fathers but unfortunately forgotten today, is the primary purpose of the Christian life. The entire Christian life demands a continual growth so prodigious that it has as its goal a perfection truly divine, for we must ultimately resemble God as a son does his father. "Be you therefore perfect, as also your heavenly Father is perfect." [16] This is said to the sons of the kingdom who, by the very fact that they are such, are already sons of God. "Unless a man be born again of water and the Holy Ghost, he cannot enter into the kingdom of God." [17] It is said of the Word

---

[15] *The Interior Castle*, fifth mansions, chap. 2; seventh mansions, chap. 3.
[16] Matt. 5:48.
[17] John 3:5.

incarnate, in the wonderful words which we read every day in the last Gospel of the Mass, that "as many as received Him, He gave them the power to be made the sons of God, to them that believe in His name" [18] through sanctifying grace.

I. INFINITE VALUE OF GRACE

This grace is not, like the infused virtues, merely received in our faculties to set these faculties to work. It is received into the very substance of the soul and makes us a new creature and so transforms and divinizes us. It gives us a manner of life which is truly divine; whence flow certain powers and energies likewise divine, by which we truly participate in the life, power, and merits of Jesus Christ. Thus are we able to perform His very works, to accomplish His divine mission, to complete, in a certain sense, the work of Redemption and the establishment of the Church. Thus do we become His brothers and members, His lawful coheirs, worthy of glory and eternal life.[19]

This eternal life consists, as St. John teaches, in being like unto God and seeing Him as He is.[20] This is nothing more than the simple expansion or development of the life of grace. The difference between eternal life and the life of grace is similar to that between an adult and an embryo; for grace, as St. Thomas teaches,[21] is the seed which, when full grown becomes eternal life. Grace is eternal life

---

[18] John 1:12.
[19] Cf. St. Thomas, *De veritate*, q.27, a.5 f.; *De virt. in comm.*, a.10; *Summa theol.*, Ia IIae, q.110, a.4.
[20] See 1 John 3:2.
[21] IIa IIae, q.24, a.3, ad 2um: "Grace is nothing else than a beginning of glory in us." In another place (Ia IIae, q.114, a.3, ad 3um), St. Thomas states: "Grace, . . . although unequal to glory in act, is equal to it virtually as the seed of a tree, wherein the whole tree is virtually." Therefore by the life of grace "we are already sons of God, we share in the divine life, we possess the Holy Ghost in our hearts. St. John tells us of the eternal life which dwells within us (I John 3:14). Glory is nothing more than grace made external, evident, and manifest to others. For that reason St. Paul says (Rom. 8:18): 'The sufferings of this time are not worthy to be compared with the glory to come that shall be revealed in us.' The more intense the awareness of the supernatural and the more fully developed that divine life, so much the more does the soul already possess that life of the world beyond the grave. The soul dwells antecedently in heaven. That divine life enables us to pass from the present to a future existence almost without any convulsive efforts. 'But our conversation is in heaven' (Phil. 3:20)." See Broglie, *Le surnaturel*, Bk. I, pp. 38–40.

inchoate and therefore merits the same name; *gratia Dei, vita aeterna*.[22]

In grace are contained the three that bear witness on earth and these three are one: [23] the Spirit who vivifies us and moves and directs us to heaven; the blood that redeemed us and merited life for us; and the water that regenerates us in Jesus Christ, burying us with Him so that we might rise with Him to a new life. Hence without Christ we can do absolutely nothing in regard to the supernatural life; but with Him we can do all things. He Himself, by the communication of His vivifying Spirit, is our true life, which gives us the status of sons of God and the power to act as such. St. Paul expresses this beautifully in his Epistle to the Romans:

> You, however, are not carnal but spiritual, if indeed the Spirit of God dwells in you. But if anyone does not have the spirit of Christ, he does not belong to Christ. But if Christ is in you, the body, it is true, is dead by reason of sin, but the spirit is life by reason of justification. But if the Spirit of him who raised Jesus from the dead dwells in you, then he who raised Jesus Christ from the dead will also bring to life your mortal bodies because of his Spirit which dwells in you. . . .
>
> For whoever are led by the Spirit of God, they are the sons of God. Now you have not received a spirit of bondage so as to be again in fear, but you have received a spirit of adoption as sons, by virtue of which we cry: Abba (Father). The Spirit himself gives testimony to our spirit that we are sons of God. But if we are sons, we are heirs also: heirs indeed of God and joint heirs with Christ, provided however, we suffer with him that we may also be glorified with him. . . .
>
> But in like manner the Spirit also helps our weakness. For we do not know what we should pray for as we ought, but the Spirit himself pleads for us with unutterable groanings. And he who searches the hearts knows what the Spirit desires, that he pleads for the saints according to God (Rom. 8:9-27).[24]

Without the communication of the vivifying Spirit, the soul is dead to the supernatural life and can have no part with Christ. From

---

[22] Rom. 6:23.
[23] See I John 5:8.
[24] St. Cyril of Alexandria, *In Isai.*: "The Son pours forth His Spirit upon us. . . , in Him we cry *Abba, Father*. Whence He calls us sons of God and of the Father inasmuch as, being regenerated through the Spirit, we are called brothers of Him who by nature is truly the Son. He says through the mouth of the Psalmist: 'I will declare thy name to my brethren.'"

this it follows that the loss of grace is the greatest calamity that can befall a man; and its acquisition, his greatest good fortune. With it, all blessings come to us, for with it comes the Author of all goods; without it all is lost, for then a man descends from the lofty and incomparable dignity of a son of God to the vile and abominable condition of a son of death, perdition, and wrath.[25] Therefore the saints teach that justification, by which the soul is created in Jesus Christ and receives the divine substance of grace, is a work greater even than the creation of heaven and earth.[26]

"When the soul loses sanctifying grace," says Bellamy,[27] "it finds itself in a condition analogous to that of primitive matter; it can be said to be an abyss where there is nothing but darkness and chaos. Dead to the supernatural life, it needs the Spirit of God to come and deposit in its bosom the seeds of resurrection and to fructify them by His omnipotent activity. Only then will the soul be able to find the order, beauty, and life which are the fruits of divine organization. Moreover, grace constitutes us sons of God; and this divine filiation is nothing other than a reproduction, however remote, of the eternal filiation of the Word. A consequence of this is that our entire supernatural life should be an image and representation of Him who is the splendor of the Father and the figure of His substance. "For in Him dwelleth all the fullness of the Godhead corporeally; and you are filled in him who is the head of all principality and power." [28]

2. REALITY OF DIVINE ADOPTION AND FILIATION

This divine filiation is not improper, metaphorical, or simply moral, as if it were due to a simple adoption similar to that among human beings. This filiation is very true and very real in an inexplicable sense and even more proper and more lofty than is imagined.

---

[25] Ven. Francesca of the Blessed Sacrament, in her life by Lanuza, chap. 1: "God has frequently shown me the state of a soul in mortal sin. Its ugliness and horror are terrible; there is no monster in all the world to which it can be compared. He has also shown me the state of a soul in grace. This is something most delightful and its fairness and beauty can be compared neither to the sun nor to any other creature."

[26] "The justification of the ungodly which terminates at the eternal good of a share in the Godhead, is greater than the creation of heaven and earth, which terminates at the good of mutable nature" (Ia IIae, q.113, a.9).

[27] *La vie surnaturelle*, p. 72.

[28] Col. 2:9.

GENERAL IDEA OF THE MYSTICAL LIFE

It resembles, even more faithfully than does natural filiation by which one man proceeds from another, the eternal filiation by which the Word is born of the Father, "of whom all paternity in heaven and earth is named." [29]

In moral adoption the son is not reborn of the adopting father, and therefore he does not participate in the being, the life, and the spirit of the father; nor is he interiorly moved by him. But the Spirit of adoption which we have received gives us not only the honorable title, inconceivable dignity, and inestimable rights, but also the mysterious and ineffable reality of sons of God. We are reborn of the Father in the likeness of His eternal Word through the working of His Spirit of love.[30]

Such charity did the Father manifest to us and such power and mercy did He exercise in us that He was not content merely with raising us from our poor and servile condition to the status of adopted sons; He went further and, in adopting us, He willed that we should be His true sons, actually reborn in Him (John 1:13) through the grace and communication of His Spirit. Thereby we are incorporated into His only-begotten Son, from whom all things redound to us as from the head to its members. We are, then, truly sons of God, participators in His divine nature, and animated with His own Spirit, as long as the Spirit of God dwells in us. Therefore, by communicating to us His Spirit of adoption and incorporating us in His Word, the Father has bestowed on us such love that we should be called children of God; and such we are.[31] As St. Augustine observes,[32] we are reborn of that very same Spirit of whom Jesus Christ was born.[33]

Lessius states [34] that through Jesus Christ, in whom dwells the fullness of the divinity, "all those who adhere to Him as branches to

---

[29] Eph. 3:15.

[30] See IIIa, q.23, a.2, ad 3um: "Adoptive sonship is a certain likeness of the Eternal Sonship. . . . Adoption, though common to the whole Trinity, is appropriated to the Father, as its author; to the Son, as its exemplar; to the Holy Ghost, as imprinting on us the likeness of this exemplar."

[31] John 3:1.

[32] *De praedest.*, 31: "One becomes a Christian by the same grace by which Christ was made. He is reborn of the same Spirit of whom Christ was born."

[33] St. Athanasius (*Contra Arianos*, II, no. 59) says: "Since by their very nature (men) are created (beings), they can in no other way become sons (of God) unless they shall receive the Spirit of Him who is the natural and true Son."

[34] *De perfectionibus divinis*, XII, 74-75.

the vine are adopted by God and made His true sons. For as soon as one adheres to Christ and is engrafted on Him through baptism, he is animated and vivified by the Spirit of Christ, which is His divinity, and is thus made a son of God. He then lives by the same spirit as that by which God lives, and by which Christ, the natural Son of God, lives, although it is communicated in a different manner. We are sons of God properly and formally, not so much by reason of any created gift, as by the indwelling and possession of the divine Spirit, who vivifies and directs our souls." [35]

So it is that "this title of sons of God is not an empty name or simple hyperbole. . . . It indicates a real supernatural dignity essential to all the just, a dignity which is the fruit of redemption and the pledge of salvation. When we attain to this dignity through sanctifying grace, in a certain measure we are to God by adoption what His Son is to Him by essence. Without identifying or fusing us with Himself, without destroying our nature, God unites us to His own nature, makes us participate in His Spirit, in His lights by faith, in His love by charity, in His activity by the power of His grace. He places in our soul a new principle of operation, the seed of a higher life, supernatural and divine, which is destined to grow and develop in time and to manifest itself fully in eternity, when we shall share in His glory and His kingdom." [36]

3. DIGNITY OF THE CHRISTIAN

From this it will be seen how marvelous is the mystical evolution which must be realized in us as a result of our regeneration and the impulse of the new life which God infuses in us. This evolution enables us to grow spiritually in grace and knowledge and in all perfection until we are completely assimilated in the only-begotten Son of God, who, that He might be our life, our light, and our model, appeared among us full of grace and truth. Compared with this progress which tends to engulf us in the infinite ocean of the Divinity and to enrich us with the treasures of the divine perfections, all human progress, however glorious it may be, is shadowy and unsubstantial.

---

[35] See Ia, q.43, a.3: "The Holy Ghost is possessed by man, and dwells within him, in the very gift itself of sanctifying grace."
[36] Bacuez, *Manuel biblique*, IV, 216 (no. 587).

GENERAL IDEA OF THE MYSTICAL LIFE

Because he rightly despises that false progress which perverts and degrades by sacrificing the moral for the material and the divine for the human, the good Christian is called antiquated and out of fashion. Actually he is so enamored of true progress that he refuses to be satisfied with perfections that are limited; he must tend with all the ardor of his soul to an infinite and divine perfection, to be perfect as is his heavenly Father.[37]

Christians, then, are a new and heavenly race of men of divine lineage, deified men, "the offspring of God" (Acts 17:29 f.), sons of God the Father, incorporated in the Word made flesh, and animated by the Holy Ghost, men whose lives and conversations ought to be altogether heavenly and divine.[38] "If God humbled Himself to become man," says St. Augustine (*Serm. 166*), "it was in order to exalt men and to make them gods," and He makes them to be so "by deifying them with His grace; because, by the very fact that He justifies them, He deifies them, making them sons of God and by that fact, gods" (*In Ps. 49*, no. 2).

"Be mindful of your dignity, O Christian," says St. Leo (*Serm. I de Nativ.*), "and having been made a participator in the divine nature, do not seek to degrade yourself with unworthy conversation nor to return to your former baseness. Remember who is your head and of whose body you are a member."

Sublime Notions of the Fathers Concerning Deification

So common were these ideas concerning deification that not even the heretics of the first centuries dared to deny them. The holy Fathers extracted from these concepts an admirable defense for the divinity of the Son and Holy Ghost against the Arians and Macedonians. The Scriptures, said the Fathers, present these two Persons to us as vivifying, sanctifying, and divinizing of themselves the souls in which they dwell and to whom they are communicated. They impress on souls the divine likeness and make them participants in

---

[37] Fonsegrive, *Catholicisme et la vie de l'esprit*, p. 19: "Is it possible to offer man a life more lofty, more stable, more active than that of God Himself? . . . There is no danger that the Catholic ideal will ever atrophy us."

[38] St. Peter Chrysologus, *Sermon 72*: "Therefore he who believes and professes himself to be the son of such a Father should live a life worthy of his lineage, should perform acts worthy of his Father, and in thought and deed should proclaim that he has become divine in his nature."

the divine nature. Yet only God, who is life, holiness, and deity by nature, can of Himself and through His own communication, vivify, sanctify, and deify.

To dwell in the soul, to vivify and refashion it, God must penetrate it substantially, and this is proper and exclusive to God.[39] No creature, says Didymus, can penetrate the very essence of the soul; the knowledge and virtues which adorn it are not substances but accidents which perfect its potencies. But the Holy Ghost dwells substantially in the soul in company with the Father and the Son.[40]

1. THE ROLE OF THE HOLY GHOST

It is the Holy Ghost, says St. Cyril, who imprints on us the divine image; and if He were nothing more than a simple dispenser of grace, then we should be made to the image of grace, and not to the image of God.[41] But no; He Himself is the stamp which impresses on us that divine image and thus He refashions us, making us participate

---

[39] St. Thomas teaches (*Contra Gent.*, Bk. IV, chap. 17): "For no creature is infused into a spiritual creature, since it is impossible to participate in a creature, and rather it is the creature that participates. Now the Holy Ghost is infused into the souls of the saints, so that they participate in Him as it were." He adds (chap. 18): "For, since the devil is a creature, as we have seen above, he cannot fill a man as though a man could participate of the devil; nor can he dwell in a man's soul participatively or substantially. But he is said to fill some men by the effect of his wickedness. . . . Whereas the Holy Ghost, being God, dwells in the soul by His substance, and makes us good by participation of Him; for He is His own goodness, since He is God; which cannot be true of any creature. This, however, does not hinder Him from filling souls of holy men by the effect of His power." He is not content with communicating His gifts to us, but He Himself comes with them in person. The Holy Doctor, always so moderate in his criticisms, holds the contrary opinion to be a manifest error: ". . . the error of those who say that the Holy Ghost is not given, but that His gifts are given," and then he adds: "The Holy Ghost is possessed by man, and dwells within Him, in the very gift itself of sanctifying grace" (Ia, q.43, a.3). He explains this by the following significant words: "We are said to possess only what we can freely use or enjoy. . . . By the gift of sanctifying grace the rational creature is perfected so that it can freely use not only the created gift itself, but enjoy also the divine person Himself" (*ibid.*, ad 1um). Speaking in another place of the power of the sacraments: "The interior sacramental effect is the work of God alone: . . . because God alone can enter the soul wherein the sacramental effect takes place" (IIIa, q.64, a.1).

[40] "Indeed, I say that it is possible for knowledge, virtues, and arts to reside in souls; not however as substances but as accidents. But it is impossible for a created nature to reside in this manner. . . . Since, therefore, it is taught that the Holy Ghost, as well as the Father and the Son, dwells in the soul and the interior man, . . . it is impious to call Him a creature" (Didymus, *De Spiritu Sancto*, no. 25).

[41] "A. Is it not the Spirit who impresses on us the divine image and sets upon us after the manner of a seal supramundane beauty? B. Not as God, but as the dispenser of divine grace. A. Then He Himself is not impressed upon us, but through

GENERAL IDEA OF THE MYSTICAL LIFE

in the divine nature itself.[42] This divine stamp or character which is impressed upon us, says St. Basil, is a living thing; it molds us within and without, penetrating into the very depth of the heart and soul, and in this way it refashions us and makes us living images of God.[43] Thus He consecrates us at the same time that He seals us and effects in us a living pledge of the heavenly heritage, as the Apostle says.[44]

He is like a divine balm which penetrates and transforms us with its unction (*spiritualis unctio*) and makes us exhale the fragrance of Christ so that we can say with the Apostle: "For we are the good odor of Christ" (cf. II Cor. 2:15). What we receive is His own divine substance and not simply the odor of balm.[45]

He is a fire which penetrates us most intimately; and, without destroying our nature, He inflames it and gives it all the properties of fire.[46] He is a light which, illuminating souls, makes them luminous

---

Him grace is thus impressed? . . . If so, then man should be called, not the image of God, but the image of grace" (St. Cyril Alex., *Dial.* 7 *de Trinit.*).

[42] "You . . . were sealed with the Holy Spirit of the promise, who is the pledge of our inheritance . . ." (Eph. 1:13 f.). "If, being sealed with the Holy Ghost, we are refashioned to God, how could that be something created, by which the image of the divine essence and the signs of the uncreated nature are impressed upon us? For the Holy Ghost does not depict the divine nature in us after the manner of a painter . . . , but since He Himself is God . . . He is impressed on the hearts of those who receive Him, like a seal upon wax, but invisibly. He depicts His own nature through a communication and likeness of Himself to the beauty of the archtype, and He restores to man the image of God" (St. Cyril, *Thesaurus, assertio 34*).

[43] "How shall the creature ascend to the likeness of God unless it share in the divine character? Further, the divine character is not such as is a human character, but it is a living and truly existing image, the cause of similitude by which all who participate therein are constituted images of God" (St. Basil, *Contra Eunom.*, Bk. 5).

[44] Cf. II Cor. 1:21 f.: "Now He that confirmeth us with you in Christ, and that hath anointed us, is God; who also hath sealed us and given the pledge of the Spirit in our hearts."

[45] St. Cyril of Alexandria, *In Joan.*, Bk. XI, chap. 2: "If the fragrance of spices transmits its strength to the clothing and transforms into itself, as it were, those things in which it resides, why cannot the Holy Ghost, since He naturally exists in God, make those in whom He resides, participants of the divine nature?" "He abounds in the faithful, not now through the grace of visitation and operation, but through the presence of His majesty; and there flows into the vessel, not now the odor of balsam, but the very substance of the sacred ointment" (St. Augustine, *Sermo 185, de Temp.*).

[46] Cf. St. Cyril of Jerusalem, *Catecheses*, 17: "If the fire which interiorly penetrates the density of iron, turns the whole thing into fire . . . , why are you astonished if the Holy Ghost enters into the innermost recesses of the soul?"

St. Basil, *Contra Eunom.*, Bk. 3: "Just as iron thrown into the midst of a fire does not lose the nature of iron; and yet, having been inflamed by the blazing fire, it will have received the entire nature of fire and in its color, heat, and activity is changed into fire; so, by reason of the communion which they have with Him who is holy by His very nature, the powers of the soul receive His entire substance and possess,

and resplendent, radiant with grace and charity as truly divine suns, for He makes them like unto God Himself and what is more, He makes them gods.[47] He is a most sweet guest (*dulcis hospes animae*) who comes to converse familiarly with us, to delight us with His presence, to console us in our labors, to encourage us in our difficulties, to advise us and prompt us to good, and to enrich us with His precious gifts and fruits. Dwelling within us, He makes us holy and living temples of God and, conversing familiarly with us, He makes us His friends and therefore His equals, to a certain extent,[48] and worthy of the name of gods.[49] And if through the indwelling of the Holy Ghost, say St. Epiphanius and St. Cyril, we are temples of God and God Himself abides in us, how can He be less than God?[50] "It is necessary that He be God," says St. Gregory Nazianzen,[51] "if He is to have the power to deify us."

"Therefore, it is not to be understood," observes St. Cyril,[52] "that any creature deifies. This is proper to God alone, who, communi-

---

as it were, an innate sanctification. The difference between them and the Holy Ghost is this, that the Spirit is holiness by nature whereas sanctification is in them by participation."

[47] Cf. St. Basil, *De Spiritu Sancto*, chap. 9, no. 23: "The union of the Spirit with the soul is not effected by His drawing near according to place. Shining on those who are purged of all dross, He makes them spiritual through union with Himself; and, as bodies become bright and shining when a ray of light falls upon them, and from their brilliance they diffuse a new luster, so souls that possess the Spirit within themselves and are illumined by the Spirit, themselves become spiritual and send forth grace to others. . . . Hence, the likeness to God and that than which nothing more sublime could be desired, that you should become god."

[48] "Friendship either discovers equals or makes them" (Seneca).

[49] Cf. St. Cyril, *In Joan.*, I, 9: "For that reason we are called gods, not only because we have been raised to supernatural glory by divine grace, but because we now possess God dwelling and abiding in us. . . . Otherwise, how are we temples of God, according to Paul, possessing the Spirit dwelling within us, unless the Spirit be God by nature?"

[50] St. Epiphanius, *Haeres.*, 74, no. 13: "If we are called the temple of God by reason of the indwelling of the Holy Ghost, who would dare repudiate the Spirit and reject Him from the substance of God, stating that we are not the temple of God because of the Holy Ghost who dwells in the souls of the just, as the Apostle clearly affirms?"

"Only the indwelling of God makes a soul a temple of God" (St. Thomas, *In I Cor.* 3:16, lec. 3).

[51] *Orat. 34:* "If the Holy Ghost is not God, let Him first be made God; and then at last He shall deify me."

But being deified oneself does not suffice to give the power to deify others; only He who is God by nature can communicate a participation in divinity. St. Thomas says: "For it is necessary that God alone should deify, bestowing a partaking of the Divine Nature" (Ia IIae, q.112, a.1).

[52] *De Trinitate, Dial.* 7.

cating His Spirit to the souls of the just, makes them conformable to His natural Son and therefore worthy to be called sons and even gods. . . . For it is the Spirit who unites us to God and by communicating Himself to us makes us participants in the divine nature. . . . If we do not possess the Holy Ghost we can in no way become sons of God. For how could we be so and how could we participate in the divine partnership if God were not within us and if we were not united to Him by the mere fact of receiving His Spirit?"

2. ABASEMENT OF THE WORD; ELEVATION OF MAN

In order to be deified in truth, the conformity of wills is not enough; there must be a conformity of nature, and we possess this if we clothe ourselves with the Son whose living image the Holy Ghost imprints upon us.[53] Putting on Jesus Christ and being made to His image, we come to form a true fellowship with Him (I Cor. 1:9); we are His friends, sharers in His divine secrets (John 15:15); His brothers (John 20:17) and even more, His very members, so intimate is the union in this divine fellowship. Thus there is given to us the power to become sons of God (John 1:12) and gods by participation. But He who is of Himself able to give us such exalted power must be God Himself in person. By humbling Himself to our level, He joins us to His own divine life and thus raises us from our servile condition of simple creatures to the incomparable dignity of gods. He enables us to call openly upon the eternal and omnipotent One before whom the heavens tremble, not now by the terrible name of Lord, but by the most sweet name of Father.[54]

St. Peter Chrysologus [55] declares: "That which the most exalted

---

[53] St. Cyril, *De Trinitate, Dial.* 5: "For the likeness of will with the Father would not form us to His natural image and similitude, but only the likeness of nature and the universal conformity flowing from His very substance would effect this in us. . . . Because we have the Son dwelling within us, and we have received the divine character and we are enriched by Him; for through Him we have been made conformable to God. That species which is the highest of all, namely, the Son, is impressed on our souls through the Spirit."

[54] St. Cyril, *In Joan.*, Bk. 12, chap. 15: "The creature is a slave and the Creator is the master; yet the creature, conjoined with its Lord, is freed from its lowly condition and raised to a better one. . . . If, therefore, we are gods and sons through grace, then the Word of God, by whose grace we have become gods and sons of God, is Himself the true Son of God. But if He also were God through grace, He could not exalt us to a like grace. For a creature cannot give to others by its own power that which it has not of itself, but from God."

[55] *Serm.* 72.

creatures never could have been able to say, that which would fill the loftiest heavenly powers with terror and consternation, we say confidently every day: 'Our Father, who art in heaven.' Thus there is established between the Creator and the creature a marvelous fellowship, making Him equal to us so that we may become in a certain way equal to Him. Who could ever have imagined such honor and such an excess of love, that God should become man so that man might become God, and that the Master should become a servant so that the servant might become a son, thereby establishing between divinity and humanity an ineffable and eternal parentage? Surely, one does not know which to admire more, that God humbles Himself to our lowliness or that He deigns to raise us to His dignity." [56]

St. John Chrysostom observes [57] that it seems far more difficult for God to become man than for man to become a son of God. But He not only humbled Himself; He did so in order to exalt us. He was born according to the flesh that we might be born according to the Spirit; He was born of woman to make us sons of God. He desires, says St. Augustine, that we should conduct ourselves as such; that we should cease to be men, for He wishes to make us gods.[58]

3. SUMMARY

These wonderful and inconceivable relations which God has deigned to establish and communicate to us are not simply moral,

---

[56] *Offic. Purif. B.V.*: "O marvelous exchange! The Creator of the human race, by taking to Himself a living body, has bestowed on us His deity." St. Athanasius, *Serm. 4 Contra Arianos:* "As the Lord became man by taking to Himself a body, so we men are deified by the Word of God."
St. Augustine, *Epist. 140 ad Honorat.*, chap. 4: "Therefore He descended that we might ascend and, remaining in His own nature, He was made a sharer in our nature that we, remaining in our nature, might be made sharers in His nature. This is not accomplished in exactly the same way, however, for His participation in our nature did not make Him inferior, but our participation in His nature made us better."

[57] *In Math., Hom. 2:* "For it is far more difficult, judging by human reason, for God to become man than for a man to be consecrated a son of God. When, therefore, you hear that the Son of God is the Son of David and Abraham, doubt not any longer that you who are the son of Adam will be the son of God. For not rashly nor in vain did He stoop to such humiliation, but only that He might raise us from our lowly state. For He was born according to the flesh that you might be born according to the Spirit; He was born of a woman that you might cease to be the son of a woman . . . and that He might make you a son of God."

[58] Cf. *Serm. 166:* "God commands this: that we be not men. . . . To this have you been called by Him who was made man because of you; for God wills to make you god." *Serm. 13 de Temp.:* "God was made man that man might be made god."

GENERAL IDEA OF THE MYSTICAL LIFE

but very real and ontological in a sense more exalted and more true than one would imagine, even more than one could either conceive or declare. The saints feel these things to a certain extent, but they do not find expressions capable of transmitting such lofty sentiments. Even the most daring language seems to them but a mere shadow of so exalted a reality; and yet they do not cease to speak to us of "participation in the divine nature itself," "transformation in God," and "deification." [59]

Truly animated by the Spirit of Jesus, who dwells in us as in His living temple and who lives in Jesus as He lives in the Father,[60] we are thus made participants in the divine nature itself, and we are truly sons of God and brothers and co-heirs of Jesus Christ. The Spirit of adoption which we have received animates us at the same time with the life of grace. He purifies us and renews and perfects us, producing in us and with us the work of our sanctification. Thus, in making us live a divine life, He deifies us, for then He Himself is "the life of our soul as the soul is the life of our body," according to the powerful phrases of St. Basil and St. Augustine, not to mention all the other Fathers.[61]

---

[59] St. Cyril declares energetically (*De Trinit.*, *Dial. 4*) that a mere moral union would be illusory and that by participating in the divine nature through the Holy Ghost we are truly in the Son as He is in the Father: "Let us acknowledge, moreover, how the Son is in the Father naturally and not, as the adversaries state, according to that fictitious relation which is based on the fact that He loves and is loved. Similarly and in the same manner we are in Him and He in us. It is not only a conjecture that we are sharers in the divine nature by our conformity to the Son through the Spirit, but we are so in very truth. . . . Shall that mystery which is within us be a fraud and a futile hope, and, as it seems, an imposture and deception, a mere expression of opinion?" *Dial. 7:* "Why are we said to be and why are we temples of God and therefore gods? Ask the adversaries whether we are indeed participants of a barren grace lacking subsistence. It is not so; not at all. For we are temples of an existing and subsisting Spirit. Moreover, on account of Him we are even called gods, especially since we are participants with Him by reason of a union, a conjunction with His divine and unspeakable nature. . . . The Spirit deifies us through Himself. . . . How can He who is not God give deity to others?"

[60] John 6:58.

[61] St. Basil, *Contra Eunom.*, Bk. V: "The Holy Ghost is not distinct from the life which He communicates to souls; so the divine life itself which He has by nature, they enjoy by participation." In another place (*De Spiritu Sancto*, chap. 26, no. 61) he states that the Spirit Himself acts as the formal principle in that divine life and is to the soul what the visual power is to the eye: "Inasmuch as the Holy Ghost possesses the power of perfecting rational creatures and of bringing them to the very peak of their perfection, He has the status of a formal principle. For he is said to be spiritual who lives now not according to the flesh but is led by the Spirit of God and is called a son of God and has been made conformable to the image

THE MYSTICAL EVOLUTION

In speaking of the indwelling by grace as an action proper to the Holy Ghost, Father Froget makes the following observation:

> The Fathers of the Church speak in exactly the same terms. The Holy Spirit is the great Gift of God and the Guest of our soul. In giving Himself to us, He makes us share in the Divine nature and constitutes us the children of God, saints, Divine beings. He is spoken of as the sanctifying Spirit, the principle of celestial and Divine life; some even go so far as to call Him the form of our holiness, the soul of our soul, the bond uniting us to the Father and the Son, as that One of the Divine persons by Whom the other two dwell in us.
>
> If Scripture and the Fathers lay so much stress upon the fact that this indwelling by grace, like the work of our sanctification and adoption, are the particular work of the Holy Ghost, is this not a sure sign, and a strong proof that the Holy Spirit has special relations with our soul and a mode of union which, in some true sense, He does not share with the other two persons? [62]

The same doctrine is taught by Petau and by Scheeben, Tomassin, Ramière, and many other modern theologians. Leaning on the patristic tradition, they maintain with very solid reasons that that work is not, as current opinion affirms, entirely common to the three divine Persons and only appropriated to the Holy Ghost, but that it is truly proper to Him. He it is who directly unites Himself with souls in order to vivify and sanctify them and, if the other two Persons dwell and work in the souls at the same time, it is by concomitance, immanence, or circuminsession, whereas He commu-

---

of the Son of God. So the operation of the Spirit is to a purified soul what the power of sight is to a healthy eye."

St. Augustine is even more decisive in affirming that God is formally the life of the soul (*Enarrat. in Ps.* 70, *Serm.* 2): "I shall say boldly, brethren, but truly: There are two types of life; one of the body, the other of the soul. And as the soul is the life of the body, so God is the life of the soul; whence if the soul departs, the body dies; and if God departs, the soul dies." On another occasion (*Serm.* 156, chap. 6, no. 6) he asks: "Whence comes the life of your flesh? From your soul. Whence comes the life of your soul? From your God. Each of these lives by its own life; for the flesh is not its own life, but the soul is the life of the flesh; the soul is not its own life, but God is the life of the soul." The statement of St. Macarius is almost identical: "The Lord truly takes the place of the soul in those on whom the grace of the divine Spirit falls. O the goodness and condescension that has been shown to the nature of man oppressed by sin!" (*De libert. mentis*, XII.)

[62] Froget, *The Indwelling of the Holy Spirit in the Souls of the Just*, Part III, chap. 1, pp. 105 f.

GENERAL IDEA OF THE MYSTICAL LIFE

nicates Himself to souls immediately and personally, although not hypostatically.[63]

However that may be, the most interesting truth of the deification of souls will remain an unquestionable fact. It is likewise indisputable that all the Fathers with one accord teach or recognize a real filiation, which is founded on an actual participation in the divine nature itself. We agree with Passaglia when he says: "The Fathers confirm that the fellowship with the divine nature, which Peter lists among the great and precious promises, is a fellowship that is not merely affected and moral, but ontological and substantial. Indeed, I make bold to contend that not even one ancient Father of the Church can be cited who would circumscribe the participation in the divine nature within the bonds and limits of a social or moral union." [64]

"The great and precious promises which are here mentioned," observes Bellamy, "oblige us to understand this participation in the divine nature in the strictest sense possible, granting always the essential difference between God and creature. . . . There is nothing that could give the Christian a loftier idea of his grandeur or remind him so eloquently of his obligations." [65]

---

[63] Petau, *De Trin.*, Bk. VIII, chap. 6, no. 8: "The three Persons certainly dwell in the just man, but only the Holy Ghost formally sanctifies him and makes him an adoptive son through His communication. . . . Let the testimonies of the Fathers and the places of Scripture be read again: . . . we shall find that a great many of them assert that this is done through the Holy Ghost as the proximate cause, and, as I have said, as the formal cause." Many of the testimonies already cited actually bear this out; and in particular, those of St. Augustine, St. Cyril of Alexandria, St. Macarius, and St. Basil. Indeed, St. Basil expressly teaches that "through this (Spirit) each of the saints is a god, for it was said to them 'I have said, you are gods and you are all sons of the Most High.' But it is necessary that He who is the cause of men's being gods should be the divine Spirit and should Himself be from God" (*Contra Eunom.*, Bk. V). St. Irenaeus (*Adv. haer.*, Bk. V, chap. 6) goes so far as to assert that according to God a perfect man is composed of body and soul and the vivifying Spirit; and when this whole composite conforms perfectly to the image of the Son, then God is glorified in His work: "God is glorified in His creature, adapting it in conformity with and after the pattern of His Son. Through the hands of the Father, that is to say, through the Son and the Spirit, man is made according to the likeness of God, but not only a part of man. . . . For the perfect man is a commingling and union of a soul which takes to itself the Spirit and a body joined to that soul, which is a creature in the image of God. . . . For man is not perfect by reason of the fashioning of the flesh alone . . . nor by reason of his soul alone . . . nor by reason of the Spirit alone . . . but the commingling and union of all these things renders a man perfect."

[64] *Comment.*, Bk. V, p. 43.

[65] *La vie surnaturelle*, p. 166.

4. STATUS OF THIS DOCTRINE TODAY

Unfortunately these sublime and consoling doctrines are utterly forgotten, as Cornelius a Lapide asserts: "Few there are who know the privilege of such a dignity; fewer still who ponder it with the gravity it deserves. Truly, each one should esteem it with reverence, and doctors and preachers should explain and inculcate it in the people so that the faithful and the saints might know that they are living temples of God, that they carry God Himself in their hearts, and that therefore they should walk divinely with God and converse in a manner befitting such a guest." [66]

Nevertheless the echo of the unanimous voice of the Fathers still resounds among modern theologians. Notwithstanding the universal forgetfulness or—why not say it?—the shameful deviations from traditional teaching, there can yet be heard some dominant and authoritative voices. It is consoling to see how many writers are beginning once again to employ almost the selfsame animated, expressive, vibrant, and pulsating language of the Fathers and the great mystics, especially since the learned admonitions of Leo XIII concerning devotion to the divine Paraclete. This augurs a happy rebirth of these fundamental doctrines which are the very soul and substance of the Christian life.

In this regard Ramière writes: "It seems that the time has come when the great dogma of the incorporation of Christians with Christ will have the same importance in the common teaching of the faithful as it had in the apostolic doctrine; a time when the point on which St. Paul based all his teachings will not be considered a mere accessory. It will be understood that this union, represented by the divine Savior under the figure of the branches joined to the vine, is not an empty metaphor but a reality; that through baptism we are truly made participants in the life of Jesus Christ; that we receive within ourselves, not in figure but in reality, the divine Spirit, who is the principle of this life; and that, without being despoiled of our human personality, we are made members of a divine body, thereby acquiring divine powers." [67]

In fact, these vital and consoling truths which so animated, in-

---

[66] *In Os.* 1:10.
[67] *Espérances de l'Eglise*, Part III, chap. 4.

GENERAL IDEA OF THE MYSTICAL LIFE

flamed, and fortified the early Christians [68] are now beginning, fortunately, to attract the attention of many apologists and theologians, who fully understand the needs and exigencies of the age and are desirous of finding an apt remedy for such evils as afflict and threaten religion. In view of the general plague of prevailing indifference and skeptical sloth and coldness which lead so many souls to defection, to ruin, and even to disloyalty and a violent, fiery opposition to the truth; at the same time taking heed of the status of subjective criticism which enslaves modern thought, we believe the fulfillment of the needs and the correct remedy for the emergencies of our time lie precisely in arousing the conscience and feeling of the faithful so that they can appreciate, experience, and live as they ought, the life which Jesus brought us from heaven.

[68] The acts of the martyrs and the customs of the first centuries offer us interesting evidences of this fact. The Christians of those times appreciated, understood, and lived the supernatural life in such a way that they liked to be called Godbearers or Christbearers. Therefore, when Trajan asked St. Ignatius: "Who is this Godbearer?" the latter answered: "It is he who carries Christ in his heart." "Then you actually bear Christ?" "Without the slightest doubt, for it is written: 'I shall make My abode in them.'"

Speaking of St. Ignatius, Tixeront says (*History of Dogmas*, I, 131 f.): "The picture which the Bishop of Antioch sets before us of the life and organization of Churches is completed by what he says of Christian life in each one of the faithful in particular. He represents it most assuredly just as he conceived it and strove to live it himself, in the ardor of love and eagerness for martyrdom, that were in his soul. Jesus Christ is its principle and center. He is our life, not only inasmuch as He brought us eternal life, but also because, dwelling personally in us, He is in us a true and indefectible principle of life. . . . He dwells in us and we are His temples; He is our God within us. . . .

"Hence the title of θεοφόρος assumed by Ignatius himself in the title of his Epistles, and the names of θεοφόροι, ναοφόροι, χριστοφόροι, αγιοφόροι, he applies to the Ephesians (9:2): hence, too, the union with the flesh and spirit of Jesus Christ, with the Father and Jesus, that he wishes to the Churches. . . .

"The condition and, at the same time, the expression of that life of Jesus in us are faith and love: 'Nothing shall be hid from you, if you have perfect faith and charity in Christ Jesus, which are the beginning and the end of life: the beginning is faith, the end, charity . . . all other things are the consequences of these for a holy life'" (Eph. 14:1). . . .

"This charity, so intense in the heart of the Bishop of Antioch, leads him also to the love of sufferings and to the thirst after martyrdom. . . . But it inspires him too with accents of an impassioned mysticism: 'My love is crucified and there is no fire in me for what is material; but there is a water living and speaking that says to me interiorly: Come to the Father.'"

St. Andronicus replied to the judge who threatened him: "I hold Christ within me"; and St. Felicitas: "I possess the Holy Ghost, who will not allow me to be overcome by the devil, and therefore I am confident." In the same manner when St. Lucy was asked by the judge, "Is the Holy Ghost within you?" replied with all simplicity, "All those who live chastely and piously are temples of the Holy Ghost."

Since the understanding of their sublime dignity lies dormant in so many Christians, there follow that indifference or coldness in their lives and the small regard which they have for that dignity, even to the extent of being ashamed of it. Such Christians make our name repulsive to those outside the Church, while actually the inner life of the Catholic Church is filled with spiritual delight for those within it and attraction for those outside it who look on it with honesty. If we would manifest and reveal to them the soul of the Church, as Blondel says, and if we would speak to them as the Apostle commands (Col. 4:5 f.), in language full of grace and wisdom, showing them the beauty, the happiness, the delights, and the grandeur of this divine life, we could attract and win, rather than repel them.

As for those who accuse us of being "antiquated and opposed to progress," it would be sufficient, to stop their mouths and even to make them change their opinion, if we were to tell them, opportunely and in the style of the holy Fathers, something of the wonderful deification of Christian souls, where all is harmony, continuity, and orderly development, without the least disconnection, incoherence, or haphazard procedure.

For that reason we deem it advisable to express in greater detail, and as our abilities permit, some doctrines of great importance which are so poorly propagated and understood even among ourselves and which are so essential in a work on the life and evolution of the Church. May God enlighten us that we may proceed with prudence!

In this first part we shall discuss the nature, elements, and qualities of the supernatural life; its principles of operation, that is, the divine powers and faculties; and the principal means of spiritual growth. Then, in the second part, we shall examine the dispositions and preparations this life requires; the obstacles it must overcome; the ways it follows in its development; the means of fostering it and of purifying ourselves so that we shall not impede it; the principal steps it traverses and the phases it presents; the phenomena it normally produces and the marvels that usually accompany it. After we have revealed its priceless riches and the perfect continuity existing between the ascetical and the mystical life, we shall finally indicate, in the third part, how this divine life is developed, manifested, and perfected in the mystical body of the Church as a whole.

CHAPTER II

The Divine Life of Grace

To see what are the principal elements of the supernatural life, we shall now consider and synthesize as far as possible the admirable data of Scripture, patristic tradition, and the testimony of spiritual souls who experienced these mysteries. In this way we shall realize more profoundly the grandeur of the gifts we have received and we shall the better be able to appreciate and preserve them and foster their development.

In our humble opinion, that clearer understanding is not attained by analyzing and systematizing this mysterious doctrine so as to make it conform to our limited intellectual capacity, nor does it consist in reducing it entirely to the level of our mental concepts, in order to fit it into some human system. This would be to disfigure it. It would deprive the mystical doctrine of that ineffable significance which one admires in its living plenitude and which surpasses all formulas, theses, and systems of either the present or the future. If used correctly, these systems do give us some analogical representation of the divine mysteries; but to attempt to define with exactness what is of itself absolute and indefinable and to try to systematize that doctrine whose unutterable grandeur confounds and reduces us to silence: this is to despoil such doctrine of its divine delight and is to give to souls, instead of the sublime truth which delights them, nothing more than paltry human evaluations which leave their hearts cold and almost make the divine mysteries despicable.

This is the reason for the scant interest which the supernatural arouses when it is presented in cold and abstract formulas. On the other hand, although the animated and vibrant expressions of Scripture and of the saints who felt these things very keenly, are lacking in precision, yet they inflame all the fibers of the soul. The more unscientific and ambiguous the expressions, the more lofty the idea which they give us of those incomprehensible realities which transcend all formulas and even our most sublime concepts. Therefore we do not intend to define or to systematize excessively but only to present in an orderly fashion to souls thirsting for light and truth, the marvelous contents of Catholic tradition concerning the divine life in souls. Realizing our own blindness, with all our heart we ask the Father of light to illumine us, saying with the Psalmist: "Send forth Thy light and Thy truth: they have conducted me, and brought me unto Thy holy hill, and into Thy tabernacles" (Ps. 42:3).

According to Scripture and the Fathers, the following elements definitely belong to the supernatural or Christian life: adoption, regeneration, justification, renewal, deification, divine filiation, the reception of new life and new energies, the development and expansion of the divine seed of grace, the indwelling of the Holy Ghost and of the entire Trinity, the friendly and intimate fellowship with the three divine Persons, etc.[1] We shall first consider these elements as a whole and then each one in particular, fixing our attentoin on one or another but never to the total exclusion of the rest, because an actual separation or excessive abstraction would result in a vivisection of the very life we are trying to analyze.

ARTICLE I

CONCEPT OF THE SUPERNATURAL LIFE

Through divine revelation and the actual experience of holy souls we know that we have received the Spirit of adoption, through which we piously dare to call our Creator by the most sweet name of Father. Actually the eternal Father has called us to share in the status of His Son. He transferred us from death to life and from darkness to wondrous light that we might enter into the intimate relations of life and fellowship with Himself, in such wise that our

[1] See Broglie, *Le surnaturel*, Part I, pp. 14 ff.; Part II, p. 7.

conversation should be in heaven and we should live in loving and familiar association with the three divine Persons.

Such is the true supernatural order, totally inconceivable to even the most brilliant intellects, had God Himself not deigned to reveal it and make it known as a fact. Such it is in reality and not as we might fathom or surmise from a comparison with existing nature. Notwithstanding the fact that traces of the supernatural are necessarily found in the natural order, any concept of the supernatural, however lofty, that we might form would at the end be something that is natural and founded on nothing more than the simple relationship of creature to Creator.

The Supernatural Order a Participation in the Divine Life

In His interior and inscrutable life, God is something more than the incomprehensible, transcendent, and unique Being whose existence is demonstrated by human reason. He is the ineffable Yahweh, the mighty and living God, one and three, inaccessible to even the most penetrating gaze and the most profound and daring feelings and desires.[1] Yet, through an inconceivable excess of love and goodness He could and did desire to abase Himself to the level of His poor rational creatures in order to make them share in His infinite life and happiness. He lowered Himself to elevate them and make them, as it were, His equals; so that they might be able to live eternally with Him in the intimate fellowship of close and cordial friendship. The true supernatural order consists, then, in God's humbling Himself to the level of His creature and the creature's being elevated, so far as is possible, to the level of the Creator. It consists, in short, in the incarnation or humanization of God and the deification of man. Such is the sublime order to which we have been raised by the divine liberality.

By birth we were sons of wrath. We were not only mere creatures without rights before our exalted Maker and absolute Lord and totally incapable of seeing Him or conversing with Him, but we

---

[1] Cf. I Tim. 6:16 "Who . . . inhabiteth light inaccessible, whom no man hath seen nor can see."

THE MYSTICAL EVOLUTION

were guilty creatures who bore the stigma of our degradation, ingratitude, and disloyalty, and who deserved to be looked upon by Him with abomination. But through a prodigy of His infinite mercy God not only rids us of the stigma which made us abominable, He ennobles us to the point of making us objects worthy of His delight. To that end He infuses in us a participation in His own being, and He transfigures us into the image of His only-begotten Son, so that we might be a living splendor of the divine Word just as the Word is "the brightness of His glory and the figure of His substance."[2] Then, seeing His own Son resplendent in us, He sees Himself in us and can look upon us with that infinite complacency which He enjoys eternally in His adorable and absolute perfections.

Such is the mystery of the supernatural life: a resemblance of and participation in the inner life of God, one and three. The august mystery of the Trinity of persons in the unity of the divine nature is the supernatural life in its essence; whereas deification—and we might even add, "trinification"—of the rational creature is the supernatural life as shared by us.[3] This is the same eternal life which was in the Father and which He manifested to us in the incarnate Word so that we might enjoy that life by entering into an intimate and loving fellowship with the three adorable Persons (cf. I John 1:2 f.).

To that end He gave us His only-begotten Son; to that end He infused in us His Spirit of adoption: that we might have life and have it more abundantly. For that reason also His adoption of us is real and not simply juridical. He gives us, together with the rights and honors, the reality of true sons. His condescension was such that He desired not only that we should be called so but that we should be His sons in very truth, in the likeness of His only-begotten Son of whom we become co-heirs and brothers. The Word Himself, by His incarnation, merited for us the power to become sons of God (cf. John 1:12).

To effect this filiation, the eternal Father regenerates us by com-

---

[2] Heb. 1:3.
[3] Gay, *De la vie et des vertus chrétiennes*, Vol. I: "The life of grace is that holy, radiant, and beatific life which is the ineffable circulation of divinity among the Father, Son, and Holy Ghost. Consequently, O Christians, a man can and even must be a god and even here below live the life of a god and for that it is necessary only that he live united to Christ . . . although he might never be or do anything that would make him be or seem to be what the world calls a great man."

THE DIVINE LIFE OF GRACE

municating to us a new life, a divine and eternal life, and by making us participate in an ineffable manner in the generation of His Word of life. Then both together instill in us their vivifying Spirit who penetrates the very depth of our souls in order to animate, renew, transform, and deify them. Thus do our souls share in the eternal spiration of the mutual love of the Father and Son, which is the Holy Ghost, the substantial and personal terminus of the operations *ad intra*, and the bond of union in the adorable Trinity.

As a result, the regenerated and deified soul enters into intimate and vital communication with each and all of the three divine Persons, and in this fellowship is echoed the mystery of the operations *ad intra*, which has been hidden from the beginning in the impenetrable bosom of the Divinity. Here is a mystery of light and love which no creature could ever have known or suspected, dreamed of or longed for, were it not for that marvelous effusion of divine light and charity.[4] As the soul is purified and ceases to place obstacles to that deifying influence—striving to grow in God and to be filled with His plenitude—its regeneration is effected and it reproduces in itself more and more clearly the enchanting image of the divine Word. So also is it filled more and more with the Spirit of love, being united to God in such a way that in Him alone it finally rests, "transformed and absorbed" (Blessed Nicholas Factor) and made one spirit with Him.[5]

1. INEFFABLE REALITIES

Human reason grows faint before such incomprehensible mysteries, but illumined hearts feel and experience even in this life that ineffable reality which cannot be expressed in words or concepts, much less in human systems of thought. What these souls manage to stammer disconcerts our weak understanding. They multiply terms which seem most exaggerated, but even that does not prove satisfactory. Always they see that such terms are inadequate and that the reality is incomparably greater than anything that could be said of it. Indeed, were it not that they possessed a lively appreciation of

---

[4] "The good which God has promised us," says St. Thomas (*De veritate*, q.14, a.2), "so exceeds our nature that, far from being able to attain it, our natural faculties could never suspect it nor desire it."

[5] See I Cor. 6:17.

their own nothingness and a firm conviction of the complete distinction between nature and personality, we would believe that they were teaching a doctrine of pantheistic identity or a truly hypostatic union, as exists between the humanity of Jesus and the Word. For that reason those who are accustomed to view and measure even the most lofty things according to the limits of their own mental capacity are easily scandalized by such semi-divine language, which only confounds their own pride. Therefore such persons do not hesitate to brand as exaggerated or even pantheistic those vibrant statements of an inflamed and illumined heart which seeks only to express as best it can what it so vividly experiences.[6]

Preserving the distinction between nature and person, the transformation which takes place in deified souls and the plenitude of divine life which they receive are unbelievably greater than can be imagined. Deeply submerged in that ocean of light, of love, and of life, they become marked with the characteristics and properties of the divine Persons in such a way that the adorable mystery of the Trinity is reproduced and shines forth in them.[7] St. Catherine of Siena said that if we had eyes to see the beauty of a soul in grace, we would adore it, believing that it was God Himself, for we would be unable to conceive of any greater nobility and glory.

Moreover, deifying grace increases with each good work which is prompted by divine charity; and the glory corresponding to each increase of grace is such that to gain it, all the labors of the world could be considered well spent.[8] How many benefits do they lose

[6] "It frequently happens," says Cardinal Bona (*Principia et doctrina vitae Christianae*, Part II, chap. 48), "that a man of the people who does not know how to read, will speak more learnedly of God and divine things than a celebrated doctor of theology, who spends all his life among books. This is due to the fact that experience excels speculation, and love surpasses knowledge. We are united to God more intimately by the affections of the heart than by the meditations of the mind."

[7] If one could clearly see the interior of a deified soul, he would see in it not only a veritable heaven but also the most august divine mysteries. Blosius, (*Institutio spiritualis*, chap. 2, appendix), repeating the statement of Tauler, says that this happened in the case of the most holy Virgin: "The very depth of her soul and her whole interior life were so godlike that if anyone could have gazed upon her heart, he would have seen God in all clarity and he would likewise have seen the procession of the Son and Holy Ghost. For never did her heart stray from God, even for the briefest moment."

[8] St. Teresa, *Life*, chap. 37: "I can say, then, that if I were asked whether I should prefer to endure all the trials in the world until the world itself ends, and afterwards to gain a little more glory, or to have no trials and to attain to one degree less of glory, I should answer that I would most gladly accept all the trials in ex-

who spend their lives on trifles, when at each moment they could be making themselves more and more like to our Savior and amassing treasures of enduring grace and glory!

Divine adoption, then, truly deifies us. It gives us a divine being, regenerates us, creates us anew in Jesus Christ, makes us participate in His own Spirit and thereby communicates to us a new and mysterious life. We receive, together with this life, a copious array of potencies and proportionate energies by which we can live, grow, and work as true sons of God, called from the kingdom of darkness to the participation of His eternal light. By means of these new powers we can discover the road to true life and thus arrive at the enjoyment of God's delightful presence.[9]

In what does that life consist; in what, those potencies? If we could define them with nice precision, they would not be supernatural nor ineffable. If, in our attempt to classify them, they were to be placed in the categories of human thought, they would then be as human as the thought which contains them. And if, knowing these potencies to be ineffable and divine, we nevertheless endeavor to narrow them to our mental capacity by reducing them to some system, then we disfigure rather than clarify them. Our effort to make them more comprehensible terminates in sterile formulas almost devoid of reality and meaning which leave the heart cold, however much the intellect is flattered and pleased.

The life of grace is not as our inquisitive reason would like to represent it; rather, it is as the divine Word communicated it to us. He who appeared among us full of grace and truth gave us an under-

---

change for a little more fruition in the understanding of the wonders of God, for I see that he who understands Him best loves and praises Him best."

[9] Ps. 15:11: "Thou hast made known to me the ways of life, Thou shalt fill me with joy with Thy countenance: at Thy right hand are delights even to the end."

Mary Agreda, *Mystical City of God*, Part I, Bk. II, chap. 13: "Remember that there are only two ways to eternity: the one, which leads to eternal death by contempt of virtue and ignorance of the Divinity; the other, which leads to eternal life by the profitable knowledge of the Most High. . . . The way of death is trodden by innumerable wicked ones (Eccles. 1:14), who are unaware of their own ignorance, presumption, and insipid pride. To those whom His mercy calls to His admirable light (I Pet. 2:9) and whom He engenders anew as sons of light, God gives by this regeneration a new being in faith, hope, and charity, making them his own and heirs of an eternal and godlike fruition. Having been made sons, they are endowed with the virtues accompanying the first justification, in order that as sons of light, they may perform corresponding works of light; and over and above they receive the gifts of the Holy Ghost."

standing of it according to the measure of our limited intellects. In order worthily to appreciate it, then, we should observe the mysterious images and marvelous expressions by which it is portrayed and explained in Sacred Scripture and in the writings of great souls who were able to express more divinely the vital influxes which they received from Jesus Christ. Above all, we should heed the voice of holy Church, the spouse of Christ and the authentic organ of His infallible truth. Ever bearing in mind those solemn definitions which mark out for us the shining path and save us from deviation, we can be certain that those admirable symbols and daring expressions in which the Church and all its worthy members appear divinized and made one with Christ, far from being exaggerations, are but pallid reflections of the ineffable reality which could never be represented adequately.

2. INCORPORATION IN CHRIST

In the first chapter of another work [10] we endeavored to explain in detail the principal symbols by which the Church is represented in Scripture and tradition so that through them we might the better be able to discover, evaluate, and admire its divine merits. So also the holy Fathers and great mystics, instead of using merely speculative and abstract formulas—except when the necessity of combatting some error warranted it—were pleased, as St. Basil mentions and as Bossuet notes, to increase the number of those concrete and vibrant expressions. So full of life are these expressions and symbols that they arouse all hearts capable of feeling these mysteries, however much they may fill us with astonishment and leave frustrated the curiosity of the intellect.[11]

[10] *La Evolución Orgánica.*
[11] Bossuet, *Lettre à une dem. de Metz:* "One must adore the divine economy with which the Holy Ghost manifests to us the simple unity of truth with a diversity of expressions and figures. . . . One must note the particular aspect of each of them in order to include them later in an integral consideration of revealed truth. Then ought we to rise above all these figures in order to find out what is even more profoundly contained in this truth. Whether considered individually or collectively, none of these figures could adequately convey this truth. Only thus can we lose ourselves in the profundity of God's secrets, where the reality is seen to be much different from what it had been surmised." St. Basil (*De Spiritu Sancto*, chap. 8) has said almost the same thing. See also Blessed Henry Suso, *La unión divina*, chap. 7; St. Teresa, *The Interior Castle*, seventh mansions, chap. 1.
Terrien, *op. cit.*, I, 56: "If the formulas which express the mystery of our deification are very numerous and infinitely varied, it is because the gifts of God are so

THE DIVINE LIFE OF GRACE

Of all these symbols there are two types that are most adequate. On the one hand there are the sacramental figures which represent the Church as the chaste spouse of Jesus Christ, made one with Him in heart and spirit in order to bring forth new sons of God. On the other hand, and more especially, there are the organic figures which represent the Church as a great living body whose head is the Savior, whose soul is His divine Spirit, and whose members are all those rational creatures who participate in the life or at least the vital motion which that Spirit of love communicates.

The participation in the divine nature which each animated member receives is sanctifying grace, making us live the selfsame life of Jesus Christ, our Lord and Savior. It enables us to reproduce in ourselves His divine likeness, to participate in His merits, to work with His power, and, under His impulse and as His members, to perpetuate His mission in the world. The mysterious faculties or powers which the divine Spirit infuses in us together with that life are the infused virtues, the faculties of our supernatural being by which we are able to work as sons of God, "created in Christ Jesus in good works." [12] Some of these faculties or powers remain habitually even in dead members to keep them united to the organism, to direct them to life eternal, and to dispose them to recover life once more and thus to rise from death to life; and these faculties are unformed faith and hope.[13] The transitory motions of the divine Consoler are those graces which are called actual. The organic functions which conserve and develop the life of the whole organism, which restore what is lost and revivify the wounded parts, are the sacraments. It is the sacraments that make the blood of the Lamb who takes away the sins of the world circulate throughout the whole mystical body.

The eternal Father adopts us and regenerates us through Jesus Christ, His only-begotten Son; He vivifies, resurrects, and glorifies us through the power of His Spirit. In the words of St. Paul: "But God, who is rich in mercy, for His exceeding charity wherewith He loved us, even when we were dead in sins, hath quickened us to-

---

inestimable and His generosity so far surpasses our rights and our concepts that all human language fails to give us any idea which accurately corresponds to their sublimity."

[12] Eph. 2:10.

[13] Faith and hope are said to be *unformed* when they reside in a soul which does not possess the theological virtue of charity. (Tr.)

gether in Christ (by whose grace you are saved), and hath raised us up together in the heavenly places, through Christ Jesus." "For we are buried together with Him by baptism into death; that as Christ is arisen from the dead by the glory of the Father, so we also may walk in newness of life. For if we have been planted together in the likeness of His death, we shall be also in the likeness of His resurrection." "And if Christ be in you, the body indeed is dead because of sin; but the spirit liveth because of justification. And if the Spirit of Him that raised up Jesus from the dead dwell in you, He that raised up Jesus Christ from the dead shall quicken also your mortal bodies because of His Spirit that dwelleth in you." [14]

Thus God enables us to participate in His own nature; He renews and transforms us so that we are like unto Him as His true sons. Through this sonship we can enter into intimate friendship and fellowship with Him and see Him as He is and become the rightful heirs of His eternal glory.

Hence the incarnate Word, as St. Mary Magdalen of Pazzi so admirably puts it, is the key to the whole supernatural order. It pleased the eternal Father to restore all things in Christ (or, as the Greek text has it, to bring back all things under the headship of Christ), the Head of both men and angels and of the entire Church, both militant and triumphant; "and through Him to reconcile all things unto Himself, making peace through the blood of His cross, both as to the things that are on earth, and the things that are in heaven." [15] For that reason the Savior Himself said that on being raised up on the cross He would draw all things to Himself. Drawing us by the bonds of His love, He leads us to life eternal; He enlightens and fortifies us for our journey, being at once the way, the truth, and the life. Indeed, were it not for Him, no one could go to the eternal Father.[16]

It is in this way alone, and not in any manner which our own crude evaluations might suggest, that we have been raised to the supernatural order and a participation in the divine nature itself. We live a life which the Spirit of Jesus Christ lovingly infuses in us, and this most sweet Consoler, since He is the Spirit of Truth, enables us

[14] Eph. 2:5 f.; Rom. 6:4 f.; 8:10 f.
[15] Col. 1:20. See also Eph. 1:10, 22.
[16] John 14:6.

THE DIVINE LIFE OF GRACE

to know this life truly [17] and makes us call God by the name of Father. He imprints on us the divine seal and fashions us in the likeness of the only-begotten Son of God. He anoints us and makes us truly anointed Christs in the image of Jesus. He dwells within us, although in a hidden manner, as the vivifying principle, and constitutes the pledge of eternal life.[18] Without destroying our nature or our personality, but rather enriching them, He renews, transforms, and deifies us, making us one with Jesus Christ, our Savior, as members of His mystical body, all of whom live one and the same life. This life resides fully in Christ as Head and thence, according to the measure of His giving and the dispositions which are found in His distinct members, it is poured forth and redounds to all. When these members, having rid themselves of all obstacles, receive this life in great abundance, the Spirit who animates them will give them clear testimony that they are sons of God and, as such, co-heirs with Jesus Christ (Rom. 8:16 f.).

Actually "they are reborn in the same Spirit of which Jesus Christ was born," observes St. Augustine,[19] and "the womb of the Church is for us," says St. Leo, "what the womb of the most holy Virgin was for Him." Whence it is that St. Irenaeus dares to call the Holy Ghost the seed of the Father, *semen Patris*, because in reality we are born into eternal life, "not of corruptible seed, but incorruptible, by the word of God," [20] who freely begot us through the Word of truth.

---

[17] St. Thomas, *In I Cor. 2*, lect. 2: "Since the Holy Ghost is the Spirit of Truth as proceeding from the Son, Who is the Truth of the Father, He inspires truth in those to whom He is sent, just as the Son sent by the Father makes the Father known, as it is written (Matt. 11:27): 'nor does anyone know the Father except the Son, and him to whom the Son chooses to reveal him.' Then . . . (the Apostle) shows that wisdom is revealed to men through the Holy Ghost."

[18] See II Cor. 1:21 f.: "Now He . . . that hath anointed us, is God; who also hath sealed us and given the pledge of the Spirit in our hearts." Eph. 1:13 f.: "In whom you also, after you had heard the word of truth, the gospel of your salvation; in whom also believing, you were signed with the Holy Spirit of promise, who is the pledge of our inheritance." A pledge, as distinct from a mere security, is the very nature or substance of that which is promised.

St. Augustine, *De verb. apost.*, Serm. 13: "What must the thing itself be if the security is such! It must be called a pledge rather than a security, for when security is given, it is taken away as soon as the thing itself has been returned. But a pledge is given of that which is promsied to be given, so that when it is realized, that which has been given is fulfilled and not changed."

[19] *De praedest.*, 31.

[20] See I Pet. 1:23.

So it is that the incarnate Word gave us the power of becoming sons of God, "who are born not of blood, nor of the will of the flesh, nor of the will of man, but of God." [21]

We know that by the baptism of regeneration we die to the world to live in Jesus Christ. We are buried with Him so that from those waters made fruitful by the power of His Spirit, we may rise to the new and glorious life which He merited for us. We are grafted on Him that we may produce fruits of glory and not of earth. We are incorporated with Him in His holy Church that we may live as His worthy members, flesh of His flesh and bone of His bones: to live, in fine, because of Him, and for Him to live in us. It is through the faithful, His own true organs, that Christ performs the mystical vital functions of that life by which He lives in His Church. In this way also He completes the work of human redemption and the salvation of the world. Vivified by His divine sap, we can produce fruits that are not human. We receive incessantly the impulses of His Spirit which place us in intimate union with the Father and strengthen the tie that binds us to the other members of the Church. By means of the sacramental functions He makes circulate through our veins His most precious blood which purifies, animates, and strengthens us.[22]

We are incorporated in Jesus Christ, animated by His vivifying Spirit, nourished with His body and blood, and washed with the water from His sacred side. If, then, we remain faithful to His grace and endeavor to keep our conversation in heaven and our life hidden with Him in God, is it any wonder that we should live because of Him as He lives because of the Father (John 6:58) and that both should reside in us so that we may be perfected in unity and loved with the selfsame love with which the divine Persons love each other (John 17:23)? In the measure that we possess this substantial Love of the Father and are made like to Christ—which is effected by the charity which the divine Consoler infuses in our hearts—we shall

---

[21] John 1:13.
[22] "As soon as we can be considered members of Jesus Christ," observes Weiss (*Apologie*, X, 16), "we cease to be natural men and are elevated far beyond our frailty, for then we are clothed in Him, His goods and powers are ours. He lives in us, and we live in Him who is our life (John 15:5; Gal. 2:20; 3:27; Rom. 13:14; Col. 3:4; Phil. 1:21). Our actions are the actions of Jesus Christ, whose life is manifest in us (cf. II Cor. 4:10 f.). Our frailty is made victorious and invincible; we find the difficult easy, the heaviest burden light (Matt. 11:30), and we produce abundant fruits (John 15:5) that will last not only for a time, but for all eternity."

THE DIVINE LIFE OF GRACE

become more sensitive and more vital organs in the mystical body of Jesus Christ, we shall receive more light and divine powers and be better able to promote the health, well-being, and general growth of the whole body.

The heart of the Church is made up of those souls who are filled with the Holy Ghost and who perceive the divine mysteries and the invisible workings of Jesus Christ on the faithful and of the faithful on others. Through this heart the Holy Ghost exercises a hidden but salutary power over the other organs, even the highest, to aid them in the discharge of their important functions. Those organs that are weak and infirm, are cured and invigorated; those that are completely dead, are enabled more easily to regain the life of grace. Because of this activity, the divine Spirit, who is truly the soul of the Church, is sometimes considered its heart. Although He is not Himself an organ of this body, He liberally pours forth His charity on the true organs and in them He secretly stores up vital energies for the good of all.[23]

As all the throbbings of the adorable heart of Jesus Christ reverberate in souls thus deified, so also do His thoughts radiate and shine with the light of life, in the illumined eyes of their heart which, aided by the Spirit of understanding, penetrate the most august mysteries.[24] If we were filled with the Holy Ghost, we would have in mind what was also in Christ Jesus. Though He was by nature God, He emptied Himself, taking the nature of a slave, being obedient to death, even to death on a cross.[25] So we ought also to humble ourselves and empty ourselves, being all to all and sacrificing ourselves for our brothers, even to the shedding of our blood for them if necessary (cf. I John 3:16). Such is the mystery of the supernatural life which the Fathers tried to synthesize in this one most extraordinary word: deification.

---

[23] IIIa, q.8, a.1, ad 3um: "The head has a manifest pre-eminence over the other exterior members; but the heart has a certain hidden influence. And hence the Holy Ghost is likened to the heart, since He invisibly quickens and unifies the Church: but Christ is likened to the Head in His visible nature."

[24] Eph. 1:18; I Cor. 2:10.

[25] Phil. 2:5–8.

THE MYSTICAL EVOLUTION

DEIFICATION AND UNION WITH GOD

Considered from a purely human viewpoint, the work of our deification would seem to be not only an exaggeration proper to dreamers and deluded persons, but to be madness. Who could conceive of this wonderful elevation of man whereby he comes to be identified with divinity? Or who could imagine that inconceivable abasement of God Himself whereby He communicates Himself to His creatures to the extent of equality or even identity and takes His delight in them, becoming man—and, indeed, an outcast of men—in order to make men gods?

The greatest prodigy of infinite Goodness and Wisdom cannot but appear as foolishness to the inflated egoistic reason. But all worldly prudence is foolishness before God. None but the pure and simple hearts to whom the Spirit of love Himself reveals them and makes them known (Matt. 11:25-27; I Cor. 1:2) can realize the profundity of these mysteries of infinite love which are hidden from even the most piercing intellects. When they see these prodigies of light and goodness they are enraptured. Perceiving the principles of divine truth, they understand how limited and insignificant are all human views; and what seems to us stupidity is to them a marvel of wisdom.

1. HARMONY OF THE NATURAL AND SUPERNATURAL

Speaking of the interpretation of deification as given by the apostles, Bainvel [26] says:

The apostles speak to us of the Christian vocation as a great mystery hidden in God and surpassing all understanding. Only the divine Spirit, who searches into the profundity of God Himself, can penetrate it; for it is something divine.[27] They represent the Christian ideal as an adoption and a divine filiation. God not only pardons us but makes us His sons, and desires that we call Him Father. The spirit of fear, which befits a slave, gives way to filial love. By nature we were slaves; by grace we are children, heirs of heaven, and coheirs with Jesus Christ with whom we become one. . . .[28] The apostles portray Him to us as the new Adam, the supernatural Head of regenerated humanity, the exemplar of all the

---
[26] *Nature et surnaturel*, pp. 66-69.
[27] See I Cor. 2; Eph. 1-2; Col. 1.
[28] Eph. 1 and 3; Gal. 4; Rom. 8.

THE DIVINE LIFE OF GRACE

predestined, our peace with God, our first-born Brother, and our very life. . . . Jesus is the Head; the Church is His mystical body; and we are the members of that body, sharing in the life of the Head and forming with Him a complete whole. Jesus is the Bridegroom and the Church is the Bride, as is each faithful soul. Beneath these images are discovered sublime and admirable realities. This entire supernatural life is ordained to the supreme good and to the vision and possession of God Himself, who "inhabiteth light inaccessible, whom no man hath seen nor can see." [29]

St. Peter says the final word, the most profound: *divinae consortes naturae*. This it is which explains our divine filiation and our incorporation with Jesus and, through Him, with the Father. This explains our life, which in a certain manner becomes identified with that of Jesus. Our destiny is to participate in the glory which is the joy of the only-begotten Son, who is in the bosom of the Father; it is to see God face to face and to know Him as He is known in Himself. What is strange about all this if we participate in the divine nature?

But since we do not as yet share fully in the divine nature, all our energies ought to be directed to a greater participation in it and to a closer union and configuration with Jesus by living entirely according to His Spirit. For this reason St. John represents as a divine seed that indefinable participation in divinity which we enjoy here on earth and which we are accustomed to call sanctifying grace.[30] This is the same concept as is found in St. Peter, but with an accessory idea, that of a life which is incipient and not yet developed. Whence the beloved disciple tells us that we are sons of God, but our future development is not yet known. *Nondum apparuit quid erimus*. "When He shall appear, we shall be like to Him, because we shall see Him as He is." [31] So grace is not yet glory; it is only the seed of glory. We have divine life within us, but we shall not possess its full development until heaven.[32] Now, there is the

[29] See I Tim. 6:16.
[30] See I John 3:9.
[31] *Ibid.*, 3:2.
[32] Lejeune, *Manuel de théologie mystique*, p. 175: "This divine life resides in our souls without our being directly aware of it. Its presence is discovered at times by the superhuman energy which it imparts to us and by the victories which it enables us to win. But during our earthly existence we do not usually perceive these divine realities directly or immediately. The veil will not be removed completely until glory. We know only, as Bossuet says, 'that the life of grace and that of glory are one and the same inasmuch as between them there is no other difference than that which exists between adolescence and maturity. Glory is nothing other than a disclosure of that life which is hidden in this world but will be fully manifest in the next.'"

Froget, *The Indwelling of the Holy Spirit*, pp. 83 f.: "God is therefore really and

laborious transformation from the old to the new man, the effort to form Jesus within ourselves, to place our activity in unison with the divine principle which ought to animate it, and to live in conformity with our divine status. Such is the basis of Christian morality and that which distinguishes it essentially from natural morality.

For that reason the apostles, following out such testimonies, exhort us to flee the world, to avoid earthly conversations, to purge ourselves of all faults and imperfections, and to strive to live entirely as Christians, as divine men, living images, brothers and members of Christ Himself, animated by His Spirit.[33]

St. Paul, in speaking of the elect, says that God has predestined them "to be made conformable to the image of His Son, that He might be the first-born amongst many brethren." [34] So it is that if we are faithful, "we . . . are transformed into the same image from glory to glory, as by the Spirit of the Lord." [35] Therefore we should strive always to put on Jesus Christ; and to such a degree that we shall eventually become one thing with Him. In this way, as St. John Chrysostom says, "we share in the selfsame parentage of the Son of God and partake of the same lineage because we possess Him and are transformed into His likeness. Even more, the Apostle is not content with saying that we have put on Jesus Christ, but he adds that we are one with Him; that is to say, we possess the same form, the same character. Can there be anything more stupendous or more worthy of consideration? He who formerly was a pagan, a Jew, or

---

substantially present to the Christian in the state of grace. His presence is not merely a presence, but a real possession, which already begins to bear fruit of enjoyment. It is a union far superior to that which binds unsanctified beings to their Creator; our union is surpassed only by the union of the two natures in the Person of the Incarnate Word; a union which, when fervently cultivated, is so blissful as to be in the true sense of the word a foretaste of heaven's joys, a prelude to happiness eternal. St. Thomas is not afraid, therefore, to assert that there is an imperfect beginning in this life itself, of the future happiness of the saints, and he compares it to the buds which are the promise and the earnest of the coming harvest (cf. Ia IIae, q.69, a.2)."

[33] Leo XIII, *Divinum illud:* "Now this wonderful union, which is properly called 'indwelling,' differs only in degree or state from that with which God beatifies the saints in heaven." Hence the life of grace is already a true commencement of the life of glory. In the words of St. Thomas (IIa IIae, q.24, a.3, ad 2um): ". . . for grace is nothing else than the beginning of glory in us."

[34] Rom. 8:29.
[35] See II Cor. 3:18.

a slave, now bears the image, not of an angel or archangel, but of the Lord of all things, since he represents Christ." [86]

This marvelous union of the infinite God with finite beings is not an absurd Gnostic emanation or a repugnant pantheistic fusion. It is an ineffable, loving, and free communication, though hidden and inconceivable, of the divine life to rational creatures, wherein the supernatural and the natural, the divine and the human, are conjoined, blended, and intermingled without being fused. God remains ever the same—God is immutable—but man, without ceasing to be man, is deified. Man's integral nature continues, but in another form. Not only is he purified and reinstated in his primitive beauty, but he is raised and elevated to the heights of divinity, brilliantly shining with true divine splendor. He is like the iron which, when placed in the furnace, loses all its dross and, without ceasing to be iron, is turned into fire.

Human reason alone could not even suspect this marvel of love, and whenever it attempts to express its vague notions in terms compatible with the human mind, it falls into great errors. But divine revelation harmonizes the extremes without confusing them, much less destroying them; and thus it extends and immensely clarifies our horizons. It enables us to see that the inner life of God is not that of a unique and absolute Being—the God of the philosophers, who is known only through the reflection of the unity of the divine nature seen in the works of creation—but that of the true living God, who, though one in nature, is three in Persons.

This admirable mystery of the divine life could never be known by philosophy. The divine works *ad extra*, which are studied by the philosopher, are common to the entire Trinity and can only indicate in some measure the unity of power and essence. But the divine life as known through revelation is the basis of the whole supernatural order and is founded not on the simple relations of causality, such as those which bind the creature to the Sovereign Creator, but on the relationship of a cordial and intimate friendship which presupposes a true likeness. Everything which flows from that friendly relationship—even the most insignificant works, such as washing dishes, serving the sick, or washing the feet of the poor for the love

[86] St. John Chrysostom, *In Gal. 3*.

of Jesus Christ—belongs entirely to the supernatural order. On the other hand, the most lofty speculations of a philosopher on the wonders and infinite perfections of the supreme being, the absolute and unknowable being who transcends all nature, if not illumined by the divine light of faith, are purely natural and without the least meritorious value for eternal life.

So it is that the two orders can be distinguished in spite of the fact that they are intermingled. The supernatural is not a violent imposition nor an interpolation of the natural, destructive of its continuity and harmony. It is an elevation of that nature, which, without losing any of its true perfections, becomes clothed in all its aspects with marvelous enchantments and powers and is truly deified, or rather, raised to a divine order. The supernatural is not, then, a disruption of the natural, but an ordination to a higher state. It is not a foreign and violent thing, but an interior, comforting, and harmonious reality, a new mode of life which entirely penetrates, ennobles, and elevates the natural, just as the rational life ennobles and elevates sensitive life, and sensitive life ennobles and elevates purely organic life.

2. THE DIVINE LIFE IN ITSELF AND IN US

The participation which we enjoy in the inner life of God: that is our supernatural life. The new relations which thereby bind us to Him and to our neighbor are a reflection of those relations which prevail among the three adorable Persons.[37] The divine Trinity, as we have said, is the supernatural life in essence; sanctifying grace, which makes us sons of God, co-heirs with Christ, and living temples of the Holy Ghost, is the supernatural life redounding to us through participation.

God is life itself, and that life is the light of men.[38] Our God is not a philosophical abstraction; He is the living God, the living One par excellence, *Vivens Pater*. Moreover, for Him to live is to know and to love, for His knowledge and love are His very life; and the adequate terminus of His operations is His own divinity. In Him there is an absolute simplicity, with perfect identity between His being

---
[37] Cf. St. Magdalen of Pazzi, *Œuvres*, Part IV, chap. 9.
[38] Cf. John 1.

THE DIVINE LIFE OF GRACE

and His operations, between the principle and the term of action, between one attribute and the other. His essence is life, His life is activity, and His actions are not only vital but they are life itself.

Yet, there is in God a personal distinction. God the Father, living in the plenitude of His life, knows Himself eternally and infinitely. Knowing Himself, He produces or utters *ab aeterno* the Word of His wisdom, the faithful, living, and personal representation of His infinite Being; and this issuing forth of the Word, expressed by knowledge and likeness, is His eternal generation. The Word is most truly the Son of God the Father, from whom all fatherhood in heaven and on earth receives its name; and He is, in turn, the model of all filiation.

The Father and the Son contemplate and love each other infinitely, in the full communication of the selfsame essence. The terminus of this impetus or spiration with which they love each other, the eternal embrace by which they bind themselves to each other, is an infinite Love which is personal at the same time that it is co-substantial. This is the mystery of that ineffable life which human reason could never discover; and, even when manifested, could never understand. But faith infallibly attests the reality of this life; and illumined souls experience it with full certitude, even in this world.[39]

God makes us participate in this same marvelous life by supernaturalizing our life to the point of deification. Through His condescension we enter into fellowship with the three divine Persons themselves, in such a way that there re-echoes in us that inexpressible mystery: the Father reproducing His Word in our hearts and both together infusing in us and breathing upon us their Spirit of love.[40] Thus each divine Person impresses on us His characteristic property and makes us participate in something of Himself. The Father gives us His divine being; the Holy Ghost vivifies and sanctifies us by pouring forth His charity in our hearts; and the Word, directly joined to our nature through the Incarnation and united with the whole Church and every just soul through the grace of His most sacred passion, fashions us to His own likeness.

---

[39] Cf. St. Teresa, *Interior Castle*, seventh mansions, chap. 1.
[40] Cf. Tauler, *Institutions*, chaps. 33 f.

THE MYSTICAL EVOLUTION

The Father has predestined us to become conformed to the image of His Son;[41] to that end He calls us and justifies us and gives us the Spirit of adoption and of promise. So, when the charity of the Father dwells in us, the Father and the Son also dwell in us.[42] We are then living temples of the entire Trinity and a "little heaven" where God reigns and is glorified. At the same time He glorifies Himself in us by letting the innermost splendors of His eternal brilliance shine forth in our souls[43] so that we become one with Him. Thus each divine Person influences the work of our deification according to His own particular property. He who possesses the Spirit of love, possesses eternal life within himself; and that is the same life as was in the Father and which He manifested to us in the Word.[44]

If many of the Christians who strive to live in grace are not aware of their own dignity and this glorious heritage of the servants of God, it is because they live in a very lukewarm manner and do not continually study the book of life, which is Jesus Christ our Savior, the model and true light of men.[45] If they would study and imitate Him, it is certain that in His holy humanity they would discover the ineffable mysteries of divinity and of the entire Trinity.[46] They would come to know the treasures of wisdom and knowledge which are hidden in Him, and they would "be filled unto all the fullness of God."[47]

3. THE IMAGE AND LIKENESS OF GOD

God respects and does not destroy the nature formed by Him to be a subject of grace. Although there cannot exist in us an absolute simplicity and identity of essence, operation, and terminus of activity, there does not, on that account, cease to exist in us a real and physical participation of His own life. When it is reproduced in us to the greatest possible extent and in harmony with our own life, it does not make us cease to be men; rather it makes us perfect men at the same time that it deifies us. This deification is so profound that

---

[41] Rom. 8:29.
[42] See John 14:23; I John 4:13, 16.
[43] Cf. John 17:22.
[44] See John 1:2-7; 3:15; 4:12 f.; 5:11 f.
[45] Cf. Isa. 54:17; 55:1-6.
[46] See John 14:9-21; I John 5:20.
[47] Eph. 3:17-19. Cf. Col. 2:2 f.

THE DIVINE LIFE OF GRACE

it penetrates to the very core of our substance; and it is so intensive and extensive that it elevates our being, our faculties, and our operations to a divine order.

To a certain extent we are by nature images of God, although only analogically and remotely. Our soul is spiritual and it knows and loves the true and the good, and therein is found a semblance of the adorable Trinity. The fullness of our natural happiness would consist in the most perfect knowledge and love which we could acquire by contemplating the divine splendors as seen solely in the marvels of creation. Yet, however perfect might be that love and knowledge, what a distance and what an impassable chasm ever remains between the sovereign Creator as He is in Himself, and us, His poor creatures!

If we had remained in the purely natural state and had not been raised to supernatural life, knowledge, and love, we could never possess formally and physically anything divine; not even divine faculties, powers, and energies. Our knowledge and love could then never attain to God as He is in Himself and we could not embrace Him with these two acts, which are the arms by which it is given to us now to unite ourselves with Him. Spiritual intuition and the intimate and friendly love of charity would be totally impossible. Instead of enjoying God as substantially and lovingly communicated to our souls, to make them participants in His own happiness, we would be forever separated from Him as He is in Himself. We would contemplate a pure abstraction, a mere concept of God, instead of His loving face. We would love a good which is far removed from ourselves, instead of loving the God of our heart and our portion forever.

But by a prodigy of love which we can never sufficiently admire, much less worthily acknowledge, He condescended to supernaturalize us from the beginning by elevating us to nothing less than His own status, to make us share in His life, His infinite power, His own operations, and His eternal happiness. He desired that we should become gods, sons of the Most High (Ps. 81:6), domestics, servants, friends, and heirs (Rom. 8:17; Eph. 2:19; John 15:14 f.) with whom He converses affably, and to whom He manifests Himself (Wisd. 6:13 f.; 8:3; John 14:17-23; I John 4:7). He willed that we should truly know and love Him in Himself and not be content with only a vague idea of a divine Being.

In the state of pure and integral nature, elevating grace was sufficient to effect this transformation and deification. But through original sin we were deprived of the divine inheritance along with the dignity of sons of God, because we lost His grace and friendship. Not only were we despoiled of His gratuitous gifts, but we were also wounded in our very nature because of the disobedience committed against the natural order. Not only did there vanish from us the supernatural divine image which deified us, but even that likeness which we had by nature was disfigured almost to the point of being effaced.

Thus we were born in the likeness of the Father of Lies and sons of wrath, with a propensity to evil and an incapacity to practice all the good which even natural reason proposes. Indeed we could not even know or love it as perfectly as nature demands. Therefore, to reestablish the primitive order, elevating grace alone was not sufficient. There was required one which would heal and reintegrate our primitive nature, at the same time that it transformed and elevated us to the divine order. It was necessary to restore the obliterated traces of the natural image of God so that upon them could be imprinted His true supernatural likeness. Thus man, created in the image and likeness of God, needed to have that image restored according to the divine likeness.

4. RESTORATION AND ELEVATION

The Lord, in His infinite mercy, instead of abandoning us as He did the rebellious angels, took compassion on our earthly weakness and decreed that where the offense has abounded, grace should abound yet more.[48] He produced the marvel of the centuries when He sent His Son not only to become incarnate and so deify us,[49] but to suffer also and so heal and purify, strengthen and teach us, pay our debts, and store up such merits for us that we were converted from debtors to creditors and were thereby raised to a much greater height than was originally ours.[50] The Word of God came to restore

---

[48] Rom. 5:20.
[49] John 1:12; St. Augustine, *Sermons 13, 166; Letter 140*; St. Athanasius, *Sermon 4, Contra Arianos*.
[50] "Both on the part of the creature and on the part of the aggrieved Creator," said the eternal Father to St. Magdalen of Pazzi (*Œuvres*, Part III, chap. 3), "the Redemption was a much greater work than that of creation. Through it the creature

nature and to enrich it with grace, by washing us with His blood in the bath of regeneration that we might be reborn and resurrected glorious and victorious over death.

So we are created anew in Jesus Christ in good works, in the image and likeness of a celestial and divine man, after having been born to the image and likeness of an earthly man. Thence the necessity of despoiling ourselves of the latter in order to clothe ourselves in the former (cf. I Cor. 15:47-49). That grace which heals and restores us must work in a painful manner to cure such deep wounds. But the more painful it is, the more glorious, since it enables us to crucify our flesh with its vices and concupiscences and to proceed in all things according to the Spirit by whom we live as members of Christ.[51] In this way we are carried progressively to perfect configuration with our Savior and model, renewing ourselves according to the Spirit of our mind, we put aside the habits of the old man in order to put on the new man, who has been created according to God in true holiness and justice.[52]

If, by living according to the flesh and not mortifying ourselves as the Spirit commands (Rom. 8:13), we have the misfortune to die as a result of losing that priceless life of grace through our own weakness and malice, we can regain it anew by being sprinkled with the blood of Jesus Christ in the sacrament of penance. This is not a rebirth, but a resurrection from death to life, for as in nature, so also in grace, one is not born more than once. And if we do not actually lose this life by grave sin, but nevertheless weaken it by light faults and thereby become sick, then that selfsame washing heals and restores us at the same time that it aids our renewal by cleansing us of the evil inclinations of the old man.[53]

In brief, were it not for sin, which overthrows the order of nature,

---

not only regained lost innocence but it acquired advantages which it did not formerly possess.... On being united to divinity, thanks to the merits of the Word, it was made worthy of the beatific vision.... So it is that certain creatures know better than do the angels themselves the divine essence, My eternal being, and the mode of union contracted by the Word with humanity, ... and that is in recompense for their virtue, which surpasses that of the angels. For these latter do not have to suffer to preserve grace, while the creature is not preserved in grace except at the cost of suffering and labor. It is just, therefore, that the creature should receive the greater reward."

[51] See Gal. 5:24 f.
[52] See Eph. 4:22-24.
[53] See St. Catherine of Siena, *Letters* 52, 57, 58, 60, 106.

nothing other than elevating grace would be required for our deification. Then, by means of the good works that we would joyfully perform under the influence of that grace and the subsequent virtues and divine inspirations, we would grow in the supernatural life until we arrived at the point where we could see God face to face by entering into His glory. But by reason of the first fall and the further degradation attendant upon new sins, we must at the same time be elevated, rehabilitated, and reborn. This rebirth in God and the restoration of nature is effected by the healing and the elevating grace of our Redeemer and Savior, the heavenly pelican who sprinkles us with His blood that we may have life and have it abundantly, and thus be truly holy and without blemish in the sight of God. To this end He is offered to us as our guide, our model, and even as our food. He is the way, the light, and the life, so that no one can go to the Father but through Him.[54]

5. THE PATH OF CALVARY AND TRANSFIGURATION

As our true and living model, Christ vivifies us without any effort on our part when we ourselves are not yet in a position to cooperate, as happens with infants. Nevertheless He does not exclude, but rather He demands our full cooperation as soon as we can give it, that we may be fashioned in His likeness and, by virtue of His blood, be able to soar to great heights. As He suffered for love of us, so does He desire that, like Him, we should suffer for love of Him; and this to our own great benefit.

The healing of our wounds, the putting off of the old man and the putting on of the new cannot be done without great violence and suffering. Inclined as we are to evil, growth in the grace and knowledge of God through meditation on His life and imitation of His works and progress along the rugged path of Christian perfection cannot be realized without fatigue and laborious efforts, at least not until we successfully root out our evil inclinations. So it is said that the kingdom of God suffers violence and only the violent carry it away (Matt. 11:12). Our God reigns from the Cross (*regnabit a ligno Deus*) and, to achieve perfect union with Him, we must follow Him along the painful and bloody paths to Calvary.[55]

---

[54] See John 14:6.
[55] Jaffre, *Sacrifice et sacrement*, p. 235: "The effects of sin which baptism does not

THE DIVINE LIFE OF GRACE

Having been lifted up there, upon the cross, it is precisely then that He draws all things to Himself. If we follow Him as our model and the true light of the world, we shall not walk in darkness but we shall possess the eternal light of life by which we shall know the Father. Knowing Him and seeing in His light the very light of His face, we shall experience the currents of everlasting life which come to us with that light, and we shall drink of the fountain of living water and the torrent of divine delights. We shall hear the most sweet voice of the Shepherd who knows His sheep and is known by them, who calls them by name and gives them life eternal.[56]

So if we grow in the grace of our Savior, we shall be deified even in this life. We shall possess the kingdom of God in our hearts; we shall live in intimate fellowship with Him; we shall possess Him and be possessed by Him, and we shall merit the name of gods. For we become gods and the sons of the living God, capable of working divinely and knowing and loving Him as He is in Himself, by receiving the grace which He deigned to communicate to us as a participation in His own life through the merits of Jesus Christ. *Gratia Dei vita aeterna, in Christo Jesu* (Rom. 6:23).

St. Dionysius says that deification is the most perfect possible assimilation and union with God.[57] It implies, on the one hand, the innermost presence of that mysterious grace which, as the internal form of our justification, purifies, transforms, sanctifies, and deifies us. On the other hand, it implies the intimate and substantial presence of the entire Trinity reigning in our hearts and giving us eternal life as well as the friendly commerce with all and each of the divine Persons through the operations of that life of grace. These operations are the acts of knowledge, understanding, desire, and love which have God Himself as their immediate object.

6. WORDS OF LIFE AND THEIR INCOMPREHENSIBILITY

To proceed philosophically, we should now examine each one of these things in particular, in order to specify in what each consists, and thus be able to form a more exact idea of the whole. But since

---

destroy, it transforms, giving them an expiatory value and uniting them with the satisfactions of Jesus Christ. Thus, after having suffered in His own body, He suffers in His mystical body, even in the infant newly born to grace."

[56] See John 10; Ps. 35:9 f.
[57] See *Eccl. hier.*, chap. 1, no. 3.

this whole ineffable subject can be aptly appreciated only by considering it in its integrity and plenitude, to try to examine each point separately would be to lose the lofty concept which we ought to form of it. Therefore, when we strive to define or formulate any of these things to our satisfaction, we despoil those notions of their divine content. Instead of the ever mysterious supernatural life, we have nothing but our sterile considerations, which leave us the more cold and unmoved as they seem to become more clear and comprehensive. St. Teresa well states that, unlike the mysterious words of the Gospel, which greatly impressed her, learned books were often repugnant to her and killed her devotion.[58] That is why, as Olle-Laprune points out, "excessive abstraction can easily cause us to lose sight of our true reality." [59]

We prefer, then, to imitate as much as possible the method of the Fathers in not abstracting, much less separating, one concept from the others. Like the Fathers, we shall always observe the reality itself, but from different points of view, multiplying the aspects and images for the sole purpose of seeing better that inexpressible and integral whole which no number of terms or concepts can exhaust.

This method necessitates the frequent repetition of the same idea; the necessity of speaking, for example, of the indwelling when treating of grace; of regeneration and adoption when considering sanctification; and of sanctifying grace when considering charity and the gifts, etc. But this same method is used in Scripture, the early Fathers, and also in the great mystics, who speak of what they themselves experience. It is always the same ineffable reality which they experience, but each time it is some new phase of its inexhaustible aspects. True, their language may not allure impatient intellects which maintain that they always hear in it the same unintelligible song, but their language does move those profoundly Christian hearts which beat intensely in the contemplation of that reality which never satisfies completely but ever arouses new hunger. *Qui edunt me adhuc esurient.* We shall observe that method even at the risk of being tedious, in the assurance that those repetitions will be useful to many souls.

[58] See *Way of Perfection*, chap. 21.
[59] *La vitalité chrétienne*, p. 149.

THE DIVINE LIFE OF GRACE

ARTICLE II

The Grace of God and the Communication of the Holy Ghost

Grace, as the Catechism of the Council of Trent says, is a divine reality which makes man a son of God and an heir of heaven. In this statement is said all that can be said. Our task is to appreciate worthily the terms of this admirable definition, considering it as but a pallid reflection of the reality itself and not as a presumptuous exaggeration.

Sanctifying Grace

Sanctifying grace truly gives us a participation in the divine life so far as it deifies us. It transforms us to our very depths and makes us like unto God as His sons in truth, and not in name only or merely in appearance.[1] It is the true divine life (*gratia Dei, vita aeterna*). So the infusion of this new type of life elevates us in our very being, not merely in appearance. St. Thomas says, "*Vivere in viventibus est ipsum esse.*"

Although grace can be called accidental with regard to man, since it can be gained or lost without his ceasing to be what he is, yet in regard to the good Christian, the *homo divinus*, it is so intimate that without it he is dead and reduced to the level of the old Adam. Grace it is which makes a man a son of God and a living member of Jesús Christ.[2]

Other gifts, although they make us change in appearance, leave us

---

[1] Louis of Granada, *The Sinner's Guide*, p. 144: "Grace acts in like manner. As a divine quality it is infused into the soul, and so transforms man into God, so that, without ceasing to be man, he assumes the virtues and purity of God."

[2] Although theologians maintain that what is in God substantially is in the soul of man accidentally, yet we can say that this "divine being" of grace is something accidental *quoad animam humanam*, but it is the very life of the soul which lives supernaturally (*quoad vero animam viventem supernaturaliter*).

St. Thomas, *In II Sent.*, dist. 26, a.4, ad 1um: "Although grace is not the principle of natural existence, nevertheless it is the principle of spiritual existence whereby the natural is perfected."

with the same nature, and for that reason they can vary in the same subject. Grace cannot be reduced to the category of the properties, for these flow from the nature itself and presuppose it. Being inseparable from the nature, they characterize it but they do not constitute it. According to our human mode of understanding, the life of grace has as its properties charity and the infused virtues and habits which always accompany it and disappear with it. These properties which flow from grace and which, for that reason, we receive with it in a rudimentary state, constitute the operative potencies of grace itself. The accidents of this order are the changing aspects, the transitory impulses, and the sudden transformations which occur in the supernatural life.

1. EFFECTS OF SANCTIFYING GRACE

Since grace elevates us in our very nature, it is received, as St. Thomas teaches, not into the potencies of the soul, but into its very essence in order to elevate it. The soul's potencies receive only the virtues and operative powers, which strengthen and transform them, ordaining them to the supernatural and making them capable of divine works.[3] This doctrine of the reception of grace into the essence of the soul is generally admitted today.[4] Giles of Rome (Aegidius Romanus), who is one of the greatest of the followers of

---

[3] St. Thomas, *De virt. in comm.*, a.10: "Grace, through which the soul possesses a certain spiritual nature, is divinely infused in man that he may be able to perform actions which are ordained to eternal life." *De veritate*, q.27, a.6: "Grace resides in the essence of the soul, perfecting it, so far as it gives to the soul a certain spiritual nature and through a certain assimilation makes it participate in the divine nature, just as the virtues perfect the faculties in regard to their operations." *Ibid.*, a.5, ad 17um: "The immediate effect of grace is to confer a spiritual nature, and this pertains to its informing a subject . . . but in conjunction with the virtues and gifts, its immediate effect is to elicit a meritorious act." Ia IIae, q.110, a.4: "For as a man in his intellective power participates in the Divine knowledge through the virtue of faith, and in his power of will participates in the Divine love through the virtue of charity, so also in the nature of the soul does he participate in the Divine Nature, after the manner of a likeness, through a certain regeneration or re-creation."

[4] Pourrat, in his *Theology of the Sacraments*, summarizes the scholastic doctrine in these words: "Habitual grace is the divine life communicated to the soul. As residing in the very substance of the soul to deify it, it is called sanctifying grace; and as dwelling in the potencies of the soul to make them capable of working supernaturally, it is identified with the infused virtues, which are in turn related to the gifts of the Holy Ghost. Sanctifying grace, the virtues, and the gifts constitute habitual grace; and all the sacraments, without exception, produce it."

THE DIVINE LIFE OF GRACE

the Angelic Doctor, proved this same doctrine with many irrefutable arguments.[5]

Speaking of man's justification by grace, Froget says:

And first, how does this deification take place? By what marvelous process does a rational creature become inoculated with the life of God? It is brought about regularly by baptism, and constitutes a real generation resulting in a real birth.

This is that new generation of which the holy Epistles make such frequent mention; it is that second birth so much lauded by the Fathers, and ever kept before our minds by the sacred liturgy of our holy religion—a generation incomparably greater than our first and merely human generation, since it transmits to us, instead of a natural and human life, a life supernatural and divine; it is a wonderful birth that transforms each one of us into that "new man" of which the Apostle speaks, "according to God, created in justice and holiness of truth" [6]—a generation wholly spiritual yet nonetheless real, the principle of which is neither flesh, nor blood, nor the will of man, but the gratuitous will of God; [7] a mysterious birth which springs not from seed subject to corruption, but from seed

---

[5] *In II Sent.*, dist. 26, q.1, a.3: "The spiritual nature which a man possesses, he possesses by grace, as the Apostle states in his Epistle to the Corinthians: 'By the grace of God I am what I am,' . . . The *esse* refers to essence just as the *posse* refers to potency. . . . Christ tells us that we have been reborn through water and the Holy Ghost. . . . But this regeneration is through grace . . . for it is through grace that we are made sons of God. . . . Therefore, as through natural generation we receive a natural being, so through spiritual generation we receive a spiritual being. . . .

"As a thing cannot perform a particular operation unless it possesses a particular essence or nature, so we cannot perform a divine operation unless we have a divine nature. Therefore the theological virtues, which reside in the faculties of the soul and which perform divine actions, . . . cannot perform those actions unless we possess that divine nature which is obtained through grace. Hence, as those virtues reside in the faculties through which we act spiritually, so grace dwells in the very essence of the soul and through it we are spiritual. . . . For we can neither act nor be acted upon spiritually unless we are essentially spiritual. . . .

"As the created image of God consists in the essence of the soul and in the three faculties (because man has been made to the likeness of God and in him there is the one essence of the soul and three faculties or powers, just as in God there is one nature and three Persons), so in man there is the re-created image, so far as grace is in the essence of the soul while the three theological virtues are in the three faculties. . . .

"As God in the act of creation first produces the nature or essence of a thing and then produces the proper and natural accidents, so in the act of re-creation He first perfects the essence of the soul through grace and then perfects the natural potencies through the virtues."

[6] Eph. 4:24.
[7] Jas. 1:18.

THE MYSTICAL EVOLUTION

incorruptible by the word of God;[8] a generation and a birth as indispensable for living a life of grace as are carnal generation and birth for natural life. For it is Truth itself who has said: "Unless a man be born again of water and the Holy Ghost, he cannot enter into the kingdom of God. That which is born of the flesh is flesh, and that which is born of the Spirit is spirit."[9] And the Council of Trent says: "Unless (men) are born again in Christ they can never be justified; it is only by that rebirth through the merit of His passion, that the grace of justification is bestowed upon them."[10]

But what at bottom is the nature of this Divine and regenerating element which baptism gives to our souls, and which makes us godlike? What constitutes this root principle of supernatural life which a sacrament confers on us and which other sacred ordinances [the other sacraments] are destined to preserve, to increase, and, should we be so unhappy as to lose it, to revive within us? And since this precious gift, the formative cause of our justification and deification, is nothing else but sanctifying grace, then what is this grace which sanctifies us?[11]

This is the great problem which our poor reason will never be able to solve. We can adequately appreciate it only by contemplating and admiring it through the sacred symbols of revelation and the sublime statements divinely inspired or canonized by the Church. Sanctifying grace is eternal life in Jesus Christ. It is the gift of God, the living water that quenches all thirst and is converted into a fountain of life and divine energies in the souls that receive it.

But Jesus said this same thing of the Holy Ghost whom His followers were to receive.[12] Therefore it is this divine Spirit who, by animating and informing us, makes us live divinely by the grace of His own communication and the communication of His grace.[13]

---

[8] I Pet. 1:23.
[9] John 3:5 f.
[10] Sess. VI, chap. 3.
[11] Froget, *The Indwelling of the Holy Spirit*, pp. 141 f.
[12] John 4:10-15; 7:39.
[13] St. Paul desires for the faithful "the grace of our Lord Jesus Christ and the communication of the Holy Ghost." According to St. Gertrude (*Exercises*, no. 5), he undoubtedly wishes to indicate to us by these words that "the communication of the Holy Ghost is in its origins identified with the grace of the Savior. We know that the Holy Ghost is given to us in baptism and confirmation. . . . There is, then, in us a body and a soul, which are the elements of the natural life; and the Holy Ghost, who is the principle of the supernatural life. And that is why St. Paul also tells us that we are temples of the Holy Ghost." Cf. St. Thomas, *In III Sent.*, dist. 13, q.2, a.2. Petau (*De Trinit.*, Bk. I, chaps. 4 ff.) attempts to prove the following proposition with a number of magnificent texts from the Fathers: "The very sub-

THE DIVINE LIFE OF GRACE

Subjectively and intrinsically this communicated grace is, according to the statement of the Council of Trent: [14] "the justice of God, not by which He Himself is just, but by which He makes us just; by which, namely, we are renewed in the spirit of our mind; and not only reputedly so, but we are called and truly are just." That grace, then, is like an impression of the divine seal within us; the unction which permeates us, soothes, beautifies, and sanctifies us and fills us with fragrance, causing us to exhale the sweet odor of Jesus Christ and to be pleasing to God. It is, in brief, a transformation or interior renewal which is effected in our very nature through the communication, animation, and vivifying presence of the sanctifying Spirit.[15]

2. GRACE AND NATURE

This grace infinitely exceeds every created faculty and all the natural powers of any creature, however exalted it may be, and this for the reason that grace is a participation of the divine life, sanctity, and justice.[16] To pass from simply human life to a life that is so exalted, we need the animation of a new vital principle that far transcends our own. We need a principle which will give us a new sort of being, a second nature with its own proper faculties or potencies, so that we shall be able to live and work divinely and produce fruits of eternal life. That second nature is constituted in us by sanctifying grace, which is rooted in the transformed souls. The faculties of that new nature are the theological virtues and the gifts of the Holy Ghost, which give us new powers or faculties at the same time that they elevate our own native potencies to produce supernatural works in accordance with the motion of the Spirit, who animates us and whose power gives to them all the value and merit they possess.[17]

---

stance of the Holy Ghost is the gift that is divinely infused to make men just and adoptive sons of God, so that He is like a certain form, so to speak, whereby the supernatural state is constituted."

[14] Sess. VI, chap. 6.

[15] See IIIa, q.7, a.13.

[16] Ia IIae, q.112, a.1: "Now the gift of grace surpasses every capability of created nature since it is nothing short of a partaking of the Divine Nature. . . . For it is as necessary that God alone should deify, bestowing a partaking of the Divine Nature by a participated likeness, as it is impossible that anything save fire should enkindle."

[17] Ia IIae, q.114, a.3: "For thus the value of its merit (i.e., of a good work) depends upon the power of the Holy Ghost moving us to life everlasting according to John iv. 14: *Shall become in him a fount of water springing up into life everlasting.*"

THE MYSTICAL EVOLUTION

The rest of the infused virtues, as also all inspirations and actual graces, are so many other dispositions or higher forces which invigorate our inherent weakness and aid us to work according to God.[18]

But the divine Consoler is not content with renewing, beautifying, enriching, and strengthening us with His graces, virtues, and most precious gifts. He even communicates Himself to us and gives Himself as the true superior principle of our happiness and new life.[19] The Spirit of Jesus Christ desires to be the true life of all Christian souls.[20]

Therefore, in addition to the elevation and transformation which the supernatural gifts produce in us there is an ineffable union with God Himself. The Giver comes with His gifts. Therefore, as when He gives us our natural being He remains with us as the author of the natural order by His essence, presence, and power, so when He gives us our supernatural being, He remains with us as the author of this order, as a loving Father, a faithful Friend, a true Spouse, and a sweet Guest of the soul. He resides in the soul as in His chosen tem-

---

[18] Froget, *The Indwelling of the Holy Spirit*, pp. 192 f.: "Let us recall, that to fit man to elicit such aids as will finally lead him to the beatific vision, God first pours into his soul sanctifying grace, which functions in the supernatural order as the human soul in the natural order. Just as the soul, by uniting with the body, transforms a vile and inert mass into a living human being, so grace, the true form of a far superior order of life, communicates to him who receives it, a new being, spiritual and Divine, which makes him a Christian and a child of God. And because being is the proper perfection of essence, just as operation is the proper perfection of the faculties, grace it is that is communicated to the very essence of the soul, which makes it participate in the Divine nature; whereas the virtues which accompany grace have their seat in the different human faculties, which they elevate and perfect by adding to their natural forces a higher and more powerful energy, which is supernatural." *Ibid.*, p. 194: "The infused virtues are therefore planted in the soul to lift up and transform our natural energies that they may be capable of performing actions beyond nature's powers and meritorious for eternal life. They are grafted on to the soul like scions or grafts of a better and nobler tree grafted upon a wild stock. In passing through the graft the natural sap is purified of its defects, so that the tree which before bore sour and wild fruits now yields sweet and delicious fruits."

[19] "And yet the Holy Ghost is possessed by man, and dwells within him, in the very gift itself of sanctifying grace. Hence the Holy Ghost Himself is given and sent." "But we are said to possess what we can freely use or enjoy as we please. . . . Thus a divine person can be *given* and can be a *gift*." See Ia, q.43, a.3; q.38, a.1.

[20] Palmieri, *Comment. in Gal.*, p. 89: "It is a life of which Christ is the principle; it is the life of Christ who operates in and through Paul himself and therefore Christ lives in him. *Vivit in me Christus*—that is, Christ is the interior principle (*per Spiritum suum*) of my thoughts and deeds."

ple and takes His delight therein; even more, He is the true principle of that divine life which He communicates. From His intimate presence, communication, and vivifying action, there results in the soul sanctifying grace, by which He enriches and beautifies it, renews, and transforms it to the very depths of its substance. He penetrates and envelops it as a fire does iron and as a ray of light shining through purest crystal.[21]

At the same time He infuses the supernatural virtues and gifts, which perfect and transform the potencies in which they are rooted, so that they may produce fruits of eternal life. As a result, it is the soul itself which, thus renewed, enriched, and transformed, works

---

[21] Blessed Henry Suso states that "the creature, since it is limited, cannot be communicated; but God, since He infinitely transcends all creatures, is communicated in essence and in such a way that in this infinite and intimate communication He gives His very substance, communicated according to the distinction of Persons" (*Unión*, chap. 5).

"The soul," says Father Juan de los Angeles (*Triunfos del amor de Dios*, II, chap. 12), "is made to participate with God Himself through a divine infiltration, that is, through grace, a divine gift which comes down from God and saturates our whole being so that we are deified."

Father Hugon, writing in the *Revue Thomiste*, March, 1905, p. 45, says: "Grace is an outpouring of the divine being in us, for God alone can communicate to us His nature and His life."

Monsabré, *Conference 18:* "The natural presence of God adds nothing to the nature of a being; but His supernatural presence transforms it. The former leaves the natural potencies with their own proper activity, but the supernatural presence raises them to a divine mode of operation. Through the former He communicates natural being to the creature, but through this other supernatural presence He makes it participate in His own being, nature, and life. . . . Grace is to the soul what the soul is to the body; that is, a form which makes the soul a supernatural being, as the soul makes the body a human being. . . . Through grace the divine substance itself is communicated to us and works in us; but we ourselves are cooperators and for that reason we can merit. . . . Whether grace is a quality or a substance does not matter. What we know for certain is that it is a permanent gift which affects the very essence of the soul and, by making it participate truly in the divine nature and life, it makes man a true son of God and it confers on him incomparable beauty and grandeur. . . . God creates in us, by means of His efficacious presence, a new life; and it is characteristic of life that it be as permanent a principle as the substance which it vivifies. . . . O wonderful mystery! I am totally penetrated by God and I share in His nature and His life. . . . How could I ever deny it . . . since His seed is within me . . . and the power of His generation is that which conserves me? (Cf. I John 3:9; 5:18.) . . . There is little that we can say, and it would avail us more to attend to the language of Scripture and to listen to the sublime interpretations of the holy Fathers. . . . Grace! It is God who is united with us as fire is united with iron and makes it like unto itself. . . . It is God who compenetrates us as rays of light in transparent bodies which receive the properties of light. . . . By means of grace man produces divine actions; and these are of more value than all those which proceed from his nature alone."

now as a beloved child of God, although all its value and merit proceed from the power of the Spirit who animates it. This entire process, as Bainvel observes,[22] is clearly illustrated by comparing it to the grafting of trees. "The ingrafted tree produces fruits which of itself it could never produce. It produces them through the juice of the sap and its natural potencies, as if they were its own. Grafting improves the fruits, but the tree is also necessary; and evidently the condition of the tree does not fail to influence the taste of the fruit."

Theologians summarize all this by saying that grace is in us as a second nature whose operative potencies are the supernatural virtues or gifts. Contrary to what Protestants suppose, it is nature itself which, by grace and the virtues, becomes renewed and transformed in such a way that it thereby produces what it was incapable of producing of itself. According to them, our nature is essentially vitiated and corrupt and from it no good can come, even with the help of grace. For that reason they deem useless and even impossible the full cooperation of man in a supernatural act. But if that were true, then sin would have penetrated more deeply than grace and there would not be that grace which more abounds, as the Apostle teaches.[23] Reparation would not only be incomplete; it would be futile. In vain would the performance of good works be recommended to us with such great earnestness.[24] Far from attempting to absorb nature in grace, Protestants have been forced to maintain the contrary extreme. They leave only the grafting without the tree, they leave grace without the cooperation of nature. Therefore the divine grafting is sterile, or rather, it cannot take root in such impious souls [25] who do not aspire to be renewed in the Spirit and who seek no more than a nominal justice, which is imputed and fictitious.[26] For that reason there remains for them nothing but natural fruits. So it is that Protestants in general have given themselves over

---

[22] *Nature et surnaturel*, pp. 154-56.
[23] Rom. 5:20.
[24] Phil. 2:12: "With fear and trembling work out your salvation." I Cor. 15:58: ". . . always abounding in the work of the Lord, knowing that your labor is not in vain in the Lord." II Pet. 1:10: "Wherefore, brethren, labor the more that by good works you may make sure your calling and election."
[25] Wisd. 1:4: "For wisdom will not enter into a malicious soul, nor swell in a body subject to sins."
[26] Wisd. 1:5: "For the holy spirit of discipline will flee from the deceitful . . . and he shall not abide when iniquity cometh in."

THE DIVINE LIFE OF GRACE

to pure naturalism, in spite of the fact that they call themselves Christians or "reformed Christians." [27]

3. OUR CREATION IN JESUS CHRIST

The New Testament frequently speaks to us of the new life which Jesus brought to us that He might fill us with it and thereby restore and revivify us. From the very beginning of his Gospel, St. John shows us the life contained in the Word, like an infinite fountain which pours forth its torrents on all those who believe in His name and who receive Him.[28] He gives them the power to become sons of God. So it is that we have passed from death to life, and not to any kind of life, but to an eternal life which remains in us.[29] The Lord vivified us who were dead by pardoning us our sins.[30] For this did Jesus come, "that they may have life, and may have it more abundantly." [31] "For God so loved the world as to give His only-begotten Son, that whosoever believeth in Him may not perish, but may have life everlasting." [32] For this was He sent into the world, that the world might be saved by Him.

This principle of supernatural life which is infused in us is called

---

[27] The famous Protestant doctor, Sabatier, like the rationalists, being unwilling to recognize that divine life which renews and enriches the human being, even ridiculed "the old and futile antithesis of the natural and the supernatural." As a result, observes Fonsegrive (*Le Catholicisme et la vie de l'esprit*, pp. 34 f.), "this disciple of Jesus is condemned to naturalism and rationalism, because he let the meaning of the doctrine of salvation grow vapid, placing all religion under natural morality, without any idea of that which he calls the kingdom of God. . . . Catholicism professes that the kingdom of heaven is nothing other than divinization, and on this fundamental belief rests the whole doctrine of the supernatural. . . . It is evident that it cannot be natural to man to be made a participant in the divine nature. Hence the necessity of grace and, presupposing the Fall, the necessity of redemption; hence the necessity of the sacraments, which, by divine power, introduce, maintain, or renew the kingdom of grace; hence the necessity of the priesthood and the Church and the superiority of religion over natural morality as that which completes and perfects the latter. . . . Through charity, the gift of grace, the divine life makes circulate through the veins of the Christian the mysterious sap of Jesus Christ: *I am the vine, you are the branches*. . . . Formerly Luther absorbed nature in grace; today the Protestants absorb grace in nature and make the supernatural disappear. But Catholicism has always proclaimed the distinction and harmony between grace and nature. Our fathers fought against Luther in defense of human nature and free will; we today must defend the dominion of the supernatural against the sons of Luther."

[28] John 1:12.
[29] *Ibid.*, 3:14 f.
[30] Col. 2:13.
[31] John 10:10.
[32] *Ibid.*, 3:16 f.

THE MYSTICAL EVOLUTION

now the seed of God, now a participation in the divine nature; and it establishes true filiation.[33] "Thus the divine life is to the soul," says Bellamy,[34] "what the soul is to the body, and even more so. The distinction of natures does not prevent grace from being truly inherent in the justified soul. It will never be proved that justification, instead of being an interior renovation, is, as the Protestants would wish it, a merely extrinsic favor of God, a conventional imputation of the merits of Jesus Christ. There is in us a true life of an order superior to that of natural life. Scripture speaks to us repeatedly of a spiritual renewal and regeneration.[35] By this regeneration the Christian is established in justice and possesses the Holy Ghost in his heart. He carries within himself the seal, the unction, and even the participation of the divine nature.[36] These energetic expressions are either devoid of meaning or they designate, as the Council of Trent teaches, something inherent in the regenerated soul." It is, then, as if we possessed a new being, created in Jesus Christ and born of God.[37] This is the vital principle that remains dormant in infants, only to become in adults a source of activity.[38]

This supernatural life does not take anything away from nature nor impede its full development. Rather it heals it, completes and perfects it. Grace raises nature from the abasement in which it finds itself; it strengthens and enriches the energies of nature and directs them to an incomparably higher goal. Grace renders easy the performance of good works and prompts us to perform more perfectly and for nobler reasons the very works which we are obliged to do according to the natural law. At the same time it enables us to work divinely and to produce the works of eternal life in conformity with our higher calling.

Grace is not, then, as the generality of Protestants falsely presume, a kind of mantle that makes us appear to be clothed in Jesus Christ but permits all the stains of sin and the ugliness of our vitiated nature to remain in our souls. Nor is it, as some of them maintain, the mere

---

[33] See I John 3:1, 2, 9; II Pet. 1:4.
[34] *La vie surnaturelle*, pp. 56 f.
[35] Eph. 4:23; Titus 3:14.
[36] Rom. 5:19; 8:11; John 3:9; II Cor. 1:21 f.; II Pet. 1:4.
[37] Eph. 2:10; John 1:12 f.
[38] St. Augustine, *De peccat. remiss.*, Bk. I, chap. 9: "The grace of illumination and justification is infused into infants. . . . It is given to them as a principle of life, although in a hidden manner; but in adults it bursts forth into activity."

THE DIVINE LIFE OF GRACE

presence of the Holy Ghost, who makes us resplendent with His divine holiness and justice, while we ourselves do not truly possess these attributes. Rather grace is something intimate and something personal; something which has been made truly our own. It purifies us, justifies us, renews us, reforms and transforms us, regenerates and re-creates us. Grace makes us like unto God, inasmuch as it makes us His sons, and therefore truly just; yet not with the same incommunicable justice by which He is just, but with a participated justice, by which we become just because He has made us so.[39]

As we received a natural being and a human life through creation, so through regeneration we receive a supernatural quality and a new Christian life. Hence justification is an added creation, a recreation, which gives us something new, not human, but divine. We have been truly created in Jesus Christ in order to live another type of life.[40] Clearly, creation refers to the very roots of substantial being and not merely to accidents and much less to appearances.

We have received with grace a new reality which is more than substantial. In its own order of being it elevates us even more than the infusion of a soul would elevate a corpse or a mineral substance. Without grace we were, in respect to divine life, like fetid cadavers or lifeless chemical substances; but with grace we are translated from death to life, from the kingdom of darkness to that of divine light. We were rough, unfinished stones in Adam's quarry and, what is worse, we were broken and deformed. Yet from those very stones Jesus Christ was able to raise up true sons of God.[41]

By the very fact that grace regenerates us, it makes us sons of Him

---

[39] If the Holy Ghost is truly the soul which gives life and unity to the mystical body of the Church and animates and directs in an orderly fashion all the members living in it, then grace is the internal and proper form of each of these elements which constitute that living body. Through grace they become interiorly transfigured according to the degree of communication and animation which they receive from the divine Spirit. And this, says St. Thomas (*III Sent.*, dist. 13, q.2, a.2), is "the ultimate and principal perfection of the entire mystical body."

"Since the Holy Ghost is given to us," says Alexander of Hales (*Summ.*, III, q.61, m.2, a.1, 2), "He transforms us into a divine species so that the soul itself is assimilated to God. . . . First there is the transforming form, and this in uncreated grace; . . . then there is the transformed form which remains in the soul after the transformation, and this is created grace."

[40] Eph. 2:10: "For we are His workmanship, created in Christ Jesus in good works, which God hath prepared that we should walk in them."

[41] Matt. 3:9; Luke 3:8: "God is able of these stones to raise up children to Abraham."

who adopts us through grace. Through grace we receive that new life, not human but divine, which is as eternal as is His own. It formally constitutes the new entity which we possess and makes us what we are in Jesus Christ.[42] Being perfect Christians, we can say that we are not now properly the sons of the old Adam, but of the new; for now we are no longer made like to the image of an earthly man, but a celestial one.[43] We are reborn through God to a new life in which everything is renewed and refashioned.[44] For that purpose we receive the Spirit of sanctification to renew us according to the spirit of our mind, despoiling us of the old man. We are now a new creature, or at least the seed or rudiment of a divine creature: *Initium aliquod creaturae ejus.*

As the rational life, which manifests itself in due time, gives us a being which is more essential or substantial than the sensitive being, and that without destroying the latter but only subordinating it; so the life of the Spirit gives us an entity which is as superior to the rational being as the divine is to the human.[45]

Since God is infinitely nobler than our humble nature, or even any other possible nature, in order to deify us, to make us like unto Himself and His true sons, He must work in us a most profound renewal and transformation. That internal and proper form by which He makes us just and godlike, not reputedly or in appearance merely, but truly so, is that which, for lack of another name, is called grace or created justice. It is so called to distinguish it from that justice by which He Himself is just and which could only be imputed to us but never communicated. But that term, although useful at times to avoid the errors of Protestantism and certain pantheistic difficulties, if taken too rigorously, is frequently an occasion of serious mis-

---

[42] See I Cor. 15:10: "But by the grace of God I am what I am."
[43] See II Cor. 3:18.
[44] Apoc. 21:5; II Cor. 5:17.
[45] Says Fr. Juan de los Angeles (*Conquista, Diálogo I*, section 5): "The Apostle dared to say while yet in mortal flesh: *I live, now not I, but Christ liveth in me,* which is as if he had said: In the spiritual order I have the accidental being of man, but the substantial being of God. Such does His Majesty desire for us, that we should be men accidentally but gods substantially, ruled by His Spirit and conformable to His will. . . . The soul transformed in God through love lives more for God than for itself. . . . It resides more where it loves than where it lives . . . , it belongs more to the thing loved than to itself. In this sense it can be said that the just are men accidentally and gods substantially for it is through the divine Spirit that they are governed and live."

takes, which reduce to our human level the inestimable gift of God.

If this grace were part of nature itself, or rather of natural creation, it would be unable to deify that nature. At best our nature, on receiving that new form, would participate with some other higher natural being; it would not enjoy the ineffable participation in the divine life itself.

Grace being a participation in eternal life, cannot perish in the state of glory; neither can charity, which will never disappear. Faith and hope, implying imperfection, will vanish in glory. Therefore these last two virtues are not inseparable properties of grace and can subsist without it. Although souls possessing only faith and hope do not have life, the Holy Ghost arouses in them certain corresponding acts in order thereby to dispose them to receive life.[46]

Communication of the Holy Ghost

To understand better the contrast between created grace and uncreated grace, which is the Holy Ghost Himself (although it should rather be said: between participated grace and grace in itself), it is well for us to recall the comprehensive and significant organic symbol mentioned previously. That grace which in itself is life eternal appeared among us and was manifested to us in time. It is communicated to us and shared by us when we are incorporated in our Lord Jesus Christ. It makes us sons of God and participants in the divine nature [47] and, by reason of that fact, gods,[48] children of the light and the light of the world.[49]

---

[46] See IIIa, q.8, a.3, ad 2um. (Here St. Thomas says: "Such as are tainted with these [mortal] sins are not members of Christ actually, but potentially, unless perhaps imperfectly, by formless faith, which unites to God, relatively but not simply—viz., so that man partakes of the life of grace. For as it is written (Jas. 2:20): *Faith without works is dead*. Yet such as these receive from Christ a certain vital act—i.e. to believe."—Tr.)

[47] See II Pet. 1:4.

[48] St. Augustine, *In Ps. 49*: "So we have been made sons of God and even gods."

[49] Matt. 5:14; Eph. 5:8; I Thess. 5:5. "If grace appeared in Jesus Christ," observes St. Gertrude (*Exercises*, no. 5), "it is because it already existed in Him. . . . When one speaks of grace, two types must be considered; uncreated grace, which is God Himself; and created or communicated grace, through which we participate in God. . . . Grace is the communication which God makes to us of that which He is by

THE MYSTICAL EVOLUTION

1. LIFE OF THE HEAD AND THE MEMBERS

In Jesus Christ as the Head resides the plenitude of the Spirit which thence redounds to all the members who offer no resistance, and in this way they are "brought to life together with Christ" (Eph. 2:5). But the participated life which is proper and immanent to each member and which is received from the Head in a special giving is something quite distinct from the fullness of life in Christ as Head, the giver and dispenser of graces. Nevertheless all grace is eternal life in Jesus Christ, of whose fullness we have all received. Hence all who truly live the life of grace can say—and that with the more truth as they live more intensely—that Christ is their life and that it is no longer they who live, but Christ lives in them.

The Savior Himself desires that all the faithful should be one with Him.[50] This was accomplished in the early Christians of whom it is written [51] that they had but one heart and one soul in God. Yet they lived and were justified, not by that capital grace by which He lives and is just and is the one who justifies, but by that grace which is derived from Him as the Head and which informs and vivifies the various members who live in Him and through Him.

The grace of God comes to us through the communication of the Holy Ghost, the Spirit of truth, who resides fully in Jesus and who is His Spirit. This communication justifies, vivifies, renews, and sanctifies us, not with the selfsame holiness with which the divine Consoler is eternally and absolutely the Holy Ghost, but with that holiness which is imparted by Him and which leaves us vivified, re-

---

nature. In other words, when we receive created grace it is through a participation with uncreated grace, which is God. Thereby we become sharers in the divine nature."

St. John of the Cross, *Living Flame of Love*, stanza II, no. 34: "The substance of this soul, although it is not the substance of God, for into this it cannot be substantially changed, is nevertheless united in Him and absorbed in Him, and is thus God by participation in God, which comes to pass in this perfect state of the spiritual life."

"The divine substance," says Fr. Godínez (*Teología Mística*, Bk. IV, chap. 11), "can be so intimately incorporated with the soul that the soul acts in imitation of divinity and knows and loves divinity. Then God is like a soul which assists our own soul, through which He produces salutary acts which neither habitual grace nor charity could produce outside this union."

[50] John 17:11-26.
[51] Acts 4:32.

THE DIVINE LIFE OF GRACE

newed, and sanctified, and makes us living members of Christ.[52]

We all drink of the same Spirit who is the fount of living water which bursts forth from our hearts unto life eternal. We all ought to live the life of Christ as so many branches grafted on this divine tree, so that we may grow in Him and put forth abundant fruit. For if we do not receive His divine sap, we shall be cut off and be cast into the fire (John 15:6).

Each member of His body, except the more vital and indispensable organs, such as the heart or the head, can degenerate and die to that life of grace but can again recover it by being revivified. But the grace itself which is received neither dies nor is revived. It withdraws, as it were, but returns again when it finds no obstacles, for grace in itself is eternal life, although communicated and restricted by time.

Grace can be compared to light, which is not destroyed when it ceases to illumine some body. When the body is removed from the light or when obstacles are placed in the way, the light follows its course or its rays are reflected. Then the object ceases to be illumined, although it can again be illumined if it is placed once more in the rays of the light. Something similar happens in the case of participated grace; as St. Thomas says,[53] "for grace is caused in man by the presence of the Godhead, as light in the air by the presence of the sun."

Sanctifying vivification is a work proper to the Spirit of Jesus Christ. That which is proper to us is to be sanctified by receiving His vivifying communication, that is, the participation of His grace; or to cease to be sanctified through our own malice; or to recover our sanctification through His goodness and mercy. That participated

---

[52] Eph. 2:20–22: "You are . . . built upon the foundation of the apostles and prophets, Jesus Christ Himself being the chief cornerstone. In whom all the building, being framed together, groweth up into a holy temple in the Lord. In whom you also are built together into a habitation of God in the Spirit."

Col. 2:19: ". . . not holding the head, from which the whole body, by joints and bands, being supplied with nourishment and compacted, groweth unto the increase of God."

St. Augustine, *Confessions*, Bk. XII, chap. 15: "Great is the difference between the illuminating Light and the light which is illumined; between creating Wisdom and created wisdom; between justifying Justice and the justice that is effected through justification."

[53] IIIa, q.7, a.13.

grace which we possess as long as we have the good fortune to be living members of the Church, the mystical body whose soul is the Holy Ghost, cannot be destroyed nor contaminated, and it possesses the power of deifying us. This grace is "a certain pure emanation of the glory of the Almighty God; and therefore no defiled thing cometh into her. For she is the brightness of eternal light: and the unspotted mirror of God's majesty, and the image of His goodness." [54] So grace is effected in us by the vivifying presence of the Sun of justice, and it is not destroyed when we force Him to withdraw from us; but it does withdraw with Him and thus leaves us in darkness or even in the shadows of death.[55]

We have already seen some of the comparisons used by the holy doctors, who understood this doctrine keenly. St. Basil, and with him St. Bernard, Tauler, and the generality of mystics, compares the deified soul to iron tested in a furnace, where, without ceasing to be iron, it becomes totally incandescent. Yet the fire or participated heat by which the iron is made igneous is one thing, and the fire which inflames the iron is another. Taken out of the furnace, the iron loses its fiery condition; but as long as the iron is inflamed, it not only appears to be fiery, but actually is. This is a weak image; yet, considering our limited capacity, it is one of the most significant examples of the mysterious operation of the divine Spirit, who is quite rightly called the fountain of life and the fire of divine love, who infuses His charity into our hearts and renews them with His loving unction.

St. Cyril of Alexandria says that He deifies us by impressing Himself on us both within and without as a living seal which reproduces in us the true likeness of the only-begotten Son of God. St. Basil [56] represents Him, now as a sculptor who makes that divine image appear in souls; now as a sun which penetrates souls and makes them radiant with His own light, like illuminated clouds, pouring forth on them life, immortality, and true holiness; again as a most precious ointment whose very essence we absorb so that we exhale the good

---

[54] Wisd. 7:25 f.
[55] Luke 1:79. Father Juan de los Angeles, *Diálogos sobre la conquista del Reino de Dios*, X, section 7: "When God enters the soul there is heat and life; when He leaves, there is coldness, bitterness, and death."
[56] *Adv. Eunom.*, I, 5.

odor of Jesus Christ.[57] St. Ambrose considers Him as a painter who copies in souls the lifelike image of the Word.[58] But no one has ever expressed what sanctifying grace is as exactly and as profoundly as did the two princes of the apostles. St. Peter calls it a participation in the divine nature in which is contained the most precious and magnificent gifts. St. Paul speaks of it as eternal life.

2. DIGNITY OF THE SONS OF GOD

So it is that sanctifying grace enters into our very substance to deify it. Since God's nature is pure life, by participating therein we cannot help but share in the divine life, in eternal life itself which resides in the Father and was manifested to us for the precise purpose of being communicated to us. Possessing divine life, we ought also to possess the divine operations conformable to it, that we may proceed as true sons of God. Thus will be understood the magnificent renewal which the Spirit of Jesus Christ works in us and which constitutes the pledge of eternal life. In this way also will be understood that mysterious rebirth through water and the Holy Ghost which was so puzzling to Nicodemus.

This rebirth raises us to a dignity which seems to be almost identical with that of the only-begotten Son of the Father, to whose image we are fashioned as His brothers and coheirs, and who is for that reason called the first-born among many brethren. Through His grace we become, in a certain sense, what He is by nature. But here there is an infinite gap which keeps the saints humble, because by virtue of their growth in God they are able to feel more keenly the vast difference between their own nothingness and the divine all; between their own miseries and the inexhaustible mercy of our most loving Savior who humbled Himself in order to exalt us.[59]

---

[57] *Op. cit.*, I, 3.
[58] *Hexaem.*, Bk. VI, chaps. 7 f.
[59] "What the Son of God was not by nature in virtue of His first birth," says St. Fulgence (*Epist.* 17), "He became through grace in virtue of His second birth, that we might become, through the grace of our second birth, that which we were not naturally through our first birth. God's human birth is a grace which He gives us. We receive also an entirely gratuitous grace when, through the munificence of a God born of man, we become participants in the divine nature."

St. Leo, *Sermo in Nativitate Domini*, 4: "Although it is from one and the same compassion that the Creator grants anything to a creature, it is less to be wondered at that men should attain to divinity than that God should descend to humanity."

3. NATURAL AND ADOPTIVE FILIATION

The divine filiation of Jesus Christ as the Word of the Father is necessary and natural; ours is the result of a free and gratuitous adoption. He was born God of God before all the ages, and through Him all things were made. We, having been born of Adam, are reborn of God and for God in the time assigned by His compassion and liberality. He, as consubstantial with the Father, is the eternal splendor of His glory and the most perfect image of His substance. In the measure in which we happily lose our earthly form by putting off the old man, we become transformed in His. We are made more like unto Him and we progress from glory to glory according as we permit ourselves to be led, fashioned, and informed by the Spirit, who makes us adopted sons of God.[60] He is from all eternity "begotten and not made"; we are re-engendered in time and made gods by participation. So He is eternally God because He cannot be otherwise; we are deified only to a degree by the grace of adoption, from which we can degenerate through our own wretched malice.[61]

We have been incorporated with Him through baptism and made His members. We became grafted on Him so that through His power we might produce fruits of glory and works worthy of eternal life. Since He is our Head, we work under His continual influence and we participate in His very divinity, His infinite power, and His life and His Spirit. This it is that gives divine energy to our faculties and infinite value to our actions.[62]

---

[60] Cf. IIIa, q.32, a.3; *ibid.*, ad 2um: "And if the likeness be perfect, the sonship is perfect, whether in God or in man. But if the likeness be imperfect, the sonship is imperfect.... Men who are fashioned spiritually by the Holy Ghost cannot be called sons of God in that perfect sense of sonship. And therefore they are called sons of God in respect of imperfect sonship, which is by reason of the likeness of grace."

[61] "When, through His deifying influence," says St. Dionysius (*Divinis nominibus*, XI), "many are made gods according to the capacity of each one, it appears that there is a division or multiplication of the one God. But He is the principle of this deification . . . and is essentially the unique and undivided God."

[62] The Church says in the Mass: "O God, make us share in the divinity of Him who desired to clothe Himself in our humanity." In the Office of Corpus Christi the Church repeats the words of St. Athanasius quoted by St. Thomas Aquinas: "The Son of God assumed our nature to make us gods."

THE DIVINE LIFE OF GRACE

4. PARTICIPATION IN THE SPIRIT OF JESUS CHRIST

Jesus as Head has the plenitude of the Spirit which He communicates to us according to the measure of His giving that we may always be moved by Him in the works of our particular ministry, without ever resisting or afflicting Him, but always following His loving impulses and faithfully cooperating with His actions, to become perfect in all things. Thus we are Christians and sons of God in the measure in which we permit ourselves to be governed and moved by the Spirit of Jesus Christ.

Monsignor Gay states that it is theologically indisputable that our Lord as man could do nothing that was not under the impulse of the Holy Ghost and dependent on Him. We also, he continues, in Jesus, through Jesus, and like Jesus, possess within ourselves the Holy Ghost, who becomes our own proper and characteristic spirit, as it is written: "But he who cleaves to the Lord is one spirit with Him" (I Cor. 6:17). In another place: "If any man have not the Spirit of Christ, he is none of His" (Rom. 8:9). On the contrary, they who are animated and governed by the Spirit [63] are true Christians, true brothers and members of Christ, and true sons of the Father. The Holy Ghost is in us as the living and permanent foundation of our supernatural being, and He becomes the principle of all the works which this holy state can produce.[64]

Bellamy adds that the Holy Ghost is in a certain sense the proper and personal Spirit of Jesus Christ who works in Him both as God and as man.[65] He constitutes, so to speak, Christ's birthright, and He is the official consecrator of Christ's holy humanity, to which is forever communicated whatever is possible over and above the hypostatic union. In us, on the other hand, the Holy Ghost is always a stranger whose coming can be slow and whose parting sudden. He gives Himself, or rather He abandons Himself, to us with great liberality, yet with a certain reserve.

Far from being perfect at the beginning, the measure of this giving can increase incessantly and in marvelous proportions, accord-

---

[63] Rom. 8:14.
[64] Gay, *De la vie et des vertus chrétiennes*, X.
[65] *Op. cit.*, p. 248. Cf. IIIa, q.8, a.1, ad 1um: "To give grace or the Holy Ghost belongs to Christ as He is God, authoritatively; but instrumentally it belongs also to Him as man, inasmuch as His manhood is the instrument of His Godhead."

ing as we abandon ourselves to Him more and more through love. There are countless grades of the divine union whose bonds can go on tightening indefinitely. This union, as it becomes more and more intimate, is augmented through an increase of sanctifying grace, or, rather, through a real and more perfect assimilation with God. Whatever may be the origin of this grace and the way it is manifested, it is always accompanied by a more intimate and more abundant communication of the Holy Ghost. So between Him and the just soul there is effected a new manner and a new grade of union, which St. Thomas calls an invisible mission of the divine Paraclete.[66] Our union with the Holy Ghost, then, is progressive.[67]

ARTICLE III

Adoption and Justification

Although our filiation is adoptive and not natural, the adoption itself is not purely juridical or, so to speak a *fictio juris*. It is something very real, for actually it is a certain participation in the eternal filiation itself. God does whatever He says. For Him, to speak is to produce; and when He calls us sons, He makes us to be precisely that.[1]

Characteristics of Divine Adoption

The first distinctive note of this divine adoption is its reality. The Angelic Doctor[2] states that God, by adopting us, makes us capable of enjoying His eternal heritage. Through it also He grants us a rebirth in His own Spirit; and thus we pass from a purely natural life to the life of grace, which is the seed of glory and a true participation in the divine nature.[3]

---

[66] Cf. Ia, q.43, a.6.
[67] Bellamy, *La vie surnaturelle*, p. 248.
[1] Cf. IIIa, q.23, a.1, ad 2um: "Wherefore as by the whole work of creation the Divine goodness is communicated to all creatures in a certain likeness, so by the work of adoption, the likeness of natural sonship is communicated to men."
[2] See IIIa, q.23, a.1.
[3] "If we are adopted sons of God," says Terrien (*Grâce et la gloire*, I, pp. 78, 98), "not in any manner whatsoever, but through a rebirth in Him, how could it be that our adoption does not imply a certain divine reality within us? Can there be any generation without a certain communication of nature between the father and the

THE DIVINE LIFE OF GRACE

The second distinctive characteristic of this adoption is that it is spontaneous, free, and loving. Men adopt because they lack children of their own in whom they can find delight, but God the Father finds infinite pleasure and delight in His only-begotten Son. He possesses a Son so lovable, so beloved, and so loving that the result of this mutual love with which they love each other eternally, is personal Love, the charity of God, the Spirit of love, who is the bond of their infinite complacency. Yet, in order that those inexhaustible delights might redound to us, God willed to communicate to us this same Spirit of love as a pledge of our true adoption. He loved us to the extent of giving us His only-begotten Son, that in Him we might possess eternal life (John 3:16).

The third distinctive quality of this divine adoption is that it is rich, precious, and fruitful, since it makes us co-heirs with Christ Himself (Rom. 8:17). It gives us full rights to His inheritance, which is not limited, paltry, and perishable, but eternal and infinite; for it is the kingdom of God,[4] or rather God Himself.[5] Such is the heritage of the servants of the Lord: the full possession of His riches, His happiness, and His own Spirit.[6] This heritage is not reserved for us for the future only; but He gives it to us immediately and permits us to enjoy even now some of its first fruits. The kingdom of God is within us. We need only penetrate into the center of our

---

son? And what would that communication be in this case but a transfusion of the infinite substance into the regenerated man? . . . Such is the constitutive perfection of the sons of God in its supreme reality. It effects in us an irradiation of the most elevated, intimate, profound, and naturally incommunicable divine substance. Therefore he who is in God's grace, as His son, is exalted above all created nature."

"How greatly this adoption exceeds that of men!" exclaims Father Monsabré (*Conference 18*). "All the tenderness of the human heart is impotent to transform the nature of an adopted son who, to his credit or discredit, preserves in his veins the blood of his progenitors. Nothing can be changed through adoption; the most that can be granted to the adopted son is a title with its accompanying rights. But God goes beyond that. He works in the very core of our substance and He re-engenders us supernaturally, communicating His own nature to us. . . . We are called His sons because we are truly that: *Nominamur et sumus*. Hence the title of gods in the beautiful expression of St. Augustine: *Si filii Dei facti sumus, et dii facti sumus*" (*In Ps. 49*).

[4] Cf. Ia IIae, q.114, a.3: "And the worth of the work depends on the dignity of grace, whereby a man, being made a partaker of the Divine Nature, is adopted as a son of God, to whom the inheritance is due by right of adoption, according to Rom. viii. 17: *If sons, heirs also*."

[5] Gen. 15:1: "I am thy protector, and thy reward exceeding great."

[6] Isa. 54:17; 55:1-6.

hearts and the very core of our souls to find God with all His infinite riches.[7] There the eternal fountain of living water bursts forth and quenches all earthly thirst. There sweetly reposes the loving Consoler, the pledge and security of everlasting life, in whom we shall find all good things and innumerable riches through His hands.[8] Thus are we filled with grace and truth in the likeness of the firstborn and model.[9]

The fourth quality of this adoption is that it is both general and particular. If human adoption takes place when there is already a legitimate heir, the true son becomes disturbed and prejudiced because of the lessening of his heritage and the division of paternal affection. But the charity of the Son of God is such that, instead of not wishing co-heirs, He acquired them at the cost of His own blood. The inexhaustible and priceless riches of His glory, far from being diminished by the addition of new heirs, seems rather to be increased on being shared by others.[10] Likewise, although He enjoys absolute happiness in the bosom of the Father, He finds its complement or redundance in the bosom of His brethren.[11] And the joy of these brethren increases in the measure in which new members arrive to

---

[7] Our Lord once said to St. Catherine of Siena, "Contemplate me in the core of your heart and you will see that I am your Creator and you will be happy" (*Life,* I, chap. 10).

Tauler, *Institutions*, chap. 34: "It is certain that God has selected for Himself a special place in the soul, which is the very essence from which the superior faculties flow. . . . There the divine image shines forth and it bears such a resemblance to the Creator that he who knows the image, knows Him. God is present most intimately in this depth of the soul, and there He continuously engenders His Word; for wherever the Father is, it is necessary that He generate. He also engenders us that we may be His sons through the grace of adoption. From this depth of the soul, then, proceeds all of a man's life, action, and merit, which three things God Himself works in man. . . . But to be aware of this rebirth and the presence of God in a way that will produce abundant fruits, they must recollect the faculties of the soul at their very source, where they touch the naked essence of the soul. There they will discover the presence of God, and with this knowledge they will be enraptured and, in a certain way, divinized. Then all the works which flow from them will be rendered divine."

[8] Wisd. 7:11.

[9] John 1:14.

[10] St. Augustine, *In Ps. 49*, no. 2: "Such is the charity of that true Heir that He wished to have co-heirs. . . . For that heritage in which we are co-heirs of Christ is not lessened by an abundance of possessors, nor is it made more limited because of the multiplicity of heirs. There is as much for many as for a few; as much for each one as there is for all."

[11] Prov. 8:31: "And my delights were to be with the children of men."

THE DIVINE LIFE OF GRACE

drink of the fountain of life and to see the light of His light.[12]

If material goods diminish and are exhausted on being distributed, spiritual goods, even in this life, are rather increased and perfected. A good teacher loses none of his knowledge by communicating it to his students. Rather he enlarges and increases his own prestige and happiness by forming great thinkers who will perpetuate his renown and render his doctrine fruitful. What will happen, then, in the case of spiritual goods that are infinite and eternal?

The essential joy of the saints, as St. Bernard says, is to possess God, to see Him, to be with Him, and to live in Him, for in Him are contained all riches and glory. Instead of this happiness being diminished, each saint enjoys it as many times over as there are lovable co-heirs, and he loves them as himself as long as they possess this integral happiness of union with God. Moreover, these co-heirs, deified as they are and totally resplendent with infinite light, see each other as most clear mirrors in which is vividly reproduced that eternal Beauty which holds them in perpetual admiration. The sight of this reflection in their own souls and in the souls of others would be sufficient of itself to keep them perpetually absorbed. So that ineffable joy is in no way lessened, but it redounds from heart to heart with never-ending echoes.

Here, then, is the great mystery of our deification through grace. Here, as St. Leo says, is the greatest of gifts: the privilege of calling God by the sweet name of Father,[13] and Jesus Christ by the name of Brother. By virtue of our adoption as sons there is restored to us that likeness to God which we would have had in the state of original justice. At the same time, through the life of grace, there is communicated to us a new image; and so faithful is this image that we are truly deified and made living reproductions of God, participants in His nature, His Spirit, and His divine life. So it is that we are His true sons and we can in all truth be called gods. "I have said: You are gods and all of you the sons of the most High" (Ps. 81:6). But we are created gods, whereas He alone is the living and eternal

---

[12] Ps. 35:9 f.: "They shall be inebriated with the plenty of Thy house; and Thou shalt make them drink of the torrent of Thy pleasure. For with Thee is the fountain of life; and in Thy light we shall see light."

[13] *Sermo 4 de Nativitate:* "This gift by which God calls man His son and man calls God his Father exceeds all other gifts."

Jahweh who, being God by nature, can make us gods by participation.[14] He is the deifying God; we are deified gods.[15]

By the same token that we ought to glory in that lofty dignity, we ought also to act in conformity with it to the end that God will be glorified in us as we glorify ourselves in Him, as St. Leo observes.[16] In all things we should act and shine forth as sons of God, that our light may illumine the rest of men and that by our good works we may glorify the heavenly Father.[17]

Sanctification and Justification

From what has been said it can be seen clearly how the soul becomes supernaturalized, transformed, and, at least initially, deified in its very essence and all its faculties through adoptive filiation, vivification by the Holy Ghost, and the indwelling of the entire Trinity. That which formerly could not perform any functions other than those of mere earthly life, and even many of those with difficulty and imperfectly, now finds itself possessed of divine potencies and energies capable of performing glorious works. Now the soul lives a truly heavenly life whose connatural goal is the full vision and possession of God.

1. THE POWER OF GRACE AND ITS MANIFESTATIONS

That sanctifying grace which lifts us to the dignity of sons of the Most High is an endless source of power which enables us to soar from earth to heaven, from the human to the divine. It is the mystical

---

[14] St. Augustine, *In Ps. 49*, no. 2: "He calls men gods because they are deified by His grace and not because they are born of His substance."

[15] Eadmer, a disciple of St. Anselm, writes in his *Liber de similit.*, chap. 66: "God makes other gods, but in such a fashion that He alone is the God who deifies and we are the gods who are deified."

St. Augustine, *Sermo 66*: "God desires to make you a god; not by nature as is His own Son, but through grace and adoption. . . . Cease, then, to be a son of Adam. Put on Jesus Christ, and then you will no longer be a man; and ceasing to be a man, neither will you be a liar."

[16] *Sermo 25 de Nativitate*, chap. 3.

[17] Matt. 5:16. "The son of adoption whose works correspond to his birth," observes Terrien (*La grâce et la gloire*, I, 272), "can truly apply to himself the words of the only-begotten Son: *He who sees me sees also the Father* (John 14:9), not to exalt himself, but to exalt Him who has done such great things in him. For I am a mirror wherein the divine face shines forth; a portrait of Himself which He has made by communicating His grace to me."

fount of living water which the Savior promised to us and merited for us and, like a jet of infinite pressure, it springs forth from our hearts unto life eternal.

Our Lord Jesus Christ, who, by infusing His grace in us, gives us the inestimable power to become sons of God, is that symbolic bridge between earth and heaven which St. Catherine of Siena saw.[18] All of us are able to pass over this bridge and thus arrive at the otherwise inaccessible heights of the divinity, where the face of the Father is seen and intimate fellowship is possessed with the divine Persons. But the generality of men are so blind and insensible that, although they have been invited to pass over this bridge, they prefer to perish by drowning or to live like crawling things, wriggling through the mire of human corruption, in darkness and the shadows of death, rather than exert a little violence on self and soar to those sublime regions of light and life where they can breathe the pure and refreshing air.

As St. John says, grace is the seed of God which regenerates us so that we may be able to live as gods even now. According to the expression of St. Peter, it is a real and formal participation in the divine nature. St. Paul calls it true eternal life, which begins to develop now and will flourish forever in glory when, being manifested as we are, we shall appear like unto God, seeing Him as He is and knowing Him as we are known by Him.

Even if our nature possessed its primitive integrity as it was in Adam, we could say little more than we have said about this mysterious deification which we should feel, enjoy, and admire in silence, rather than seek to describe. Since our nature was deeply confused, wounded, and corrupted through sin, to be deified it must not only be elevated, but also renewed, cured, purified, and restored to its primitive integrity so that the natural image of the Creator may once again shine forth in it in full splendor. Then upon this natural image there must be superimposed the likeness of the living God, one and three, as He is in Himself.

Hence it follows that purely elevating grace is not sufficient, but there is required a type of grace which heals at the same time that it elevates our nature. Hence also the laborious and most fruitful work of purification and renewal must accompany this entire process

---

[18] *Dialogue*, chaps. 21–31.

of deification, or rather of illumination and union, and this even after a soul has worked hard and long. Even the most valiant saints found this work of purification very painful, for there is no one who does not feel unspeakable sorrow and agony in stripping himself "of the old man with his deeds, and putting on the new"; [19] to purge himself of every trace of the old leaven of malice and iniquity in order to become "the unleavened bread of sincerity and truth." [20]

Without this work of purification, which so commends itself to our cooperation and generous efforts, we would enjoy nothing more than a painless and easy growth comparable to that of well-fed and healthy children. We would receive and react to the beneficent and delightful impulses of the vivifying Spirit without any resistance or obstacle and even with great satisfaction and pleasure. But as those vital impulses are tasted and enjoyed more and more intensely we experience the bitterness and pain of extricating ourselves from vicious habits and from the seeds of malice which are so deeply rooted that they cannot be completely eradicated save at the cost of poignant suffering. Especially at the beginning, when we are still full of evil, we must use the greatest possible self-violence so that the seeds of malice will not dominate us. We must die to ourselves that we may live for God alone, for it is only after we have been greatly purged of the taste for earthly things that we can have a palate healthy enough to taste and enjoy divine things.[21]

Since grace is eternal life, the introduction of this new life produces in us a profound renewal and transformation. It is indisputable that we die to the supernatural life if we have the incomparable misfortune to commit a grave sin and that we rise from death to life when we return to the friendship of God through sincere repentance. For, as we are reborn through baptism, through penance we are resurrected. We recover the life which was lost and we again become living members of Christ, holy temples of God, and saints in the incipient stage.

As a result of sin, which places an obstacle to grace and which must be destroyed by justification, the infinite goodness and mercy of the Father stand out in greater contrast. Although He looks upon

---

[19] Col. 3:9 f.
[20] See I Cor. 5:8.
[21] St. Augustine, *Confessions*, VII, chap. 16.

sinners as His enemies, He yet desires to deify them and is ready to offer them life even after they have renounced it so ungratefully.[22] This fact should prompt us to correspond with God by a more fervent and disinterested love, seeing what love He has shown in offering us pardon so frequently and so readily and in bidding us to share in His glory. Yet He also desires that we truly merit glory, although from Him comes the power of meriting. Therefore, in crowning our works, says St. Augustine, He crowns His own gifts.[23]

Although grace instantaneously vivifies us and translates us from the shadows of death to the kingdom of light, destroying the sin which made us archenemies of God, it does not, on that account, completely destroy the *fomes peccati*, the disordered concupiscence which inclines us to evil. By dint of our own efforts and with the help of grace, we must subdue and conquer it, expurgating and rooting out the ferment of evil, all remnants of vice, and every seed of sin and corruption. And since vicious habits are so deeply rooted in us and have become, as it were, a second nature, thence follows the painfulness of the task in banishing them entirely. Thence the ceaseless vigilance and sacrifices entailed in the work of our purification; thence our inability to progress in sanctity and justice without exerting violence to rid ourselves of all obstacles.

2. FALSITY OF IMPUTED JUSTICE

Those unfortunate heretics who reduce the whole function of grace to the covering of our sins by the mantle of Christ and make of justification a petrification of souls in the uniform molds of a sanctity that is imputed and not real, have little knowledge of these mysteries of renewal. They are unable to understand the cries of pain which this renewal extracts from even the most generous and heroic souls. According to these heretics, restoration in justice is simply an amnesty granted to all who trust in the merits of the Savior. Without any change in the internal disposition of the sinner, the deserved punishment is remitted and he is permitted to enter into the society of the sons of God. Radically he continues to be a servant of sin. He is a whitened sepulcher, filled with the same stench and corruption as before, retaining all his evil desires and his evil life.

[22] Eph. 2:5.
[23] *Ep. 194*, no. 19.

If anyone does not truly live in Christ, he cannot grow in Him. Not possessing true justice, he will be unable to augment it by good works and the faithful practice of the Christian virtues. Therefore these heretics were consistent in their error by denying the necessity of good works and considering them useless and even derogatory of the merits of Jesus Christ.

One need not spend time in pondering over these things because it is evident how contrary all this is to divine revelation and Christian experience. The Savior came into this world that we might possess eternal life and that we might be made sons of God by being reborn in Him and that we might live a life that is more and more divine.[24] Therefore He translated us from death to life; from the power of darkness and the slavery of sin to the bright and glorious liberty of the sons of God,[25] making us true sons, and not sons in name only.[26]

This filiation interiorly transforms us to the point of deifying us, and deification is impossible without a true interior justification which destroys the sin that has caused an estrangement between God and ourselves.[27] Through the grace of justification we are changed from enemies and sons of wrath into true sons and friends of the eternal Father, and then it is that He takes delight in us. "The love of God," says the Angelic Doctor,[28] "infuses and creates goodness."

3. JUSTIFICATION A RENEWAL AND CONTINUAL GROWTH

The Council of Trent [29] teaches: "Justification is not merely the remission of sins, but it is also the sanctification and renovation of the inner man." So it is, according to the teaching of St. Augustine, that "He who justifies us also deifies us, because in justifying us, He makes us sons of God." [30] Therefore the divine Lamb "who takes away the sin of the world" (John 1:29) purifies us and with His own blood cleanses our conscience of dead works to serve the living God.[31] He is come "that transgression may be finished, and sin may

[24] John 1:3, 10.
[25] Col. 1:13; I Pet. 2:9.
[26] See I John 3:1-11.
[27] Isa. 59:2.
[28] See Ia, q. 20, a. 2.
[29] Sess. VI, can. 7.
[30] *In Ps. 49*, 2.
[31] Heb. 1:3; 9:14.

THE DIVINE LIFE OF GRACE

have an end, and iniquity may be abolished, and everlasting justice may be brought." [82]

For that reason we ought also to repent and be converted, that our sins may be blotted out (Acts 3:19). Then the Lord, who through His mercy blots out our sins (Isa. 43:25), will pour upon us clean water and cleanse us from all our filthiness (Ezech. 36:25). Even the saints beg Him to wash them yet more from their iniquity and cleanse them from their sin for they know that He will wash them and they will be made whiter than snow and He will give them joy and gladness (Ps. 50). [83] Through the ardor of charity their "sins shall melt away, as the ice in the fair warm weather." [84] The Lord will put away our iniquities and He will cast all our sins into the bottom of the sea (Mich. 7:19). [85]

The Apostle, after reminding the faithful of the most sorrowful state in which they formerly found themselves, adds: "And such some of you were; but you are washed, but you are sanctified, but you are justified in the name of our Lord Jesus Christ and the spirit of our God." [86] And this divine Spirit of sanctification, through whom we are created for eternal life by receiving His divine grace, continually renews the face of our hearts.[37] He charges us to be renewed in the spirit of our mind and to put on the new man (Eph. 4:23 f.) and to make sure our calling and election by means of good works (II Pet. 1:10) through which we cooperate as much as possible in our renewal.[38]

In this way, using the waters of grace which wash and give fertility, we shall grow luxuriant, like a tree planted near the running waters which shall bring forth its fruit in due season (Ps. 1:3). We

---

[82] Dan. 9:24.

[83] Ps. 50:12: "Create a clean heart in me, O God; and renew a right spirit within my bowels."

[84] Ecclus. 3:17.

[85] Ps. 102:12: "As far as the east is from the west, so far hath He removed our iniquities from us."

[86] See I Cor. 6:11.

[87] Ps. 103:30.

[88] Rom. 12:2: "Be reformed in the newness of your mind." Eph. 4:22-24: "To put off, according to former conversation, the old man, who is corrupted according to the desire of error. And be renewed in the spirit of your mind; and put on the new man, who according to God is created in justice and holiness of truth." I Pet. 2:9: "You are a chosen generation, a kingly priesthood, a holy nation, a purchased people; that you may declare His virtues, who hath called you out of darkness into His marvelous light."

shall flourish like the palm tree and prosper like the cedars of Lebanon (Ps. 91:13).[39] Thus does divine wisdom fructify in us and we begin to exhale, not the stench of whitened sepulchers, but the sweet odor of Christ (II Cor. 2:15).[40]

After we have been reborn of the Holy Ghost and renewed in Him, we shall be truly spiritual [41] and that to such an extent that He can then say to our souls, "Thou art all fair, O my love, and there is not a spot in thee." [42] Growing in all things according to Him, we shall "be filled unto all the fullness of God" (Eph. 3:19).[43]

Such is and ought to be the process of our deification. We are not

---

[39] Ecclus. 24:15-32.
[40] Titus 2:11 f.: "For the grace of God our Savior hath appeared to all men, instructing us, that, denying ungodliness and worldly desires, we may live soberly and justly and godly in this world."
[41] John 3:6: "That which is born of the Spirit is spirit." II Cor. 3:18: "But we all beholding the glory of the Lord with open face, are transformed into the same image from glory to glory, as by the Spirit of the Lord."
[42] Cant. 4:7.
[43] St. Augustine, *De peccatorum meritis et remissione*, Bk. II, chaps. 9-12: "Men become sons of God when they begin to live in newness of spirit, and to be renewed as to the inner man after the image of Him who created them (Col. 3:10). For it is not from the moment of a man's baptism that all his old infirmity is destroyed. Renewal begins with the remission of all his sins and so far as he possesses a taste for spiritual things. All things else are accomplished in hope, even to the full renewal which we shall experience at the resurrection of the dead. This, too, our Lord calls a regeneration, though not such as occurs through baptism, but a regeneration wherein there is brought to perfection in the body that which has begun in the spirit.... We have therefore even now begun to be like Him, having the first fruits of the Spirit; but yet we are still unlike Him by reason of the remnants of the old nature.... Finally, we shall possess this adoption completely, and the sinful man within us will totally disappear, and no one will be able to find any trace of him."

St. John of the Cross, *Ascent of Mt. Carmel*, Bk. II, chap. 5: "And thus, when the soul rids itself totally of that which is repugnant to the Divine will and conforms not with it, it is transformed in God through love, ... therefore must the soul be stripped of all things created, and of its own actions and abilities—namely, of its understanding, liking and feeling—so that, when all that is unlike God and unconformed to Him is cast out, the soul may receive the likeness of God; and nothing will then remain in it that is not the will of God, and it will thus be transformed in God.... Wherefore God communicates Himself most to that soul that has progressed farthest in love; namely, that has its will in closest conformity with the will of God. And the soul that has attained complete conformity and likeness of will is totally united and transformed in God supernaturally.... In thus allowing God to work in it, the soul (having rid itself of every mist and stain of the creatures ...) is at once illumined and transformed in God, and God communicates to it His supernatural Being, in such wise that it appears to be God Himself, and has all that God Himself has. And this union comes to pass when God grants the soul this supernatural favour, that all the things of God and the soul are one in participant transformation; and the soul seems to be God rather than a soul, and is indeed

so many mummies under the illusory wrappings of an imputed justice, nor are we solidified in a changeless mold. Rather we are obligated to cooperate with the grace which vivifies us in order to increase it and to make fruitful the gifts we have received. Therefore we ought to grow in the grace and knowledge of God, and we ought to die more and more to ourselves in order to live more and more perfectly in Him. We must be renewed from day to day and continually purify ourselves of the traces of the old ferment of iniquity and be cleansed of the earthly dust which imperceptibly clings to us. By truly cooperating with the grace which heals, purifies, and deifies us; by being washed and inebriated with the blood of Christ in the sacraments of penance and the Eucharist; and by sharing His sufferings, we can repair the evils of our fallen state and, by virtue of His most precious blood, arrive at a much greater height than we could have attained in the state of original innocence.[44] Indeed, many saints believe that even had man retained his original innocence the divine Word would have become incarnate in order to deify us and to serve as the key to the supernatural order,[45] but He would not then have suffered for our redemption. By the same token, we would not now have the good fortune of sharing in His triumphs, which are as sublime as they are bloody and as glorious as they are sorrowful, for we would not be able to follow Him valiantly along the arduous path to Calvary.

God by participation; although it is true that its natural being, though thus transformed, is as distinct from the Being of God as it was before."

Fr. Juan de los Angeles, quoting Tauler, says: "Having abandoned its own proper form and being transformed and elevated beyond all possible images, the soul arrives at a state which defies all representation by created things. It is completely deified and in all that it is and all that it does, it is God who is and works in it. All that God is by nature, the soul is through grace and, although it does not cease to be a creature, it is wholly divinized or deified and has the appearance of God. ... The created spirit is dissolved and submerged in the uncreated Spirit. ... Now nothing remains but pure divinity and essential unity" (*Triunfos*, II, chap. 7).

[44] See Blessed Henry Suso, *Eternal Wisdom*, VII.

[45] Sauvé, *Le culte du Cœur de Jésus*, 24: "To unite us not only to the works of God, to the ideal and to the memory of God, but to God Himself; to establish a vital relationship between our soul and the inner life of God, such is in very deed the purpose of the Incarnation and the love of God as manifested in this mystery. It was to make possible this union, these vital relations with God Himself and the most holy Trinity, that the infinite Life in the bosom of the Father desired to unite Himself to human nature and thus it was that He came to be the source of the divine life."

THE MYSTICAL EVOLUTION

4. CATHOLIC DOGMAS AND TRUE PROGRESS

Our dogmas, which are the true laws of eternal life, far from being incompatible with true progress (which is the modern accusation), presuppose and intimate a progress so prodigious that it knows no limit other than deification. They would make men like unto God in being, life, knowledge, love, and work. They would unite men to God in such a way that they are engulfed in Him and transformed into Him.[46]

Actually, the modern accusation can be made only against those outside the Church who reduce justification to a mere imputation of the merits of Christ. According to them, good works are unable to contribute anything to its increase, and evil works, however horrible they may be, cannot impede it, as long as faith remains. As if faith without good works performed under the influence of the Holy Ghost were not dead.[47]

Catholicism, "instead of giving to its heroes the immobility of statues cast in the mold of an imputed, uniform, and immutable justice, incessantly spurs them to activity. It stimulates their most generous efforts and encourages them in the struggle. Nor does it hesitate to place the infinite ideal of sanctity at a distance far beyond even the most perfect." [48]

Catholicism continually commands all men in the words of St. Paul to "walk worthy of God, in all things pleasing, being fruitful in every good work and increasing in the knowledge of God." [49] The desire of the Church is expressed in the words of St. John: "and he that is just, let him be justified still; and he that is holy, let him

---

[46] See II Cor. 3:18: "But we all . . . are transformed into the same image."

[47] Jas. 2:26: "For even as the body without the spirit is dead, so also faith without works is dead."

[48] Bellamy, *La vie surnaturelle*, p. 284. "If there is any doctrine," he adds, "that favors the true development of human activity and impresses on liberty a continuous ascent to the supreme good, it is certainly the Catholic dogma of variable justification and progressive sanctity with no limit but the infinite. Grace, then, truly merits the name of supernatural life and has, therefore, the phases of growth and virility. It is comparable to an edifice in which each good work is a stone and the stories are always ascending until the roof touches the heavens."

Jaffré, *Sacrifice et sacrement*, pp. 135 f.: "We are but the beginning of a divine creature, and we must offer to God what we are in order to become that which as yet we are not."

[49] Col. 1:10.

THE DIVINE LIFE OF GRACE

be sanctified still." [50] The Apostle admonishes us: "For you were heretofore darkness, but now light in the Lord. Walk, then, as children of the light. For the fruit of the light is in all goodness and justice and truth; proving what is well pleasing to God; and have no fellowship with the unfruitful works of darkness, but rather reprove them." [51] "For if you live according to the flesh, you shall die; but if by the Spirit you mortify the deeds of the flesh, you shall live." [52] So we shall live by God's grace as communicated to us by the Holy Ghost, and this is eternal life in Jesus Christ. Living in Jesus and animated by His Spirit, we shall be His members and true sons of God.

If we work as true sons, the seed of eternal life will be happily developed in us. We shall continue the work of Jesus and we shall be other Christs, or better still, we shall be Jesus Christ Himself as reproduced in us. We shall effect the growth and perfection of that mystical body to which we belong; for, as St. Augustine says, "The sons of God are the body of His only-begotten Son. He is the Head and we, the members. Together we constitute the Son of God." [53] Rightly does he exclaim in another place, "Let us admire and rejoice, for we have become Christ; since the Church is, as the Apostle says (Eph. 1:23), His body and His fullness." [54]

In spite of this, Sabatier, the famous professor of Protestant theology at the Sorbonne, never ceased to proclaim the "quietude and sterility of Catholicism" and the "progress and fecundity of Protestantism" in his fantastic notion of "direct union with God without the need of a Church or the shackles of good works." His subsequent history resulted in what would logically follow: he imprudently broke away from the Son of God, since he would not share the life of His mystical body. In the beginning, Sabatier recognized the divinity of the Savior as a "fundamental dogma without which Christianity would be reduced to a purely philosophic system." At the end, he denied this dogma and was content to recognize only God the Father. In line with his thought, he should also have denied the

---

[50] Apoc. 22:11. I Pet. 3:15: "But sanctify the Lord Christ in your hearts."
[51] Eph. 5:8-11.
[52] Rom. 8:13.
[53] *In Joan.*, X, 3.
[54] *Loc. cit.*, XXI.

THE MYSTICAL EVOLUTION

Father, as did many of his confreres, for the idea which he had of the Father was more pantheistic than Christian.[55]

Actually, no one can know the true God the Father except through the Son; [56] so neither does anyone hear the Son, if he does not hear His Church.[57] The Church announces to all men, with St. John, the eternal life which was in the Father and which was manifested to us, so that all might form one society with us and that our society might be with the Father and His Son Jesus Christ. "He that hath the Son, hath life. He that hath not the Son, hath not life." [58]

Sabatier praises Protestantism because it is conformable to the worldly type of nature, work, and thought. But the truly Christian spirit is incompatible with the mundane spirit. "We know that we are of God, and the whole world is seated in wickedness. And we know that the Son of God is come; and He hath given us understanding, that we may know the true God and may be in His true Son. . . . Whosoever is born of God, committeth not sin; for His seed abideth in him, and he cannot sin.   Behold what manner of charity the Father hath bestowed upon us, that we should be called and should be the sons of God. Therefore the world knoweth not us because it knew not Him." [59]

"As all things of His divine power which appertain to life and godliness are given us, through the knowledge of Him who hath called us by His own proper glory and virtue. By whom He hath given us most great and precious promises, that by these you may

---

[55] In 1868, when seeking for some sort of theology, he said that the divinity of the Lord is the capital question which distinguishes the Gospel from that which is not. "If Jesus Christ is only a man, then, however great He might be, Christianity loses its characteristic of absolute truth and becomes a mere philosophy. If Jesus is the Son of God, Christianity is a true revelation. . . . I believe and confess with St. Peter that Jesus is the Christ, the Son of the living God" (*Revue de theol.*, May, 1897). But after he became a professor of Protestant theology, he no longer believed in Christ. "I do not know," he wrote (*Relig. et cult.*, p. 192), "whence Jesus Christ comes or how he entered into this world."

[56] Luke 10:16.

[57] "The voice of God and that of the Church are one and the same thing, for He it is who speaks through the mouth of the Church, our Mother, in the teachings, counsels, and commands which she gives us" (Tauler, as quoted by Denifle in *Das Geistliche Leben*, chap. 7).

[58] I John 5:11 f. Cf. *ibid.*, 1:1-3.

[59] See I John 5:19 f.; 3:9 f., 1 f.

THE DIVINE LIFE OF GRACE

be made partakers of the divine nature, flying the corruption of that concupiscence which is in the world." [60]

We should exercise ourselves in every manner of virtue and good works and through them glorify the Father and become resplendent with His light. Then we shall not appear empty and without fruit in the presence of Jesus Christ. But he who neglects this "is blind and groping, having forgotten that he was purged from his old sins. Therefore, brethren, labor the more, that by good works you may make sure your calling and election. For doing these things, you shall not sin at any time." [61]

Simple faith, without works in opposition to those of the world, is not only dead, but it will bring about greater condemnation. Those who are content with faith alone deny Christ in practice and show themselves to be completely worldly. Therefore do they talk much of the world, and the world listens to them and does not hate or persecute them as it does good Catholics. The Protestants do not deserve this deference which rightfully belongs to the servants of Christ.

"They are of the world; therefore of the world they speak, and the world heareth them." [62] "Now we have received not the spirit of this world, but the Spirit that is of God; that we may know the things that are given us from God. Which things also we speak, not in the learned words of human wisdom, but in the doctrine of the Spirit, comparing spiritual things with spiritual." [63]

All things in the kingdom of God are hidden mysteries which the wise of this world know not, nor can they know. But we Catholics, who are sons of God, know them; and we experience them because God revealed them to us and made us feel them through His Spirit, who penetrates all things. He did this that we might not be seduced by the snares of the world nor be infected by its harmful influence. To the world, which lacks understanding, those lofty truths which constitute the life and experience of the Church seem foolish and extravagant. Actually the foolishness is in him who loses himself in the search for vain appearances, illusions, and snares; he who does not

---

[60] See II Pet. 1:3-5.
[61] *Ibid.*, 1:9 f.
[62] See I John 4:5.
[63] See I Cor. 2:12 f.

see the Truth nor discover the Light of the world, nor do the *unum necessarium*.[64] But he who has a living faith and hope becomes holy, just as God is holy; [65] and perfect, just as the heavenly Father is perfect.[66]

APPENDIX

1. Incorporation with Christ and Progressive Renewal

"Our incorporation with Christ is not merely a transformation and metamorphosis. It is also a true creation, the production of a new being with new rights and duties. 'Do you not know,' asks the Apostle (Rom. 6:3-8), 'that all we who have been baptized into Christ Jesus have been baptized into His death? For we were buried with Him by means of baptism into death, in order that, as Christ has arisen from the dead through the glory of the Father, so we may walk in newness of life. For if we have been united with Him in the likeness of His death, we shall be so in the likeness of His resurrection also. For we know that our old self has been crucified with Him, in order that the body of sin may be destroyed, that we may no longer be slaves to sin; for he who is dead is acquitted of sin. But if we have died with Christ, we believe that we shall also live together with Christ' " (Prat, "La morale de St. Paul" in *Revue practique d'apolog.*, May, 1907, p. 140).

According to St. Paul, as Prat observes (*ibid.*, pp. 141-46), baptism buries us with Jesus Christ, causing us to die to ourselves in order to rise with Him to a new life. He grafts us on Himself that we may be able to partake of the divine sap through union with His mystical body. In that sacramental bath of regeneration there is a death and a resurrection; a burial and a return to the light. These four qualities which are effected by the rite which symbolizes them, should endure and continually increase.

Death to sin is the definite characteristic of baptism because Jesus, by His death, destroyed the rule of sin and, by making us live with Him, He also enables us to share in His triumph. Unlike physical death, spiritual death is capable of increase. Further, merely to pre-

---
[64] See I Cor. 2.
[65] See I John 3:3.
[66] Matt. 5:48.

serve this death to sin is not enough; it must be intensified. "For you are dead, and your life is hid with Christ in God. . . . Mortify therefore your members" (Col. 3:3–5). The Christian ought to press ever forward in the mortification of Jesus. Likewise the life of grace ought not only to be maintained but also developed, strengthened, and renewed. "Therefore, if you be risen with Christ, seek the things that are above. . . . Mind the things that are above, not the things that are upon the earth" (Col. 3:1 f.).

Our burial in Christ ought to follow a similar pattern. Hence, after reminding us that we have been baptized in Christ and have put on Christ, the Apostle does not weary of telling us also that we must continue to put on Christ more and more (Gal. 3:27; Rom. 13:14). Finally, although baptism is itself a sort of enlightenment, St. Paul implores for the neophytes new lights which are ever more brilliant and he invites them to pass from glory to glory (Eph. 1:18; II Cor. 3:18).

The new life which we receive in baptism brings with it a new series of operations and establishes in us four new relations with their corresponding duties. These are, namely: 1. filiation to the Father; 2. consecration by the Holy Ghost; 3. mystical identity with Jesus Christ; and 4. supernatural solidarity with the other members of Christ.

From the filial relation flows the obligation of honoring and imitating the Father as His beloved sons. We must strive to be perfect and holy like unto Him in order to please and glorify Him and thereby make ourselves deserving of the eternal and glorious heritage.

From the possession of the Spirit of adoption there follows the obligation of not afflicting or suppressing Him and especially of not destroying or profaning His temple. In return He will enrich us with His charisms, His gifts, His fruits, the sacramental graces, and the graces proper to our state in life. He will pour forth on us His unction and His light and will engrave the divine law on our hearts with indelible characters of love, and this law will become an internal and autonomous norm of our lives. Thus is explained the enigmatic statement: "But if you are led by the Spirit, you are not under the law" (Gal. 5:18). The Christian can obey the law without being under the law, for the law is no longer for him an exterior yoke but an inner principle that animates and moves him. Far from enslaving or oppressing him, "the law of the Spirit of life, in Christ Jesus, hath delivered me from the law of sin and of death" (Rom. 8:2). For that reason St. Augustine says that we must die to all that is death in order that we may live in the true life alone (*Confessions*, Bk. VIII, chap. 11).

The relation of mystical identity with Christ brings us to a conformity with Him in all things and likewise to a perfect harmony with the rest of His members. St. Paul therefore urges us not only to imitate Christ in Himself and His saints and faithful followers (I Cor. 11:1), but to mold ourselves to Him and to be transformed in Him. We must put on Jesus Christ and be filled with His sentiments until we realize perfectly that ideal: "And I live, now not I; but Christ liveth in me" (Gal. 2:20). To put on Jesus Christ, to be transformed to His likeness, to live in Him (Rom. 6:11), and to grow in Him (Eph. 4:15): these are all various expressions of the same idea. They infer much more than the simple imitation of Christ. They imply the effort to assimilate more and more to ourselves the divine sap of the Redeemer.

St. Paul describes the constitution of that mystical body, whose Head is Jesus and whose soul is the Holy Ghost, and he shows the need for a diversity of members enjoying the one life. From this he deduces the reciprocal obligations of charity, solidarity, and justice which each member must contribute to the common good (cf. I Cor. 12:12–27; Rom. 12:4 f.; Eph. 12: 4–16; Col. 2:19). All must strive to arrive at the perfection of the Head. That there may be harmony and proportion in the mystical Christ, each one of the faithful must endeavor to grow according to the measure of Jesus Christ and they must endeavor to hold as the ideal His own plenitude.

2. Adoration and Reparation

"Were it not for sin, everything could be comprised under *adoration*. But sin has desolated the world and our soul, and therefore *reparation* is necessary. Nor is it sufficient to make reparation for ourselves alone... The soul which is not engaged in making reparation for others, loves but little. It does not understand the heart of Jesus. Reparation for our own sins can be a work of fear. What is performed for others is a work of love and, if any fear inspires it, it is what is prompted by charity. Rightly ought we to fear for the great number of terrible sinners on whom the stroke of divine justice is to be inflicted" (Sauvé, *Le culte du C. de J.*, elév. 52).

3. Creation and Restoration in the World; the Intervention of Mary

"Here is a mystery which I desire to reveal to you," said the eternal Father to St. Magdalen of Pazzi. "Even if Adam had not sinned, the Word would nevertheless have become incarnate. But He would not in that case have enjoyed the title of Victor nor would He have enjoyed the honors of triumph. The glory which you would have then received would be only partially merited . . . and My goodness and mercy would not have shone forth so brilliantly. Moreover, eternal glory and the beatific vision and all the goods which flow therefrom would not have been granted you to such a high degree. The blood of the Word, flowing over your souls, has made them much more pure and beautiful and at the same time much more suitable for the divine union. The sight of that blood moves Me to bestow on you still more love and to communicate to you a greater knowledge and more perfect enjoyment of My divinity. . . . There is the same difference between the glory which I now give you and that which I would have given you had My Word not died in satisfaction for your sins, as there is between the merits of the Redeemer, which are the sole basis of your hope, and those merits which are purely human. . . . So, you see, My much loved daughter and beloved spouse of My only-begotten Son, how useful Mary has been to you through her *fiat* by which she gave the Word to you. She was for you a source of very great blessings" (*Œuvres*, III, chap. 3).

"In this instant was decreed first of all, that the divine Word should assume flesh and should become visible. . . . This hypostatic union of the second Person of the most holy Trinity I understood necessarily to have been the first incentive and object on account of which, before all others, the divine intelligence and will issued *ad extra*. . . . It was also befitting and, as it were, necessary, that if

God should create many creatures, He should create them in such harmony and subordination, as would be the most admirable and glorious within the reach of possibility. In conformity with this, therefore, they must be subordinate to a supreme Chief, who should be as far as possible united immediately with God, so that through Him they may have communication and connection with His Divinity. For these and for other reasons (which I cannot explain), the dignity of the works of God could be provided for only by the Incarnation of the Word; through Him creation should possess the most beautiful order, which without Him was impossible." Then follows "the decree and predestination of the Mother of the Divine Word incarnate; for here, I understand, was ordained that pure Creature before aught else whatever. Thus, before all other creatures, was she conceived in the divine mind." In regard to the creation of the angels, the saintly visionary writes: "As they are created first of all for the glory of God, to assist before His divine Majesty and to know and love Him, so secondarily they are ordained to assist, glorify and honor, reverence and serve the deified humanity of the eternal Word, recognizing Him as Head, and honoring Him also in his Mother, the most holy Mary, Queen of these same angels." In the final instant was decreed the creation of mankind and "the fall of Adam was foreseen and in him that of all others, except of the Queen, who did not enter into this decree. As a remedy was it ordained, that the most holy humanity should be capable of suffering" (Ven. Mary Agreda, *City of God*, I, 1, chap. 4).[1]

ARTICLE IV

INDWELLING OF THE HOLY GHOST

The doctrine on grace is clarified by that of the indwelling of the Holy Ghost, the Master and Vivifier of souls. We know that sanctifying grace not only justifies and vivifies us, blotting out our iniquities and calling us from death to life; but it truly sanctifies and deifies us by creating us anew in the likeness of Jesus Christ. The

---

[1] A classification of the divine decrees into six "instants" and what God decreed to communicate *ad extra* in each of these instants. (Tr.)

THE DIVINE LIFE OF GRACE

life which it bestows on us, though but a seed needing development through our faithful cooperation, is true eternal life. Although it does not transform us into God in such a way that our being, our work, and the terminus of our operations are one and the same thing (for this is impossible because of our nature), nevertheless it brings God Himself, together with all His treasures, to reign in our hearts. So we shall enjoy both Him and them if we wish to avail ourselves of such condescension.

Grace and the Divine Indwelling

In the measure in which we are united with God in this friendly commerce by the bonds of true and intimate knowledge and filial love and are inflamed with the fire of His charity, in that measure shall we succeed in purging ourselves of all earthly dross. Being transformed from glory to glory, we shall cleave to Him and be one spirit with Him (I Cor. 6:17).

Thus, living in God and by God, we can even now have all our conversation in heaven, for from that moment we exercise the functions characteristic of eternal life and we are able to make better use of them as time goes on. These functions are to know God as He is in Himself, to love Him with the same love with which He loves Himself and us, to possess Him as He possesses Himself, and to lose ourselves in the abyss of His eternal happiness.[1]

Then we no longer tend to God as something which is outside ourselves. We possess Him here on earth in essentially the same way as the way we hope to possess Him in glory. To enjoy Him beatifically it is sufficient to develop that seed of eternal life which has been sown in our souls, to remove the earth that covers it, and to clear away the obstacles that impede its growth, and to fix all our attention on Him.[2] We should enter within ourselves and converse

---

[1] St. Thomas, *III Sent.*, dist. 27, q.2, a.1, ad 9um: "Since men are made deiform through charity, so they are more than men and their conversation is in heaven."
[2] Sauvé, *op. cit.*, no. 27: "Theologians unanimously call grace the seed of glory. It needs but be developed and it will divinely blossom into the beatific vision of God, and therefore he who possesses it will be in heaven. We are now sons of God, although our filiation is not yet manifested. Although all these riches will not shine forth until glory, when we shall be perfectly like unto God and shall see Him face to face as He is in Himself; yet even now this mystery of filiation is in our soul

with the God of our heart, who is our portion forever.[3] Discovering His glorious kingdom in our heart and drinking at the fount of living water which springs from life eternal, we shall see that our happiness lies in union with Him and we shall swoon with love. This fountain is the Spirit whom we have received [4] and from whom incessantly flow the graces from which our souls receive moisture, are beautified, purified, and made fertile.[5]

1. PRESENCE OF GOD IN THE JUST SOUL

Though God is and must be in all places by His power, presence, and essence as Creator, First Mover, and Conserver of all things, He is not omnipresent as a friend through the loving indwelling, but only in rational creatures who accept His divine familiarity.[6] This requires a prodigious elevation which will enable them to converse with Him, not as lowly slaves to their mighty and powerful Lord, nor as simple creatures to their supreme Maker, but in a certain way as to an equal, a true friend and sweet guest, or as to a father or a most loving spouse. It is necessary, then, that they depart from the condition of slavery to enter into that of friendship and familiarity. "God not only does not dwell in each and every creature to which He is present; but in the very ones in whom He dwells He does not dwell in all in the same measure." [7] Whence comes the greater or less perfection of the saints but from the fact that God dwells in them more or less perfectly?

---

together with the divine likeness and union with God Himself. The divine Persons dwell in us and are united to us, spirit to spirit and heart to heart so that this is already heaven, but a hidden one. How important for us to have a knowledge of this indwelling, which is so noble and so delightful!"

Tauler, *Institutions*, chap. 6: "If the omnipotent God is within us and more intimate to us than we are to ourselves, why is it that we do not feel His presence? The reason is that His grace cannot work in us; and it cannot work because we do not seek it devoutly, eagerly, and with a humble heart; because we do not love God whole-heartedly and with all our affection; . . . because the eye of our intellect is filled with the dust and dirt of transitory things; . . . because we do not wish to die to our sensuality and to be converted to God with our whole heart. That is why the light of divine grace does not operate in us."

[3] Ps. 72:26.
[4] John 7:38 f.
[5] St. Augustine, *Confessions*, Bk. X, chap. 20: "For when I seek Thee, my God, I seek the blessed life. I will seek Thee that my soul may live. For my body liveth by my soul, and my soul liveth by Thee."
[6] John 1:11 f.
[7] St. Augustine, *Epist. 187 ad Dard.*, no. 41.

And the more pleasant and copious this abode of God in the saints, the more animated they are by His Spirit and the more inflamed with the fire of His charity, which is translated into good works. "If anyone love Me," says the Savior, "he will keep My word, and My Father will love him, and We will come to him and will make Our abode with him." [8] "If we love one another," adds the beloved disciple, "God abideth in us, and His charity is perfected in us. In this we know that we abide in Him, and He in us, because He hath given us of His Spirit." [9] So charity, as the Angelic Doctor observes, is not a virtue proper to man as such, but so far as he is made God.[10]

God cannot tolerate those who love and serve Him with lukewarmness and He begins to vomit them out (Apoc. 3:15) because they possess Him only in part. Yet He incessantly knocks at the doors of all, desiring that they receive Him whole-heartedly, so that He may celebrate with them the banquet of friendship (*ibid.*, 20). Though most close their doors to Him and are deaf to the sweet voice which says: "Give Me thy heart," as many as receive Him He makes fellow citizens of the saints and, what is more, His servants and true sons.

2. VIVIFYING ACTION OF THE HOLY GHOST

That loving indwelling, although common to the three divine Persons, who can never be separated, is attributed in a singular manner both in Scripture and in the Fathers to the consoling Spirit as though He exercised in it a very special mission, while the Father and the Son assist by concomitance.[11] St. John indicates this to us, and the Savior Himself gave us to understand the same thing when He said: "If you love Me, keep My commandments. And I will ask the Father, and He shall give you another Paraclete, that He may abide

---

[8] John 14:23.
[9] See I John 4:12-14.
[10] Cf. Ia IIae, q.62, a.1, ad 1um: "A certain nature may be ascribed to a certain thing in two ways. First, essentially; and thus these theological virtues surpass the nature of man. Secondly, by participation; . . . and thus, after a fashion, man becomes a partaker of the Divine Nature: so that these virtues are proportionate to man in respect of the Nature of which he is made a partaker."
[11] "It can be said without presumption," says St. Magdalen of Pazzi (*Œuvres*, Part I, chap. 33), "that through baptism we are made children of God and that the Third Person of the most Blessed Trinity descends upon us as He is inseparably united with the other two, so that the entire Trinity dwells in us and finds pleasure in us."

with you forever, the Spirit of truth, whom the world cannot receive, because it seeth Him not nor knoweth Him. But you shall know Him, because He shall abide with you and shall be in you. I will not leave you orphans; I will come to you. Yet a little while, and the world seeth Me no more. But you see Me because I live, and you shall live. In that day you shall know that I am in My Father, and you in Me, and I in you. . . . But I tell you the truth: it is expedient to you that I go. For if I go not, the Paraclete will not come to you; but if I go, I will send Him to you." [12]

The divine Spirit who abides eternally in the faithful is the one who gives testimony of the truth (John 15:26 f.) and convicts the world of sin (*ibid.*, 16:8) and bears witness that Christ is the truth (I John 5:6). And if, animated and moved by Him, we hearken to His voice and do not afflict Him, He will also testify to us that we are sons of God and therefore heirs, for His communication gives us that divine being as such [13] and deifies us, impressing on us the living image of the Word.[14] He is the Spirit, Lord, and Vivifier, in whom we believe and whose communication, derived as it is from Jesus Christ, our divine Head, makes us living members of the Church and holy temples of God.[15] He is the Spirit of adoption through whom we confidently call God by the name of Father and who makes us live and act in conformity with our dignity as sons.[16] Communicating Himself to us, He pours forth divine charity in us,[17] He enables us to guard the divine deposit,[18] and as the Spirit of revelation and knowledge He discloses to us the most lofty mysteries of God and the unutterable grandeurs of Jesus Christ and teaches us the way of life.[19] Finally, He dwells in us as the living

---

[12] John 14:15-21; 16:7.
[13] Rom. 8:14-17.
[14] See II Cor. 3:18.
[15] See I Cor. 3:16 f.; 4:19.
[16] Rom. 8:9-16; Gal. 4:5-7.
[17] Rom. 5:5. "Charity is called God and the gift of God, for substantial Charity gives accidental charity. When it signifies the Giver, it is called substantial Charity; when it signifies the gift, it is called accidental" (St. Bernard, *Epist. 11 ad Guidon*, no. 4).

"In justification a double charity is given us, created and uncreated; the one by which we love, the other by which we are loved" (St. Bonaventure, *Comp. theol. verit.*, Bk. I, chap. 9).

[18] See II Tim. 6:20 f.
[19] See I Cor. 2:10; Eph. 1:17; 3:5-15; Ps. 142:10.

THE DIVINE LIFE OF GRACE

pledge of eternal life, a prevention against corruption and the seed of our resurrection and immortality.[20]

All these and many other similar passages, whose obvious meaning must be maintained at any cost as long as there is no evident inconsistency, seem to make it very clearly understood that the Holy Ghost resides in souls in a proper and singular manner. The holy Fathers, as we have already noted, instead of weakening that interpretation, rather seek to emphasize it to show the vivifying action of the divine Comforter.[21]

In conformity with this, the pure and simple souls who are able to penetrate to some extent these mysteries of divine love through the illuminated eyes of the heart, know and understand how the Father and Son reign and sweetly repose in us as in their sanctified temple. These two divine Persons delight in seeing the work of renovation which their Spirit produces in us. They desire that we heed Him as the director, comforter, counsellor, and master, who, at the same time that He pours forth divine charity in us, also inspires and prompts us and teaches us all truth.[22]

3. MISSION, GIVING, AND INDWELLING OF THE HOLY GHOST

Scripture repeatedly states that the Holy Ghost has been sent to us, and in almost the same manner as it is said of the Son.[23] St. Thomas observes that a mission implies, together with the original procession, a new and special mode of presence of the person who is sent in those who receive him.[24] At other times it is said that the Holy Ghost is given,[25] and this giving also supposes a unique possession on the part of those who accept Him, to the extent that they can freely enjoy the gift received. Whence the holy doctor states

---

[20] See II Cor. 1:22; 5:5; Rom. 8:11.

[21] Louis of Granada, *The Sinner's Guide*, Bk. I, chap. 5: "The doctors of the Church and theologians conclude that the Holy Spirit resides in a special manner in the soul of a just man.... Entering such a soul, God transforms her into a magnificent temple. He Himself purifies, sanctifies, and adorns her, making her a fitting habitation for her supreme Guest."

[22] St. Augustine, *Soliloquies*, chap. 32: "Thou art true light and divine fire, O Master of souls.... As the Spirit of truth, Thou teachest us all truth through Thy communication."

[23] John 14:26; 15:26; 16:7; Gal. 4:6.

[24] Cf. Ia, q.43.

[25] John 14:15; Rom. 5:5.

that "the Holy Ghost is possessed by man and dwells within him, in the very gift itself of sanctifying grace. Hence the Holy Ghost Himself is given and sent." [26] Again, St. Thomas says: "But we are said to possess what we can freely use or enjoy. . . . Thus a divine person can be given, and can be a gift." [27]

Scripture also expressly states that this divine Spirit dwells in us as absolute master and makes us holy temples of God which cannot be violated without incurring divine indignation. "Know you not," asks the Apostle, "that you are the temple of God, and that the Spirit of God dwelleth in you? But if any man violate the temple of God, him shall God destroy. For the temple of God is holy, which you are." [28] Later, he adds: "Know you not that your members are the temple of the Holy Ghost, who is in you, whom you have from God, and that you are not your own?" [29]

To beautify this temple the divine Spirit pours the charity of God into our hearts. To consecrate and increase it—Sanctifier and Vivifier that He is—He deifies us and fashions us in such a way that we become "a habitation of God in the Spirit." [30]

Since this divine Giver comes to us together with His precious gifts, with which He enriches us, and which adorn, strengthen, and deify our faculties while He vivifies and deifies our very soul, it seems certain that, according to the correct understanding of the Fathers and Scripture, we must admit a mission, a giving, and an indwelling proper in a special manner to the Holy Ghost. He is the Gift par excellence who dwells in us not only as a comforter and sweet guest, but as a perpetual fount of living water.

He has been given to us that He might possess us and we might possess Him, and in this way He realizes in us very singularly the mystical work of our deification.[31] Possessing Him, we possess the very charity of God which sanctifies His dwelling-place. We are then able to observe faithfully His commandments, loving Him with

---

[26] Cf. Ia, q.43, a.3.
[27] Cf. Ia, q.38, a.1.
[28] See I Cor. 3:16 f.
[29] See I Cor. 6:19.
[30] Eph. 2:22.
[31] St. Athanasius, *Epist. ad Serap.*, I, no. 24: "Participation in the Holy Ghost is a participation in the divine nature. . . . If He descended upon men, it was to deify them."

THE DIVINE LIFE OF GRACE

a true filial love. Then shall we be loved by the Father with the selfsame love with which He loves His Son, and together they will come to us to make our hearts their glorious dwelling place.[32] Therefore he who remains in charity, abides in God and God in him.[33] The Spirit of charity frees us from the slavery of vices and sins and gives us that true liberty which can be only where He is.[34]

The Loving Presence of the Trinity

Although the doctrine of the indwelling or vivifying presence as something proper and special to the Holy Ghost is a doctrine still very much discussed, it is certain that He dwells in us as a sweet guest, and with Him, either directly or by concomitance, the entire most Holy Trinity.

Therefore, as St. Teresa observes,[35] in our hearts there is a true heaven, for God dwells there in all His glory. Though a Lord of such infinite majesty condescends to be fashioned to our measure, yet He enjoys perfect liberty, and He has the power to enlarge the palace of our soul. St. Teresa marvels and laments, as does St. Augustine, at having delayed so long in realizing and recognizing this invaluable treasure which was buried within herself;[36] at not having known how to converse lovingly with so amiable a com-

---

[32] John 14:23.
[33] See I John 4:16.
[34] Gardeil, *Gifts of the Holy Ghost in the Dominican Saints*, p. 6: "The Holy Ghost does not cause in us the love of God as an exterior agent which becomes foreign as soon as it has finished operating. He produces it as an interior cause dwelling in this love, for the Apostle says that 'He has been given to us.' His activity is like that of a soul, ever present in that which it does and whose operation never ceases. So long as the just soul loves God, it does not act alone; it has, deep in its heart, the Spirit of God, and it is this Spirit that causes the soul to utter, with all truth and efficacy, the name of filial love, 'My Father!'"
So the law of Christ is to the Christian what the natural law is to man. It is not an exterior imposition, but a condition within the being itself. It is not a yoke which oppresses, but an interior norm of health and life which is necessary for normal growth.
[35] *Way of Perfection*, chap. 28.
[36] St. Augustine, *Soliloquies*, chap. 31: "I wandered aimlessly like a lost sheep, seeking Thee in exterior things, when all the time Thou wert in my very being. I grew fatigued in looking all about me, while actually Thou wert within me, because I had a desire for Thee. I have walked through the streets and squares of the cities of the world searching for Thee and I have not been able to find Thee, because I sought in vain outside myself for that which was within my soul."

panion and treating God as Father, Brother, Lord, and Spouse; and of having been neglectful in preparing well this habitation of His glory.

1. IGNORANCE OF THIS DOCTRINE

What must we say of the generality of Christians who have never thought of this enchanting mystery? Perhaps many of them would exclaim with the Ephesians: "We have not so much as heard whether there be [within us] a Holy Ghost." Actually it often happens that, although the little ones desire the bread of doctrine, few there are who impart it to them.[37] Formerly even children knew that they were living temples of the Holy Ghost and that they should live as such, for that doctrine was inculcated in them with great insistence in order to fashion them in the true spirit of Jesus Christ. Nowadays very little is said about this dogma which is so fundamental in the Christian life. As a consequence the spirit is quenched in many souls who are ignorant of the words of eternal life.

In the beginning, as we have already pointed out, it was common for Christians to call themselves by the name *Christoforos, Theoforos, Agioforos,* and so forth, that is, Christ-bearers, God-bearers, or bearers of the Holy Ghost. But today even many ecclesiastics and religious, when they read or hear that we are members of Jesus Christ and that His Spirit dwells in us, take these expressions in a figurative sense. As a result they pay no attention to the divine Guest who inspires us and teaches us all truth and who seeks thereby to do no less than deify us.[38]

---

[37] Lam. 4:4.
[38] Weiss, *Apologie*, Vol. IX, appendix 1: "When the Savior says that through grace He Himself comes into our soul, together with the Father and the Holy Ghost, and makes His abode in us (John 14:23), it is not to be understood in a figurative sense, nor as if the Divinity worked in our hearts only by means of His gifts. Instead, God Himself, not content with conferring His gifts, comes to dwell in us in a singular manner. Formerly, youths and even children were found to be so convinced of this indwelling of God that they considered it as something very obvious, as is manifest from the lives of St. Lucy, St. Inez, and St. Agueda. But now there are very few, even among the theologians, who understand this clearly. When we read in the Apostle that 'Jesus Christ is our Head and each one of us a member of His body,' we probably exclaim in admiration, 'What a beautiful image!' But for the servants of God this was the absolute truth."

Weiss adds in appendix 2: "The Holy Ghost is the focal point, the center, the origin, and the heart of supernatural thought and life. He manifests Himself at each step as a guide to one who desires to penetrate the very depths of the supernatural.

THE DIVINE LIFE OF GRACE

But this requires our loving cooperation, for, as St. Augustine says, "He who created thee without thyself will not save thee without thyself." Much less will He make us perfect if we do not cooperate with Him. Therefore, with much love He says to us: "My son, give Me thy heart: and let thy eyes keep My ways." [39] But we shall be unable to correspond as we should with the impulses of the Holy Ghost if we do not love Him whole-heartedly and heed Him or if we do not have a clear notion of His activity. As a result we shall close our ears to His holy inspirations, and resist Him when He sweetly leads us to solitude in order to speak to our hearts and, like a loving mother, to feed us at the breast.[40]

With good reason, then, spiritual souls lament the lack of devotion to the Holy Ghost, without whom it is impossible for true piety to flourish. Since Leo XIII, in his encyclical *Divinum illud*, sought to remedy this evil by calling the attention of theologians, apologists, and preachers to a more zealous promulgation of this salutary and necessary doctrine, the vital action of the divine Paraclete is becoming better understood and one can hope for a great spiritual renewal.

2. THE BEAUTY OF THE HOUSE OF GOD

This special mission, this giving, indwelling, and vivification on the part of the Holy Ghost, and that friendly and substantial presence or immanence of the entire Trinity within us cannot be caused, certainly, through any change in God Himself, for He is immutable. It is a change effected by Him in us when we are reborn, renewed, justified, and sanctified. This change is productive of a supernatural organism of which sanctifying grace is the essence, the substance, which deifies us. The properties or faculties of this organism are the virtues, the gifts, and the other powers which are infused in us after the manner of habits, through which we are able to act divinely. Finally, the graces *gratis datae* and various transitory inspirations are classified as accidents in relation to this supernatural structure.

By these divine aids and the continual exercise of the Christian

---

And only he who familiarizes himself with Him can orientate himself in that sublime world. Without a knowledge of His activity, a man sees in the supernatural truths nothing more than disconnected and incomprehensible fragments. To him alone who seeks to find the light of that beneficent sun, is disclosed a new world, lofty and full of unity and life."

[39] Prov. 23:26.
[40] Osee 2:14; Isa. 66:12.

virtues we increase the talents which the Lord has entrusted to us. We grow in His grace and knowledge. We contribute to the development of the mystical body of the Savior and we ourselves are fashioned into living and holy temples of God in the Holy Ghost.

The life of grace, the ardor of charity, and the splendor of all the other virtues constitute the beauty of the house of God, and He dwells there with so much the more delight as He sees it more deified and more radiant with His eternal brilliance. When that divine dwelling place, that new city of God, reaches the required perfection, there will shine forth in it no light other than that which emanates from the wounds of the Lamb who takes away the sins of the world.

The saints went into ecstasy and swooned away in contemplating the inexpressible beauty of the house of God, which caused them to exclaim: "How lovely are Thy tabernacles, O Lord of hosts!" [41] This divine beauty cannot be other than the grace of our Savior and the communication of His Spirit whereby we are rendered pleasing in the eyes of the Father, for when we are thus honored and deified He sees Himself resplendent in us. How could we help but love and seek to obtain what merits so much esteem from the omnipotent God? Rather we should say with those souls who have a vivid experience of these truths: "I have loved, O Lord, the beauty of Thy house and the place where Thy glory dwelleth."

That happy place where we are able to enjoy God on earth is the center of our hearts, the depth of our souls.[42] Let us enter within ourselves; let us close the doors of our senses to all earthly vanities; let us heed the voice that calls us to this sweet retreat and we shall find the kingdom of God and see His glory. God is there with His

[41] Ps. 83:2.
[42] This depth or center of the soul is called by various names: *apex totius affectus* (St. Bonaventure); *vertex animae seu mentis* (St. Thomas); *fundus vel centrum animae* (Plotinus); *intimus affectionis sinus, cordis intima, mentis summum, mentis intimum, cubiculum vel secretum mentis* (Richard of St. Victor); *claustrum animae* (Hugo de Folieto).
Fr. Juan de los Angeles, *Diálogos*, I, 3, 4: "Blosius, Ruysbroek, Tauler, and others say that this center of the soul is more intrinsic and more lofty than its three superior faculties or powers, since it is the origin and principle of the others. . . . The interior of the soul is its very essence, sealed with the image of God, which some saints call the center; others, the interior; others, the apex; and still others, the mind. St. Augustine calls it the height, but the moderns speak of it as the depth. . . . No created thing can fill this inner chamber, but only the Creator with all His majesty and grandeur; and there He has His peaceful abode as in heaven itself."

loving and glorious presence as long as we remain in true charity. He is inherent in our being and in our work as the beginning and immediate end of our supernatural life and all its characteristic functions. In the measure in which these are perfected and purged of the vicious habits of the old man by the ceaseless increase of light and the riddance of obstacles that impede our vision, we shall be truly renewed in the Spirit and we shall find that God is "all in all."

APPENDIX

The Kingdom of God within Us

"Consider now what your Master says next: 'Who art in the Heavens.' Do you suppose it matters little what Heaven is and where you must seek your most holy Father? I assure you that for minds which wander it is of great importance not only to have a right belief about this but to try to learn it by experience. . . . Remember how St. Augustine tells us about his seeking God in many places and eventually finding Him within himself. Do you suppose it is of little importance that a soul which is often distracted should come to understand this truth and to find that, in order to speak to its Eternal Father and to take its delight in Him, it has no need to go to Heaven or to speak in a loud voice? However quietly we speak, He is so near that He will hear us: we need no wings to go in search of Him but have only to find a place where we can be alone and look upon Him present within us. Nor need we feel strange in the presence of so kind a Guest; we must talk to Him very humbly, as we should to our father, ask Him for things as we should ask a father, tell Him our troubles, beg Him to put them right, and yet realize that we are not worthy to be called His children.

"Avoid being bashful with God, as some people are, in the belief that they are being humble. . . . A fine humility it would be if I had the Emperor of Heaven and earth in my house, coming to it to do me a favor and to delight in my company, and I were so humble that I would not answer His questions, nor remain with Him, nor accept what He gave me but left Him alone. . . . *Remember how important it is for you to have understood this truth—that the Lord is within us and that we should be there with Him.*

THE MYSTICAL EVOLUTION

"If one prays in this way, the prayer may be only vocal, but the mind will be recollected much sooner; and this is a prayer which brings with it many blessings. It is called recollection because the soul collects together all the faculties and enters within itself to be with its God. Its Divine Master comes more speedily to teach it, and to grant it the Prayer of Quiet, than in any other way. . . .

"Those who are able to shut themselves up in this way within this little Heaven of the soul, wherein dwells the Maker of Heaven and earth, and who have formed the habit of looking at nothing and staying in no place which will distract these outward senses, may be sure that they are walking on an excellent road, and will come without fail to drink of the water of the fountain, for they will journey a long way in a short time. . . .

"This may not be evident at first, if the recollection is not very profound—for at this state it is sometimes more so and sometimes less. . . . But if we cultivate the habit, make the necessary effort and practice the exercises for several days, the benefits will reveal themselves, and when we begin to pray we shall realize that the bees are coming to the hive and entering it to make the honey, and all without any effort of ours. . . . When no hindrance comes to it from outside, the soul remains alone with its God. . .

"And now let us imagine that we have within us a palace of priceless worth, built entirely of gold and precious stones—a palace, in short, fit for so great a Lord. . . Imagine that within the palace dwells this great King, Who has vouchsafed to become your Father, and Who is seated upon a throne of supreme price—namely, your heart. . . . If we took care always to remember what a Guest we have within us, I think it would be impossible for us to abandon ourselves to vanities and things of the world, for we should see how worthless they are by comparison with those which we have within us. . . .

"I think, if I had understood then, as I do now, how this great King *really* dwells within this little palace of my soul, I should not have left Him alone so often, but should have stayed with Him and never have allowed His dwelling-place to get so dirty. . . Being the Lord, He has, of course, perfect freedom, and, as He loves us, He fashions Himself to our measure. . . .

"When a soul sets out upon this path, He does not reveal Himself to it, lest it should feel dismayed at seeing that its littleness can contain such greatness; but gradually He enlarges it to the extent requisite for what He has to set within it. It is for this reason that I say He has perfect freedom, since He has power to make the whole of this palace great. The important point is that we should be absolutely resolved to give it to Him for His own and should empty it so that He may take out and put in just what He likes, as He would with something of His own" (*Way of Perfection*, Bk. XXVIII, *passim*).

"Do not think that it is sufficient for you to think of Me for only one hour each day. He who desires to hear interiorly My sweet words and to understand the secrets and mysteries of My Wisdom must be always with Me, always thinking of Me. . . . Is it not shameful to have the kingdom of God in one's soul and to depart from it in order to think of creatures?" (*Eternal Wisdom*, XV.)

ARTICLE V

Grace and Glory

We know that God is as intimate to us as is our very soul. Even more, He is, according to the saints, the life of our soul and the soul of our life.[1] "For in Him we live and move and are" (Acts 17:28). Deified by the vital communication of His Spirit and the participation in His divine nature, we can and should live and work divinely as sons of the light.

Since operation follows nature, the mode of activity characteristic of the just, so far as they possess God and are clothed in His divine nature, is a knowledge and love which correspond to that eternal life which is divine grace. Through this knowledge and love just souls touch, embrace, and possess God Himself in His very substance and not merely by a remote and analogical representation, which is the only way He can be possessed by natural knowledge and natural love.[2] Although the simple rational creature can know its

---

[1] Denifle, in *Das Geistliche Leben*, chap. 2, quotes Eckhart as saying: "He is very close to us and we are far removed from Him. He dwells in the center of our soul, and we on the very edge. He is our friend, but we treat Him like a stranger."

[2] St. Thomas, *In II Cor.* 6:16: "God is in the saints though the activity by which

transcendent Maker only by induction, tracing the reflections of His attributes in the marvels of nature without seeing the attributes themselves, nevertheless, once it has been elevated to the divine order, it can to some extent directly perceive the divine realities themselves.

Once we are deified and made sons of God, we can in one way or another exercise the functions proper to eternal life which are due to us as His sons, for with this participation in the divine nature, and in proportion to it, there are communicated to us its characteristic operations. Thus, it will not remain dormant nor shall we possess it in vain; but rather, as the seed of glory, it will grow and fructify. Therefore, in the measure that we physically and ontologically share the divine nature, we also share its corresponding operation and, since the former participation is real and formal, so also should be the latter.

Eternal Life, Inchoate and Perfect

According to our imperfect mode of knowledge and expression, the activities proper to God are to know and love Himself as He is in Himself, in His absolute unity and His ineffable Trinity. So the operations of the divine life as shared by us ought to tend proportionately, as to their only worthy object, to the divine essence, not as a sterile abstraction, but as it is in itself, touching the one and triune God and reaching out to Him with those two powerful supernatural arms of knowledge and love which He deigned to communicate to us.

For us to grasp to some extent the supernatural truths which far surpass our natural capacity, it is sufficient that we be illumined by the light of faith which presents them to us, however dimly and enigmatically, as incontestable facts. But worthily to appreciate these truths, we need to penetrate them, to know and feel them by a living faith which is accompanied by the gifts of understanding and wisdom. This demands a high degree of purification.[3]

To supply as best we can for the irreplaceable experience of the

---

they attain to God and, in a sense, comprehend Him, which is to love Him and know Him." *In I Sent.*, dist. 37, q. 1, a. 2: "The creature attains to God in His very substance when he adheres to the First Truth by Faith and to Perfect Goodness by charity."

[3] See St. John of the Cross, *Dark Night of the Soul*, Bk. II, chap. 16.

THE DIVINE LIFE OF GRACE

mystical states which is enjoyed through those most precious gifts as a prelude to glory, we shall consider what faith and sound theology teach us.[4] For if we succeed in forming some approximate idea of what the life of grace is in its complete development as it is manifested in heaven, we can deduce what it ought to be during this laborious period of growth which precedes glory.[5]

1. HAPPINESS OF THE SAINTS ON EARTH AND THE BLESSED IN HEAVEN

The activity of eternal life consists in knowing and loving God the Father and Jesus Christ whom He sent; that is, in contemplating clearly the most august and most profound secrets of the divinity and the ineffable mysteries of our redemption and deification. Such is the everlasting activity of the blessed who enjoy the infinite treasures of the paternal heritage, contemplate the bottomless abyss of uncreated Beauty, and love the absolute Goodness. They are in a perpetual ecstasy, submerged in the sea of divine delights, and amid the most pleasant surprises that can be conceived, they discover at each instant new and indescribable enchantments. They can find no bottom or end to that unsounded ocean of wonders.

But the blessed are all this in the measure that they are deified. They are eternally happy because they have been made gods, and they are now at the terminus of their mystical growth, where is brought to its complete and glorious expansion the mysterious seed of eternal life which they received at their regeneration. They are totally renewed and transformed from sons of Adam to sons of the Most High through the power of the Spirit, who made them like to the Word and like unto God.

Essential beatitude consists not only in activity but also, and even more so, in being. The divine activity of the blessed is a necessary and immediate consequence of the divine good which they now possess in its due perfection.[6] Truly deified, they possess the highest Good and they are able to know Him, see Him, feel and enjoy Him at will, loving and embracing Him as He is in Himself, yet always in the proportion that they are deified. Intuitive vision, in which

---

[4] Sauvé, *Etats mystiques*, p. 2.

[5] Cf. IIa IIae, q. 24, a. 3, ad 2um: "Grace is nothing other than a beginning of glory in us."

[6] See St. Dionysius, *Eccles. hier.*, chap. 2.

are simplified the acts of wisdom and knowledge, and the joyful love which necessarily follows it, are the two functions characteristic of eternal life in its plenitude. Lacking this love, the saints would be happy without fully realizing that they were so, without taking delight in their happiness, and without reaping the benefits of the good which they possess.[7]

The functions proper to life are its necessary complement. So, although a person can possess God without realizing the fact very clearly, owing to the many obstacles here on earth which prevent his seeing it, these obstructions totally disappear when the soul, freed from "the corruptible body which is a load upon the soul and the earthly habitation which presseth down the mind," [8] has attained the total purification of the eyes of the intellect.

Even here on earth, the saints who are more deified are truly happy in the midst of all their pains and bitterness, in their poverty, tears, hunger, thirst, and persecutions. Although their consolations and joys abound to such an extent that by comparison all pains are to be reckoned as nothing, nevertheless these sufferings are sufficient to prevent them from participating in a joy which is proportionate to their sanctification. These souls can even now be equal to or greater than many who dwell in heaven for they can surpass the latter in charity, at least radically, and therefore in grace also and in the extent of their deification and essential union with God.[9] However, they do not have an equal joy because, not seeing God face to face, as do the blessed, they cannot know Him in the measure that they love and possess Him. Hence follows that blind, instinctive, and ineffable love which they experience to such a high degree that it seems irresistible in its fiery vehemence. Such souls, as sorrowful as they are happy, would a thousand times quit this life if they were not sustained by Him who can do all things.

---

[7] St. Thomas, *Quaestiones disputatae, De veritate*, q.29, a.1: "The first union without the second does not suffice for beatitude, for even God Himself would not be happy if He did not both know and love Himself, because He could not then take delight in Himself, and this is required for beatitude."

[8] Wisd. 9:15.

[9] Cf. Ia, q.117, a.2, ad 3um: "Certain men even in this state of life are greater than certain angels, not actually, but virtually; forasmuch as they have such great charity that they can merit a higher degree of beatitude than that possessed by certain angels."

THE DIVINE LIFE OF GRACE

Thence comes the incredible value of all their actions, however small and humble they may appear. Since they are saints, they sanctify and ennoble the most natural and lowly deeds, just as the lukewarm enervate and make base those acts of theirs which could be very great.[10] It also follows from this, as a great mystic points out, that we ought not to be so much concerned with what we do as with what we are, for the value of our deeds will depend upon what we are in ourselves.[11] Therefore St. Francis de Sales said that a great saint can merit more in a lowly occupation than can an imperfect man in the most noble and glorious works.[12] Even when sleeping, the true servants of God can love and merit more than others who are praying or working for the good of souls, because even during sleep their deified hearts keep vigil, praying and loving intensely, although the saints themselves are not aware of it.

---

[10] Spiritual masters unanimously teach that God measures our works principally by the spirit or intention with which they are performed.

[11] Tauler, *Institutions*, chap. 14: "Truly, men ought to consider, not what they do, but what they are, for if they are interiorly good, so also will be their works. If deep within their souls they are just and upright, their works will be just and upright. Many measure their sanctity by their works, but that is not as it should be. Sanctity consists and ought to consist in being. For however holy be our works, they do not sanctify us as such; on the contrary, in the measure that we are holy and our soul and intention are holy, we shall sanctify our works. All our efforts and diligence, whatever we do or refrain from doing, should always be ordained to this one thing: that God be magnified, that is, made great within us. The better we achieve this, the greater and more divine will be our works."

The Lord said to Father Hoyos (*Vida*, p. 97), "I desire the hearts of My humble but generous servants. The surest sanctity is that which most resembles Mine. I always deal with man as one among many, making Myself all to all, although I am infinitely superior to all in works. Merit lies, not in doing much, but in loving much. Sometimes much is done when it would have been better if there had been less action and more love."

Weiss, *Apologie*, IX, 12: "Everything does not depend upon austerity of life or the number of exterior deeds. Otherwise factory workers would be far ahead of us on the road to sanctity. Sanctity does not depend upon the number of pious exercises, but upon the spirit and interior perfection with which they are performed. Christians are told to walk according to the spirit (Gal. 5:16), because God is spirit and therefore He desires true followers in spirit and in truth (John 4:23). Life should be diffused from within, from the spirit, through good works. That is how the saints proceeded, and in that way they obtained magnificent results. Why did they live in continual silence? Why did they perpetually keep their eyes cast down? Because their whole world, their relationships and their principal spheres of activity, were all within themselves. There, within themselves, they have much to do, not with themselves, but with the Holy Ghost who has made of them His temple."

[12] *Treatise on the Love of God*, Bk. IX, chap. 5.

The Spirit who animates them pleads for them with unspeakable groanings.[13] Since they are more closely united with God, they cannot help but please Him more in all that they do.[14]

2. VISION OF GOD IN THE WORD THROUGH THE HOLY GHOST

We know for a certainty, since it is defined as a truth of faith, that after death all the just who have completed their purgations and are strengthened by the *lumen gloriae* will see God face to face; that is, they will contemplate the divine essence intuitively and without any obstacle or medium. The existence of that *lumen gloriae* was declared in the Council of Vienna against the Beghards, but in what that mysterious light consists and how the beatific vision is brought about by it, is still disputed among theologians.

Nevertheless, all agree in this, that God is not seen by means of any created species, image, or representation which objectively presents God to the intellect. Such an image would always be infinitely removed from the reality; and therefore, as St. Thomas asserts, "to say that God is seen through some likeness is to say that God is not seen at all." [15] Yet, since the human intellect cannot know anything without a representing idea, in order to see God it is necessary that the Divinity itself be united to the intellect so intimately that it serves as an idea. So it is said that the divine essence itself takes the place of the intelligible form.[16]

On the other hand, that our intellect may receive this divine idea, its capacity must be vastly extended. Otherwise there would be a disproportion and, according to the principle that whatever is re-

[13] "A soul which is entirely united to God," said our Lord to Blessed Henry Suso (*Eternal Wisdom*, chap. 28), "glorifies Me continuously. Whatever it is doing, either interiorly or exteriorly, whether it meditates, prays, works, eats, sleeps, or keeps a vigil: its smallest action is an act of praise that is pleasing to God."

[14] St. Francis de Sales, *op. cit.*, Bk. VII, chap. 3: "Imagine that St. Paul, St. Dionysius, St. Augustine, St. Bernard, St. Francis, St. Catherine of Genoa, or St. Catherine of Siena were still on this earth and, fatigued with the many labors which they had performed for the love of God, were asleep. Imagine, on the other hand, a good soul, but one not so holy as these others, who is at the very same time engaged in the prayer of union. Who do you think is more united, more closely bound to God, those great saints who are asleep or this soul which is at prayer? Those much loved lovers, certainly, because they have more charity and their affections, although dormant to a certain extent, are in a certain way inseparably abandoned to their Master and fixed on Him. . . . The particular soul excels in the exercise of union; the saints, in the union itself. . . ."

[15] Cf. Ia, q.12, a.2.

[16] *De veritate*, q.8, a.1; *Supplement*, q.92, a.1, ad 8um.

THE DIVINE LIFE OF GRACE

ceived is received according to the mode of the recipient, the divine reality would become disfigured and brought down to the level of our capacity.

"Nothing can receive a higher form," says St. Thomas, "unless it be disposed thereto through its capacity being raised: because every act is in its proper power. Now the divine essence is a higher form than any created intellect. Wherefore, in order that the divine essence become the intelligible species to a created intellect, which is requisite in order that the divine substance be seen, the created intellect needs to be raised for that purpose by some sublime disposition" (*Contra Gent.*, Bk. III, chap. 53).

What could this disposition be but the divine intellectual power itself? Anything other than this, however lofty and noble it might be, would not be superior to any created power and there would thus remain the same disproportion. Says Terrien: "For the beatific vision it is necessary that the created intellect be made to the likeness of the uncreated by an assimilation which exceeds every other intellectual light." [17] An assimilation so perfect as to be adequate for the vision of God Himself can be effected only by the infinite power of His Spirit who animates us and deifies the soul and all its potencies. We have received the Holy Spirit precisely "that we may know the things that are given us from God," [18] and by His gift of understanding He strengthens our intellect in such a way that it "searcheth all things, yea, the deep things of God." [19] Here, then, is the sovereign power which disposes our hearts to "ascend by steps" and carries us subjectively "from virtue to virtue" until we see God Himself.[20]

---

[17] *La grâce et la gloire*, II, 164.
[18] See I Cor. 2:12.
[19] *Ibid.*, 2:10.
[20] See Ps. 83:6–8. In conformity with this, St. Thomas states (*III Sent.*, dist. 23, q.1, a.3, ad 6um): "The vision which supplants faith pertains to the perfect gift of understanding." He adds (*ibid.*, dist. 34, q.1, a.4): "In heaven, understanding, whose function it is to apprehend spiritual things, attains to the divine essence through facial vision." In yet another place (IIa IIae, q.8, a.7), St. Thomas says: "Again, the sight of God is twofold. One is perfect, whereby God's Essence is seen; the other is imperfect, whereby, though we see not what God is, yet we see what He is not. . . . Each of these visions of God belongs to the gift of understanding; the first to the gift of understanding in its state of perfection, as possessed in heaven; the second, to the gift of understanding in its state of inchoation, as possessed by wayfarers."

John of St. Thomas, *In Iam IIae*, q.68: "The gift of understanding is given by

What, objectively, is this divine idea, this faithful expression of the divine essence, but the very Word of God? What is the Word but the most perfect and adequate image, the eternal idea, the living word, the very face of God and His substantial manifestation? He is the eternal splendor of the Father and the figure of His substance; light of light, light of glory on whom the angels love to gaze, the sole luminary in the city of God where none other is needed.

Hence the Word, to whose image souls are configured and who is immediately united to their intellects, is the eternal light which objectively enlightens them, the true *lumen gloriae* in whom they see the face of God. He is the absolute and adequate idea in whom they see the divine essence faithfully and without any intermediary. But that we may see the divine essence and receive such an idea, it is necessary, we repeat, that our intellects be strengthened subjectively and their capacity enlarged. Further, to perceive the divine essence as it is and worthily to appreciate it, our very soul with all its faculties must be deified.[21] This cannot be effected through any created power which would be of the same condition or incapacity as the soul itself. It can be done only through divine power; that is, through the loving Spirit who strengthens us from within and fortifies our weakness.

Deified by the animation of the divine Paraclete, we can fix our gaze on the Word of divine wisdom, who is intimately united with pure and holy souls. In the Word of wisdom these souls see the divine essence itself, and they see the eternal principles of all things. Seeing the divine Word, they see the very face of God and they also see

---

the Holy Ghost to know and penetrate spiritual things through an experimental knowledge of God and His mysteries. But the most excellent and clearest knowledge is the vision of God."

[21] Monsabré, *Conference 18:* "The medium proportionate to the vision and possession of the divine essence can be nothing other than the divine essence itself. ... If we are said to see and possess God and to be happy in and through Him, we cannot achieve this without a transformation of our nature and a participation in the nature and life of God. ... In order to be divinely happy, a transient help is not sufficient but there is required a divine state which can produce a divine operation. ... We must share in the divine power by which God possesses Himself immediately and naturally and by means of which the creature is elevated, in a certain manner, to the divine being and is made a participator in the divine nature in a greater or less degree (St. Thomas, Ia IIae, q.112, a.1). It is necessary that we bear within us the life of God as the principle of a new being and that this life be in us the root of all our supernatural operations as our rational nature is the root of all our natural operations."

THE DIVINE LIFE OF GRACE

reflected there, as in an infinite and spotless mirror, all things else more clearly than if they were to see the things in themselves. Thus, in the eternal light of God they see the eternal God: *In lumine tuo videbimus lumen;* and they see all in the Word: *Omnia in Verbo vident.*[22]

When, therefore, our hearts are perfectly cleansed, through the power of the Spirit of renewal and understanding, who purifies, illumines, and vivifies them, we shall be able to see God face to face. We shall see Him as He is, because we shall then be like unto Him, and we shall be so united with Him that we shall become one with Him. "We know that, when He shall appear, we shall be like to Him, because we shall see Him as He is."[23]

Such seems to be the true meaning of the holy Fathers who, as Petau notes,[24] never spoke of any type of created light to explain the beatific vision.[25] Their whole doctrine, according to Thomassin[26] is contained in these two statements: *The intelligible idea, in which the soul sees God, is the Word Himself;* whence the current expression: to see God in the Word. *The interior power, which enables the soul to see, is that of the Holy Ghost, intimately united to the intellect and vivifying and strengthening it.* "That," he adds, "is

---

[22] St. Augustine, *Soliloquies,* chap. 36: "Thou art that light in which we must see the light; that is, we must see Thee in Thyself with the splendor of Thy countenance.... To know Thy Trinity is to see Thee face to face. To know the power of the Father, the wisdom of the Son, the clemency of the Holy Ghost, and the one and indivisible essence of the same Trinity is to see the face of the living God."

[23] See I John 3:2. *Dark Night of the Soul,* Bk. II, chap. 20: "And, as we say, this vision is the cause of the perfect likeness of the soul to God, for, as St. John says, we know that we shall be like Him. Not because the soul will come to have the capacity of God, for that is impossible; but because all that it is will become like to God, for which cause it will be called, and will be, God by participation."

"Filled with God," says St. Augustine (*Sermon 243 in die Pasch.,* 14, no. 5), "they will see divinely."

[24] *Theol. dogm.,* Vol. I, Bk. VII, chap. 8, no. 3.

[25] Ia, q. 12, a. 5: "But when any created intellect sees the essence of God, the essence of God itself becomes the intelligible form of the intellect. Hence it is necessary ... that the power of understanding should be aided by divine grace. Now this increase of the intellectual powers is called the illumination of the intellect. ... And this is the light spoken of in the Apocalypse (xxi. 23). *The glory of God hath enlightened it*—viz., the society of the blessed who see God. By this light the blessed are made *deiform*—that is, like to God."

Blosius, *Inst. spir.,* chap. 12, no. 4: "So by a transcendent understanding the soul flies back to its idea and to God, its principle, and there is effected the *lumen in lumine*.... For when the uncreated light leaps up, the created light vanishes. Therefore the created light of the soul is transformed into the light of eternity."

[26] *De Deo,* Bk. VI, chap. 16.

how they see God through God, for the Holy Ghost is the power by which He is seen, and the Son is the species in which He is seen."

In this way it is actually true that no one goes to the Father except through the Son, who is the way, the truth, and the life;[27] nor can anyone know Him save him to whom the Son deigns to manifest Him.[28] And He will manifest the Father by manifesting Himself to all who love Him, for whoever sees the Son sees the Father.[29] When souls are configured and united with the Word by the power of the Holy Ghost, He will give them the selfsame glory and delight that He receives eternally from the Father, so that they may be absorbed in unity as are the three divine Persons.[30] United to God in this manner, they will possess the same Spirit that He possesses, and God will be their "all in all."

3. UNION OF BEATIFIC LOVE

Speaking of the actual union of love between God and the soul in heaven, Froget says: "There we shall see Him in Whom we have believed; we shall possess Him in Whom we have hoped and Whom we sought after while in this world; we shall at last enjoy fully, without fear of loss, and for all eternity, Him Who is the supreme Good. Then will the work of our deification be complete; then shall we be perfectly like unto God, imbued through and through with Him—divinized."[31]

Thus, God Himself in His very essence will reside in the innermost recess of our mind. In an ineffable manner, which we would seek in vain to try to explain, He will contribute to the production of that act which is vital par excellence, and intense and intimate to the highest degree: the beatific vision. He will be at once the beginning and the immediate terminus of our activity. Could there be conceived a presence more intimate and more real than that of God in our intellect? With what great reason could we say that we touch Him, we communicate with Him, we embrace Him sweetly in His very essence; and He, in turn, compenetrates us with Himself in that happy act of the beatific vision!

[27] John 14:6.
[28] Matt. 10:27.
[29] John 14:9-21.
[30] John 17:21-26.
[31] *The Indwelling of the Holy Spirit*, p. 76.

THE DIVINE LIFE OF GRACE

Yet even greater is the union produced by love. For this union not only corresponds to the plenitude of knowledge but of itself it is more unifying than is knowledge.[32] And so the soul, inflamed with the fire of divine love, is totally imbued and inundated and it sweetly perishes in the immense sea of the divinity. And since the joyful love of heaven implies the absolute lack of all evil and the full and unending possession of the Sovereign Good loved with the whole heart, the blessed in heaven sing without the least hesitation: "I found him whom my soul loveth: I held him: and I will not let him go" (Cant. 3:4).

Our wise and beloved brother and good friend, Father Gardeil, has this to say of the plenitude of the supernatural life:

Here God is all in all—not the God of the Philosopher, the First Cause, the Perfect Being—but God as He is in Himself, God the Father, God the Son, God the Holy Ghost. The blessed behold the wonderful spectacle of the Father begetting the Son through all eternity.... They see the Holy Ghost, the mutual love of the Father and the Son. ... The blessed behold the inmost essence of the Divinity, see in their first origin all those perfections of the creature which enchant us.... This is but a feeble notion of what the blessed see face to face, without comprehending its immensity, since it is boundless. There is nothing which touches, draws, or enchants us upon this earth, nothing of the good and the beautiful, which is not found in the ocean of the Divinity—though infinitely enlarged, infinitely more beautiful and more consoling.

In the presence of this spectacle, the eye and the heart are open wide and the Infinite penetrates them without difficulty. Just as we allow ourselves, without resistance, to be penetrated by the good things of this world, the scholar by truth, the artist by harmony, the friend by the thought of his friend, giving them a permanent home in the depths of our very selves, so that they dwell and remain intimately and profoundly there, in a way as true as that offered by material dwelling together, just so does God penetrate into the inmost recesses of the blessed. There He dwells and remains. It is a spiritual habitation of which lively thought and love form the foundation, the roof, and the walls. It is the only dwelling in which can live the incorporeal Being, the Pure Spirit, the Subsistent Thought and Love who is God. Such is the supernatural life when achieved, the life eternal in heaven.[33]

[32] Cf. Ia IIae, q. 28, a. 1, ad 3um.
[33] *The Gifts of the Holy Ghost in the Dominican Saints*, pp. 24-26.

THE MYSTICAL EVOLUTION

Identity of the Life of Glory and the Life of Grace

What is said of that intimate communication of God in glory can be applied in a lesser degree to the communication of God through grace, for the latter is the seed of the former. To be manifested in its plenitude it does not require any essential change, but only that it complete the development of its latent power and manifest clearly what it already is. At its basis, the supernatural life is identically the same in this exile as it is in heaven. The union with God which is communicated through grace to the essence of the soul, will remain the same for all eternity as it is at the end of life, for from that moment on it cannot be augmented. The union of charity is also identical, for this virtue is not destroyed as are faith and hope; but it will remain as an eternal bond of union, without diminishing or increasing the least bit after death.

1. UNION OF FAITH, HOPE, AND CHARITY AUGMENTED BY THE GIFTS

So it is that there can be souls on earth in a higher degree of grace and charity and, therefore, more intimately united with God than many of the souls who are now in glory. Glory merely manifests what we were and permits the full enjoyment of the Good possessed, and that without any obstacles. Only the union of knowledge here on earth is less; and so also, the joy consequent upon that knowledge. For faith, together with hope, although it goes straight to God in His reality, shows Him to us from afar off and in shadows and enigmas. When perfected by the gift of understanding, it penetrates, even here on earth, into the profundity of God and partly removes the shadows. When further perfected by the gift of wisdom and the various forms of the *sensus Christi*, which are expansions of this precious gift, we can in a certain sense feel, touch, see, and taste God in Himself.[34] With the development of the Christian life the knowledge of faith tends to be perfected by these two gifts and the other gifts and spiritual senses.

[34] Cf. John of St. Thomas, *In Iam IIae*, q.68, disp. 18, a.1.

THE DIVINE LIFE OF GRACE

2. PRESENT GLORY OF THE SONS OF GOD

Let us soften the brightness of the mysterious picture of the life of glory and we shall then have the picture of the life of the sons of God on earth. Father Gardeil explains this beautifully:

The life eternal is in the order of things accomplished what the present supernatural life is in the order of things which have not yet reached their conclusion though tending efficaciously toward that goal. Let me explain. It is the same reality which lies at the root of heavenly life and the supernatural life on earth; but, above, we possess it unveiled, never to lose it; while, here below, we have it veiled and may unhappily lose it. But, once more, apart from the difference between faith and sight, the possession is just as real. God dwells in our hearts as really as in the hearts of the blessed, since, in truth, we love Him and this love which we have now will not change after our entry into heaven. "Charity never dies," says St. Paul. Thus, the just man, the saint on earth, performs now, in the sight of God, the same triumphant act through which it will possess God in heaven. God already dwells in his love. His heart is a veritable heaven, although invisible and hidden from all eyes. Such, in its profound reality, is the supernatural life on earth.

But, to go still deeper into the springs of this mysterious life, who has been able to deposit this heavenly love in the heart of man, living in the world? Of ourselves we cannot produce even a particle of love for God as He is in Himself. First of all, we cannot naturally know God in such a way: He must be revealed to us. But how can we love naturally what we do not know naturally? Further, even after He has been revealed to us, how dare we love Him? I mean with the love of friendship, a love given and received, in a word, an efficacious love, not the false and discouraging love which one has for an inaccessible being, a love which is only a shadow of love. Yet it is with this given and efficacious love that the blessed love God. God has stooped down to them and what they could not do He has given them the power to do. He has made them participants of the love wherewith He loves Himself. The divine act has become, so far as it is possible, the act of the blessed. And as the Father and the Son love one another through the Holy Ghost, so the blessed love God through the Holy Ghost. But, since the love of the blessed for God is already in us in a state of efficacious tendency, it follows that God stoops down to us to make us participants of the love whereby He loves Himself, to raise our small love to the loftiness of His Heart. Thus it follows that the Holy Ghost, the consubstantial love of the

Father and the Son should, in a certain way, be at the bottom of our love of God. For, once more, we really love God, and it is by the Holy Ghost alone that one can love God.

The Holy Spirit, then, dwells in us in an especial way, though the whole Blessed Trinity dwells there as the object to which our faith and our love efficaciously tend. The Holy Ghost adds an especial way to this already intimate way of living in a soul. He resides at the bottom of the supernaturalized heart as the principle of the movement by which it tends toward the Holy Trinity. He is, so to speak, the heart of our heart. And, as the heart makes itself known in a man by an inclination which induces it, by a bias which orients it and draws it powerfully toward the good, so the Holy Ghost, as an inherent bias to our charity, orients us, draws us, and carries us along toward the Holy Trinity, the common center of the aspirations of the blessed in heaven and of the just on earth.

It is with the expansion of this force, hidden in the depths of our supernaturalized heart, that the Gifts of the Holy Ghost are connected. They are one of the two ways, and the most divine one, by which the activity of the Holy Ghost operates in the souls of the just.[35]

3. THE DELIGHTS OF DIVINE FRIENDSHIP

So charity and a living faith, accompanied by the gifts of the Holy Ghost, contract the substantial and loving presence of the Trinity in our souls as in the souls of those in heaven. Actually, charity is a love of intimate friendship between God and men, and such love demands continual association and affective and disinterested communication of pure and faithful benevolence. God our Lord, whose love is to do good, treats us this way. He loves us not for selfish reasons, but out of pure goodness and liberality, in order to lavish on us His inexhaustible riches.[36] If He asks for all our love and our whole hearts,[37] it is not to make us unhappy but that we may find our rest and happiness in Him.[38] If He takes His delight in us

---

[35] *The Gifts of the Holy Ghost in the Dominican Saints*, pp. 26–28.
[36] See Ia, q.44, a.4, ad 1um.
[37] Prov. 23:26.
[38] "O who shall grant me to rest in Thee," exclaims St. Augustine (*Confessions*, I, 5). "When shall I have the happiness of having Thee come into my heart to possess it entirely and to inebriate it with Thy Spirit so that I shall forget all my evil ways and embrace and be closely united to Thee who art my only good? What am I to Thee that Thou shouldst command me to love Thee and if I love Thee not, be angry at me and threaten me with greater woes? . . . Then tell my soul: *I am thy salvation*. So speak that I may hear and hearing, let me come in haste to embrace Thee."

(Prov. 8:31), it is because He sees that we share in His own goodness.

Since friendship either presupposes likeness or creates it, God, who desires to assimilate us to Himself as much as possible, communicates to us His inner life, His Spirit of love, so that we become participators in His divinity.[39] He establishes with us a friendship as close and cordial as that of a father, spouse, and brother, and it is so firm that on His part it would never be broken if we, unfortunately, would not break it by sinning. As true friendship tends to the presence of the beloved and the most intimate communication possible, so the friendship of God, which incomparably exceeds human friendship, contracts that ineffable communication of the Spirit of love, who pours forth in our souls divine charity that we may be able to love God with the selfsame love with which He loves us and with which the three adorable Persons love one another.[40] Therefore Scripture often repeats that if we love God He will abide in us and we in Him, thereby entering into friendly association with the sovereign Trinity.[41] Since God can remove all the obstacles impeding the union to which that friendship tends, it follows that on His part He will take care to strengthen the communication and presence of indwelling as much as possible. So charity, as the Angelic Doctor

---

[39] St. Francis de Sales, *The Love of God*, Bk. III, chap. 13: "Love not finding us equal, equalizes us; not finding us united, unites us."

[40] Blessed Henry Suso, *Unión*, chap. 5: "The Holy Ghost is the spiritual love who resides in the will as a bond and as a divine impetus which inspires and urges us on; He is the Charity of God.... In Him are transformed those who love God and are attracted to the light, and this in so intimate a manner that it is neither known nor understood except by experience. Come, then, to this God, One and Three ... but come without stain, without self-interest, and with a most pure love. To sinners He is a terrible God; to those who serve Him in hope of a reward He is a liberal God, omnipotent and majestic; but to those who banish servile fear and love Him with a pure love, He is a tender and complacent friend, a brother and a spouse. To be united with Him you must prepare your spirit and your body, renouncing the flesh and sensuality, subjecting the senses, seeking after the things of the spirit, and persevering in recollection and prayer. Such is the way to arrive at the higher Spirit, who is God, and to be united with Him. Then you will feel that this divine Spirit inspires you, calls you, invites you, and attracts you; ... When you find that you cannot perceive this, divest yourself of self.... Resign yourself and abandon yourself wholeheartedly to God and His power.... Throw yourself on Him with loving trust and remain buried in Him, forgetting yourself and losing yourself quite completely, not as to your spirit but as to your sensuality and the possession of your body and soul. And when you are thus elevated, lost in the immensity of the divine essence, you will then be united and transformed in the Spirit with God."

[41] John 14:23; I John 3:2-4; 4:12-16, etc.

teaches,[42] presupposes the possession of God already present in the soul, for it is a communication so intimate that it makes Him dwell in us and us in Him. By charity He resides in us as the soul of our supernatural life and as the beginning and immediate end of that vital act which does not cease, even at death, but will remain the same for all eternity.

We possess Him as present to us even now in a certain manner through the knowledge which a living faith and the intellectual gifts permit us to have of Him. But if, as St. Augustine says, to know God is to possess Him, this knowledge cannot be an indiscriminate kind; it must be vital and, as it were, experimental. It is not enough to have merely a cold and abstract speculative knowledge, which terminates in a sterile idea, but there is required a knowledge so living and throbbing that it touches the reality itself.

So God dwells in Christian children, but not in the great pagan philosophers; and He might dwell with great pleasure in humble and illiterate women, but not in famous theologians who are haughty in their pompous dialectic and their arrogant science. If they do not live in God and by God, they do not know Him as He is in Himself (I John 2:4; 4:9); nor can they converse amiably with Him or be on friendly relations with Him.[43] If they do not bind Him to their hearts by charity, they cannot possess Him in truth, no matter how much theological knowledge they possess. So it is that if God is to abide in us and if we are truly to possess Him, the acts of a dead faith are not enough, even if they flow from a semi-vital impulse of the Holy Ghost and are directed to God.[44] We must above all live in Him through grace, possess Him as the inner and immanent principle of action and life. Then through those same acts the indwelling and possession of God will become more intimate and complete.[45]

The acts of a vital and ardent faith make one feel to some extent the loving and adorable presence of the highest Truth, which we possess even now. And in the measure that the gift of wisdom is de-

---

[42] *Contra Gent.*, Bk. IV, chap. 21. Ia IIae, q.66, a.6: "But the love of charity is of that which is already possessed."

[43] St. Augustine, *Manual*, chap. 20: "He who would wish to possess knowledge of God, should love Him and he will know Him. In vain does anyone attempt to read, meditate, preach, or pray if he does not love God."

[44] John 1:5.

[45] Cf. IIa IIae, q.28, a.1, ad 1um: "Nevertheless, even in this life, He is present to those who love Him, by the indwelling of His grace."

THE DIVINE LIFE OF GRACE

veloped or made manifest, together with the acts of this living faith and the loving presence of God, so also does one begin to taste and see how sweet is the Lord, how delightful is His conversation, and how intimate His fellowship, which does not cause us disgust or bitterness, but joy and gladness.[46]

The Supernatural Life, the Kingdom of God on Earth

We have now to consider how the supernatural life is eternal life and divine life and why it is called also the kingdom of heaven and the kingdom of God on earth. "Life and kingdom," says Father Hugueny,[47] "are a phase of that development which begins here in time and will have its full expansion on the day of the coming of Christ in glory and the renewal of the world." This same thought is contained in the words: "then is the kingdom of God come upon you"; "the kingdom of God is within you"; "Come, ye blessed of My Father, possess you the kingdom prepared for you." [48]

The whole man participates in the supernatural life although it is received into the soul. By it he enters into such an intimate union with God that God's life becomes his own.[49] So it is that to those who are risen are attributed thrones, rule, and the power to judge, which are things proper to God. The symbols of the Apocalypse (the fruit of the tree of life, the hidden manna, the new name which is known only to him who receives it and which is the name of God Himself) all paint for us the ineffable quality of eternal life which is the very life of God Himself. If man enters this life so fully as to share in the divine attributes, it is because he is truly made a son of God. But the prerogatives which are peculiarly characteristic of the Son are the knowledge and love of the Father. Therefore divine filiation and the vision and love of God constitute the essence and the activity of eternal life.

---

[46] Wisd. 8:16.
[47] "A quel bonheur sommes nous destinés," *Revue Thomiste*, January, 1905.
[48] Matt. 12:28; 25:34; Luke 17:21.
[49] Cf. IIIa, q.2, a.10, ad 2um: "Habitual grace is only in the soul; but the grace—i.e., the free gift of God—of being united to the Divine Person belongs to the whole human nature, which is composed of soul and body. And hence it is said that the fulness of the Godhead dwelt corporeally in Christ because the Divine Nature is united not merely to the soul, but to the body also."

THE MYSTICAL EVOLUTION

1. MANIFESTATION OF THE DIVINE LIFE

St. Paul shows us the intimate and natural bond existing between that eternal life and the life of a Christian. The life which the Christian will possess, when, in view of the whole world, he receives the crown of justice, will not be entirely new. It will be the manifestation, the free and glorious expansion, of the divine life which now works mysteriously in the souls of the just. The new life which the believer received on that day when, after having been crucified and buried with Christ through baptism, he rose again from the baptismal waters, is the life of the risen Christ, a life entirely animated by the Spirit of God, which is also the Spirit of Christ. But, however active it might be at the beginning, this life does not attain its complete and manifest development until much later.

At baptism the life of sin, of the flesh, and of the old man loses its power of directing the activities of the faithful soul. In this sense it is said to die, for a life which has lost the power of directing its activity is no longer a true life, since it is no longer the first principle of movement.[50] But the organism over which the new life presides is still impregnated with the earthly tendencies of its carnal principle, and it remains subject to the limitations and impotencies of the world of corruption.[51] Under these conditions, the divine life of the faithful soul remains buried and hidden just as the life of Christ Himself is hidden, working in a mysterious manner toward the realization of His kingdom in this world and without manifesting anything of the glory and splendor that belong to it. But there will come a day of the great manifestation of the Son of Man, and then the life of His faithful followers will receive its full development and splendor. "When Christ shall appear, who is your life, then you also shall appear with Him in glory" (Col. 3:4).

St. John teaches that eternal life begins in this world, as does the

---

[50] "Actually," says Bacuez (*Manuel biblique*, p. 388, no. 733), "the natural life is not killed at baptism, but the Christian life ought to predominate in such a way that it alone appears to exist."

St. Francis de Sales, *Love of God*, Bk. VI, chap. 12: "As the stars without losing their light do not shine in the presence of the sun, but the sun shines in them and they are hidden in the light of the sun, so the soul, without losing her life, lives not herself when mingled with God, but God lives in her."

[51] Rom. 6:3-20; 8:9-18; Gal. 2:20; 4:1-17.

THE DIVINE LIFE OF GRACE

kingdom of God.[52] We have passed from death to life by a spiritual resurrection of which the true bodily resurrection at the end of time will be a consequence and a manifestation. Meanwhile, although lacking the privileges of glory, the Christian life is even now the eternal life, for it contains the essential element of that life which is divine filiation, and future glory will be a simple manifestation of this filiation. For that reason "the expectation of the creature waiteth for the revelation of the sons of God" (Rom. 8:19).

This divine filiation is not, then, a simple movement of loving trust on the part of the creature in the Creator, nor is it the mere communication of a gift superior to the natural condition and powers of that creature. It is a communication of the very life of God under the immediate action of His Spirit, who is the life of God and the life of Christ (Rom. 8:14–16). The life received in this communication is so intimate a participation in the divine life that its production is not called creation but generation.[53]

St. Paul affirms that this filiation is so intimate that it gives us, over and above the gifts of God, the selfsame rights of the eternal Son: we are "sons, heirs also; heirs indeed of God, and joint heirs with Christ." [54]

Among the goods reserved for the heirs of God, the most characteristic and those which are so exclusive to the Son that they are communicated only to those whom He wishes to have as sharers in His privileges, are a knowledge and love of God such as the Father has of the Son. "No one knoweth the Son but the Father; neither doth anyone know the Father but the Son, and he to whom it shall please the Son to reveal Him." [55] This knowledge is an operation characteristic of eternal life, just as divine filiation is its constitutive element. "Now this is everlasting life, that they may know Thee, the only true God" (John 17:3). The knowledge of God proper to a son who is already in full exercise of his rights and in full possession

---

[52] John 5:24–29; I John 5:11–13. Loisy, *L'Evangile*, p. 190: "St. John associates the idea of life in God with that of life in the kingdom and he thus conceives the eternal life as future and yet present. This idea is that of a deification of man ... effected through the partial communication of the divine Spirit whereby believers are united to God in Christ as Christ Himself is united to the Father."

[53] John 1:13; 3:3–8; I John 2:29; 3:9; 4:7; 5:4; I Pet. 1:3 f.; 2:2.

[54] Rom. 8:17.

[55] Matt. 11:27.

THE MYSTICAL EVOLUTION

of his heritage is the intuitive vision of God Himself. We shall possess this vision when we shall be manifested as we are, when we are like unto Him, seeing Him as He is and knowing Him as He knows us.[56] But now we know Him through loving Him: "And everyone that loveth is born of God, and knoweth God. He that loveth not, knoweth not God; for God is charity" (I John 4:7 f.).

Father Hugueny summarizes this doctrine as follows:

> The love of the Father places us in immediate possession of life and the dignity of the sons of God, but this life is not apparent to the eyes of the world. On the day of the great revelation that likeness will be so accentuated that there will redound to the body itself a life and a glory which will make this likeness manifest. This external splendor is not the essential element of our likeness to God for this likeness requires a more elevated activity, an operation impossible to one who does not enter into transcendent communication with the divine Being. We shall see Him as He is, and therefore we must be like unto Him and share in His very nature. Therefore the only ones who can know Him thus, that is, His sons, cannot help being love, as He is love. It is impossible for them to continue as His sons if they do not love Him with a filial love, if they do not have the desire to fulfill the will of the Father (John 4:32–34), if they do not strive to become pure as He Himself is pure and if they do not sacrifice for the salvation of their brethren with a love like that which God had for us in giving us His Son (I John 3:3; 4:9–11). This love is an activity characteristic of eternal life as is filial knowledge, that is, faith or vision. As long as the Christian does not renounce that life, there is nothing that can separate him from the charity of God, which is in Jesus Christ (Rom. 8:38).
>
> In order not to lose that life, but to protect and develop the divine seed (John 3:9), we should gird our body with the mortification of Jesus so that the life of Jesus will be manifest in our mortal flesh, knowing that He who resurrected Christ will also resurrect us with Him. Therefore we should not be dismayed, for although this outer man is weakened, the interior man is strengthened from day to day. The momentary and passing tribulation marvelously produces in us an eternity of glory. We know that if our earthly dwelling place, this mere tent, is destroyed, we have in heaven an eternal mansion which is the work of God. This firm hope of a resurrection is what consoles us at the thought of our temporal dissolution. Therefore do we weep because we desire to clothe ourselves in our heavenly garment without removing, if it were possible,

[56] See I John 3:1–3; I Cor. 13:10–12.

the earthly vesture. As long as we are in this earthly tabernacle we are prostrate with weeping, because we do not wish to be despoiled, but reclothed so that what is subject to death will be absorbed in life. . . . As long as we are in the body, we walk apart from the Lord—for we walk by the light of faith and not of vision—but we prefer to absent ourselves from the body and to be present to the Lord (II Cor. 4:10–17; 5:1–8).[57]

2. LONGINGS FOR DISSOLUTION AND UNION WITH GOD

This separation from the body is an evil; but, for the Apostle, it is preferred to the loss of the vision of his Lord for whom he sighs ardently. These longings increase in him, as in all the saints, growing more and more, in the measure that he feels more keenly that the fetters of the flesh hinder his ardent charity. So it is that he cries out: "Who shall deliver me from the body of this death?"[58] But also, in the measure that he identifies himself with Christ and lives the life of Christ Himself, so much the more will he resign himself and conform to His holy will, even though it means that he must continue to be separated from Him. Therefore he says to the Philippians: "For to me, to live is Christ; and to die is gain. And if to live in the flesh, this is to me the fruit of labor, and what I shall choose I know not. But I am straitened between two: having a desire to be dissolved and to be with Christ, a thing by far the better. But to abide still in the flesh is needful for you."[59]

That is how, according to St. Irenaeus, spiritual men live for God, for they have within them the Spirit of God who elevates them to a divine life. St. Augustine says that the pure soul desires the coming of its Spouse and yearns for His most pure embrace. No longer does the soul have to struggle to say: "Thy kingdom come." Formerly, fear made the soul say these words with dread; but now it can say with David (Ps. 6:4 f.): "But Thou, O Lord, how long? Turn to me, O Lord, and deliver my soul." There are many who die patiently; but he who is perfect continues to live patiently, when he would be pleased to die. That is the way the Apostle endured life patiently. But unless the soul truly desires the happy day of deliverance, it does not possess perfect charity. A soul inflamed with

---

[57] Hugueny, *op. cit.*, pp. 662–71, *passim*.
[58] Rom. 7:24.
[59] Phil. 1:21–24.

the fire of divine love cannot help but yearn for the possession of God, and it will even be necessary for Him to mitigate the ardor of those desires.[60]

"To be born of God," says Broglie,[61] "and to become His sons, is the origin of this sublime state. To live a divine life in God and with God, is its development. And what will its completion be but to see God and to be transformed in Him?"

ARTICLE VI

Familiar Relations with the Divine Persons

Faith enables us to know not only God's attributes as reflected in creatures but also His inner life; the gifts of understanding and wisdom give us the power to penetrate into the divine mysteries and to taste them; charity places us in intimate communication with the three divine Persons and permits us to know Them and converse with Them as we ought. From this it follows that through grace we enter into a most singular relationship with each of these Persons and not merely with the Trinity as a whole or with the simple unity of the divine nature. But we could hardly be able to recognize each Person in particular or communicate with Him unless there were some contact with the proper activities by which each is distinguished.

Fellowship with God and Participation in His Life

The works of grace are not like those of nature. The latter, as realized *ad extra*, are referred to the absolute unity of the divine omnipotence and are common to the three Persons, however much they may be appropriated to one or other of them according to our way of speaking. But the works of grace, since they make us enter into the joy of the Lord, into the intimate and secret life of the Divinity, and into friendly and familiar fellowship with the Father, Son, and Holy Ghost, raise us to a participation in those ineffable

---
[60] *In Evang. Joan.*, Tr. 9.
[61] *Surnaturel*, I, 34.

communications which are effected *ad intra*, in the very bosom of God. Thus some of these communications must be proper to one Person; and others, at least very singularly appropriated.

1. Proper Attribution and Appropriation

Ordinary appropriation consists in attributing in a special manner to one Person, actions or properties which in reality are common to all three, and the reason is that they possess a certain likeness or analogy to the truly proper activities of that particular Person. Thus we attribute to the Father eternity, omnipotence, and justice; to the Son, beauty, wisdom, and mercy; to the Holy Ghost, charity, goodness, peace, and joy. Yet actually these attributes are common to the three Persons and are applied to a particular Person only by appropriation. They pertain, not to the hidden mystery of the personal relations, but to the unity of the divine nature as known through created things. The personal relationships are known to us only by revelation; but unaided natural reason can, to some extent, trace and recognize the common attributes through the works *ad extra* which are common to the entire Trinity.

The following attributions are entirely proper to each Person, as are the names Father, Son, and Holy Ghost: the eternal Father is the Father of our Lord Jesus Christ and also our Father who is in heaven; the Son is the Word of the Father, the eternal splendor of His glory and the image of His substance, the uncreated Wisdom, the Only-begotten who is in the bosom of the Father, the First-born among many brethren and our Brother also; the Holy Ghost is personal Love, the subsisting Charity of God, the great gift of the Father and the Son. The same thing is true in regard to many other titles that are intimately connected with these and are attributed almost continually by Scripture and tradition to one Person and not referred to the others, except in a different manner or in a less proper sense. So it is, we believe, when we call the Holy Ghost a sweet Guest, the intimate Vivifier, Sanctifier, Director, and the Inspiration of the soul.[1]

---

[1] "Although the works of the most holy Trinity which are effected extrinsically are common to the three Persons, yet many of them are properly attributed to the Holy Ghost, so that we may understand that they redound to us through the im-

THE MYSTICAL EVOLUTION

Doubtless, in these continual appropriations there is something very special which we are unable to define or even indicate; something so ineffable that it cannot be spoken, but something that serves as the fundament for the singular relations which enable us to know and converse lovingly with each one of the divine Persons with whom we enter into that mysterious fellowship of eternal life, that life which was in the Father and which He manifested to us that we might be associated with Him and His only-begotten Son. Thus, by means of the illumined eyes of a heart inflamed with charity and by means of the savory experience which the gift of wisdom gives to them, the great saints see, feel, and know for certain—although they cannot explain it—that each divine Person does His proper work in the soul and influences our sanctification according to His personal character.[2] This happens to such an extent that in their deified hearts the adorable mystery of the Blessed Trinity redounds and shines forth.[3]

---

mense charity of God. . . . It can be perceived that those effects which are referred properly to the Holy Ghost arise from the great love of God for us" (*Roman Catechism*, I, a.8, no. 8).

"Sanctification," says Broglie (*Surnaturel*, I, 30), "is always attributed to the Holy Ghost."

"Although these effusions," says Gay (*Elévat. sur N.S.J.C.*, XII), "are the work and gift of the entire Trinity; nevertheless it is easy to see that each of them embodies some characteristic proper to one of the three Persons in such a way that it can and ought to be regularly appropriated. So it is in the Creed: creation is appropriated to the Father, redemption to the Son, and sanctification to the Holy Ghost."

[2] "That which was from the beginning, which we have heard, which we have seen with our eyes, which we have looked upon and our hands have handled: of the Word of life: for the life was manifested; and we have seen, and do bear witness, and declare unto you the life eternal which was with the Father, and hath appeared to us: that which we have seen and have heard, we declare unto you, that . . . our fellowship may be with the Father, and with His Son Jesus Christ" (I John 1:1-3).

Fervent souls who resign themselves totally to the hands of God and without any desire other than that of pleasing Him "receive three signal favors from the three Persons of the most holy Trinity; from the Father, a strength almost invincible in action, in suffering, and in temptations; from the Son, rays and splendours of truth, which shine without ceasing into their soul; from the Holy Spirit, a fervour, a sweetness, and a consolation full of joy" (Lallemant, *Spiritual Doctrine*, Prin. II, sect. 2, chap. 2).

[3] Tauler, *Institutions*, chap. 33: "God the Father will accomplish without ceasing the generation of His Word in these souls and they will experience this ineffable generation within themselves. Their spirit will undergo a certain alteration, elevation, and exaltation in the singular presence of a peaceful eternity and the departure from creatures and perishable things. They will begin to consider all things tasteless that do not proceed from this generation and they themselves will be changed

THE DIVINE LIFE OF GRACE

Actually, deification establishes between the soul and God a multitude of marvelous relations. Although these relations cannot be portrayed adequately by any manner of expression, yet the Fathers attempt to explain them by a variety of images which, if taken together, will give us a more approximate and true concept by which we can soar above all symbols to ponder and admire in silence what cannot be expressed in words or represented by any kind of images. Some of those terms used by the Fathers to help us recognize the true character of each Person imply something proper to the particular Person, and others merely indicate an appropriation which is more exclusive than ordinary appropriation.

Whereas the operations of the divine nature *ad extra*, since they are common, are appropriated to one or another Person only by a remote sort of analogy, the operations of grace, which are vital activities, share in the life and communications *ad intra*. Further, since these operations of grace are of a social nature, they are of themselves either proper or especially appropriated to one Person and not to the others nor to the unity of the divine nature.[4]

---

to conform to it. The soul and all its multiple activities will be reduced to a marvelous unity." See also Blosius, *Spiritual Instructions*, Appendix, chap. 2; St. Mary Magdalen of Pazzi, *Œuvres*, I, chap. 28.

Blessed Henry Suso, *Eternal Wisdom*, chap. 32: "From the generation and filiation of God proceeds the true interior and exterior abandonment of chosen souls. Being sons of God, . . . they participate through grace in the divine nature and divine activity, for God always produces a son like to Himself in nature and operations. The just man who delivers himself up to God triumphs over time and possesses a blessed life which is transformed in God. . . . Through perfect renunciation the soul is lost in God to its eternal gain; it is buried in the divine essence and is no longer distinct from God, nor does it know Him through images, light, or created forms, but in Himself. . . . It is a marvelous exchange in which the soul, in the abyss of the Divinity, is transformed into the unity of God in order to be lost to itself and blended with Him, not, however, in regard to its nature, but in regard to its life and faculties."

"The life of grace," writes Gay, (*op. cit.*, I, 67), "is the ineffable circulation of divinity among the Father, Son, and Holy Ghost."

[4] St. Thomas, *Contra Gent.*, IV, chap. 21: "It is fitting that all that God effects in us should proceed at once from the Father and the Son and the Holy Ghost as from an efficient cause; but the word of wisdom by which we know God is properly representative of the Son and, likewise, the love by which we love God is properly representative of the Holy Ghost."

"When the Holy Ghost is given," says the same holy doctor (*In I Sent.*, dist. 14, q.2, a.2, ad 3um), "there is effected in us a union with God according to the mode which is proper to that Person, namely, through love. . . . Whence, this knowledge is quasi-experimental."

In Ia, q.43, a.5, ad 2um: "The soul is made like to God by grace. Hence for a divine person to be sent to anyone by grace, there must be a likening of the soul

THE MYSTICAL EVOLUTION

We do not venture to say precisely which of these operations are proper and which are appropriated, for not even those who could have done so much better than we, have attempted it. Indeed, to strive to define these things too accurately would be to run the risk of falling into dangerous intellectualism. We shall be content to indicate a few of the principal operations which the saints have insisted on, so that souls who are beginning to understand the reality of these awesome communications will recognize and better appreciate the truth. Then they will not be frightened on seeing that what astonishes them with its excellence and divinity is, through the goodness and wisdom of God, quite possible and even easy; that that communication which seemed to them far beyond their capabilities and even impossible, is impressed on them with the indisputable evidence of a fact.

2. ROLE OF EACH PERSON IN ADOPTION AND DEIFICATION

The basis for all these relations is adoptive filiation, which can be said to be common to the three divine Persons so far as they all contribute to this mysterious work, yet each in His own manner. This filiation, like the subsequent deification, is not an instantaneous and invariable thing, but it is continuous and progressive. We become more and more properly sons of God as we conform ourselves more and more to the Only-begotten, with whom we ought to be made one.[5] In this continuous operation, apart from what is common to

---

to the divine person who is sent, by some gift of grace. Because the Holy Ghost is Love, the soul is assimilated to the Holy Ghost by the gift of charity; hence the mission of the Holy Ghost is according to the mode of charity. Whereas the Son is the Word, not any sort of word, but one Who breathes forth Love. . . . Thus the Son is sent not in accordance with every and any kind of intellectual perfection, but according to the intellectual illumination, which breaks forth into the affection of love. . . . Thus Augustine plainly says (*De Trin.*, iv., 20): *The Son is sent whenever He is known and perceived by anyone.* Now perception implies a certain experimental knowledge; and this is properly called wisdom (*sapientia*), as it were a sweet knowledge (*sapida scientia*)."

In this way the entire Trinity is the efficient cause of the incarnation of the Word "because the works of the Trinity are inseparable. Yet the Son alone assumed the form of a slave in His own Person" (*Symb. fidei*, Conc. Tolet. XI). We could also say that the entire Trinity is the efficient cause of our justification, although the Son alone is the meritorious cause and the Holy Ghost alone the quasi-formal cause. So it is that there are sins which directly offend the Father, the Son, or the Holy Ghost, such as, respectively, lukewarmness, ignorance, or malice; and these are unpardonable as long as the spirit remains opposed to God (Matt. 12:31 f.; Luke 12:10).

[5] See St. Augustine, *De peccat. mer. et. rem.*, Bk. II, nos. 9 f.

the Trinity as a work *ad extra*—which is to act upon a pure creature so as to elevate it to the divine order—there is in the terminus of this elevation something characteristic of each Person, since each of them, in accordance with the popular expression of the mystics, performs I Its special work in our continuous renewal and sanctification.

Although the making or producing of a natural effect in the creature is a work common to the entire Trinity,[6] our being made sons of God is not an effect of this type. Rather it is a deification whereby there is communicated to us that intimate participation in the divinity itself through which we are created anew in Jesus Christ. We are reborn, not from something extraneous to God, not from a corruptible seed, but from an incorruptible one, the seed of the eternal Father. That mystical seed which abides in us and preserves us from sin [7] can truly be said to be the vivifying Spirit Himself who is communicated to us, according to the daring and energetic expression of St. Irenaeus, as the living and vivifying seed of the Father. To the Father, therefore, is attributed this second creation and renewal.[8]

On receiving the divine participation through the regeneration of water and the Holy Ghost and a rebirth in God Himself,[9] we can, through the power which Jesus Christ merited for us and granted to us, become sons of God. That rebirth and transformation which we experience on passing from being sons of Adam to the status of sons of the Most High, does not entail any action on His part, but rather a communication, so intimate and so vital that it becomes a true sharing in the eternal generation. And this, properly speaking, is not to make or effect a simple change in us in the way that God makes or produces an effect in other creatures, but it is to engender us to the image of His only-begotten Son. Therefore, although the Gospel says (John 1:12) that we are made sons of God—"*Dedit eis potestatem filios Dei fieri*"—it is not to be understood in the sense that God actually makes us such, but that He engenders us, adopts us or regenerates us through Jesus Christ.[10] It is in this way that we are reborn from an incorruptible seed through the word of God, for God has

---

[6] See IIIa, q.23, a.2; *In Rom.* 8, lec. 3.
[7] See I John 3:9; 5:18.
[8] Ps. 103:30.
[9] John 1:13; I John 3:9; 4:7; 5:1-18.
[10] Deut. 32:18; Jas. 1:18; I John 5:1.

engendered us in the Word of His truth. Hence adoptive filiation becomes a participation in the eternal sonship of the Word, who is engendered and not made.

Engendered from all eternity, the Word is most truly the Son and the model of all other sons. As First-born among many brethren (Rom. 8:29), He requires that these brethren must in some way, like Himself, be engendered and not made. As in the work of the Incarnation, in spite of its termination *ad extra* and the concurrence in it of all the three divine Persons, the Word alone took on human flesh, and the Father alone is the Father of our Lord Jesus Christ even as man. So, in the work of our adoption and regeneration, notwithstanding its being a work *ad extra*, we must recognize something in it that is proper to the eternal Father, from whom flows all paternity in heaven and on earth. Again, in the anointing of Jesus Christ and in our own, we must recognize another work which is proper to the Spirit, the consecrator and sanctifier.[11]

It is the Son by nature and excellence, our Savior and Model and the true Mediator between God and man, who merited for us this communication of the Holy Ghost. He shared in our nature that we might be able to participate in His and thus enter into fellowship with Him.[12] So it is that He gives us the power to become sons of God by being reborn in His Spirit. This rebirth will be in the measure that we are renewed in the Spirit of adoption and sanctification, and this renewal will be in the measure that we despoil ourselves of the earthly man.[13]

[11] Luke 4:18; Acts 10:38; II Cor. 1:21; I John 2:20.
[12] "If the Word became flesh and the eternal Son of the living God became a son of man," says St. Irenaeus (*Haer.*, Bk. III, chap. 19, no. 1), "it was in order that man, by entering into fellowship with the Word and receiving the status of adoption, might become a son of God."
[13] John 1:12 f.; 3:5-8; Eph. 4:22-24; Col. 3:9 f. *Ascent of Mount Carmel*, Bk. II, chap. 5: "And it is this that St. John desired to explain, when he said: *Qui non ex sanguinibus, neque ex voluntate carnis, neque ex voluntate viri, sed ex Deo nati sunt* (John 1:13). As though he had said: He gave power to be sons of God—that is, to be transformed in God—only to those who are born, not of blood—that is, not of natural constitution and temperament—neither of the will of the flesh—that is, of the free will of natural capacity and ability—still less of the will of man—wherein is included every way and manner of judging and comprehending with the understanding. He gave power to none of these to become sons of God, but only to those that are born of God—that is, to those who being born again through grace, and dying first of all to everything that is of the old man, are raised above themselves to the supernatural, and receive from God this rebirth and adoption, which transcends all that can be imagined. . . . He that is not born again in the Holy Spirit

THE DIVINE LIFE OF GRACE

But it is the Father who more properly adopts us and constitutes us His sons through Jesus Christ, for He it is who freely engendered us through the Word of truth.[14] This act of generation is proper to the person of the Father [15] as also is the corresponding act of adoption through the Son, through whom He has brought many sons into glory.[16] Thus He predestined us and adopted us and blessed us through His Son, through whom we receive grace and charity in the Spirit of sanctification.[17]

In brief, the Father regenerates us for eternal life [18] and makes us share in His very own nature in order to make us like to the image of His only-begotten Son; [19] the Son gives us the power to become sons of God and His own brothers and co-heirs; and both together call us and translate us from death to life by communicating to us their Spirit of love,[20] who vivifies us with that life of grace which is the seed of glory and imprints upon us the seal of Christ.[21] So this work is in a certain way common to the whole Trinity; and yet, as

---

will not be able to see this kingdom of God, which is the state of perfection; and to be born again in the Holy Spirit in this life is to have a soul most like to God in purity, having in itself no admixture of imperfection, so that pure transformation can be wrought in it through participation of union, albeit not essentially."

[14] Jas. 1:18.
[15] Cf. IIIa, q.23, a.2.
[16] Heb. 2:10 f.
[17] Eph. 1:3-6: "Blessed be the God and Father of our Lord Jesus Christ, who hath blessed us with spiritual blessings in heavenly places, in Christ. As He chose us in Him before the foundation of the world, that we should be holy and unspotted in His sight in charity. Who hath predestinated us unto the adoption of children through Jesus Christ unto Himself, according to the purpose of His will, unto the praise of the glory of His grace, in which He hath graced us in His beloved Son."
Eph. 2:18: "For by Him we have access both in one Spirit to the Father."
I Cor. 8:6: "Yet to us there is but one God, the Father, of whom are all things, and we unto Him; and one Lord, Jesus Christ, by whom are all things, and we by Him."
[18] See I Pet. 1:3 f.
[19] Rom. 8:29.
[20] See I John 3:14.
[21] "The Son of God," says St. Cyril of Alexandria (*In Joan.*, I, 1), "came to give us the power of being by grace what He is by nature and to make common what is proper to Himself. Such is His kindness to men and such is His charity.... Made participants in the Son through the Holy Ghost, we have received the stamp of His likeness and we have been conformed to the divine image.... We are, then, sons of God by adoption and by imitation; while He is so by nature and in the fullness of truth. Here lies the difference: on the one hand there is a natural dignity; on the other, a favor by grace.... We have received the power to become sons of God, and we have received it from the Son; whence it is manifest that we were born of God by adoption and through grace, whereas He is the Son by nature."

the Angelic Doctor states (IIIa, q. 23, a. 2, ad 3um), it is attributed to the Father as author, to the Son as meritorious cause and model, and to the Holy Ghost as vivifier and deifier, who imprints in us the living image of the Word. Yet it is attributed particularly to the Father since it is more intimately connected with His personal character.[22]

Hence, strictly, it seems that it should be said that our adoption is proper to the Father through the Son, through whom we receive grace—indeed, the grace par excellence which is the communication to us of the Spirit of adoption. The Father "hath predestinated us unto the adoption of children through Jesus Christ. . . . In whom we have redemption. . . . In whom you were signed with the Holy Spirit of promise: who is the pledge of our inheritance" (Eph. 1:5-13). Therefore we give thanks to the Father—*ex quo omnia*—to the Son who is our older Brother, Head, and Mediator—*per quem omnia*—and to the Holy Ghost, who is the common life of love—*in quo omnia.*[23]

3. DIVINE INDWELLING

If the right to call God by the name of Father is, as St. Leo maintains, the greatest of all gifts, it is because in it are epitomized all things else and all things are ordained to this filiation. And if adoption, although common, is not attributed equally to the three Persons, we can say much the same of the consequent indwelling. The Father, in union with the Son who is in His bosom, dwells in us as in His temple, which is sanctified by the communication of His Spirit of love who consecrates us by His unction [24] and rebuilds us by His charity, thereby making us a fitting dwelling place of God.[25] Thus

---

[22] St. Thomas, *In III Sent.*, dist. X, q. 2, a. 1, ad 2um.
[23] St. Augustine, *Meditations*, chap. 31: "I invoke Thee, O glorious Trinity, Father, Son, and Holy Ghost: God, Lord and Consoler; fountain, river, and torrent; one from whom all things proceed, one through whom all things were made, and one in whom all things have their being; living life, life from the living, and vivifier of the living; one of Himself, one of the other, and one from the other two . . . from whom, through whom, and in whom all things are blessed."
Ibid., chap. 33: "Glory be to the Father who created us; glory be to the Son who redeemed us; glory be to the Holy Ghost who sanctified us; glory be to the most high and undivided Trinity whose works are inseparable."
[24] St. Thomas, *Comm. in II Cor.* 6:16: "A temple is a place dedicated to God for His indwelling."
[25] Eph. 2:21 f.

THE DIVINE LIFE OF GRACE

do we become like so many living stones in this temple so far as we are like so many other gods deified by the eternal One.[26]

Likewise the loving Consoler and Sanctifier of souls (cf. I Pet. 1:2) contracts with souls a union which is most singular, as the better informed and more experienced theologians are beginning to admit, either implicitly or explicitly.[27] However, it is not accurate to say that it is impossible there should be any type of union with a divine Person other than the hypostatic union. For, since these ineffable realities do not fall within the scope of our weak intellects, neither do they admit of our customary distinctions. Consequently no one can declare such things impossible, and, if we would wish to appreciate them adequately, we must adhere, not to what appears to us more reasonable and less astonishing, but to the testimony of Sacred Scripture and the Fathers and to the inner experience of holy Church. We shall find that they always present the Holy Ghost to us as the consecrator and vivifier who dwells in us as the life of our soul and the soul of our life.[28]

This union, which is so intimate that it makes us one with Christ and united in the Spirit in God, is not hypostatic, as neither was the union of the Holy Ghost with Christ, in whom He resided fully and from whom He redounds to all the living members of the mystical body. If we can have, as we undoubtedly do, so singular a mystical union with the incarnate Word as that of members with the Head; if the sacramental union which we enjoy when we receive the Holy Eucharist worthily is a real and immediate contact with His Person, and yet these are not hypostatic; why then can we not have with His Spirit, which is the divine soul of the Church, a union or relation which is similar to that between the members of the body and its soul?

This mystical union with God which enables us to receive and feel His vital influx; this loving indwelling and sweet cohabitation of

---

[26] St. Augustine, *Enchiridion*, chap. 56: "The temple of God is constructed of gods made by the uncreated God."

[27] Cf. Ramière, Gay, Broglie, Bellamy, Prat, Weiss, Gardeil, Hugueny, etc. Pope Leo XIII teaches that "although the indwelling is effected by the presence of the entire Trinity ... yet it is peculiarly ascribed to the Holy Ghost" (*Divinum illud munus*).

[28] Gardeil, *The Gifts of the Holy Ghost*, p. 15: "The supernatural order is gratuitous in all its degrees, and the greatest arguments of fitness are not comparable in value to a single word spoken by God."

God with souls, which places us in familiar relationship with the entire Trinity and gives us a fellowship with the Father and His true Son through the communication of the Holy Ghost: all these make it possible for us to share in the divine life, action, and power. Therefore the functions characteristic of the life of the sons of God, which are to know and love Him as He is in Himself, have for their object not only the unity of the divine nature or the Trinity in common, but also each one of the divine Persons. "Now this is eternal life: that they may know Thee, the only true God, and Jesus Christ, whom Thou has sent" (John 17:3). "But you shall know Him [the Paraclete], because He shall abide with you, and shall be in you" (*ibid.*, 14:17). This sweet knowledge, which is not from hearing but is much like intuitive knowledge and intimate experience, entails very special relations.[29]

4. DIVINE PATERNITY

The eternal Father is our true Father—*ex quo omnis paternitas in coelo et in terra nominatur*—whom we all ought to salute by saying: Our Father, who art in heaven, reign in our hearts in such a way that we shall always do Thy holy will, and Thy Name will be sanctified in us. This kingdom of God which is within our very selves is the communication of His Spirit,[30] and the daily bread which we ask is the bread of life which He sends us from heaven and which we truly consume.

The Savior and His apostles teach us to bestow on Him always that loving name of Father as is seen in these examples: "Go to My brethren and say to them: 'I ascend to My Father and to your Father'" (John 20:17). "Blessed be the God and Father of our Lord Jesus Christ, who according to His great mercy hath regenerated us" (I Pet. 1:3). "Behold what manner of charity the Father hath bestowed upon us, that we should be called and should be the sons of God" (I John 3:1). "And because you are sons, God hath sent the Spirit of His Son into your hearts, crying: Abba, Father" (Gal. 4:6). "Grace be to you, and peace from God the Father, and from the Lord Jesus Christ" (Eph. 1:2).

For that reason the Church always invokes God by that sweet

---

[29] Cf. *Interior Castle*, seventh mansions, chap. 1.
[30] See Ia IIae, q.69, a.2, ad 3um.

THE DIVINE LIFE OF GRACE

name through His only-begotten Son and the power of His Spirit. For no one can go to the Father except through the Son; nor yet, as St. Irenaeus says, can he know the Son save through the Holy Ghost, the Spirit of truth and charity who gives testimony of Him. Moreover, neither to the Son nor to the Holy Ghost, as such, is given the name of Father except rarely and then in a less proper sense.

This name "Father" is given to the loving Paraclete only once by the Church, in the Sequence for the feast of Pentecost, wherein He is called the Father of the poor: *Veni Pater pauperum.* As the Consoler, the Holy Ghost acts rather in the role of a mother, who caresses us and clasps us to His bosom to speak to our hearts.[81] Again, He is like an eagle who protects us, warms us beneath His wings, and teaches us how to fly.[82] Moreover, it is well known that in Hebrew the expression for Spirit of God (*ruaj-elohim*) is feminine.[33]

The Church never gives to the Son the title of Father, but that of Lord and Savior. Yet, as the Spouse of the Church, He is the "Father of the world to come" (Isa. 9:6) and the Father of all faithful Christians, even though they are not in grace, just as the Church is the true mother of the just and of sinners. With the Church He regenerates us in the waters of baptism through the power of His vivifying Spirit.

But the Father sent to us and still gives us His only-begotten Son to redeem us, to bring us to life together with Himself, and to adopt us.[84] So the Son is the one sent from God, the Messias, Redeemer, Mediator, Savior, Master, Model, the Way, the Truth, and the Life, Shepherd of our souls, Lamb of God who takes away the sins of the world, Head of the mystical body of the Church, Cornerstone of the house of God, etc.

The glorified Son sent us and still gives us, in union with the Father, the Spirit which proceeds from both of Them.[85] So the Holy

---

[81] Isa. 66:11 f.; Osee 2:14.

[82] Ps. 16:8; 35:8; 56:2; 60:5; 62:8; Deut. 32:11.

[33] In a certain sense, we have been born of the Holy Ghost as is seen in the statement of the Lord: "Amen, amen, I say to thee, unless a man be born again of water and the Holy Ghost, he cannot enter into the kingdom of God. That which is born of the flesh is flesh; and that which is born of the Spirit is spirit. . . . So is everyone that is born of the Spirit" (John 3:5-8).

[84] John 3:16 f.; Gal. 4:4 f.; Eph. 1:5; 2:5 f.

[85] John 14:15-18; 15:26 f.; Rom. 8:15; I Cor. 6:19; Gal. 4:6.

Ghost is the great Gift of God and the perpetual Consoler whom the Father and the Son have given and sent that He might nourish and vivify us and inspire us and teach us all truth.

Relations with the Word

If from the eternal Father is derived and denominated all paternity in heaven and on earth, then from His only-begotten Son, the divine Word, is derived and denominated all filiation by reason of His eternal filiation. Indeed His sonship, since it is a natural one, is the prototype of ours, which is adoptive. "Wherefore, as by the work of creation," says St. Thomas, "the Divine goodness is communicated to all creatures in a certain likeness, so by the work of adoption the likeness of natural sonship is communicated to men." [86] Our filiation is attributed to the Son as its exemplar, according to the words of the Apostle: "For whom He foreknew, He also predestinated to be made conformable to the image of His Son, that He might be the first-born amongst many brethren" (Rom. 8:29).

1. Christ as Our Brother

His filiation is infinitely more excellent than ours, for His is eternal, natural, and necessary, whereas ours is temporal, gratuitous, and free, and He is God by nature whereas we are but men deified by grace. Nevertheless He who by reason of His infinite superiority is the only-begotten,[87] desired to be also the first-born, not disdaining to accept us and recognize us as His brothers.[88] "He who calls the Father of Jesus Christ 'our Father,'" says St. Augustine (*In Joan.*, no. 3), "what can he call Christ but 'our Brother'?" This most noble fraternity with Jesus Christ obliges us to be His faithful imitators and to participate in His glorious actions so that we may thereby glorify the common Father.[89] Therefore we should make ourselves like to Him as our true exemplar, adjusting our life and conduct to

---

[86] Cf. IIIa, q. 23, a. 1, ad 2um.
[87] John 1:14.
[88] Heb. 1:6; 2:11; John 20:17.
[89] "He desired to be our Brother and when we say *Our Father* to God, this is made manifest in us. For he who says *Our Father* to God, says *Brother* to Christ. Therefore he who has God for his Father and Christ for his Brother need not fear the dreadful day" (St. Augustine, *Enarr. in Ps. 48*).

THE DIVINE LIFE OF GRACE

His, until we faithfully copy in ourselves His divine image and reproduce within ourselves all His sacred mysteries.[40]

By reason of His eternal filiation, Christ is the elder Brother of all the sons of God, whether men or angels. By reason of His temporal filiation, in which He assumed our human nature and not that of an angel, He became our Brother in a twofold sense and thus He tightened the bonds of this fraternity in a loving manner when He appeared entirely like unto us.[41]

This self-abasement of the Son of God, which so confounded the pride of Lucifer, who refused to adore Him in human form, ought to fill us with a noble pride and prompt us to eternal gratitude and a most faithful cooperation with such a dignity. St. Augustine says: "He lowered Himself that we might be exalted; and retaining His own nature, He made Himself a sharer in ours that we might be made sharers in His. He did not lessen Himself by descending, but we better ourselves by ascending." [42] "Just as the Lord," says St. Athanasius, "became man by putting on a human body, so we men are deified by putting on the Word of God." [43]

[40] Blessed Henry Suso, *Eternal Wisdom*, chap. 30: "He who wishes to turn to God and become a son of the Eternal Father must abandon self and be entirely configured to Jesus Christ in order to arrive at the beatific vision. . . . Among My chosen souls I have some who live in complete forgetfulness of the world and self; and they preserve a virtue that is as stable, as immutable and, as it were, as eternal as God Himself. Through grace they are transformed into the image and unity of their principle, and so they neither think of nor love nor desire anything other than God and His holy will."

Bacuez, *op. cit.*, p. 215, no. 587: "The perfection of the Christian consists in being despoiled as much as possible of everything that he has received from the sinful Adam and of being reclothed, animated, and filled with the virtues, gifts, and perfections which the Savior deigns to communicate to him. . . . If all the faithful would cooperate with their calling, Jesus Christ would live in them and reproduce in each one of them, together with His affections and virtues, the likeness of His mysteries. Then it could be said of each member of the Savior that it is, like the Head and Model, crucified, dead to the world, risen, and glorified."

[41] Heb. 2:14-17.

[42] *Epist. 140 ad Honorat.*, chap. 4.

[43] *Sermo 4 contra Arian.* St. Catherine of Genoa, *Dialogues*, III, 9: "O Lord, what dost Thou call souls that are dear to Thee? 'I say to them: *You are gods and sons of the Most High*' (Ps. 81). O Love! By this word Thou dost destroy whatever is earthly in those who love Thee and Thou dost lift them to Thyself. Man disappears and only Thou livest. . . . Be eternally blessed, my God, who hast thus divinized us. . . . And since Thy name is the Omnipotent (Exod. 6), Thou dost fulfill in us also the prophecy which was spoken of Christ: that He should have no will but that of His Father (Isa. 53). Yes, Lord, since we have been called by Thee to follow after Christ, to be other Christs, we must strive to do nothing but what Thou dost

THE MYSTICAL EVOLUTION

The Incarnation, effected in the womb of the most pure Virgin through the working of the Holy Ghost, is the reason and basis of our regeneration, which is realized through the operation of the same Spirit and under the protection of the same Virgin in the womb of the Church, which symbolizes a second Eve and is the mother of all true believers. Therefore the most holy Virgin, as also the holy mother Church, had to receive a most copious communication from the Holy Ghost so that it might redound to us.[44] And since the Father predestined us to be conformed to the image of His Son so that Christ might be the first-born among many brethren, He also "predestinated us unto the adoption of children through Jesus Christ . . . to re-establish all things in Christ." [45] And so He sent His Son to us through the woman, to redeem us and to give us the adoption of sons.[46]

In this way we receive from the incarnate Word the power to become sons of God, being reborn in His sacrament of regeneration through the power of the vivifying Spirit, who remains eternally in His Church.[47] Therefore in order to be justified and deified we must be reborn in Him and live in the bosom of the Church. So the Council of Trent teaches (Sess. VI, no. 3): "Unless they be reborn in Christ they cannot be justified, for by that rebirth through the merits of His passion, the grace which justifies them is given them." St. Paul teaches the same thing: "For you are all the children of God by faith in Christ Jesus. For as many of you as have been baptized in Christ, have put on Christ." [48]

---

wish. O how wonderful is the power of this love which changes a poor and weak creature into a god! How beautiful is this servitude of love which reigns in sweetness and grace to free us from the slavery of corruption and to make us enter into the liberty of His glory (Rom. 8), to be reclothed in His power, grandeur, and majesty, and to make us share His happiness, to live His life in a certain sense, and to shine with Him like stars in a glorious eternity."

[44] Mary of Agreda, *Mystical City of God*, Bk. I, chap. 13: "If these gifts existed in Christ, our Redeemer and Lord, as in their fountainhead, they were in Mary as in a lake or ocean, from whence they are distributed over all creation: for from her superabundance they overflow into the whole Church. This is referred to by Solomon in the book of Proverbs, when Wisdom is made to say that she builds for herself a house on seven pillars, etc. and in it she prepares the table, mixes the wine and invites the little ones and the uninstructed, drawing and raising them up from their childhood to teach them prudence" (Prov. 9:1-2).

[45] Eph. 1:5, 10.
[46] Gal. 4:4 f.
[47] John 1:11; 3:5 f.; 6:64; 14:16-18.
[48] Gal. 3:26 f.

Thus, through baptism we are engrafted on Jesus as on the true tree of life so that by means of the divine vigor we can produce fruits of virtue and glory.[49] Incorporated in Him, our souls are espoused to Him in faith and charity in such wise that they are one with Him and animated and impressed with His very Spirit.

But since the communication of the Holy Ghost can and ought to be increased incessantly, when the Savior—now glorious since His passion and absent from us in order to test our faith—sees us longing for Him and desirous of imitating Him, He sends the Holy Ghost to us anew and even more fully in order to transfigure and glorify us. For this reason, when taking leave of His disciples, He said to them: "But I tell you the truth: it is expedient to you that I go. For if I go not, the Paraclete will not come to you; but if I go, I will send Him to you. . . . But when He, the Spirit of truth, is come, He will teach you all truth. . . . He shall glorify Me."[50] And so to whomsoever truly believes and lives in Him, Christ promises the communication of His Spirit in such plenitude that "out of his belly shall flow rivers of living water."[51]

2. CHRIST, THE GOOD SHEPHERD AND CORNERSTONE

As the Good Shepherd who lays down His life for His sheep, He lets us hear His soft voice and loving call, which beckons us to the shelter of contemplation. There He feeds us with the living words which proceed from the mouth of the Father, and He manifests Himself to us and gives us eternal life, for He came that we might have life and have it more abundantly.[52] He is at once the shepherd and the gate through which we enter into the sheepfold, that is, the

---

[49] Rom. 6:5; 11:24; John 15:5.
[50] John 16:7-14.
[51] John 7:38. Lallemant, *Spiritual Doctrine*, Prin. IV, chap. 2, a.4: "It was necessary that the Incarnate Word should enter into glory, before He sent the Holy Spirit as Comforter. The interior comfort which the Holy Spirit bestows is much more profitable than the bodily presence of the Son would have been. Therefore He said to His disciples, *It is expedient to you that I go.* . . . The unction which He pours into souls animates them, fortifies them, aids them to win the victory; it sweetens their troubles, and makes them find their delight in crosses."

"One small portion of divine consolation," says Richard of St. Victor, "can do more than all the pleasures of the world. These latter never satisfy the heart, but one small drop of the interior sweetness which the Holy Ghost infuses into the soul will cast it into ecstasy and cause in it a holy inebriation."

[52] John 10:10-28.

house of God. He is the pasture on which we graze; the bread of life which descended from heaven; the way, the light, and the life.

He is likewise the basis for our strength and the cornerstone of the living temple of God. By His own blood and the charity of His Spirit He joins and unites all the stones of this temple, ourselves, if in Him we grow in sanctification. In the words of the Apostle: You are "built upon the foundation of the apostles and prophets, Jesus Christ Himself being the chief cornerstone. In whom all the building, being framed together, groweth up into a holy temple in the Lord. In whom you also are built together into a habitation of God in the Spirit." [53]

3. CHRIST AS SPOUSE OF OUR SOULS

He is espoused with our souls and, by the full communication of the Holy Ghost, He ratifies this mystic espousal and changes it into a marvelous spiritual marriage so that our souls desire nothing except what He desires. He unites them so entirely to Himself and so transfigures them to His divine image that they become one thing with Him.

Thus He is not only espoused to our souls, but we are incorporated with Him as intimately as are the leafy branches with the vine. He makes us His living members, in which He Himself lives and acts. He is, in truth, the head of the whole mystical body of the Church, "head over all the Church, which is His body, and the fullness of Him who is filled all in all." [54]

Although we are many Christians, we are one body in Jesus Christ and members, one of another.[55] Living in this way, we are perfected in unity, He in us and we in Him, and we are loved by the Father with that selfsame love with which the Father loves His Son. We are able to give to the world testimony of the truth; [56] for we have been changed into Christ Himself, He being the Head and we His members. "Behold, we have become Christ," exclaims St. Augustine,

---

[53] Eph. 2:20–22. See St. Catherine of Siena, *Letters*, no. 34; St. Mary Magdalen of Pazzi, *Œuvres*, III, chap. 2, sec. 3.
[54] Eph. 1:22 f.
[55] Rom. 12:5; I Cor. 10:17; 12:12–17.
[56] John 17:23.

THE DIVINE LIFE OF GRACE

"for He is the Head and we the members and the whole comprises the living body, both He and ourselves." [57]

4. CHRIST, THE HEAD OF THE MYSTICAL BODY

From Him as the trunk, the shoot from the root of Jesse, in whom we are engrafted, comes to us all the sap that nourishes and vivifies us, flowing from the vine to the branches. From Him as Head come all the holy impulses and inspirations, thoughts, movements, and instincts, which foster the development of the Christian life. From Him proceed all the mysterious influxes which His Spirit communicates to us. From Him flows all the power of the sacraments, which are the transmitting organs of that divine blood which washes us, purifies us, vivifies us, heals us, fortifies us, resuscitates us, renews and comforts us, feeds us and makes us advance in deification through a growth that is of God.[58] We are flesh of His flesh and bone of His bone and, finally, one with Him.

The Church is His true and holy spouse, since it is His mystical body and He is her Bridegroom and the Bridegroom of all just souls, for He is the Head which governs and gives life. "The Bridegroom is the head," says St. Augustine, "and the bride is the body," and together they constitute but one organism. So this union with Him is so intimate that we become one Spirit and one body and this to such an extent that where He is, there also are His members and servants [59] and whatever we do it is He who does it through us.

Although the simple union which is His as the Bridegroom might seem but slightly intimate to the worldly-minded, who do not feel or suspect or even attempt to believe the ineffable communications of His most tender love, the union portrayed by the symbol of an organism forces us to recognize a union superior to any other that could be imagined. For if this union of espousal incomparably exceeds, as we shall see, that of human espousals, then that union which is Christ's as Head of the mystical body is also, in a certain way, more intimate than the natural union of our head with our body. He is the true "head over all the Church, which is His body, and the

[57] *In Joan.*, no. 9.
[58] Col. 2:19.
[59] John 12:26.

fullness of Him who is filled all in all." [60] He is the fountain of grace and life,[61] and from His fullness we have all received the measure of life and energies which is suitable to us.[62]

Although Christ possesses that capital and fontal grace, He does not actuate and manifest it in Himself and for Himself alone as Head, but He diffuses it throughout His whole body. He manifests it in divers ways, according to the exigencies of time and place and the needs of the various members who are continually appearing, under the perpetual influence of the Spirit of renewal,[63] and in whom He is formed anew.[64]

Therefore all those new organs through which Christ acts and suffers what He could not suffer in His own Person are properly His body and His fullness, for it is He who acts and suffers in them so far as they are Christians. He gives them their being, their activity, and their suffering. Hence the Apostle completed in his flesh whatever was wanting to the sufferings of Christ, and he did this for the good of the Church. We should all do likewise so that the greater prosperity and progressive increase of the mystical body may not be impeded. "Although the sufferings of Christ as the Head were complete," says St. Augustine, "the sufferings of His body were wanting." [65] We are that body of Christ and we are His members. "The plenitude of Jesus Christ consists in the Head and all the members." [66]

"The Church," says Bossuet, "is Jesus Christ extended and communicated, Jesus Christ entirely, Jesus Christ perfect man, Jesus Christ in His plenitude." [67] Therefore His faithful are part of Him-

[60] Eph. 1:22 f.
[61] Ps. 35:10.
[62] John 1:16.
[63] Wisd. 7:27.
[64] Terrien, *op. cit.*, I, 300: "When we are born into the divine life and grow in it, it is Jesus Christ who is reborn and grows in our souls. 'My little children,' says the Apostle (Gal. 4:19), 'of whom I am in labor again, until Christ be formed in you.'"
"Each one of us is formed in Christ," says St. Cyril of Alexandria (*In Is.*, IV), "through our participation in the Holy Ghost. . . . He it is who forms Christ in us when, through sanctification and justification, He impresses the divine image on us. So it is that the character of the substance of God the Father shines forth in our souls through the Spirit, whose sanctifying power refashions us according to the divine Model."
[65] *Enarr. in Ps.* 86, no. 5.
[66] St. Augustine, *Tract. 21 in Joan.*, nos. 8 f.
[67] *Lettre a une dem. de Metz.*

self, part of His body, and deserving of the name of Christ. "How grand is the excellency of the Christian!" says St. Anselm. "He can make such progress in Christ that he bears His very name." [68]

But the good Christian is not only another Christ; he is Jesus Christ Himself. For there is only one Christ, and to bear His name worthily is to be a living member of His body which, with the Head, forms the one Christ. "For the Head in union with the body," says St. Augustine, "forms one Christ." [69]

The body of the Church and all its members receive from Jesus Christ the divine life which they possess, the life of grace, the communication of the Holy Ghost with the charity of God, and all the supernatural forces and energies by which they work and suffer. Since they are what they are through Him and they do and merit through Him whatever they merit and do, it follows that the divine head is more essential to them, more influential, more intimate, than that which is proper to the human body, for the human head is not the principle of the natural organism as Christ is of the mystical body. All that we are or can be as Christians, as sons of God and members of the Church, we are through our Savior. Through Him we are perfected in unity and, though many and diverse, we form but one living body,[70] just as He is one with the Father.[71]

So much does Christ desire to strengthen this union that He is ceaselessly working to this end, dwelling in our hearts through a living faith and giving us more and more fully the communication of His Spirit.[72] If we follow His sweet inspirations and do not resist His grace, we shall be united with Him to the point of being flesh of His flesh and bone of His bone and we shall possess the same Spirit as He Himself possesses.[73] Even more, through the continual

---

[68] *Meditations,* I, no. 6.
[69] *Sermo 14 de verbis Domini.*
[70] Rom. 12:5.
[71] John 17:21-23.
[72] Eph. 3:17.
[73] "From this marvelous benefaction by which all the justified are made living members of Christ," says Ven. Louis of Granada (*Sinner's Guide,* Bk. I, chap. 5), "it follows that the Son of God loves them as such. . . . He has a tender solicitude for them . . . and constantly infuses into them the power which flows from the Head to the members. Finally, the Eternal Father looks upon them with loving eyes because He sees them as living members of His only-begotten Son, united and incorporated in Him through the communication of His Spirit. Therefore, their works are pleasing to Him and meritorious, because they are the works of the living members of His Son, who works all good in them. Possessing such great dignity as

activity of this vivifying Spirit, who imprints the divine image on us and makes us more and more clearly like to Christ, we shall ultimately be transformed in Him and become one with Him.[74]

Thus Jesus Christ is continually formed in us and we are renewed in Him. Through Him we are despoiled of self and reclothed in Him until we become but a simple expansion or continuation of Himself.[75] Thus do we become one thing with Him and form that marvelous union so sublimely enunciated by His sacred lips in the sermon in the supper room (John 17).

From this union flows a prodigious communication of life, works, treasures, and merits, for all that is His He has communicated to us, and whatever we have is His. He came into the world and lived and died for us; and we live, work, and die for and in Him.[76] As His members, we participate with Him in the same vivifying Spirit who is the distributor of graces.

From this most loving union follows the enormity of the crime of heresy or schism which despoils the body of our Savior and dislocates His members. St. Augustine says that whoever thus separates the faithful of the Church, tears, not the seamless garment, but the very flesh of our Lord. Hence, this sin is greater than that of homicide, for it spills the blood of souls and tears off members from the body of Jesus Christ.

The Divine Spouse

There is nothing that can so fill us with admiration and astonishment and at the same time inflame us with the throbbing desire of corresponding with divine love as these awesome mysteries of union

---

they do, it follows that when these souls ask favors of God, they do so with very great confidence, for they realize that they ask not for themselves alone but also for the Son of God Himself, who is honored in them and with them. . . . The good that is done to the members is done also to the Head."

[74] See II Cor. 3:18.

[75] Gal. 2:20; 3:27; 4:19; Rom. 6:3-11. Gay, *De la vie et des vertus chrétiennes*, I, 60, 64: "In each soul is reproduced in miniature the mystery of Christ, the absolute type of which Christian souls are so many faithful copies." So it is that the entire Trinity "forms Christ in us and fashions us into Christ, or rather, makes of us true Christs, for it desires that each Christian soul as such should become a member and a miniature image of the absolute and sovereign Christ, who is the unique object of its pleasure, the sole basis of all its works, and the one medium of all the operations of God."

[76] Rom. 14:7 f.

THE DIVINE LIFE OF GRACE

with God. It seems that He finds such delight in dwelling with the children of men (Prov. 8:31) that He wishes to contract with us all the relations possible and even the most cordial and intimate that can be imagined. Not content with being a most merciful Father, a most faithful Friend, and a most tender and loving Brother, He desires also to be the sweet Spouse of souls. He espouses them to Himself forever in faith and justice so that they may know Him and love Him with a most pure love and thus cooperate in His work of mercy and goodness.[77] Once they are purified of all earthly affection and of all stain, He pours out on them the riches of His most exquisite love and He floods them with the torrents of divine delights.[78]

The various relations which exist among men are inadequate to express the relationship which God desires to contract with us. Therefore, He is not content with calling the soul daughter, sister, spouse, guest, tabernacle, living temple, etc. He wishes to form one body with us so that we may truly be "members of His body, made from His flesh and from His bones" (Eph. 5:30). He desires to be

---

[77] Osee 2:19 f. "Our Lord," says St. Mary Magdalen of Pazzi (*Œuvres*, II, chap. 13), "is at the right hand of the Father as God and as man. He is in our souls as Spouse, King, Father, and Brother according to the purity, love, and particular dispositions which He finds in each soul."

"The soul," observes Massoulié (*Traité de l'amour de Dieu*, II, chap. 14), "sometimes regards God as a Father who is preparing the eternal heritage for it, and it directs itself to Him with confidence, asking Him to bestow His kingdom on it. When it finds itself separated from Him, it complains lovingly and asks Him not to abandon it, but to comfort and protect it. At other times, the soul considers the eternal Word a faithful friend and seeks to learn from Him the laws of true friendship. Again, it regards Him as a spouse and consecrates its most tender affections to Him and swears eternal fidelity to Him. Yearning to possess Him completely, with Magdalen it casts itself at His feet and kisses them, embraces them, and washes them with its tears, and asks pardon of all its infidelities. Then, with perfect confidence in Him and mindful of the mercies received, it kisses the generous hand which has lavished such blessings upon it. And as its love and affections increase from day to day it even dares to ask Him that He refuse not a still greater testimony of His love and that He be so intimately united with it that it will never more be separated from Him. In the attempt to be assimilated to Him completely, it renounces all vanities, and it has a dread of pleasure, and it strives more and more to imitate His humility, His meekness, and His patience, knowing that this perfect conformity will make of it a true spouse. When it has no will other than that of the divine Bridegroom, it is actually one spirit with Him."

[78] Ezech. 16:8-10: "And I swore to thee, and I entered into a covenant with thee, saith the Lord God: and thou becamest Mine. And I washed thee with water, and cleansed away thy blood from thee; and I anointed thee with oil ... and I clothed thee with fine garments."

our head, our life, our light, and our very food, fully entering into us to be our delight, to be our all, and all ours.

1. ESPOUSAL OF THE WORD WITH JUST SOULS

But if God wished to be called the spouse of souls, this sweet title is especially befitting the Son, who hypostatically united Himself to human nature in order to unite us to the divinity.[79] Hence, our union with the Word is very often compared to that of matrimony, and in the mystical states the spiritual espousal represents the supreme grade of union with Jesus Christ and the most complete transformation in God which is possible in this life.

The greatest of the prophets was the first to give the Savior the name of spouse. "St. John the Baptist," says Bossuet, "discloses to us a new characteristic of Jesus Christ which is the most tender and the most sweet: that of the Spouse. . . Christ is espoused with holy souls, bestowing on them gifts and chaste delights. He is enjoyed by them and He enters into them, giving them not only all that He has but all that He is." [80] In another place, where Christ is given that title, He is compared to the son of a king who has come to the world to be espoused with souls.[81] Finally, the beloved disciple sings of the eternal nuptials of the Lamb which are begun in grace and consummated in glory.[82]

Scripture is so filled with this subject that one book is dedicated to singing the mutual love of Jesus and the holy soul. "Consider," says Bellamy, "those inspired pages of the Canticle of Canticles. When you perceive the ardent effusions of a love that is not of this world, then you will understand something of the mysterious union by means of which the just soul lives the life of Jesus Christ. . . . At its basis it is an allegorical poem of sanctifying grace." [83]

This mystical union of Jesus Christ with souls, which is symbolized by human matrimony, is incomparably more intimate and

---

[79] "He who becomes the true spouse of souls," says Ribet (*Mystique*, I, 311), "is the Word, clothed in our humanity. This union of the incarnate Word with souls is the expansion and completion of His union with human nature. For He united Himself to the flesh only to be united with souls, to make them share in His life, and through them and with them to draw all creation to His Father."
[80] *Elév. sur les myst.*, sem., 24, no. 1.
[81] Matt. 9:15; 22:2.
[82] Apoc. 19:7.
[83] *Op. cit.*, p. 219.

THE DIVINE LIFE OF GRACE

loving than that to which it is compared because it works, not with a human love, but a divine love. Human matrimony makes two to be one flesh; this divine love makes many to be one spirit.[84] Thus St. Paul says to the Ephesians: "This is a great sacrament: but I speak in Christ and in the Church" (5:32). Again, in the Second Epistle to the Corinthians, he says: "For I espoused you to one husband that I may present you as a chaste virgin to Christ" (11:2).

Thus St. Augustine says that all just souls and all the particular Churches, which are the delight of the King of glory, constitute but one kingdom, for He loves them all with an undivided love as He loves His own body.[85] As the mystics experienced with astonishment, He loves each particular soul as if there existed no other in the world, and He is ready to shed His blood for it.[86] Although there are many sisters and spouses who wound His heart (Cant. 4:9), one alone is His immaculate dove (*ibid.*, 6:8).

"The spouse," says St. Bernard, "is the enamored soul." [87] In another place he says: "All of us have been called to these spiritual nuptials in which Jesus Christ is the Bridegroom and we ourselves the bride. All together we are that bride, and each soul in particular is also a bride. The bride is very inferior to the Bridegroom; nevertheless, through love of her, the Son of the eternal King descended from His glory and gave up His life.   Whence comes to you such honor that you should become espoused with Him whom the angels love to contemplate and whose beauty is reflected in the sun and the moon? What will you render to the Lord for that inestimable benefit of being associated at His table, His kingdom, and His

---

[84] In the words "one spirit" we have, as Bellamy points out, "the precise formula of our relationship with Jesus Christ, under a daring symbol. This union is so intimate that it in some way approaches the hypostatic" (*op. cit.*, p. 221).

[85] *Enarr. in Ps. 44*, n. 23.

[86] Blessed Henry Suso, *Eternal Wisdom*, chap. 7: "I am Infinite Love which is not limited by its unity nor dissipated by its multiplicity. I love each soul in particular as if it were the only one. I love thee and concern Myself with thee as if I loved no others and you were the only one in the world."

St. John of the Cross, *The Living Flame*, stanza 2, no. 32: "For the soul now feels God to be so solicitous in granting it favours and to be magnifying it with such precious and delicate and endearing words, and granting it favour upon favour, that it believes that there is no other soul in the world whom He thus favours, nor aught else wherewith He occupies Himself, but that He is wholly for itself alone. And, when it feels this, it confesses its feeling in the words of the Songs: My Beloved is mine and I am His (Canticles ii, 16)."

[87] *Sermo 7 in Cant.*, n. 3.

couch? With what arms of reciprocal charity ought you to love and bind yourself to one who so loved you that He refashioned you in His side when He slept the sleep of death on the cross?" [88]

The love of human spouses is as nothing when compared with this love that is built, not on the flesh, which profits nothing, but on the spirit which vivifies all things.[89] So intimate is its union that it establishes a most perfect communication of life and merits.

"In His immense desire to unite Himself more closely with us," writes Terrien, "the divine Word clothed Himself in our nature for the purpose of celebrating these mysterious nuptials. And that the spouse might not be too unworthy of Him, He formed her from His side—from His heart, which was opened on the cross. Thence she came forth, vivified after her birth in the blood of the Bridegroom. From that source she received all that makes her what she is: glorious, holy, immaculate, flesh of His flesh and bone of His bone. Whence she is the spouse; the body of Christ; a spouse because she is His very body." [90]

2. CHARACTERISTICS, INTIMACY, AND FRUITS OF THIS UNION

St. Bernard says that Christ took the name of spouse because there was no other title more fitting to indicate the sweetness of His love and the mutual affection of that union in which all things are common.[91] But we do not think of anything earthly when we discuss this love which is entirely spiritual and divine. It is as pure as the very charity of God Himself, and its fruits are fruits of honor and riches, for they are the fruits of the Holy Ghost, who is the bond of this union.

It was this love that animated the admirable virgin, Inez, who at the age of thirteen disdained the seductions of this world and exclaimed joyfully in the face of her persecutors: "I have another Lover who gave me His ring as a pledge of His faith and adorned me with the most costly jewels. I am espoused to Him whom the

---

[88] *Sermo 2, Dom. I post oct. Epiph.*, n. 2.
[89] John 6:64.
[90] *La grâce et la gloire*, I, 338.
[91] St. Bernard, *In Cant. Serm.* 7, no. 2: "There have never been found such tender names by which the sweet affections between the Word and the soul can be expressed as those of bridegroom and bride, wherein everything is common and nothing is proper or divided. The one heritage for both, the one dwelling place, the one table, the one couch, and even the one flesh."

THE DIVINE LIFE OF GRACE

angels serve. Loving Him, I am chaste; touching Him, I am pure; possessing Him, I am a virgin. . . . To expect me to submit would be to injure my Spouse. He first loved me, and I am His. Why do you wait, O sword? Let this body perish which can be desired by carnal eyes!"

In this union of Jesus Christ with souls, as Bellamy says (*op. cit.*, pp. 230–33), are found the principal characteristics of matrimony. The Savior gives us the three essential gifts which every bridegroom bestows upon his bride: his name, his goods, and his own person.

From Christ we receive the name of Christian and, on making us Christians, as St. Augustine states, He also makes us Himself, for in Him we are at once men of Christ and Christ Himself, since the complete Jesus Christ is made up of Head and members.[92] Therefore, as Le Camus points out, "Christians form the illustrious family, the living image, and the indefinite expansion of Christ across the ages. *Christianus alter Christus.*" [93]

Together with His name, Christ gives us His rich gifts: all the fruits of His redemption. These gifts are so precious that, as St. Peter teaches, through them we are made participators in the divine nature. We receive them all in common as an undivided inheritance that each soul can dispose of as mistress; yet not in the same degree for each soul, but in the measure of the giving on the part of Christ. If we do not derive from them the corresponding fruit, the fault is ours. Whenever we respond to His generosity with ingratitude and indifference; whenever we do not strive to cultivate the gifts received and do not contribute to the common good as we have the power to do, then we loosen the loving bonds by which Jesus unites us to Himself.

But "He is not content with giving us His goods; He gives us Himself also. In grace He gives us His divinity; in the Eucharist, which is the crowning of grace, He gives us His holy humanity also; that is, His entire sacred Person with the natures in which it resides. Here is the perfection of love, and St. John Chrysostom (*In Hebr.*,

---

[92] St. Augustine, *In Joan.* XXI: "Admire and rejoice; behold we have become Christ. He is the Head, and we the members; together a complete man, He and ourselves." *Enarr. II in Ps. 26*: "We appear as the body of Christ, for we are all united in Him. We are of Christ and we are Christ because in a certain sense the complete Christ is both Head and body."

[93] *Œuvre des apôtres*, chap. 12.

Homily 6) is correct in calling it a type of consubstantiality which, although it undoubtedly maintains the distinction of persons and natures, makes this union as close as is possible. Could we ever dream here below of anything more intimate than this mysterious alliance in which, according to the beautiful expression of St. Paul (Gal. 2:20), it is not now the Christian who lives, but Jesus Christ in him?"[94]

Thus the three goods of Christian matrimony (*fides, proles et sacramentum*) are found exalted to an almost incredible degree in the marriage between Christ and just souls. Faith, the first of these goods, cannot weaken on the part of Him who, far from breaking or loosening the bond, is ever ready to retie it or tighten it more. He welcomes back the faithless spouse who recognizes her errors; He confers caresses on her; and she begins to serve Him again with greater fervor. On the part of the bride, if she strives to correspond with this divine love, not even death can break this sweet chain which binds, but it will be strong enough to endure for all eternity. Almost the same effects follow from the mystical death as from the corporal death. Souls that have died completely to the world and to themselves and that have merited to contract the indissoluble marriage, receive, as we shall see, the firm assurance of remaining united forever with their divine Spouse.

Procreation or fructification does not kill, spoil, or weaken that mutual affection or cause it to be lost. Rather it augments and strengthens it in such a way that it increases the vigor of the bride and gives her new enchantments so that she ever retains her youth and gains even greater fertility. The more fruitful the soul in good works and the more it fructifies for God, the more vigorous and beautiful and radiant in glory does it become and the more pleasing it is to the divine Spouse. The more that love flourishes in fruits of

---

[94] Bellamy, *loc. cit.* St. Mary Magdalen of Pazzi, *Œuvres*, IV, chap. 5: "O beloved Spouse, it is necessary that I feed on Thy body and Thy blood for that is the bond of union which unites us. Oh, union, union! Who could ever understand it? The mere idea of a union in which the perfect is united to the imperfect to make it like to itself would fill the heavenly choirs with wonder. . . . O sweet union by which the soul becomes another Thee through a participation in Thy divinity! This union makes two things one and yet preserves each in its proper nature. . . . When the soul finally discovers these marvelous operations, it cannot cease lamenting that it has known and admired them so little."

glory, so much the more vital and vehement will be the reciprocal affection and so much the more will this mutual union be strengthened and consolidated until the soul hears these tender words: "Thou art all fair, O my love, and there is not a spot in thee. Come from Libanus, my spouse . . . thou shalt be crowned. . . . Thou hast wounded my heart, my sister, my spouse" (Cant. 4:7–9). The soul is called "sister" inasmuch as she is now the worthy daughter of the eternal Father; being deified, she can aspire to the kiss of the Word of God.

When, having placed Him as a seal in her heart and on her arm, her love is made as strong as death, so that the many waters of tribulation, far from quenching it, enliven it (Cant. 8:6 f.); then, inflamed with zeal for the glory of her Spouse, she will not refuse labors and sacrifices by which she may gain souls in whom He can find divine pleasure. Indeed she will gladly endure tribulation in order to give Him new sons and new brides who will conscientiously serve Him, bless Him, adore Him, praise Him, and love Him.

Instead of wishing to be unique in His love, she will greatly lament that not all hearts of creatures are capable of loving the supreme goodness of the Spouse as He deserves. The new brides do not cause any envy nor do they deprive her in the least of the affection of the Beloved. Rather the reciprocal love increases on both sides. She is so much the more loved, honored, and glorified as the more numerous and better are the associates whom she attracts to bring in her wake to the presence of the heavenly King (Ps. 44:15 f.). Her love burns the more brightly as other hearts are more and more inflamed, in which there shines forth nothing but the adored image of the common Spouse. Thus does charity increase in intensity with the extension of the beloved object.[95]

This union, then, merits the name of matrimony by which it is so often represented, except that it exceeds matrimony as the reality exceeds the symbol. According to the teaching of St. Thomas:

[95] St. Teresa, *Exclamations*, II: "O powerful love of God, how different are Thy fruits from those produced by love of the world! For love of the world desires no companions, thinking that they may take from it what it possesses. But love for my God increases more and more as it learns that more and more souls love Him. . . . And thus the soul seeks means of finding companionship and is glad to abandon its own enjoyment, thinking that this may help others in some degree to strive to attain it."

Just as the thing signified exceeds the sign, so does the love and union of God in souls excel the love of bridegroom for bride.... In this union faith is more inviolate, the indissolubility greater, the fruit more profitable.... Great is the fidelity of God to the soul, as is said in Osee: "And I will espouse thee to me in faith"; and in the Canticles: "My beloved to me, and I to him." He is more faithful than any spouse for He is even with the soul that lacks faith.... And so, just as the species is not diminished because many individuals share in it, so, O my soul, God loves you in such a marvelous manner as if all His love were reserved for you.... In human marriage, a separation eventually comes, at least, at death; but in that marriage which God celebrates with you in Baptism, ratified by a holy life and consummated in glory, there is no separation. You ought, then, to say with the Apostle: "Who will separate us from the charity of Christ?" And to rapt and unitive souls, he addresses the following: "I am certain that there is nothing that can separate us from that charity." The offspring also, which is good works, is more profitable and varied. This offspring proceeds from God and the soul together—from grace and free will and not from either of them alone.... This is the offspring which, far from causing injury to the mother, obtains for her eternal life.[96]

This mysterious union of espousal with the divine Word is as real as it is ineffable. In the mystical life it is experienced with indescribable delights which are not to be measured, but only to be admired in silence, for they escape human language. The soul discovers the infinite enchantments of her heavenly Spouse and recognizes the treasures of life and glory with which He enriches her. She is aware of the intimacy of this union and communication and she enjoys the sweetness of love with which she is favored.

"The soul and Jesus," says Gay, "are two in one spirit and they form a perfect union. The whole undiminished life of the Spouse is transferred to that of the bride, with all its states, all its mysteries, all its titles, all its excellencies, virtues, and actions, with all its sufferings and merits. From all this is made a type of matrimonial goods, of property common to both the spouses, although the bride does not dispose of them without the permission of the Spouse. This is pre-

[96] *Opusc.* 61, chap. 13. We ought to note that, although this work is listed among those of the Angelic Doctor, it seems not to be authentic. Yet it carries authority, since it is based on his doctrine.

cisely the hidden meaning of the divine words: 'I will . . . sup with him, and he with Me' " (Apoc. 3:20).[97]

3. SINGULAR DIGNITY OF CONSECRATED VIRGINS

Though all just souls are truly spouses of Christ, yet the Catholic Church reserves this sweet name especially for the holy virgins, who are its most perfect symbol, and even more especially for those consecrated to God by the vows of religion, which are like three loving bonds which unite them still more closely with the Redeemer. Crucified with Him, they contract a most singular union, which can be rightly appreciated only by the inflamed and illumined hearts that feel keenly the excellence of these mysteries.

Therefore these consecrated souls delight in frequently renewing their sacred promises with all possible solemnity in order thus to tighten and consolidate the chains of love. They know how much this rededication pleases their divine Spouse, and they realize the benefits that accrue to them when they offer themselves anew to God as a holocaust.[98]

Since souls thus consecrated are the blessing of the world and the delight and pleasure of that heavenly Lover who grazes among the lilies, it is not strange that they should be despised by the wicked and highly esteemed by the good. Following in the blood-stained footprints of the Crucified, they cannot help but share in His affections and hates. He who despises such souls is already judged, and whoever loves them loves Jesus Christ in them. Therefore holy Church

---

[97] *Op. cit.*, p. 58.
[98] Uriarte, *Vida del P. Hoyos*, p. 99: "The soul receives inexplicable benefits from this renewal of vows. All the virtues are augmented; grace is increased in proportion to the disposition of the individual; charity attains to new perfections; and the union is strengthened beyond that which the soul formerly possessed. It is, moreover, a great glory to the Most Holy Trinity and extremely pleasing to the three divine Persons, since by the three vows the soul enjoys a union with God which bears a resemblance to that existing between the three divine Persons. It is united to each Person by each of the vows and in a manner that cannot be explained. The most sacred humanity of Christ is pleased and overjoyed to see the soul follow in His footsteps. The holy Virgin receives accidental glory and rejoices as if her own vow of virginity were renewed."

Tauler, *Institutions*, chap. 13: "Whoever considers obedience as tedious or difficult shows that he has not arrived at an understanding of what obedience is. As divine delight far exceeds all natural delight, so is obedience far more pleasant than all self-will, for God gives Himself as the reward for all things that are done or omitted for His sake."

has always regarded the virgins of the Lord as the children of His predilection, and she celebrates their religious consecration, which is a figure of the eternal nuptials of the Lamb, with a solemnity rivaling the consecration of her priests as the dispensing ministers of the divine mysteries.[99] Hence it is that from the time of St. Dionysius [100] to that of St. Peter Damian,[101] religious profession, which is today so much despised by those who are Christian in name only, was considered a sort of sacrament or a quasi-sacrament.

The faithful fulfillment of the obligations which that profession implies, in addition to the continual practice of the ordinary virtues of the Christian life, leads to a perfect union of conformity with the divine will. Then the most loving Spouse of souls, seeing that they are now fully animated with His Spirit and, as true daughters of God, are docile to His loving impulses, begins to manifest to them more clearly the mysteries of that intimate union which they have contracted with Him. Further, that they may better understand these mysteries, He deigns to celebrate, before the heavenly court, the symbolic ceremonies of the mystical espousal in a visible manner and with a solemnity which is not proper to earth.

To reach that happy state, they must attain a high degree of purity and be completely divested of the old man in order to reclothe themselves splendidly with the likeness of the heavenly and divine Man. They must die to self in order to live only for God. As long as they have not accomplished this, the Lord will visit them as a physician to heal their wounds and to cure their diseases and feebleness or, at most, as a loving father, to console and encourage them, but He will not yet bestow on them those ineffable communications which are reserved for the faithful spouse.[102] No soul can hope to enjoy the

---

[99] In the ceremony of the consecration of virgins, as found in the *Pontificale Romanum*, the Bishop addresses them as follows: "I espouse you with Jesus Christ, the Son of the eternal Father. . . . Receive this ring as the symbol of the Holy Ghost so that, remaining faithful to your heavenly Spouse, you may receive the eternal crown." And the virgins sing: "I am espoused to Him whom the angels serve. . . . My Lord Jesus Christ has given me His ring as a pledge of His love and with His crown has adorned me as His spouse."

[100] *De Eccl. hier.*, chap. 6.// [101] *Sermo 69.*
[102] St. Bernard, *Sermo 32 in Cant.*: "The Word visits certain souls as a physician bringing salves and salutary ointments, and such souls are as yet imperfect. Other souls He visits as a loving spouse, kissing and embracing them and binding them to Himself by the splendor and tenderness of His ineffable unifying love; and such

consolations of the espousal without first being made like to Him who is the true Spouse of blood (Exod. 4:25). But that soul which is resolved to refuse Him nothing, cost what it may, will persevere firm and confident that its hopes will not be frustrated.

APPENDIX

Excellency of This Union

Fray Luis de Leon, *Nombres de Cristo*, II, 4: "It is well worthwhile to consider the exceedingly great tenderness with which Christ has treated men. He is our father, our head, and He rules us as a shepherd and cures us as a physician. He is united to us and joins us to Himself by many other titles of intimate friendship. Yet, not content with all those, He adds still another bond or tie and desires to be called and to be our spouse. As a bond, He is the closest possible bond; as a delight, the most pleasant and sweet; as a unity of life, that of the greatest intimacy; as a conformity of wills, the greatest union; as love, the most ardent and burning of all loves. Not only in words, but in very deed is He our spouse. The intimacy of love and fellowship and the unity of body which characterize the union of a man and a woman, are but frigidity and pure indifference when compared to the union in which this spouse is united to our soul. In a human union there is no communication of spirit, but in that union with Christ the very Spirit of Christ is given and communicated to the just soul. . . In the human espousal, one body does not receive life from the other; in the spiritual espousal our flesh lives through its union with the flesh of Christ. . . . He instills in us His operative power and, if we let ourselves be directed by it and offer no resistence, then He works in us and we work with and through Him. We then produce whatever is befitting His being, which has been placed within us, and whatever is due the exalted qualities and noble

---

souls are more perfect souls. These souls feel that in this embrace of the Spouse they are totally permeated with the sweetness of His holy love. . . . That soul alone enjoys the kisses and embraces of the Spouse which seeks the Spouse with many vigils and prayers, with much labor and tears. Yet, once He is found and when you think that you possess Him, He suddenly steals away; but if you return once again to your prayers and tears, He willingly suffers Himself to be possessed again. Yet he is never held for a long time, but He slips through your hands, as it were. However, be constant in your groanings, and you can surely expect His return."

birth that we have received from Him. Having become another Christ, or rather, having been transformed into Him, all operation flows from Him and from us as from one principle, so that it is fittingly called a work of Christ. . . This same flesh and body which He took from us, He unites to the body of the Church and to all her members who worthily receive Him in the Sacrament of the Altar, drawing His flesh to their own and making it as much as possible one with their own."

Froget, *The Indwelling of the Holy Ghost*, pp. 155 f.: "In Holy Scripture this union is compared to that of the husband and wife, and mystical writers speak of it as a spiritual espousal or marriage. This shows how intimate, sweet and fruitful it is.

"It is indeed a close, intimate, and profound union far greater than that which exists between man and woman, for nature at its best is but the shadow of grace. In marriage we have bodily union, here we have the compenetration of the soul by God. And if it is true to say of married persons that they are two in one flesh, the Apostle declares that 'he who is joined to the Lord is one spirit' (I Cor. 6:17).

"How sweet and chaste this union is! When placed side by side with it the marriage union seems cold and full of sorrows. The joys of the marriage state are fleeting, the pleasures in themselves of the lower grade; here everything is noble, lofty, and lasting; glory, purity, love, and other ineffable delights, which baffle all description and which fill the human heart to overflowing.

"Lastly, this is a fruitful union, whence are born holy thoughts, generous affections, bold and daring enterprises, and that whole series of works of perfection known as beatitudes and gifts of the Holy Ghost.

"This blessed union, begun on earth, will be consummated only in heaven. Although, as St. Paul remarks, the soul is already betrothed to Christ; it is already the spouse of the Holy Ghost. The Third Person of the Trinity has already given to the soul its faith and troth, as it were, the wedding ring of the union. He has clothed it with the gold-embroidered robes of grace and charity; He has adorned it with the precious stones of His gifts and of the infused virtues; and He has given Himself to it, although in an obscure manner, as the pledge of the eternal bliss of heaven. Yet this divine Spirit must complete His work in paradise by granting to the soul that rich dowry known as vision, as comprehension, and as fruition; vision, which is to take the place of faith; comprehension, which will enable the soul to grasp the Sovereign Good, the object of its constant desires here below; and fruition, which will perfect and consummate its happiness.

"The work of supernatural transformation which is going on throughout the Christian's life, will then come to an end, for our assimilation with God will be henceforth perfect. Already deified on earth in its essence by grace, it will in heaven be deified in its intelligence by the light of glory, and in its will by perfect charity; the soul in heaven will be admitted to a face-to-face contemplation of God, and will possess in the fullness of joy Him who is Sovereign, subsistent Truth and sovereign Good."

Relations with the Holy Ghost

From what has already been said, we can understand to some extent how numerous are the ineffable relations which the just soul contracts with the divine Spirit, whose mysterious work cannot be explained in words, because it does not fall within any human concepts. It can be deduced or conjectured only partially and imperfectly from the unique titles that He Himself, through the mouth of His prophets, continually attributes to Himself.

He is personal Love; the Charity of God; the Peace of the Lord that ought always to be with us; the hypostatic Sanctity and Sanctifier; the uncreated Grace; the divine Unction; the Seal of Jesus Christ; the Spirit of adoption and revelation; the Creator, Renewer, Regenerator, Vivifier, Illuminator, Consoler, Director, and Transformer of souls. He is the great Gift par excellence.

1. THE HOLY GHOST AS THE SPIRIT OF LOVE

He is personal Love because God is charity as well as wisdom, and personified charity is the Holy Ghost, as personified wisdom is the Son of God, the eternal Word of the divine intelligence. But the Son is not merely any kind of word, says St. Thomas.[103] He is not an empty, cold, and abstract word as the word of human reason often is, but He is the Word that breathes forth love. For the Father

---

[103] Cf. Ia, q.43, a.5, ad 2um.

and the Son, knowing each other infinitely, cannot do less than love each other with an infinite love. "Emitting," says St. Francis de Sales, "with the same will and the same impetus, . . one breathing or spirit of love, they produce and express a breath which is the Holy Ghost." [104]

So this sovereign Spirit is the eternal expression of the mutual love of the Father and the Son, the perfect fruition of Their love. He is the close embrace which unites Them eternally, the ineffable kiss of love which They eternally give to each other. "The Savior communicated the Spirit to His disciples," says St. Bernard, "in the form of a breathing, which was equivalent to His kiss, so that we might understand that the Spirit comes from the Father and the Son as a true mutual kiss." [105]

This, then, is the most sweet kiss of His mouth which the enamored soul seeks with such ardor from the divine Spouse. The soul is lovingly united with Him through that ineffable communication of His Spirit in which are contained all the wonders of the charity of God.[106]

From this notion springs the ancient custom of the Church of giving to the faithful the *Pax Dei* in the form of the kiss of peace, which represents the mutual communication of the Holy Ghost. It is the Holy Ghost who will perfect our unity as members of that Church in the likeness of the divine Persons.[107]

The Holy Ghost, as Spirit of Love, is symbolized by the dove, the emblem of faithful, pure, simple, and fruitful love. The Spouse calls the holy soul "My dove" because He sees that it is radiant and filled

---

[104] *Sermon for Pentecost.*
[105] *In Cant. Serm.* 8, no. 2.
[106] Juan de los Angeles, *Triunfos*, II, chap. 14: "Surely the soul is blessed, a thousand times blessed, in that kiss of God by which He joins the soul to Himself without any medium. It is transformed and deified, and, dying to itself and to all that is not God, it lives only for God. . . . Many souls have been carried away by the sweetness of the kiss of God and in this ecstasy have been deified."
[107] Luis de León, *op. cit.*, II, chap. 4: "So, as in the Divinity the Holy Ghost, who is spirated by the persons of the Father and the Son jointly, is love and is, as we say, the sweet and strong bond of both, so also the Holy Ghost, infused into the Church and united to all her just members dwells in them, vivifies them, inflames them, excites their love, delights them, and makes them one with Himself."
St. Mary Magdalen of Pazzi, *Œuvres*, IV, chap. 9: "Charity is like a chain of gold which unites Me to souls and unites them to others in Me with a union like that of the three divine Persons. This is the grace which My Word so fervently begged of Me for them in His last discourse on charity: 'That they may be one as We are one.'"

THE DIVINE LIFE OF GRACE

with the love of the Spirit. This is that affection for God spoken of by St. Irenaeus [108] which leads us to the Father by means of the Word. Through the Holy Ghost we ascend to the Son, and through the Son to the Father.[109] The Spirit is that love as strong as death, whose lamps are lamps of divine fire and flames.[110] How vividly those souls feel this who are inflamed by the Spirit! [111]

2. GIFT OF GOD AND FOUNT OF LIVING WATER

"That Love which is of God and which is God," says St. Augustine, "is the Holy Ghost Himself, through whom is poured forth in our hearts the charity of God which makes us guests and temples of the Trinity. Hence it is that the Holy Ghost is also rightly called the Gift of God. And what is this Gift but the charity which leads us to God and without which no other gift could lead us to Him?" [112] So this loving Spirit, who makes us exclaim "Father!" is that Gift par excellence in which are contained all divine gifts. If we could know the Gift of God, how could we help but appreciate it above all earthly treasures?

If we but understood it well, it is certain that we would wholeheartedly desire to satiate ourselves in that fount of living water which takes away all earthly thirst and gives life eternal. Surely we would ask God to give us this mysterious water and we would obtain it. This vital and vivifying water, which the Lord speaks of, not

---

[108] *Haeres.*, IV, chap. 2.
[109] *Ibid.*, V, chap. 36.
[110] Cant. 8:6.
[111] St. Mary Magdalen of Pazzi, *op. cit.*, I, chap. 33: "Through this Spirit, O Lord, Thou dost transform souls into Thyself in such a way that they are no longer contained in themselves, so to speak. Rather, since love has transformed them into Thee and Thee into them, they have become identical in Spirit with Thee. O the grandeur of the Word! O privilege of the creature! O ineffable grace of the Holy Ghost! If this grace were but known, it would excite the admiration of all, and all would desire to be thus united with Thee."
St. Catherine of Genoa, *Dialogues*, III, 11: "O holy Love! Thou dost inflame us in the fire of Thy love until we are consumed. Who could believe it? What liberality! We are now nothing more than love in Thee; but we are unable to give an account of this superhuman, sublime, and totally divine work. We were earthly, but we became heavenly . . . (cf. I Cor. 15). We lost the nature which we received from Adam and now we have no other life than that of Jesus Christ. . . . We are spiritual, as is this divine Savior; and since the Spirit is of Himself indivisible, man finds himself united to God in such a way that he need not know whence this union proceeds or where it leads while he yet remains in this earthly pilgrimage. It is sufficient for him to be submerged in the ardors of charity which impel him (II Cor. 5)."
[112] *De Trinitate*, Bk. XV, chap. 32.

only to the more advanced, but even to the Samaritan woman,[113] is the Spirit, who gives us unending life. Therefore, Christ adds, addressing His words to all the world: "If any man thirst, let him come to Me and drink. He that believeth in Me, as the Scripture saith, 'Out of his belly shall flow rivers of living water.' Now this He said of the Spirit which they should receive, who believed in Him." [114]

This Spirit is called living water because He satiates, refreshes, washes, purifies, renews, and gives life, vigor, and robustness. The Apostle considers Him as living water when he says: "In one Spirit we have all been made to drink." [115] He is called the Gift of God, the Gift of the Most High, or simply, the Gift, as is evident from the words of St. Peter: "You shall receive the gift of the Holy Ghost." [116] According to His personal character, as St. Thomas says, it is fitting that He should be given and that He should be the Gift par excellence. "Actually, He proceeds," states St. Augustine, "not as one born, but as one given, and for that reason He is not called son, because His origin was not a birth but a giving." [117] And because He is the first "giving," which contains all others, the primitive Church used to designate Him by that name alone. "In His goodness," writes St. Irenaeus, "God has given us a Gift; and this Gift, superior to all gifts because He contains them all, is the Holy Ghost." [118] Thus, to the original Gift and to the Spirit of Love are attributed all other gifts—graces, charismata, inspirations, divine impulses, lights, fervor, conversion, pardon, regeneration, renewal, sanctification, and, in brief, the adoption and indwelling, with all its works of love and its goodness in general.[119]

---

[113] John 4:10-14.
[114] Ibid., 7:37-39.
[115] See I Cor. 12:13.
[116] Acts 2:38.
[117] De Trinitate, Bk. V, chap. 14.
[118] Haer., IV, 33.
[119] See Terrien, La grâce et la gloire, I, p. 408. Froget, The Indwelling of the Holy Spirit, pp. 125 f.: "The Holy Ghost comes to act, God being essentially active, or as theologians phrase it, Pure Act. Far from being unfruitful, the presence of this sanctifying Spirit of our soul bears abundant fruit. The purpose of His mission, the great work that He comes to perform and that He will succeed in performing if we are docile to His inspirations and do not refuse Him our cooperation without which nothing can be done, is to wrest us from the empire of darkness and translate us into the kingdom of light; to create a new being within us and transform our entire soul by clothing it with justice and holiness; to infuse into us, together with His grace, a life infinitely superior to the natural life; to render us partakers of the

THE DIVINE LIFE OF GRACE

3. SOURCE OF ALL SANCTITY

As personal Charity, He is the hypostatic sanctifying Holiness, and for that reason is He called the Holy Ghost.[120] "He is denominated as holy," teaches Leo XIII, "because, being supreme Love, He directs souls to true sanctity, which consists precisely in the love of God."[121] Says St. Basil: Because He is holy by essence, He is the source of all sanctity. Whether it pertains to angels, archangels, or all the heavenly powers, all are sanctified by the Spirit who has sanctity by nature and not by grace. Hence He alone bears the name Holy.[122]

When He sanctifies us, He purifies us and gives light to the eyes of our hearts so that they may gaze upon divine truth. Thus, as the same doctor adds: "The road to the knowledge of God passes from the Spirit alone, through the Son alone, to the Father alone. In an inverse order, natural goodness and essential sanctity are derived from the Father, through His only Son, and finally through the Holy Ghost."[123] Therefore St. Cyril of Alexandria calls Him "the sanctifying power which, proceeding naturally from the Father, gives perfection to the imperfect."[124]

Thus is He manifested to us, transforming us and impressing on us the outline of the Word of the Father and the living image of the divine essence.[125] In this way He is the vivifier, renewer, and illumi-

---

divine nature, children of God and heirs of His kingdom; to strengthen our native powers by endowing us with new energies; to bestow His gifts upon us; and to render us capable of performing acts that will be meritorious of eternal life. In a word, His mission consists in laboring efficaciously, incessantly, and lovingly in the work of our sanctification."

[120] Petau (*De Trinitate*, Bk. VIII, chap. 6, no. 7) says that the most celebrated of the Greek fathers considered the sanctifying or vivifying quality as something just as personal to the Holy Ghost as is filiation to the Son and paternity to the Father.

[121] *Divinum illud munus.*

[122] *Epist. 8*, no. 10; *Epist. 159*, no. 2.

[123] *De Spiritu Sancto*, no. 47.

[124] *Thes. Patrum Graecorum*, LXXV, 597.

[125] St. Cyril of Alexandria, *In Joan. 17:* "Transforming souls into Himself in a certain manner, the Spirit of God imprints on them a divine image and traces in them the likeness of the supreme substance."

Further, to configure us the better with Him who is our Head and Model, the Holy Ghost wishes to form us, like Christ, in union with the most holy Virgin. So, St. Louis-Marie Grignion de Montfort (*True Devotion to the Blessed Virgin*) says: "God the Holy Ghost being barren in God—that is to say, not producing another divine Person—is become fruitful by Mary, whom He has espoused. It is with her, in her, and of her, that He has produced His Masterpiece, which is a God made

nator. He is the life of our souls, as St. Augustine [126] and St. Basil [127] call Him, for when He animates souls with the grace of His communication, He refashions their very form, or rather He bestows on them a superior and divine soul which is the grace of His sanctification. He is the life which was in the beginning in the Word and which is the light of men [128] and the source of all supernatural action. St. Athanasius says: "We are made partakers in the Word by the Holy Ghost, through whom we participate in the divine nature and through whom we are renewed." [129]

The Holy Ghost imparts the regenerative power to the waters of baptism and there He creates us anew in God. He gives us the divine form of grace and causes us to be reborn to eternal life.[130]

That we may enter into the kingdom of God, or that this kingdom may enter into us, we must be reborn of water and the Holy Ghost.[131] The liturgy clearly states this fact on Holy Saturday when it says: "O almighty and eternal God, . . . send forth the spirit of adoption to regenerate the new people, whom the font of baptism

---

Man, and whom He goes on producing in the persons of His members daily to the end of the world. The predestined are the members of that adorable Head. This is the reason why He, the Holy Ghost, the more He finds Mary, His dear and inseparable spouse, in any soul, becomes the more active and mighty in producing Jesus Christ in that soul, and that soul in Jesus Christ.

"It is not that we may say that our Blessed Lady gives the Holy Ghost His fruitfulness, as if He had it not Himself. For inasmuch as He is God He has the same fruitfulness or capacity of producing as the Father and the Son, only that He does not bring it into action, as He does not produce another divine Person. But what we want to say is, that the Holy Ghost chose to make use of our Blessed Lady, though He had no absolute need of her, to bring His fruitfulness into action, by producing in her and by her Jesus Christ in His members."

[126] *Serm.* 156, chap. 6, no. 6.
[127] *De Spiritu Sancto*, chap. 26.
[128] John 1.
[129] *Epist. I ad Serap.*, nos. 22-24.
[130] St. Cyril of Alexandria, *Il In Joan.*: "It is the Holy Ghost who calls us from nothingness to being. . . . He restores the image of God when He impresses His lines in our souls and transforms them, so to speak, with His own proper quality." The same saint says in another place (*In Is.*, chap. 44): "Jesus Christ is formed in us by virtue of a divine form which the Holy Ghost infuses in us through sanctification."

In this way do souls who are filled with the Holy Ghost, inflamed with zeal for the glory of God, and who work for the conversion of sinners contribute to that spiritual creation or formation of Jesus Christ. Therefore St. Mary Magdalen of Pazzi said (*Œuvres*, I, chap. 6) that every zealous soul re-creates God in those who have lost Him, because the return of these souls to God is like a new creation of God within them.

[131] John 3:5 f.

THE DIVINE LIFE OF GRACE

brings forth; . . . Graciously behold the face of Thy Church, and multiply in it the number of the regenerate . . . that by command of Thy majesty it may receive the grace of Thy only Son from the Holy Ghost. . . . May He by a secret admixture of His divine power render this water fruitful for the regeneration of men, to the end that a heavenly offspring, conceived in sanctification, may emerge from the immaculate womb of the divine font, reborn new creatures: and that all, however distinguished either by sex in body or by age in time, may be brought forth to the same infancy by grace, their spiritual mother. . . . May the power of the Holy Ghost descend into all the water of this font and make the whole substance of this water fruitful for regeneration . . . that all who receive this sacrament of regeneration, may be born again new children of true innocence." [182]

Thus it is He who fecundates the baptismal waters and communicates to the Church the power of regeneration, as is evident from this precious inscription which was placed by order of Sixtus III in the baptistery of St. John Lateran:

> *Gens sacranda polis hic semine nascitur almo*
> *Quam foecundantis Spiritus edit aquis.*
> *Virgineo foetu genetrix Ecclesia natos*
> *Quos, spirante Deo, concipit amne parit.*
> *Fons hic est vitae qui totum diluit orbem,*
> *Sumens de Christi vulnere principium.*

St. Irenaeus (*Haer.*, IV, 31) dares to call the Holy Ghost "the living and vivifying seed of the Father" because He causes us to be reborn of the Father and by His communication He makes us true sons of God.[183] Also, according to the expression of St. Augustine,

---

[182] Prayer at the blessing of the font. Terrien, *La grâce*, I, 24: "There is nothing so instructive as the formulas and symbols which the Church has used since the beginning to portray the spiritual rebirth of her children. Baptism is called a regeneration. The baptized, of whatever age they may be, are to the Church infants newly born, 'as newborn babes' (I Pet. 2:2). In Christian inscriptions we see this expression applied to men of thirty or forty years (cf. Mabillon, *De re diplom.*, Suppl. 5; Martigny, *Antiq. chrét.*, baptême, III). In certain places, immediately after baptism, they were given honey mixed with milk, the food of infants. . . . The instructions which the Bishop addressed to them were sermons 'to children': *Ad infantes.*"

[183] St. Thomas, *In Rom.* 8:14, lect. 3: "It must be considered how those who are acted upon by the Holy Ghost are sons of God. And this is evident from their similitude to carnal children, who are generated by the seed which proceeds from the

we are reborn from the same Spirit as was Christ. St. Leo says that the baptismal font is to us what the virginal womb was to the Savior.[134]

4. SPIRIT OF ADOPTION AND MYSTICAL UNCTION

Since the Holy Ghost gives us that divine form which makes us sons of God (for sonship consists in being animated by Him), He is also the Spirit of adoption which makes us call God by the name of "Father." [135] "He is," says Terrien, "the one who, forming us in the image of the Word, makes us adopted sons of the Father. . . . He it is who, when united to our souls, enables us to work as sons of God; who, by His intimate presence and operations, gives us testimony that we do not bear that glorious title in vain. The possession of Him makes us realize that we abide in God and that God dwells in us." [136]

He is the living seal of Christ which, when imprinted on our souls, makes us living images of God. He is also the mystical unction which permeates us with the divine life and transforms our hearts into so many other sanctuaries of the divinity. Thus do we become living temples of God wherein the Holy Ghost dwells as in His proper dwelling place and where "with Him and through Him the Father and the Son come to dwell." [137] "Know you not," asks the Apostle, "that you are the temple of God and that the Spirit of God dwelleth in you? . . . Or know you not that your members are the temple

---

father. But the spiritual seed proceeding from the Father is the Holy Ghost. Therefore through this seed some men are generated into sons of God. Whoever is born of God cannot sin, because the seed of God abides in him (I John 3)."

[134] *Serm. in Nativ. Dom.*, 5: "The Son became a man like us in order that we might become consorts in His divinity. The origin which He had in the womb of the Virgin, He placed in the baptismal font; . . . The power of the most High and the overshadowing of the Holy Ghost which was given Mary that she might bring forth the Savior, was given to the water that it might regenerate believers."

[135] Rom. 8:14-16; Gal. 4:6-7.
St. Thomas says (IIa IIae, q.45, a.6, ad 1um): "Likewise the Holy Ghost is called the *Spirit of adoption* in so far as we receive from Him the likeness of the natural Son, Who is the Begotten Wisdom."

[136] *Op. cit.*, I, 388. See also I John 4:13. St. Thomas says that both holiness and adoptive filiation must be attributed to the Holy Ghost (IIIa, q.32, a.1): "For by Him men are made to be sons of God. . . . Again, He is the *Spirit of sanctification*, according to Rom. i. 4. Therefore, just as other men are sanctified spiritually by the Holy Ghost, so as to be the adopted sons of God, so was Christ conceived in sanctity by the Holy Ghost, so as to be the natural Son of God."

[137] Terrien, *op. cit.*, I, 408.

THE DIVINE LIFE OF GRACE

of the Holy Ghost?"[188] This unction and consecration soften, purify, illumine, and inflame our hearts. They preserve us from error, manifest the truth to us,[139] and make us docile and willing to hear it and practice it.

5. INFLUENCE OF THE HOLY GHOST ON CHRIST AND THE FAITHFUL

To the Holy Ghost is necessarily attributed, as Terrien says, all the gifts of grace and whatever pertains to our sanctification. He makes God approach to us and makes us come closer to God, as is evident from the activity of the Spirit in Christ, the Head, and in the faithful, who are His members. Speaking of this influence of the Holy Ghost on the Head and members of the mystical body, Terrien continues (*loc. cit.*):

It is remarkable to see with what minute care the Gospel portrays the influence of the divine Spirit on the mission of the Savior. He formed Christ in the immaculate womb of the Virgin; through Elizabeth, Anna, and Simeon, He announced Christ as the long-awaited King;[140] He descended visibly at the baptism in order to give official testimony before the precursor and the people.[141] He led Christ into the desert to prepare Him for the great work of His apostolate;[142] and through this same Spirit, the God-man worked His miracles so that to resist them with obstinacy is to sin against the Holy Ghost.[143] Even more, if Jesus Christ is offered for us as a bloody victim, it is through the Holy Ghost;[144] and if He continues His work of redemption in the world by the testimony of the apostles, it is the Holy Ghost who provides this testimony.[145] Lastly, if the Church remains to perpetuate the mission of Christ until the end of time, it is through the Spirit that Christ establishes it, fashions it, preserves it, and renders it everlastingly fruitful.[146] Thus, from beginning to end, the Holy Ghost reigns in Christ for the realization of His work of grace, of love, of restoration, and of health. And if He influences the Head in this way, can He not do likewise in regard to

---

[188] See I Cor. 3:16; 6:19.
[139] See I John 2:20, 27.
[140] Luke 1:35-68; 2:25.
[141] Matt. 3:16; John 1:29-34.
[142] Luke 4:1.
[143] Matt. 12:28; Luke 11:20.
[144] Heb. 9:14.
[145] John 15:26.
[146] Acts 1, 2, etc.

the members? Even before God has taken possession of a soul, it pertains to the Holy Ghost to prepare it for His entrance. To this are ordained all those interior illuminations and impulses, called prevenient graces, with which He touches hearts.[147]

But His actions and blessings do not cease here. In all that infinite variety of graces which divine goodness so liberally bestows on us, there is not one which is not from the Holy Ghost.[148] When, after being made sons of God, we are transformed from glory to glory, He it is who works this wonder.[149] The unutterable groanings with which we plead for mercy and by which we touch the heart of God; [150] all the salutary acts which cause merit; charity, joy, peace, benignity; all sanctity, piety, meekness: [151] these are so many effects and fruits of His presence in the very essence of our souls. Residing in us, He renews us entirely,[152] activates our spiritual life, assists us in our weakness, consoles us in our afflictions, and is saddened by our infidelities. He is within us as the beginning and pledge of our future happiness.[153]

All the tradition of the East and the West is in accord in attributing the divine indwelling to the Holy Ghost in a very singular manner and in affirming that in Him and through Him the Father and the Son are united to souls through His abiding in them.[154] "Through

[147] *Conc. Trid.*, Sess. VI, can. 5.
[148] See I Cor. 12; Heb. 2:4.
[149] See II Cor. 3:18.
[150] Rom. 8:26.
[151] Gal. 5:22-23.
[152] Titus 3:5.
[153] Rom. 8:14-26; Acts 9:31; Eph. 4:30; II Cor. 7:22. Ven. Louis of Granada, *The Sinner's Guide*, Bk. I, chap. 5: "What could be more priceless or more desirable than to have within oneself such a guest, such a governor, such a guide, such a companion, tutor, and helper? Yet, He who is all things, works all things in the souls in which He dwells. First of all, as a *fire* He enlightens our understanding, inflames our will, and raises us from earth to heaven. Then as the *dove*, He makes us simple, meek, docile, and friends, one to another. . . . As a *cloud*, He protects us from the heat of the flesh. . . . As a *moving wind* He drives and inclines our will totally to the good and separates and disinclines it from evil. . . . All our goods and all our benefits ought to be derived from this divine Spirit. If we are separated from evil, it is He who delivers us and if we do good, we do so through Him. If we persevere, it is because of Him and if we receive any reward for the good that we do, it is He who gives it to us."
[154] St. Augustine, *Meditations*, chap. 9: "O Divine Love of the supreme Deity, holy communication of the omnipotent Father and His most blessed Son . . . I believe that in whomever Thou dost deign to dwell, Thou dost also make that one the temple and habitation of the Father and the Son. Blessed is he who merits to lodge Thee! since through Thee the Father and the Son also make him their mansion. Come, then, most benign Consoler of the afflicted soul. . . . Come, Sanctifier of sinners and Healer of our wounds. Come, Master of the lowly, Destroyer of the proud . . . and singular glory of all the living."

the Holy Ghost," says St. Athanasius, "we participate in the Word and we enter into communication with God the Father. . . . And so it is evident that the unction and the seal which are in us are not anything created, but they are of the same nature as the Son because it is the Son who unites us to the Father through the Holy Ghost who resides in Him."[155] "When we possess the Holy Ghost," he says in another place, "who is the Spirit of God, we are truly in God and God dwells in us."[156]

As St. Basil affirms, "union is effected through the Holy Ghost, for God sent into our hearts the Spirit of His Son whereby we cry *Abba*, Father."[157] St. Augustine, in turn, says: "Through the Holy Ghost the Trinity dwells in us. . . . For this Spirit who has been given us, makes us dwell in God and God in us. . . . Also He is the Charity of God, and he who perseveres in charity remains in God and God in Him."[158]

The Holy Ghost anoints us by His communication and thus converts us into anointed ones of the Lord, and true Christs. He stamps us invisibly with the impress of the Word, the true light of life, and imprints it on the sensitive plate of our hearts. Then, little by little, as the active agent of the sufferings of Christ causes us to die with Him that we may rise gloriously with Him, we lose the image of the earthly man and carry within us the likeness of a heavenly man, resplendent with divine brilliancy.[159]

---

[155] *Epist. ad Serap.* I, nos. 23 f.
[156] *Orat.* 3, *contra Arian.*, no. 23.
[157] *De Spiritu Sancto*, chap. 19.
[158] *De Trinitate*, Bk. XV, chap. 18. St. Cyril of Alexandria, *In Joan*, Bk. XII, 17: "The Savior effects our return to God by means of sanctification and a participation in His Spirit. For it is the Spirit who unites us with God, and to receive Him is to become sharers in the divine nature. And we receive Him through the Son, and in the Son we receive the Father."

St. Mary Magdalen of Pazzi, *Œuvres*, IV, chap. 2: "Thou art wonderful, O divine Word, in the Holy Spirit whom Thou dost send to the soul and by means of whom the soul is united to God, knows God, tastes God, and finds delight in God alone. This effusion of the Holy Spirit is so necessary to the soul that without it the soul would be a devil; it would feed in the pasture of the demon and would enjoy what he enjoys. O how numerous are these demons who expose Thy servants to such great dangers! . . . Pour forth in all hearts this effusion of Thy Spirit; and if it is necessary that there always be evil ones in the world to test the good, then grant that those evil ones be also tested by others and that their adversity lead them back to Thee."

[159] Rom. 6:3-11; I Cor. 15:45-49; II Cor. 3:18; 4:10-14; Col. 2:2; Eph. 4:23 f.; Phil. 3:10 f.

So this sovereign Spirit who, by His vivifying substance, anoints us and impresses on us the mystic seal and gradually manifests it more and more, is a preservative against corruption. He is the germ of immortality, the pledge and dowry of glory, and the cause of our future resurrection. "And if the Spirit of Him who raised up Jesus from the dead dwell in you, He that raised up Jesus Christ from the dead shall quicken also your mortal bodies because of His Spirit that dwelleth in you." [160]

At the same time that He is the unction and living seal, the Holy Ghost is also the secure pledge. And as the beginning and seed of a glorious immortality, He constitutes the dowry of eternal life and everlasting heritage.[161] For the dowry is substantially a part of what is promised and pledged. "Now He that confirmeth us with you in Christ and that hath anointed us, is God; who also hath sealed us and given the pledge of the Spirit in our hearts." [162]

Dwelling in holy souls, the Spirit makes them "friends of God and prophets"; [163] and remaining in Himself the same, He renews all things. He makes them friends because He is the charity of God and this charity He pours forth in their hearts in such a manner that they can love God with the same love as that with which He loves them: the love of true friendship. So it is that they abide in God and He in them.

Since friendship is a love of benevolence, there proceed from it, on the one hand, pardon; and on the other, adoption, which is attributed to the Holy Ghost, by whose power the offenses committed against God are forgiven,[164] and through whose communication we are adopted as sons of God. The Spirit Himself testifies to this: "You have received the spirit of adoption of sons, whereby we cry: Abba (Father). For the Spirit Himself giveth testimony to our spirit that we are the sons of God." [165]

The faithful friend communicates his secrets and permits the sharing of all his own goods. So it is that the Spirit of love should be

---

[160] Rom. 8:11.
[161] St. Basil, *Adv. Eunom.*, Bk. V: "When the Spirit of God enters into a soul, He pours forth in it life, immortality, and holiness."
[162] See II Cor. 1:21 f.
[163] Wisd. 7:27. See also II Cor. 5:17.
[164] John 20:20–23.
[165] Rom. 8:15 f.

the revealer of the divine mysteries,[166] the pledge of the heritage of God,[167] and the dispenser of all graces [168] through which He renews all things.[169] Hence we are commanded to "be strengthened by His Spirit with might unto the inward man" and to "be renewed in the spirit of your mind; and put on the new man." [170] Then shall we be filled with spiritual powers with which we can work divinely, subjugating our passions and enjoying the glorious liberty of the sons of God.[171]

Owing to this renewal by the Holy Ghost, even the tongues of children are apt for uttering the great mysteries; or better, He Himself utters them through the mouth of His prophets. "By the Spirit he speaketh mysteries." [172] "For it is not you that speak, but the Spirit of your Father that speaketh in you," [173] "who spoke by the prophets." [174]

As distributor of all the graces and gifts of Christ, He communicates to each of the faithful, according to the measure of the giving of the Head, divine life, power, and strength. Thus He organizes and develops the mystical body of the Church, of which He is the soul, as St. Augustine says: "What the soul is to the body, the Holy Ghost is to the body of Christ, which is the Church." [175] And since

---

[166] See I Cor. 2:10; Eph. 1:17-19.
[167] Rom. 8:17; Eph. 1:14.
[168] See I Cor. 12.
[169] Ps. 103:32; Wisd. 7:27.
[170] Eph. 3:16; 4:23 f.
[171] Rom. 8:21; II Cor. 3:17. Grou, *Manuel*, p. 36: "When anyone has succeeded in dominating his passions, he finds himself actually freed from all that is not God, and he sweetly enjoys the liberty of God's sons. He feels pity for the miserable slaves of the world, and he congratulates himself that he is freed from his bondage. Standing peacefully on the shore, he sees others who are tossed about by the waves of the sea of iniquity, driven by a thousand contrary winds, and always at the point of perishing in the tempest. He, however, enjoys a profound calm; he is master of his desires and actions, and he does what he desires to do. No ambition, no covetousness, no sensuality seduce him; no human respect restrains him. Neither the opinions of men nor their criticisms, mockery, or sneers are able to deter him one jot from the right path. Adversities, sufferings, humiliations, and all manner of crosses, whatever they may be, have nothing of fear or terror for him. In brief, he is one who has been raised above this world with its errors, its attractions, and its terrors. What does it mean to be free, if not precisely this? Even more, it is a freedom in respect to oneself, for not being influenced by imagination or inconstancy, he remains firm in his perfect resolutions."
[172] See I Cor. 14:2.
[173] Matt. 10:20.
[174] Nicene Creed. See St. Thomas, *Contra Gent.*, IV, chap. 21.
[175] *Sermo 266 in Pent.*, chap. 4.

THE MYSTICAL EVOLUTION

He is the true soul of this marvelous organism and the higher and divine life of each of its members who are not in sin, in Him is found all the power of the vital functions, both common and particular, of the body as a whole and each organ in particular. Therefore it is the Holy Ghost who effects the entire wonderful work of our justification, sanctification, and deification, from beginning to end.[176] By holy inspirations, He disposes us to receive the life of grace. He it is who introduces it, preserves it, develops it, and gradually makes it manifest in the measure that He transforms us from glory to glory.[177]

Thus, considering the adorable mystery of the Most Blessed Trinity, we see that the primordial origin of life is in the eternal Father,—*ex quo omnia*—for in Him is the fount of life. From the Father, it passes through the Son—*per quem omnia*—in whom it is the selfsame life. Finally, it proceeds entirely to the Holy Ghost—*in quo omnia*—and He it is who diffuses this life into our souls, makes them participants in the divine nature, and pours into our hearts the very charity of God.[178] In this way we enter into communication with the inner life of the entire Trinity and into relation with each one of the three adorable Persons.

But that divine life which the Spirit of love infuses in us needs a subject, a human-divine organism, with organs and arteries which will distribute this life and perform the required vital functions. That subject or organism is Jesus Christ in union with His Church, and the arteries of life are the sacraments.

The Holy Ghost began His sanctifying mission in the incarnation of our Lord. He was an active principle in the formation of the

---

[176] St. Magdalen of Pazzi, *Œuvres*, I, chap. 28: "O Lord, Thy divine Spirit produces no effect in the world more wonderful than when He renews it and gives it new life. He has exalted Thee by entering into the hearts of Thy chosen ones. By uniting Himself to them, He makes them do Thy works, and in this way art Thou exalted in them as much as is possible. In them Thou dost come to be another self, thanks to the union which they enjoy with this divine Spirit. Thou art particularly glorified in all Thy priests, who possess this Spirit, for each priest has become as another god in Thee, as another Word (Ps. 81:6). Although there is but one God by essence, there are thousands of gods through communication, participation, and union."

[177] See II Cor. 3:18.

[178] St. Athanasius, *Epist. ad Serap.* I, no. 19: "The Father is the fount, the Son the river, and the Holy Ghost that from which we drink. But by drinking the Holy Ghost, we also drink Christ." See also St. Augustine, *Meditations*, chap. 31.

sacred body and its union with the soul, as well as the infusion of capital or fontal graces, for it is admitted that the mystery of the Incarnation was effected in the womb of the holy Virgin through the operation of the Holy Ghost. But besides the fashioning of the natural body of Christ, the Holy Ghost formed, in the likeness of Christ, the mystical body which is the Church. In this mystical body, of which He is the soul, He exercises all the vital functions which are necessary to reproduce in the various members whatever will integrate the whole series of mysteries of the life, passion, death, and resurrection of the Savior.[179]

The natural body of Christ, when it reached its plenitude and finished its proper work, ascended gloriously into heaven, but the mystical body yet remains and will remain as long as the world endures. It is still in the process of growth and must perfect itself in the pattern of Jesus Christ through the power of His Spirit of love.[180]

So both of them, the divine Word and His Spirit, immediately and directly influence the progressive development of the union, incorporation, vivification, purification, illumination, sanctification, and deification of each one of the members and living organs of the holy Catholic Church. Yet, even here, each one acts according to His own manner: Christ as the Head of the mystical body, and the Holy Ghost as its soul.

APPENDIX

The Marvelous Work of the Holy Ghost

We have come across a manuscript written by an unlettered person who was very experienced in the things of God. Many things

---

[179] St. Leo, *Sermo in Nativitate Domini*, 6: "The generation of Christ is the origin of the Christian people.... All the sons of the Church are distinct by succession of time, but since all the faithful by being born at the baptismal font, were crucified in the passion of Christ, resurrected in His rising, placed at the right hand of the Father through His ascension, so also, were they generated in His nativity.... For whoever has been regenerated in Christ and has lost the traces of his former origin, becomes a new man through that rebirth, not now through the generation by a carnal father, but through the seed of the Savior. Therefore He became the Son of Man that we might become sons of God."

[180] Eph. 4:7-24.

contained herein, if correctly interpreted, will clarify some of the points we have already indicated. For that reason we reproduce it in part.

"I am going to speak of the great debt we owe to the Holy Ghost, the Third Person of the Most Blessed Trinity, the least loved and the least known. . . . It would have availed us little that the Father created us and preserved us in existence; and that the divine Word redeemed us and freed us from slavery, obtained for us the pardon of our sins, opened for us the gates of heaven, . . . and willed to elevate us to the dignity of sons of God, if the Holy Ghost had not come and will continue to come until the end of the world to vivify and sanctify us with His grace and His gifts.[1]

"This great work, greater in its beginning than the whole of creation, was begun by the Father and continued by the Son, who devoted every moment of His life to it from the instant of His incarnation: all the fatigue, labor, and privation of His public life; all the contempt, abuse, contumely, sorrow, and agony of His passion; the abandonment by His Father, and the death itself which He suffered. We creatures cannot understand suffering such as this; not even the most privileged intellects can comprehend it. It surpasses all other suffering even as the bottomless oceans surpass the little streams that run through the meadows. Those souls which arrive at a most intimate union with God are the only ones that have a certain and clear idea of what this suffering is. Yet for all that Jesus Christ suffered for our good, it would have availed little had not the divine Spirit come to teach us with His light, to animate us with His grace, and to communicate His gifts to us. By these means He sanctifies us and places on us the seal of predestination which we have forfeited through sin. Through the merits of our adorable Redeemer, it is given to us anew.

[1] Weiss, *Apologie*, Vol. IX, conf. 3, app. 1 and 2: "Alas, that we must suffer the derision with which Renan (using a phrase of Feuerbach) pities that divine Person who is so forgotten by His worshipers. . . . If we reminded ourselves more often of the Holy Ghost, we would find ourselves repaid quickly with such spiritual progress as none of them ever fancied. . . . He who does not close his eyes to the light, will understand that all the power of the Church, her heart and blood and vital energy and all the manifestations of her life, are nothing other than the Holy Ghost working in her. He it is who lives and works in the sacraments, which are channels of life, instruments of grace, and means of salvation and sanctification. . . . The spiritual life will never be able to flourish until the Holy Ghost is better known and loved."

"All divine works are performed by the three divine Persons of the august Trinity. They are begun by the Father, continued by the Son (Word), and perfected by the Holy Ghost. . . . Therefore Jesus said to His disciples: 'It is expedient to you that I go.' He knew well that in spite of all the works performed for the instruction of men, in spite of all the means used to make them understand the truth and love it, they would never bear fruit until the divine Spirit should descend upon them. Christ desired to go to His Father so that the Holy Ghost might come and conquer for Him those men whose intellects were so darkened and whose hearts were so sensate. . . And so it happened, for although they saw Him resurrected by His own power and saw Him ascend into heaven, they remained in ignorance and obscurity until the promised Comforter came upon them. And it could not be otherwise, since it is the Holy Ghost who proceeds from the other two and is, as it were, the very essence of Divinity;[2] who is (I speak thus in order to make myself understood) the chest wherein are buried all the treasures of God. Since He is the steward of the riches contained in the divine essence, Jesus Christ was eager to sit at the right hand of the Father so that this divine Spirit who proceeds from the two Persons might descend as soon as possible to conclude and perfect the work which is continued but not consummated by Christ. This activity is reserved for the Holy Ghost as something proper to Him.

"It is sad to see a mighty work begun and pursued with great effort, fatigue, and privation and then not brought to fruition. This is the reason why the Redeemer desired to be bathed in the baptism of blood. He wished to be lifted up on the holy wood of the cross so that from it He might be able to win for us, not heaven, which had been given to us antecedently through His redemption, but to win for us something far greater than heaven. To redeem us, one tear shed in favor of man, or one sigh from that loving heart was sufficient. Why, then, was He lifted up on the cross to suffer such torments, were it not that we were to imitate Him in this? And further, if He submitted to the crucifixion, why did He prolong His life for three hours, in each one of which He suffered more than He did during the whole of the thirty-three years He spent on earth? . . . O greatest Good and immense Wisdom! . . . He was lifted

---

[2] Actually He is the charity of God, and God is charity.

up on the cross to effect our elevation from our fallen state and that to our great advantage. He remained there for three hours until He obtained from His eternal Father that we should no longer be looked upon as creatures descended from Adam, but that He should adopt us as sons, treat us as sons of adoption. This was effected without delay.

"But that loving heart, thirsting for our good, while He was in the midst of those terrible agonies just before He died, cried out: 'I thirst.' . . . The Blessed Mother well knew that it was not a bodily thirst which her Son desired to quench. It was a divine thirst to do good to man by raising him to the greatest dignity that any creature could possess. . She understood very clearly, through a communication from the Word, exactly what her Son desired and petitioned. At the foot of the cross, her eyes fixed on Him, her hands joined in prayer, and her heart filled with courage, she united with her blessed Son in praying for man and effecting what her Son desired. And what could be granted us that is greater than to become sons of God by adoption?

"That ardent love desired above all that it should possess man; it desired that we should be gods by grace, something that we could not acquire through our own nature. It desired that this grace should fructify even in this life; that in this mortal life we might be able to possess the chains of union with the divine essence and that this might be communicated to us through the gifts of the Holy Ghost. We have nothing by which we may merit such graces; on the contrary, we have many reasons for being abhorred by God. But Christ, melting with love toward the human race, exclaims from the depths of His blessed soul: 'Father, forgive them, for they know not what they do.'

"Forgetful of self in such terrible agony, He begs and urges His eternal Father to grant what He seeks. But since He who suffered was the incarnate Word, He could see that the justice of God was opposed to the concession of this grace to all men because of the contempt they had shown Him and the mockery they had manifested. Then Jesus Christ turned His loving gaze to the few chosen ones and, locking them all in Himself, that heart which hungers for the salvation of men presented them to His Father, saying: 'Let all these

THE DIVINE LIFE OF GRACE

whom I present to Thee be assimilated to Me. Let them form one body, with Me as the Head and our vivifying Spirit as the soul which vivifies and animates them. And as many as with a good will associate themselves with this mystical body, give to them the power to live our life in time and in eternity. To all men let there be affectionately granted that which I entreat of You. My Father, place the attribute of mercy which resides in Me, before that of justice which resides in Thee. As long as mortal life endures, let My attribute work, and after death let Thine work.'

"There, upon the holy wood of the cross, before Christ expired, the holy Church was established and from that time on the Holy Ghost remained as the soul and life of that Church. The Spirit would impart to the Church His gifts whereby the faithful could produce fruits by which the Church would become beautiful; He would impart to them His charity whereby might be bound in a most perfect and intimate union all the souls gathered together in Him; He would make them sharers in His riches without rule or measure.

"When all this was accomplished, the dying heart of Christ was comforted by the strength of love, and He exclaimed: 'It is consummated. Father, into Thy hands I commend My spirit.' He miraculously prolonged His life until He could accomplish for men what He desired. He desired not only to redeem us; a sigh would have accomplished that. What He really desired was to make us gods by grace, obtaining from the eternal Father that He send the divine Spirit to us here on earth.

"When He had completed that work which belonged to God made man for the love of man, He ascended to sit at the right hand of His Father. It remained only for the Holy Ghost to perfect the work.[3] Without the Holy Ghost, this mystical body of the Church, whose Head is our Redeemer, would not have life, because the Holy Ghost is the soul and life of this body. The members would not be able to go to Jesus Christ and be united to Him without the Holy

---

[3] St. Augustine, *Manual*, chap. 26: "Moved by mercy, God sent His Son to this world to redeem His servants. He also sent the Holy Ghost to adopt them as sons. He gave His Son as the price of our ransom; the Holy Ghost, as a pledge of His love. Finally, He gave Himself as the heritage of those men whom He adopted as sons. . . . That men might be born of God and might become His sons by adoption, God first became man and took human nature."

Ghost, even though Christ is their Head. . . . Jesus said that we could not go to the Father except through Him, and we cannot go to Christ without the help of the Holy Ghost.

"So degenerate did the human race become through the sin of our first parents! So weak and powerless! So obscure of intellect! So dead was the beautiful life of the soul! We were rendered so incapable of doing good that our ruin was mortal and complete. Our sins were pardoned through Jesus Christ. Through Him we were once more heirs of glory. But the weakness into which we fell when our first parents were despoiled of grace, . . . the power and tyranny acquired by those passions which formerly were subjected to reason, these are the spoils of Satan when we lost grace.

"Since this loss of grace was not owing to violence, that first state of innocence is not given to us again. But does that mean that we have no way of recovering it? O, holy and divine Spirit! You have been given to us for this very purpose, and not only to recover that former state, but one more glorifying to our heavenly Father and more profitable to ourselves. By means of the grace and the gifts which you deny to no child of Adam who seeks them wholeheartedly and is disposed to receive them; by means of that grace and those gifts by which we are united to the mystical body whose Head is Christ,—a condition absolutely necessary for the attainment of that state—you make it possible for us truly to aspire to and achieve the celebration of our espousal and marriage with the King of eternal glory, the only-begotten Son of the living God, who is consubstantial with the Father and before whom all the powers of heaven and earth are as if they were not.

"Although it is not ours by nature to be gods, we cannot aspire to anything more grand, more glorious, more perfect. And all this—the striving, the actual possession, the inamissibility—these are within our power. He who wishes to attain it need only ask wholeheartedly and persistently that the Holy Ghost come and be his Master. Without a doubt it will be effected because the divine Spirit hungers to do good for us.

"Anyone who begins to call upon Him from the heart, is not made to wait; he is heard immediately. The teachings of the divine Spirit are not such as lead us step by step along the ways of God, but His charity is such that in a very short time it enables us to run or even fly. If we are docile in following His teachings, He enables us to undertake the way of pure and disinterested love wherein the most delicate of lovers, Jesus Christ, is immediately enamored and imprisoned. He does not tire nor does He ever take His gaze from the actions performed by souls in this way. However small the action may be, it is like a magnet attracting this sweet Lover. Since He is love, this is what He seeks, this is what He desires, this it is in which He is most glorified. He finds no action too small or without merit. . . He does not look at the greatness of the deed, nor the sacrifice with which it is performed. The measure of the greatness of our acts is not the great works we do for Him but the love with which we do them and the love which, through them, we give to Him.

"We have stated that we can do nothing without the Holy Ghost. We inherited from our first parents the sorrowful state of desolation into which they were thrust after losing their innocence. Our intellect, obscured and darkened, cannot now know or sufficiently grasp truth. To see it, to distinguish it, and to understand it; to avoid the confusion of errors and lies, we need the light of the Holy Ghost.

"In this state of ruin we have also inherited a great weakening of the will so that we cannot of ourselves go to God unless carried by the Holy Ghost. We are so prone to evil that if we are not instructed by Him we know not how to do anything agreeable to God. We are like children who never come to the point of calling upon our heavenly Father nor of asking forgiveness for our sins and asking for the things we need, unless the divine Comforter comes to our aid. Were it not for Him, what great blunders we would perform in our petitions! We would ever go into the presence of God like a tender child who as yet does not know how to talk and, not knowing how to ask or seek those things that are needed, we would suffer many privations. . . .

"But if this child, so incapable of all things, is placed under the care and solicitude of a tender mother, she will teach him to talk so that soon he can ask for the things he needs. She holds him by the arms and helps him to walk time after time. Later she is careful to see that he walks always in her presence because, when she is not present, he falls into many perils. When he cries, it is an annoyance to all but the mother, and she interprets this crying as a sign of hunger and thirst and she consoles him with a million caresses. She does

THE MYSTICAL EVOLUTION

it with greater and greater pleasure, without ever tiring. When the child is older, with what love she counsels him, speaking from her heart and telling him the things he must seek and desire so that they will be most profitable to him! . . . If a mother is so necessary in the natural life, she is not less so in the spiritual life.

"The role of the mother in the spiritual life is that of the Holy Ghost, and His solicitude and love for the members of the mystical body surpasses that of all earthly mothers. And on the part of the soul great docility is required just as it is necessary for the natural child, so that the parents may receive the fruits of consolation for the labors they have expended on their child."

CHAPTER III

Participation in the Divine Activity

Divine charity is not limited to the deification of our nature, but this deification extends to all our faculties so that our operations also may be divine. In this way we proceed, or are able to proceed, in all things as worthy sons of the light, brothers and faithful imitators of Christ, the Sun of justice. We are able to produce copious fruits of eternal life and to shine forth in such a way that the heavenly Father is glorified through our works.[1]

Whether the life of grace is communicated to us in all its definitive plenitude or simply as a pledge of glory, we need only preserve it in that state if we are to be deserving of the paternal heritage. This is what happens to those Christians who die before they reach the age of reason or, rather, to those who die in the very moment that they are justified, without having had the opportunity to make fruitful the grace they have received.

The Operation of Grace

Yet grace is given to us as a seed which is to be developed so that we shall not only have life, but we shall have a life which is ever more rich and abundant.[2] But if, through our own fault, grace is not developed, then we become unworthy of it and we are despoiled of the divine talent which we have kept buried and dormant, when we should have exerted ourselves to make it fruitful of divine things.[3]

As long as a man lives, he ought to perform actions which are in

[1] Matt. 5:16; Col. 1:10.
[2] John 10:10.
[3] Matt. 25:24-30; Rom. 7:4.

conformity with his nature and ordained to his ultimate end. Now, grace is like a second nature, for it is the root principle of that higher order of operations whose ultimate goal is eternal life.[4] Hence the inescapable obligation we have of working in all things for the good, the supernatural good, as long as we have time.[5] Hence also the necessity of working out our salvation with fear and trembling,[6] since we know that we can lose it through our indolence. Finally, there follows the obligation of assuring our vocation and election by means of good works, so that we may preserve ourselves from sin and merit entrance into the kingdom of the Savior.[7] We ought, then, always to abound in the work of the Lord, knowing that our work is not in vain in His presence,[8] for each one will receive a reward proportionate to his work.[9]

"Eternal life," as the Council of Trent teaches, "is to be offered, both as a grace mercifully promised to the sons of God through Christ Jesus, and as a reward promised by God Himself, to be faithfully given to their good works and merits. For this is the crown of justice which after his fight and course the Apostle declared was laid up for him, to be rendered to him by the just Judge, and not only to him, but also to all that love His coming." [10] As St. Augustine says, "He who created thee without thyself, will not save thee without thyself." [11]

We are, then, obliged to cooperate in our justification and sanctification because God wishes to reward our merits by crowning His own grace, that is, the power which He communicates to us to perform good works. When we received the divine grace of His Son, we received it as a most precious seed of life which we must foster and not let perish. We began the life of grace in the status of newborn babes who crave pure spiritual milk, that by it they may grow to salvation,[12] which is the status of perfect manhood. We must

[4] Gay, *La vie et les vertus chrét.*, I, 65: "Grace is above all a principle of action. It is life, and life is given us that we may live; it is a power, and power is given us to be used; it is a seed, and this seed is given us that it may fructify."
[5] Gal. 6:10.
[6] Phil. 2:12.
[7] See II Pet. 1:10 f.
[8] See I Cor. 15:58.
[9] *Ibid.*, 3:8.
[10] Sess. VI; can. 16.
[11] *De verb. apost.*, Serm. XV, chap. 11.
[12] See I Pet. 2:2.

grow and develop in total conformity with Jesus Christ,[13] and that to such an extent that He Himself is formed anew in us.[14] If, on the other hand, we do not strive to grow, we shall perish, because we shall be contradicting the plans of divine Providence.

"It is part of the order of divine Providence," says Terrien, "that no being receives from the very first instant the final perfection which it ought to achieve. In all things there must be growth, with the concomitant tendency to a better state. Everything here below is subject to this law. All things must pass from a less perfect to a more perfect state, from incipient goodness to consummate goodness. This is true in the works of nature, the production of art, and the wonderful works of grace itself. . . . This law of progress governs all things that have come from the hand of God." [15]

1. NECESSITY OF INFUSED POWERS

But to progress in the divine life, we must perform divine operations and realize divine functions. To do this we need in every case faculties of that same order which actually are given to us in germ with the divine life itself. In the natural order we possess the array of cognoscitive and affective potencies or faculties, both rational and sensitive, which flow from the very essence of the soul and are like so many immediate principles of operation enabling us to fulfill the functions of a properly human life. So also in the supernatural order, we need another set of potencies which corresponds to the life of grace and by which that life is manifested in such a way that we work and advance as true sons of God and not merely as men.[16]

Hence, with the supernatural entity we receive a whole series of new faculties which, in a certain manner, spring from grace itself as potencies that not only perfect and ennoble the natural faculties, but elevate, transform, and divinize them. They bestow on these natural faculties an entirely new power and transcendental energy which of ourselves we could never possess. Thus we are made capable of performing operations far superior to the abilities of our own poor

---

[13] Eph. 4:13-16.
[14] Gal. 4:19.
[15] Op. cit., I, 154.
[16] "As from the essence of the soul flow its powers, which are the principles of deeds, so likewise the virtues, whereby the powers are moved to act, flow into the powers of the soul from grace" (Ia IIae, q.110, a.4, ad 1um).

nature or those of any nature whatever. The new powers and energies thus received are, together with actual graces and transitory inspirations, the infused virtues and the gifts of the Holy Ghost, which render us capable of working habitually as deified men and even as vitalized organs of the Spirit of God.[17]

Nor are these superior potencies merely virtual and latent powers which are proper to nature; powers which nature itself possesses in germ, only to be developed and manifested in time. No, they are entirely new and so superior that only God could communicate them to us. He it is who bestows them on us and manifests them in us in the measure in which He renews us. "Behold, I make all things new."[18] Thus the functions and operations of grace develop in us connaturally and ordain us to eternal beatitude, just as the natural potencies develop our human functions and lead us to temporal happiness.

It is certain that a transitory divine impulse would be sufficient to stimulate and invigorate these natural faculties and powers and make them produce an act in some way supernatural. Such an act would not, however, be connatural or even truly vital, for, as a divine operation, it would not spring from that inner principle which is the life of grace. Not flowing from the life of grace, it would not be able to contribute to the increase of that life; nor would it be per se meritorious of eternal life. No impulse that is forcibly impressed on us without our assimilating it, can be called our own and hence it is not meritorious. We must possess those higher potencies as something proper and connatural to us so that the acts of such potencies will be truly our own. At the same time they must be totally dependent on grace so that they will be meritorious and give an increase of glory.

Hence, although faith and hope are infused habits and connatural, if they are dead they are incapable of any merit. Even when, through a mysterious impulse of the Holy Ghost they produce acts disposing

---

[17] Terrien, *op. cit.*, p. 156: "The nature of the sons of God is not simply human. ... It is a nature elevated and transfigured by grace, a deiform nature which is proper to a divinized being. ... And the knowledge of a son of God ought to be equivalent to the loftiness of being which he possesses through grace."
St. Cyril, *Thesaur.*, Bk. II, chap. 2: "Since we possess the same activity as does God, we must also share in His nature."
[18] Apoc. 21:5.

the sinner to receive life anew, they still do not merit any glory, because those are not vital acts and proper to the sons of God.[19]

2. NATURAL AND SUPERNATURAL POTENCIES

Grace does not destroy nature nor oppose it, but rather perfects it by being accommodated to it. Thus grace rectifies and completes nature to the extent that it elevates and transforms it. So it is that those supernatural energies, to be made manifest in all their splendor, presuppose the necessary development of the natural functions to which has been given a new luster and upon which have been imposed virtualities and greatly superior powers for accomplishing the works of eternal life.

Further, since eternal life is compatible with natural life, the supernatural potencies, energies, and powers are, in a certain sense, analogous to those of nature. In the natural life, in addition to the powers of growth, we have cognitive, affective, and operative faculties which are developed and perfected by right use and the subsequent acquisition of the habit of those virtues which are integrated in the four cardinal virtues. Moreover, we have certain instincts communicated to us by the Author of nature for the realization of those indispensable acts which could not be well directed by our own proper knowledge.

So also, in the life of grace, serving a similar but far superior function, we have the three noble virtues which are called theological. These are the great faculties of the life of grace by which we are directed and ordained to God, knowing Him in Himself, tending to Him, and desiring and loving Him with our whole heart. We have also the four principal infused virtues which correspond to the cardinal virtues, and these direct the progress of our life to the supernatural end in regard to the means and our relation to our neighbor.[20]

[19] If we wish to be divinely happy, we must do works that are worthy of God (Col. 1:10), and we must work in a divine manner. But, according to the lofty doctrine of St. Dionysius (*Eccl. hier.*, chap. 2), to work divinely, a transitory aid is not sufficient. There is needed a divine birth, a divine existence, and a divine state which can produce a divine operation. It is necessary that we share in that divine power through which God is possessed immediately. See Monsabré, *Conf.* 18.

[20] Sauvé, *Le culte du C. de J.*, no. 25: "The virtues and gifts are faculties of the new man and through them he lives in God, in whom he is rooted. . . . His faith perceives Him as infinite Truth; on Him, as infinitely good and infinitely desirable, he casts the anchor of his hope; and as the infinite goodness, charity embraces Him and loves Him in Himself. . . . But since the soul in grace must continue to live in

THE MYSTICAL EVOLUTION

We have, finally, certain instincts by which God Himself moves us and directs us to eternal life in regard to those things which could not be well regulated by ourselves through the simple light of faith and the norms of ordinary prudence, and these are the gifts of the Holy Ghost whereby the work of the virtues is completed and the communications of God and the marvelous effusions of His infinite love are perfected.

The knowledge of this mechanism of the supernatural life should fill us with admiration, astonishment, and enchantment. The study of our organic and rational life is of vital interest to the physiologist. What, then, should not the knowledge of the organs, functions, phenomena, and, in brief, of all the means employed by the Holy Ghost to cause and promote the sanctification of the soul, mean to the Christian? [21]

But all this is more easily conjectured and surmised than explained, because it is as indescribable as it is admirable and in no way can it be expressed by words or even by human concepts. And if, because of the imperious demands of our natural condition, we often appeal to certain systems of thought, it is not done in an effort to confine or restrict the divine to these systems, but only to aid in their explanation. As St. Thomas says, we seek only "in our own weak way, to declare the truth which the Catholic faith professes, while weeding out contrary errors." [22]

For that reason we ought not to attend too much to the material element of our expressions. The servile interpretation of the letter which kills (II Cor. 3:6) is one of the causes responsible for the fact that these enchanting mysteries are so poorly appreciated and regarded with such scant interest. Their vitalizing appeal cannot be translated into words nor understood by systems of thought. They can be perceived and appreciated with a certain degree of exactitude only through the sacred symbols that divine revelation offers us, and even then they are vague and tenuous. Revelation presents the sacred mysteries to us in this manner for the precise purpose of preventing us from adhering too closely to their material aspect and to help us perceive something of the spirit which palpitates beneath them. This

---
nature and in society by means of the natural faculties, we have other virtues which regulate and deify our relations with men and with created things."
[21] Cf. Froget, *The Indwelling of the Holy Spirit*, p. 193.
[22] *Contra Gent.*, Bk. I, chap. 2.

PARTICIPATION IN THE DIVINE ACTIVITY

spirit is manifested to us more and more clearly in Christian experience under the internal direction of the divine Paraclete and the external direction of Holy Mother the Church.

3. THE TWO SUPERNATURAL PRINCIPLES OF OPERATION

A consideration of the organic symbol will enable us to see how our souls derive two immediate principles of operation from that most loving Spirit who vivifies us. One of these principles consists in the infused virtues that elevate and transform our natural potencies and enable them to perform works deserving of eternal life. Although they are supernatural, these virtues are, as it were, connaturalized, so that they are exercised in a human manner, under the directive norm of reason illumined by a living faith. Without this faith, the soul is not able to perceive clearly the light, warmth, and energies which the divine Spirit infuses into it through these virtues. Hidden in the inner recesses of the soul, He does not disclose His sweet presence, but He gives the soul full liberty of action in the exercise of these virtues, as if they were something natural and proper to the soul itself. Hence it appears to be one's own reason which works, governs, and directs all things.

There is yet another principle of activity that the Holy Ghost infuses in us, and this consists in His most precious gifts, which are a sort of divine instinct making us apt to receive and second His highest impulses. They make us docile in complying with His sweet sighs and quick to follow and actuate His loving inspirations by which He manifests Himself to some degree. By means of the gifts, we work in a superhuman manner, yet it is not ourselves who work, for we do no more than follow His motion. He it is who works in us and through us by communicating Himself to us in a singular and divine way.[23]

---

[23] Gardeil, *The Gifts of the Holy Ghost*, pp. 28-31: "Every superior force has two modes of employing its action. First, it may raise up in the being subject to itself, fixed, permanent organs which divide among themselves, under its direction, the various fields of activity which are necessary to attain the end which it purposes. . . . It leaves each organ to act according to the laws which it has traced out for it; it seems to adapt itself to each one's mode of action. It is thus that the Holy Ghost, residing at the source of our entire activity by charity, creates for Itself the fixed organs of Its operations in the infused virtues, in prudence, justice, fortitude, temperance, and in all the lesser virtues which are like the secondary organs, the tissues and cells of these supernatural organs. He contents Himself with unifying them, leaving them to attain their functions according to their special modes of

THE MYSTICAL EVOLUTION

From the presence and animation of the Holy Ghost and from the exercise of His gifts, together with the virtues, there result the twelve delightful fruits which He produces in souls and which enable them to recognize Him. Then, as a final touch and culmination of the mature fruits, there come the eight beatitudes, which are, each of them, the permanent and perfect possession of one of the principal evangelical virtues together with the corresponding gifts and fruits. Or they may be said to be so many different aspects of the happiness which the sons of God enjoy in the midst of their pains and bitterness. Such souls are happier and more animated as they appear more wretched and dead in the eyes of the world, because in the blessed

---

action, analogous to those of the human moral virtues which bear the same names. The direction of the Spirit is not lessened by the power which He leaves to these ministers of His power, which hold from Him the vivifying impulse which forms the basis of the life of the just, which performs, noiselessly and naturally, works of a kind which are nonetheless divine since the Holy Ghost ceases not to be at their deepest source.

"But if the vital force of the germ, essentially immersed in the matter to which it gives life, is in some sort exhausted in its first activity, such is not the case with a vital force which is independent and necessarily transcendent such as God is in relation to His creatures. The divine activity goes beyond the activity of all the organs which He has been pleased to create in order to realize it. Just as the head of a state, the absolute master of his realm, is not bound to act through subordinates in order to work his pleasure in such and such a part of his government, although, ordinarily, he allows them to act of themselves, so is the Divine Spirit who is the absolute master of the government of souls in regard to a supernatural end, the possession of the Trinity. We should expect, on His part, direct interventions, whether it be to aid the infused virtues, the ordinary organs of His government, for example, in certain extraordinary cases such as grave temptations which the ordinary virtue cannot overcome, or, simply because, being able, He wishes to do so, or to promote, here and there in our lives, works of an excellence which surpasses the common measure.

"It is for these operations that the Gifts of the Holy Ghost serve as a base of operation. Of course, God could have justified us without our consent. He could have entered at will into our supernatural organization, making use of us as mere instruments for His work. . . . It is with such operations that we connect prophecy, the gift of miracles and all those graces which are given to man not for his own sanctification but for that of others. But since He is concerned here with our personal sanctification, God did not will that, even if He acted upon us directly, without passing through the normal organs, we should be not only without merit but without cooperation with His spontaneous inspirations. Hence this sanctifying germ has caused the Gifts of the Holy Ghost to spring up in our hearts. By them our supernatural organism is, as it were, doubled. The extraordinary, the divine and spontaneous, is in some manner acclimated. . . .

"The Gifts of the Holy Ghost are not actual interventions of the Holy Ghost in our life, but habitual dispositions placed in our soul which lead it easily to consent to His inspirations."

PARTICIPATION IN THE DIVINE ACTIVITY

shadow of the Cross of Christ they taste of the immortal fruits of the tree of life.[24]

Who can describe the divine impulses which such souls continually experience and the vital energy and vigor which they receive under the vivifynig breathing of the Holy Ghost? In his marvelous work on the Christian life and the virtues, Bishop Gay describes the effects of this activity of God on souls:

This active and beneficent irradiation of God in the creature in whom He dwells is something ineffable. We call it an irradiation, and it actually is such because His eminent gifts, emanating originally from the very substance of God, are not only reflected, but also, in the expression of the holy Fathers, impressed and engraven upon our souls. Such is the mystery which is realized in us, in the inner core of our being . . . where the kingdom of God resides. . . This irradiation and divine activity is effected especially in the essence of the soul. There it pours forth the root grace which we call sanctifying. This grace, since it is at once the condition and first effect of His supernatural presence, authorizes and disposes us to receive all His other blessings. By means of this grace He redeems the soul and frees it from the slavery of sin. He reintegrates it, renews it, rejuvenates it, purifies it, and makes it docile to all the inspirations with which He favors it and all the impulses which He communicates to it. By this grace God takes, as it were, the roots of the soul and engrafts them on Himself. He makes the soul capable of being saturated with His most holy sap and of diffusing this sap throughout all the marvelous faculties by which it is expanded, as the trunk of a tree is by its branches These natural potencies, so numerous, so varied, and now so marvelous, acquire a divine perfection through that internal diffusion of vigor, according to the status, office, and proper function of each potency. They all receive new superior qualities which are essentially supernatural and which make them equally flexible and energetic, docile and strong, transparent and focal points of radiation. They bestow on the soul a greater passivity for the reception of God and a greater activity in serving Him and fulfilling His wishes. Such are, in the first place, those supreme virtues that we call theological . . . , which are the first reflection or immediate expansion of grace. Then come the infused virtues, both intellectual and moral; then the gifts of the Holy Ghost . . . which place the soul in a position to exercise the virtues divinely, and which are converted into the fecund seeds of the

[24] Cant. 2:3.

fruits that God desires to gather in us. Although the sacrament of confirmation alone communicates the plentitude of these sacred gifts, the mere state of grace also implies their presence in the soul. Actually there is no just soul that does not possess them more or less perfectly.[25]

"Merely to be in the state of grace, as is a little child after Baptism," says Father Froget, "is to possess all supernatural virtues in root and essence, only awaiting the full use of reason for their development according to the will of God in each particular case." [26]

The Supernatural Virtues

The virtues proper to the Christian life are called infused. They are so called because we are totally incapable of acquiring them, in spite of any efforts we may make. God Himself deigns to grant them to us together with His grace, so that through them we may perform divine works. Together with grace, they grow and develop. With grace also they disappear, excepting faith and hope, which remain in the sinner as the basic roots of ability to regain life and are lost only by the grave sins which are directly opposed to them.

These virtues are called Christian because they are proper to the members of Jesus Christ, and they are not manifested in all their splendor except in perfect Christians. They are also called supernatural because they surpass the needs and capabilities of our nature and are implanted in us to elevate and transform our natural powers, thus making them able to produce fruits of life, or rather works deserving of unending glory.

"They are grafted on to the soul like scions or grafts of a better and nobler tree grafted upon a wild stock," says Father Froget. "In passing through the graft the natural sap is purified of its defects, so that the tree which before bore sour and wild fruits now yields sweet and delicious fruits." [27]

So also our poor nature can be admired for producing such rich and extraordinary fruits and delicate flowers without itself knowing how it produces them. Although they are not natural, they are nonetheless proper to the soul so far as they proceed from it in some man-

[25] Gay, *op. cit.*, chap. 2.
[26] *The Indwelling of the Holy Spirit*, p. 191.
[27] *Op. cit.*, p. 194.

ner. Nature, in union with grace, forms a perfect whole and, as it were, a single principle of action.[28]

1. DIVISION AND NUMBER OF SUPERNATURAL VIRTUES

These virtues are either theological, those which ordain us directly to God; or moral, those which direct us in regard to the means of arriving at our ultimate end through the faithful fulfillment of the obligations of our life. The former are: *faith*, by which, accepting divine revelation, we know God in Himself as the principle and end of our supernatural life; *hope*, by which we tend to Him as our ultimate end and, confiding in His promises, strive to reach Him; *charity*, by which we love Him above all things and cherish Him as a loving Father in whom rests all our good. These virtues have for their object, as has been said, the union and possession of God, and they effect, as much as is possible in this life, the operations which are characteristic of eternity.

Charity ever remains the same. It is certain that faith presents God to us, but remotely and in a veiled manner. It permits us to see Him only enigmatically, through symbols and representations or human analogies. Yet faith is perfected by the gifts of understanding, science, and wisdom, by which the divine Reality is attained, touched, and tasted. Hope, as a tendency to something still afar off, disappears on the arrival at the goal and is exchanged for full joy and possession, as faith is exchanged for the face-to-face vision. But for the present, hope serves us as a firm anchor, cast into the interior of heaven, so that the tempests of this life cannot separate us from God.[29]

The moral virtues are reduced to the four *cardinal* virtues because on them all the others hinge and in them all the others are contained. "There are four virtues," says St. Augustine, "which should direct our life... The first is called *prudence*, and it enables us to distinguish good from evil. The second is *justice*, by which we render to each what is his due. The third, *temperance*, by which we restrain

---

[28] Terrien, *op. cit.*, I, 291: "The complete principle of operation is not grace alone, nor nature alone, but nature transformed and vivified by grace. In a word, it is the rational nature divinized. 'Yet not I, but the grace of God with me' (I Cor. 15:10)."

[29] Heb. 6:19: "The hope ... which we have, as an anchor of the soul, sure and firm, and which entereth in even within the veil."

our passions. The fourth, *fortitude,* which makes us capable of enduring hardships. These virtues are given to us by God together with grace in this vale of tears." [80] So we have seven principal infused virtues to which there corresponds a like number of gifts of the Holy Ghost.

2. THE THEOLOGICAL VIRTUES

That the three theological virtues are divinely infused is indisputable, for the Council of Trent has so declared.[81] Further, as St. Thomas points out,[82] in order to tend properly to our supernatural end, we must know it, desire it, and love it. This desire implies the firm confidence of obtaining it, a confidence founded on the divine promises known to us by faith. Therefore, according to the Council of Trent, faith is the principle and foundation of our salvation: "Faith is the beginning of human salvation, the foundation and root of all justification, without which it is impossible to please God and to come to the fellowship of His sons." [83] The Apostle calls faith "the substance of things to be hoped for." [84]

Without the light of faith, the movement toward eternal life would not be connatural to us, free, and autonomous, because we do not rationally move except to that which is in some way known to us. And since faith pertains to things that exceed our natural capacity, it must be infused in us supernaturally as are also the firm confidence with which we hope for those things and the invincible love with which we strive for them. Yet, since that knowledge is made connatural to us, it is expressed in a human manner; that is, through images, representations, and analogies. It is enigmatic and not intuitive, as will be the knowledge in glory. Therefore faith will vanish in heaven and give place to the face-to-face vision; yet here on earth it is not so intimately bound up with grace that it cannot exist without it. Faith remains in sinners, but it is a dead or unformed faith. It is a weak light which cannot shine forth from within because it lacks grace, which is its life-giving source. Its light is produced en-

---

[80] *In Ps. 83,* no. 11.
[81] Sess. VI, can. 7.
[82] *De veritate in comm.,* 2.12.
[83] *Loc. cit.,* can. 8.
[84] Heb. 11:1.

PARTICIPATION IN THE DIVINE ACTIVITY

tirely from without by the divine Spirit who, without dwelling in the soul and without inflaming the heart, continually enlightens the intellect in order to direct it to the good and to establish the hope of the recovery of grace and the practice of good works.

Thus these two supernatural virtues that remain in a sinner as pledges of the goodness and mercy with which God invites him anew to salvation, prepare him for the recovery of grace, if he does not resist. But by these two virtues alone he cannot be saved, for the simple reason that they are dead. Indeed, they give good grounds for a terrible condemnation if the soul does not strive to revive them. "And that servant who knew the will of his Lord, and prepared not himself and did not according to his will, shall be beaten with many stripes."[35]

This unformed faith presents God very remotely and not as the internal principle of life. Yet at the same time it shows Him as the greatest good, not only lovable and extremely desirable in Himself, but attainable through His many helps. Thus it excites the soul to desire Him truly and to confide in His infinite goodness. If the errant soul is docile to these promptings and adjusts its conduct to the Gospel norms; if it does not resist grace (which God will not refuse as long as the soul places no obstacle in the way), but pleads for it as is fitting, then that grace will actually be infused and in such wise that God will vivify those inclinations and make them efficacious by the heat of charity. Then, when charity inflames, impels, urges, and attracts the soul forcibly to God as the only center of all its aspirations, the soul will truly advance and even run toward glory.

Possessing charity, we are already in God and He in us. Therefore it is the greatest of all the virtues,[36] because it makes us possess God as the King of our hearts and unites us to Him in such a fashion that this loving union will be eternal if we ourselves, through our malice, do not destroy it.[37] Even natural death, which breaks all other bonds, cannot break the bond of charity. Rather it tightens it, strengthens it, and makes it indissoluble. Charity of itself has

---

[35] Luke 12:47.
[36] See I Cor. 13.
[37] See Ia IIae, q.66, a.6: "In this way charity is greater than the others. Because the others, in their very nature, imply a certain distance from the object; since faith is of what is not seen, and hope is of what is not possessed."

nothing of imperfection which can make it, like faith and hope, the virtue of the wayfarers alone. It pertains both to the wayfarers and to the blessed.

So it is that there can be in the world many souls, hidden and obscure, who possess a deep charity, and because of that charity are greater lovers of God and more loved by Him than many of the angels and saints in heaven. However, these latter cannot now lose charity because they have reached the fullness of their respective evolution. But since they have reached their terminus, they can no longer increase their charity. In us, on the other hand, charity can be either lost or increased. Therefore we should increase it by ceaseless use or else expose ourselves to losing it entirely.[38]

Charity is the measure of sanctity and grace and the focal point of all spiritual activity that is meritorious of life.[39] Since it is a sort of emanation from uncreated love Himself in whom the divine Persons are loved, charity is a virtue which is proper, not to men, but to gods.[40]

---

[38] St. Augustine, *Trad. 5 in Epist. Joan.*: "Charity is born to be perfected; therefore, as soon as it is born, it is nourished; when nourished, it is strengthened; when it is strengthened, it is perfected; and when it reaches its perfection, what can be said of it? 'For me, to live is Christ; to die is gain.'"

[39] Gardeil, *op. cit.*, pp. 4-6: "In this word 'charity' we find our entire supernatural psychology concentrated. . . . The theological virtue of charity is, as it were, the point of penetration by which God, already dwelling in the essence of the soul, spreads over its power, and from this center He directs the operations of the infused virtues. It is through the heart, where there is gathered all that is unfolded in the activity of man, that God begins the deification of our intellect and will. . . . The supernatural virtues, on the contrary, are established in our faculties at a single stroke. God, infinitely powerful, dispenses with human activity which can do nothing in this regard, and inserts these divine graftings on the pristine native stock supplied by our nature. Sustained in being by the power from which it draws sap, the infused virtue transforms its activity. . . . Charity, so far as it is the proper effect of the Holy Ghost, surpasses all other virtues. . . . In fact, the infused virtues, as faith and hope, prudence and justice, fortitude and temperance, operate under the influence of divine love. That is to say, that the Spirit of God, the soul of our charity, finds in these virtues channels by which He may spread the love which He inspires in the hearts of the just through all the parts of man, intellect or will, and even the passions themselves."

St. Augustine, *De moribus Eccl.*, chap. 15: "Virtue is the order of love. . . . Whence it is fitting to define temperance as the love of God keeping one entire and incorrupt; fortitude as love readily enduring all things for God; justice, serving God alone and thereby commanding well those things which pertain to men; prudence, correctly discerning those things which will lead to God or impede progress to Him."

[40] St. Thomas, *Quaest. un. de carit.*, a.1, ad 3um: "Charity is not a virtue of man as man, but so far as he is God through participation in grace."

PARTICIPATION IN THE DIVINE ACTIVITY

Through these three virtues which are called theological we are made participants in the vital activity of God, just as through grace we are made participants in the divine Being.[41] By them we are directed with ease to our supernatural ultimate end and we are enabled to fulfill our principal obligations.

3. THE MORAL VIRTUES

But here, as in all things else, we still need direction concerning the means conducive to that ultimate end and the equipment for fulfilling our other obligations toward our neighbors and ourselves. This is effected by the moral virtues which guide the whole activity of our life, and in a more special manner, this guidance comes from the cardinal virtues, which are the nucleus of all the others. Thus, as the three theological virtues direct our intellect and our heart to God, Christian *prudence* directs us in regard to ourselves and our neighbors, so that we may know in particular cases what is to be done or omitted. We are thus able to treat others as God wishes them to be treated. *Justice* induces us to give to each what is his due. *Fortitude* and *temperance* enable us to triumph over the strategies of our three enemies, the world and the flesh and the devil, and to overcome the obstacles that would impede us from pursuing our journey toward heaven.

To these four principal virtues are subordinated other partial or secondary moral virtues which contribute, each in its own way, to the regulation and sanctification of the more minute details of our lives. Among these, the principal ones are *piety* and *religion*, which, as parts of justice, teach us to deal with our neighbors as brothers and to give to God, our Father and Lord, the worship due Him.[42] But all these virtues, in order to contribute to our sanctification, must be supernatural and therefore infused. Otherwise they could not produce those fruits of life that surpass the powers of pure nature.

4. NECESSITY OF ACQUIRED AND INFUSED MORAL VIRTUES

Because of the parallel between the moral virtues which direct the supernatural life and the other virtues of the same name which regu-

---

[41] See Ia IIae, q. 110, a. 4.
[42] Lallemant, *Spiritual Doctrine*, IV, chap. 5, art. 5: "Religion and piety both lead us to the worship and service of God; but religion considers Him as Creator, and piety as a Father: and in this the latter is more excellent than the former."

late human life and which can be acquired even by the pagans through the simple repetition of acts, some theologians (Scotus, for example) thought that it was not necessary for the Christian to be infused with new virtues which seem to have the same objects as the natural virtues. Such theologians maintained that it would suffice that these natural virtues, even though acquired by our own efforts, be informed by divine charity, which would then make their operations meritorious of eternal life.

Although charity does sanctify all our actions, however small, and makes them meritorious, yet if these acts flow from a natural principle, then they do not cease to be intrinsically natural. And, if natural, they are of themselves disproportionate to the supernatural end and incapable of producing effects which are properly divine.

Therefore, although it is not contained in an express definition of the Church, the doctrine generally admitted today is that, in addition to the moral virtues naturally acquired, there are other infused virtues which bear the same name. Although these virtues appear to have the same objects materially, their objects are nevertheless formally distinct, and therefore the infused virtues produce acts of a transcendent order. So St. Augustine teaches in the passage already quoted. So also does Scripture teach us, when speaking of the effects of wisdom: "for she teacheth temperance and prudence and justice and fortitude, which are such things as men can have nothing more profitable in life." [43] Similar indications can be found also in other scriptural passages.[44] The Catechism of St. Pius V, which is highly esteemed in the Church, says that with grace the noble cortege of the virtues is divinely infused into the soul.[45]

It is necessary, as St. Thomas states, that effects be proportionate to their causes and that there be a harmony between the supernatural and the natural. Therefore, just as the moral virtues naturally acquired for the direction of our life are contained in germ in the principles of our rational faculties, so also in the order of grace, where, instead of natural principles, we have the infused theological virtues, it is necessary that there be contained other infused habits which have for their object the supernaturalizing of our whole moral

[43] Wisd. 8:7.
[44] See Prov. 8:14; Gal. 5:22 f.; II Pet. 1:4-7.
[45] Part II, *De baptismo*, no. 51.

life and the production of acts intrinsically directed to eternal life.[46] In other words, we need certain virtuous habits that will be to the theological virtues what human habits are to the natural principles from which they proceed. Only in this way can our entire moral life be deified.

Since the human virtues are in no way proportionate to the theological, Terrien states that any other explanation would result in "the oddity of a man transfigured in his being and made deiform by grace and yet incompletely deified in his moral life. Man's moral life should also manifest the dignity of the sons of God, but in this instance it would be excluded from that glorious transformation, for the immediate principles of the moral life would be purely natural, as happens in the case of sinners. . . . If the sons of men have their own proper virtues, should not a son of God also have virtues peculiar to his new status? Being supernaturalized by faith, hope, and charity in regard to his movement to the ultimate end, should he not also be supernaturalized in regard to his movement to the proximate and intermediate ends which are so indispensably connected with charity? Reclothed as he is in a new entity which makes him a god, it is necessary that man's moral life correspond to that being and proceed from principles which transcend purely natural activity."[47]

Since "by grace God gives us a new being by which we are reborn to a new and divine life," says Scaramelli, "He ought also to give us not only the infused habits of the theological virtues, but also the infused moral virtues. It is expedient that this supernaturalized nature be equipped with the potencies and powers by which a man can exercise connaturally, as it were, the acts that are proportionate to the nobility of his being."[48]

Therefore in the good Christian there must be two orders of the moral virtues. First, those purely human virtues which are acquired by the repetition of acts and which regulate his life in accordance with the norm of reason alone; secondly, those virtues that are not acquired but are supernatural and infused by God with grace. These latter are also conserved and developed together with grace, but when grace is lost, so are they also lost. The infused moral virtues

---
[46] Cf. Ia IIae, q.63, a.3.
[47] Terrien, *op. cit.*, I, 163.
[48] *Direttorio mistico*, I, no. 51.

regulate the Christian life according to the norm of supernaturalized reason, that is, the norm illuminated by faith and taught by the Gospel.

These virtues, since they are infused, are not acquired by our own efforts; nor do we cooperate in their reception save by the acceptance of them. Yet, since they are planted in us as a seed or in a virtual state, it is our duty to cultivate and develop them by proper use and by means of the watering of divine grace. We also root them within ourselves more firmly by struggling against difficulties. Beginning as they do in an embryonic stage, although they are even more real than the other virtues, yet they do not exclude the opposite habits or the difficulty entailed in their use. Therefore it is necessary that they be organically formed through exercise and struggle; and this is effected as the spirit more and more subjects the flesh and builds up other virtuous habits which are incompatible with vicious tendencies.

Although these infused virtues have the same material object as the acquired virtues, they transfigure that object and give it a new being by the very fact that they have an origin, end, power, and mode of working that are very superior and of a distinct order. The habits acquired by our own industry do not confer any new power but merely give, with the contracted habit, a greater facility in doing good in conformity with the order of reason. But the supernatural virtues infused by God give us an entirely new power by which the efficacy of our natural energies is increased and transformed. In this way we are able to produce connaturally the fruits of eternal life.

To substantiate this fact, we need merely to point out the difference in the operations of these two classes of moral virtues. Human prudence, so often associated with worldly prudence or prudence of the flesh, leads to death, but Christian prudence is always united to the Spirit, who is life and peace.[49] Natural justice gives to each His own; Christian justice gives good for evil or in double measure. Natural fortitude, attentive to human appraisals, seeks to overcome certain difficulties which impede the fulfillment of duty; Christian fortitude, without any other appraisal than that of the glory of God, enables one to perform the most difficult enterprises, and seeks thus to triumph over all enemies, even that enemy which dissimulates

[49] Rom. 8:6.

most: self-love.[50] Finally, human temperance tends to maintain the equilibrium of natural health and the necessary subordination of the appetites to reason. Christian temperance, as ordained to eternal salvation, is not content with moderating the gross pleasures of the animal man, but repels and disdains them. It is not satisfied with governing the body; it castigates it and reduces it to servitude [51] until proud reason has been subjugated and rendered docile to the Spirit.[52]

Speaking of Christian temperance, Terrien says that "its delights are found in the Cross and its object is angelic purity. To live in the flesh as if there were no flesh; this is the temperance of the sons of God. Certain it is that to arrive at such renunciation, they must have recourse to charity, for only souls possessed of divine love can perform such heroic acts. But, although love directs such acts, it is not love alone that produces them, for each of the virtues has its proper object." [53]

Only these virtues can teach souls that wisdom which is not overcome by evil [54] and which is not found in the land of them that live in delights.[55] They are proper only to just Christians, whereas the natural virtues can be possessed by sinners and pagans. Indeed, it seems that sinners and pagans can practice the natural virtues with even greater perfection or with less difficulty than do many of the newly justified faithful or those who live lukewarmly. Whence it is that some impious persons glory in the fact that they possess certain human virtues in a more perfect degree, apparently, than many good Catholics. This is sometimes the cause of pharasaical scandal or "scandal of the little ones."

The infused virtues neither replace nor supplant the natural virtues, but they presuppose them or work to the acquisition of them in order to perfect, complete, and transform them. Consequently these infused virtues do not obviate the labor entailed in the acquisition of the natural moral virtues, a labor that is always painful; but they impose it more forcefully at the same time that they give us the

---

[50] St. Gregory, *Moral.*, VII, chap. 9: "The fortitude of the just consists in governing the flesh, restraining self-will, extinguishing love of this world, and disdaining the pleasures of the earth."
[51] See I Cor. 9:27.
[52] See II Cor. 10:5; Ia IIae, q.63, a.4.
[53] Terrien, *op. cit.*, I, 165.
[54] Wisd. 7:30.
[55] Job 28:13.

strength to bear it. He who does not truly try to acquire and consolidate the natural virtues is much disposed to lose the supernatural virtues, together with grace.[56] Thus, hardened sinners, when they are converted, receive the supernatural virtues by infusion, but not the natural virtues. To develop and make fruitful the former (since they are received only in seed), they must exert themselves to acquire the latter by the laborious and continual repetition of acts. The acquired moral virtues will then serve as a support and a defense for overcoming difficulties and for destroying contrary vices.

So it is that some of the unfaithful can perform certain acts of human virtues with greater facility than many of the just who are but little advanced and who have not as yet tried to uproot evil habits. These habits are not rooted out except by the contrary acts by which the virtues are acquired and strengthened. Those souls, therefore, who before their conversion received a good training in which they cultivated many virtuous habits, find later on that they are able to practice good with more facility than those who receive grace in a coarse, base nature which is full of evil tendencies.

With grace and the infused virtues is given to us the power to conquer evil inclinations until we overwhelm and scatter them by force of combat; but generally, even though they are deadened, they are not entirely uprooted until we have resisted them for a long time. They are completely destroyed only by the performance of the opposite good acts whereby the habit of the natural virtues is acquired and the infused supernatural virtues are increased. Under these circumstances both the natural and the supernatural virtues increase at the same time.

It follows from this that the greater part of one's time, especially in the beginning of the purgative way, must be spent in rooting out vices and implanting the natural virtues in order to ensure progress in the supernatural virtues. But the vices often reappear, even after they seem to have been uprooted, and vitiated nature finds on all sides new seeds of corruption. Also, human virtues can always be increased and strengthened in order to work more perfectly and to overcome greater difficulties. Therefore throughout one's spiritual life there is always need to correct the defects of nature and to perfect it in its own order at the same time that it is elevated and

---

[56] See *Interior Castle*, seventh mansions, chap. 1.

PARTICIPATION IN THE DIVINE ACTIVITY

perfected by the supernatural virtues and is integrated and transfigured by the continual influxes of divine grace.

With the help of grace, a person can eventually re-establish himself in his primitive integrity at the same time that he is enriched and deified. Without grace the true perfection of natural virtue is absolutely impossible, for only the divine Physician of souls can cure the wounds and restore full health to the poor nature of Adam, fallen as it is.

That is why there can be no more perfect men than there are perfect Christians. As St. Augustine says,[57] to live as perfect men, we must be sons of God. The children of this world, however well and easily they seem to practice certain virtues, always vitiate them with hidden defects, usually presumption and vainglory. However good and incorrupt they may seem to be, they are still whitened sepulchers.

In the great conversions, as that of St. Augustine, the supernatural virtues are communicated in a very high degree and with an abundance of grace, so that they make easy and delightful the practice of good and the avoidance of evil. But, although the vices are deadened and made to appear abominable, as was the case with St. Augustine, they are not completely uprooted until one experiences the great struggles. These usually follow the first sensible fervors, because inveterate vices, as we have said, are not usually destroyed except by the repetition of contrary acts, which produce the corresponding habit of the natural virtue. Also, since this habit of natural virtue can be acquired up to a certain point without grace, it is not lost with the loss of grace as happens in the case of the supernatural virtues.

Another consequence is that Christians somewhat advanced in perfection, if they have the misfortune to fall into serious sin, on recovering themselves and rising through penance, do not usually find such difficulties in the practice of good as they felt in the beginning of their spiritual life. In spite of their fall, they retain the good natural habits which they have already acquired. Since these acquired habits are closely united with the supernatural virtues (which ought to inform them to such an extent that there seems to be one principle of activity), it is often difficult for us to discern whether a certain action is natural or supernatural; whether it is ordained

[57] *Epist. 2 contra Pelag.*, I, no. 5.

simply to a human end and produced by a human principle, or whether it is informed by some infused virtue and directed to something divine. All the Christian virtues, when connaturalized in us, are exercised in a human manner under the rule of reason and without our being conscious of the divine element. Yet this divine element must inform the rule of reason so that our actions may be worthy of eternal life.

The Gifts of the Holy Ghost

So far as he is rational, man is master of his acts and, within his own sphere of activity, can determine to do one thing or another.[58] Therefore his actions have a moral aspect because they are free. But free will is not of itself a sufficient guaranty to ensure his procedure in all things with the desired rectitude. That a man's faculties may be directed to good in such a way that they can practice it promptly, continually, and with facility, they must be perfected by the respective virtuous habits which make them docile to the rule of reason. In the natural order, this is effected by the acquired virtues; in the supernatural order, it is effected by the infused virtues. Thus reason, either alone or illumined by faith and directed by Christian prudence, is the mover and regulator of our moral life, whether that life is purely human or whether it is Christain (in the ordinary sense and in contradistinction to the spiritual or "pneumatic" life).

1. COMPARISON OF THE GIFTS AND THE VIRTUES

In the ordinary Christian life—"psychic" life as it is sometimes called—the theological virtues direct us to God as our ultimate end. Infused prudence enables us to regulate our particular acts according to a just mean. The remaining infused virtues perfect, complete, and transform the natural virtues so that, under the ceaseless influx of grace, we can proceed in all rectitude, in peace with our brothers and ourselves, overcoming all obstacles which impede our advance to heaven.

In spite of the grace of God which inundates us from within and without and which vivifies us and in spite of the many virtues and

---

[58] Cf. Ia IIae, q.9, a.4, ad 3um.

divine powers or impulses which fortify us in the performance of good, it is our reason that seems to control our progress, presiding as mistress over the whole course of our life. God truly abides as a loving Father and as King and Lord in the core of our souls, which are His living temples, and He vivifies them by His grace. But His loving presence is hidden from the gaze of our consciousness just as our own soul is hidden. Even His activity is concealed from us in the infused virtues, which have been grafted upon our souls to be used as our very own.

Hence, even when we are filled with life and divine energies, we cannot, without a special revelation,[59] know with certitude whether we are deserving of love or hate;[60] whether we are in the state of grace or at enmity with God. Man does not know this, but only the Spirit who penetrates all things and can, if He pleases, give testimony of this truth.[61] We can have only moral certitude of this fact by reason of our tranquillity of conscience, our horror of sin, our love of virtue, sacrifice, and holy things, our conformity with the divine will, our resignation to the dispositions of Providence, etc.[62] But unless God divinely demonstrates it to us, we cannot know with certainty that we possess Him.

He dwells in us not only as a hidden God (Isa. 45:15), but as a God who is the prisoner of love. We can make use of His gifts and Himself, together with the graces and virtues which He communicates to us, as if they were our own. According to the vital expression of St. Thomas, the Holy Ghost is given us in the very gift of sanctifying grace so that we may freely enjoy His benefits.[63] So it is that we can use such treasures without adverting to the fact that we possess them.

Speaking of this presence of the Holy Ghost within us with sanctifying grace, Father Gardeil says:

[59] Council of Trent, Sess. VI, can. 9. See Ia IIae, q.112, a.5.
[60] Eccles. 9:1.
[61] See I Cor. 1:10-12; Rom. 8:16.
[62] St. Thomas, *Opusc. 60, De humanitate Christi*, chap. 24: "The primary indication that one is in the grace of God is the testimony of conscience (II Cor. 1:12). The second is the hearing of the word of God, not merely to listen, but to do; whence (John 8:47): 'He that is of God, heareth the words of God.' . . . The third sign is an internal taste for divine wisdom which is a certain foretaste of future happiness."
[63] Cf. Ia, q.43, a.3.

First, then, we must answer that charity and the infused virtues are really and properly active virtues. Now, the active virtues essentially appertain to the perfection of the active human powers; and the Holy Ghost, dwelling within through charity, acts in us according to the manner of the human virtues, adapting Himself to the mode of action of our human faculties.

The just man, enriched with the supernatural virtues, remains the true and principal author of his supernatural operations. He alone directs the movements of his intellect and heart; his reason continues as the head of his entire supernatural psychology. As a fire unconsciously warming the heart, the Holy Ghost is strongly but sweetly spread abroad in the faculties through the virtues, or as a hidden light, illuminating without revealing its source. It is "the fountain of life, the fire, the charity, and spiritual unction." This changes nothing in the ordinary functioning of our inner world, though everything is changed in regard to the end toward which our activity tends and the vigor employed in aspiring to it. Such is the role of the Holy Spirit inasfar as His actions are performed by the virtues.[64]

If the Holy Ghost did not assist us with His gifts, He would not be the immediate regulator of our supernatural life. From this arises the obscurity of our faith and the imperfection of our charity which is ruled by that obscure knowledge. So the Holy Ghost desires to become a prisoner of the imperfections of our love. Father Gardeil continues:

If the theological virtues are regulated by man's narrow and limited mode of comprehension, with more reason this should be true in regard to the infused moral virtues. But the rational nature of man places the perfection of morals in a just mean, equally removed from the extremes of excess and default which may be found in the matter of his activity, whether this activity be either exterior actions or interior passions. The loftiness of the supernatural end can raise the level of this just mode. It will not hinder it from consisting in the adaptation of human actions and passions to the supernatural end, which adaptation requires the reduction of the possible excesses of these human acts to the just proportion which makes them apt to reach their end. *To find* this just mean in relation to the divine end marked out by faith, desired by hope and willed by charity, is the rule of infused Prudence. *To realize* the just mean already determined by infused Prudence in the domain of volun-

[64] *The Gifts of the Holy Ghost*, pp. 7 f.

tary acts or the passions will be the roles of the infused virtues of Justice, Fortitude, and Temperance. Here again the Holy Ghost seems to sift through a sieve the brilliance of His action. Our entire practical moral order is governed by prudence as the order of conscience and the intentions was regulated by faith.

Thus it is apparent that obscurity and the just mean are the human veils under which the activity of the Holy Ghost is hidden.[65]

Yet, the Holy Ghost does not always hide His activity thus, for charity frequently moves Him to manifest His generous hand and even to disclose His divine face. Even when our poor reason possesses this noble assortment and glorious exercise of the supernatural virtues, it is not sufficient to guide us securely to the port. Nor is it sufficient to remove the most serious obstacles, to conquer extraordinary difficulties, or to discover and avoid the hidden snares which our astute enemies lay for us at all times. Much less is human reason able to raise us up to the sublime summits of perfection where the splendors of eternal light shine forth.

But the loving Consoler, who ordinarily dwells in us in a hidden manner, vivifying us with His grace and inflaming us with His love, is able and desires to remedy our inherent weakness, to supply for our deficiencies and to correct our ignorance. All this He does by inspiring, moving, prompting, advising, dissuading, nourishing, and restraining us; by teaching us to pray and to work as we ought; by pleading for us and working in and through us. And He does all this wherever and whenever He wishes throughout the course of our spiritual life. We experience His sweet breathing and delicate impulse without actually adverting to who it is that comes to us or whence He leads us.

The Holy Ghost can and sometimes does (when He so desires or when circumstances demand) take the reins of our government directly into His own hands. At such times He supplants, with great profit to us, the direction and norm of our reason. He manifests Himself more or less clearly, not now as imprisoned in our charity, but as He really is and as Holy Church acclaims Him, the true Lord and Vivifier who desires to work through us as so many organs of Himself, just as He willed to speak through the holy prophets. He does this with some earlier, with others later, all according to His divine

---

[65] *Op. cit.,* pp. 9 f.

good pleasure. But we can safely say that He does so quasi-normally when human direction, remaining faithful to His grace, has already given of itself as much as it can give and has arrived as far as the lights and divine forces which it has assimilated will enable it to go. At that point there will be a certain degree of union, called the union of conformity and, to arrive at greater perfection, it will be necessary that He Himself move and direct the soul. [66]

2. THE GIFTS AND THE MYSTICAL LIFE

When the soul arrives at that happy state in which it has broken the bonds of its passions and all other earthly chains which bind it, it begins to enjoy the sweet liberty of the sons of God. It then lives entirely according to the Spirit and has no desire other than that of divine things. Dead to self and completely submissive to God, it realizes with happy surprise that it is now living a higher type of life and that God, who deigns to accept the sincere and total abandonment which the soul has repeatedly made to Him, is now in loving and absolute control and possession. In this state, the soul experiences certain violent and sweet impulses, which carry it along without its knowing where, but surely to some height for which ordi-

---

[66] Surin, *Catéchisme spirit.*, I, chap. 1: "The perfect man is he who, having acquired great purity of heart and a true union and familiarity with God, faithfully follows the movements of grace and the direction of the Holy Ghost."
St. John of the Cross (*The Living Flame*, stanza IV, no. 14) says: "Where He dwells with the greatest content and most completely alone is in the soul wherein dwell fewest desires and pleasures of its own; for here He is in His own house and rules and governs it. And the more completely alone does He dwell in the soul, the more secretly He dwells; and thus in this soul wherein dwells no desire, neither any other image or form of aught that is created, the Beloved dwells most secretly, with more intimate, more interior and closer embrace, according as the soul, as we say, is the purer and more completely withdrawn from all save God. . . . But this is not always so when these awakenings take place, for then it seems to the soul that He is now awakening in its bosom, where aforetime He was, as it were, sleeping; for, although it felt and enjoyed His presence, it experienced it as that of the Beloved asleep in its bosom; . . . Oh, how happy is this soul that is ever conscious of God resting and reposing within its breast! Oh, how well it is that it should withdraw from all things, flee from business and live in boundless tranquillity, lest anything, however small, or the slightest turmoil, should disturb or turn away the bosom of the Beloved within it! He is there, habitually, as it were, asleep in this embrace with the bride, in the substance of the soul; and of this the soul is quite conscious, and habitually has fruition of Him, for, if He were forever awake within it, communicating knowledge and love to it, it would be already living in glory. . . . In other souls, that have not attained to this union, He dwells, secretly likewise; and He is not displeased, since after all they are in grace, though they are not yet perfectly prepared for union. Such souls are not as a rule conscious of His presence."

mary light, force, and direction are insufficient. It senses certain loving inspirations which cut and sweetly wound the soul like so many penetrating darts of divine fire, which heal and vivify at the same time that they burn, destroying by their heat whatever remains of worldliness.

The soul then finds itself impelled to fly without even knowing whether it has wings. In the straits and afflictions in which it finds itself, it desires with a great anxiety, and understanding is given it. The soul calls out, and the Spirit of Wisdom hovers over it. Preferring Him to all the kingdoms and riches of the world (Wisd. 7:7 f.), the soul soon perceives that this good Spirit of God will lead it to the port of salvation (Ps. 142:10), and that He will vivify it and teach it to do the divine will in all things.

Where formerly the soul asked for wings of a dove to fly and be at rest, it now perceives that there is given to it much more than was asked, for it now discovers that it is filled with fortitude and is equipped with other wings, even more vigorous, so that it rises like an eagle to the lofty and serene regions of divine light and flies higher and higher without tiring, living completely engulfed in the ethereal region of infinite delights.[67]

But to attain this, the soul must experience that mystical metamorphosis which is a transformation so prodigious that it entirely renews the soul and penetrates its very depths. The soul is thus changed from a creeping caterpillar, which moves so slowly and laboriously and feeds on earthly things, into an agile butterfly, brilliant and airy, which can be nourished by nothing but the most exquisite nectar of the virtues, for it is animated now by instincts that are entirely celestial.[68]

---

[67] Isa. 40:31: "But they that hope in the Lord shall renew their strength, they shall take wings as eagles, they shall run and not be weary, they shall walk and not faint."

[68] *Interior Castle*, fifth mansions, chap. 2: "It sets no store by the things it did when it was a worm—that is, by its gradual weaving of the cocoon. It has wings now: how can it be content to crawl along slowly when it is able to fly? All that it can do for God seems to it slight by comparison with its desires. It even attaches little importance to what the saints endured, knowing by experience how the Lord helps and transforms a soul, so that it seems no longer to be itself, or even its own likeness. For the weakness which it used to think it had when it came to doing penance is now turned into strength. It is no longer bound by ties of relationship, friendship, or property. Previously all its acts of will and resolutions and desires were powerless to loosen these and seemed only to bind them the more firmly; now it is grieved at having even to fulfill its obligations in these respects lest these should cause it to sin against God. Everything wearies it, because it has proved that it can

THE MYSTICAL EVOLUTION

This beautiful comparison by St. Teresa helps us better to understand the mystery effected in the soul which abandons, or through some vital power finds itself forced to abandon, the norms of reason for those of the Spirit. Such a soul is entirely made like to Christ and exchanges the image of the earthly man for that of a heavenly one so as to live entirely in accord with the latter and not at all with the former.[69]

This renewal is prepared for in the night of the senses wherein the senses are gradually subjected to the rule of reason, and the higher impulses of the Holy Ghost are noted with greater frequency. But when this divine breathing ceases (which happens often and sometimes for a long period), the soul, abandoned by the Spirit of God, weakens and finds itself forced to return to its ordinary creeping life. Once again it has to walk on foot, aided only by the virtues and directed by the obscure light of faith and the rules of prudence. But then the Spirit breathes again, and the soul finds itself created anew, and the face of its heart is renewed.[70] When this renewal is complete,

---

find no true rest in the creatures. . . . It is not surprising, then that, as this little butterfly feels a stranger to things of the earth, it should be seeking a new resting place. But where will the poor little creature go? . . . Ah, Lord! What trials begin afresh for this soul! Who would think such a thing possible after it had received so signal a favour? But, after all, we must bear crosses in one way or another for as long as we live. And if anyone told me that after reaching this state he had enjoyed continual rest and joy, I should say that he had not reached it at all. . . . Oh, the greatness of God! Only a few years since—perhaps only a few days—this soul was thinking of nothing but itself. Who has plunged it into such grievous anxieties?"

[69] Surin, *Catéchisme*, I, chap. 7: "The soul which is transformed in Jesus Christ presents an entirely new creature similar to the resurrected man, with his new instincts and operations and the rehabilitation of all his faculties. God inundates all the powers of such a soul, even the inferior ones, and He fills it with His gifts in such wise that the body is, as it were, embalmed and the whole man lives a heavenly life. The imagination is filled with supernatural phantasms; the appetites, with the divine impulses which the Holy Ghost communicates. The intellect is radiant with light; the memory is occupied with divine things; and the will is a burning brazier which keeps the body agile and docile to the Spirit. Such is the condition of man in this divine transformation. His virtues are clearly manifest; faith is elevated, hope is vital, and charity is flaming; the moral virtues are divinized, and there is nothing of earth in this man. . . . The principle of the divine operations thus effected in the soul is the Holy Ghost, who works in it through His gifts. These gifts supplant the natural instincts, which are, in a certain sense, annihilated by grace. The Spirit impresses on them all their movements. The subjects of these operations are the interior faculties, but, animated as they are by the Holy Ghost, they remain outside themselves and under the complete control of the Spirit who moves and vivifies them, using them as instruments, yet not dead ones, but living."

[70] Ps. 103:29 f.

PARTICIPATION IN THE DIVINE ACTIVITY

as happens after the passage through the great darkness, the sweet breathing of the Holy Ghost refreshes the soul continually, and the current of the river of His living water beautifies forever this city of God wherein the Most High has sanctified His dwelling place, never more to abandon it.[71] As at the beginning of creation, so now the loving Spirit broods over the black chaos and makes the divine light shine forth in the soul.

To realize in full this happy transit by which the soul passes to such a new and happy life, it must withdraw, whether it wishes or not, into the mystic cocoon which is woven in the obscure night of the spirit, where, amid the most formidable darkness, the soul is inert, immovable, and incapable of any self-initiative. There it dies totally to self and revives to God. It is buried there with Jesus Christ and, though it appears to be destroyed and to undergo a total dissolution, actually it is ceaselessly acquiring new divine energies. In the measure in which it loses the traces of its earthly operations, it develops new spiritual organs which must now be actuated continually and led entirely and directed completely by the divine Spirit. Thus the soul, though it appears to be a slave, proceeds always with the true liberty of the sons of God.

Those who are thus actuated and guided by the Spirit of God, are His faithful children.[72] And in order that, under the holy impulses of His prudence, they may not resist, even unwittingly, those impulses of the Holy Ghost, they must be completely reduced to that painful incapacity for all things. Thus, amid mortal agony they become fully renewed and are made truly spiritual—pneumatics.

St. John of the Cross says:

Therefore, O spiritual soul, when thou seest thy desire obscured, thy affections arid and constrained, and thy faculties bereft of their capacity for any interior exercise, be not afflicted by this, but rather consider it a great happiness, since God is freeing thee from thyself and taking the work from thy hands. For with those hands, howsoever well they may serve thee, thou wouldst never labor so effectively, so perfectly and so securely (because of their clumsiness and uncleanness) as now, when God takes thy hand and guides thee in the darkness, as though thou wert

---

[71] Ps. 45:5 f.
[72] Rom. 8:14-21.

blind, to an end and by a way which thou knowest not. Nor couldst thou ever hope to travel with the aid of thine own eyes and feet, howsoever good thou mayest be as a walker.[73]

If we are to follow with docility the rule of Christian reason, we must be equipped with the habits of the whole array of the moral virtues, both acquired and infused. Moreover, in order not to oppose but to accept worthily the motion and direction of the Holy Ghost, we need, as St. Thomas states, other habits which are superior to these and proportionate to the Spirit.[74] Such are His gifts, which dispose us to receive His ineffable impulses, inspirations, and promptings and enable us to cooperate with them and put them into practice.[75]

3. NECESSITY OF THE MOTION AND PROMPTINGS OF THE HOLY GHOST

Human reason alone, although it can often direct us and ordinarily does, is not sufficient of itself to lead us securely to the gate of eternal life. This is proved by the holy doctor from the fact that here and now we do not possess eternal life in a perfect manner with its respective principles of operation. Therefore we need a superior motion and direction which can supply for our deficiencies and carry us with assurance to that happy goal which faith obscurely proposes to us.

"But in matters directed to the supernatural end," says St. Thomas, "to which man's reason moves him, according as it is, in a manner, and imperfectly, actuated by the theological virtues, the motion of reason does not suffice, unless it receives in addition the prompting or motion of the Holy Ghost . . . because, to wit, none can receive the inheritance of that land of the Blessed, except he be moved and led thither by the Holy Ghost. Therefore, in order to accomplish this end, it is necessary for man to have the gift of the Holy Ghost." [76]

Father Froget enlarges on this point in the following manner:

---

[73] *Dark Night of the Soul*, Bk. II, chap. 16.
[74] See Ia IIae, q. 68, a. 1.
[75] *Ibid.*, a. 3: "The gifts are perfections of man, whereby he becomes amenable to the promptings of the Holy Ghost."
[76] *Ibid.*, a. 2.

PARTICIPATION IN THE DIVINE ACTIVITY

In so far as he is informed by the theological virtues—although in an imperfect way—he can accomplish, with the ordinary help of grace, some meritorious acts; and he can begin to advance and push forward to the eternal shores. But because he is powerless either to know all that it is important to know, or to accomplish all that it will be useful or necessary to do; and because, also, he has not the possession of the acquired or the infused virtues in sufficient volume to furnish a remedy against the ignorance, the stupidity, the hardness of heart and the other miseries of our nature—for all these reasons he is unequal to the task of overcoming all the difficulties which may present themselves and to proceed securely to heaven, without a special assistance, and, therefore, without the Gifts of the Holy Spirit.

How many times in the course of his life, does a Christian find himself in the presence of certain serious crises, of important resolutions to be taken (even of a choice of a state of life to be made), of adopting a line of conduct to be followed in such and such grave circumstances, in a word in need of knowing exactly what is expedient for his eternity! It is, therefore, necessary that we be now and again *specifically* directed and protected by Him Who knows all, Who can direct all.[77]

So the gifts come to the aid of the virtues in difficult matters and whenever it is necessary to act with divine heroism. They give a superabundance where formerly the virtues were not sufficient for the task. Hence they exceed the virtues both in capacity and in the manner of operation. They complete and perfect them, giving them a divine luster. The gifts excel the moral virtues so far as they ordain us directly to God and in a certain manner unite us with Him, though

---

[77] *The Indwelling of the Holy Spirit*, pp. 224 f. Blessed John of Avila, *Trat. 4 del Espíritu Santo*: "O joyful Consoler! O blessed breathing which guides our ships to heaven! Treacherous indeed is this sea which we traverse, but with such a wind and such a pilot, we sail securely. How many ships are lost! How many contrary winds and great dangers abound! But when this sweet Consoler blows, He directs the ships to a safe port. And who can count the benefits which He bestows on us and the evils from which He protects us? This wind proceeds from and then returns to the Father and the Son. From Them He is spirated and through Them He is infused in His friends; through Them He leads His friends and guides them and for Them He loves His friends. . . . Heaven and earth bless Thee, O Lord God Almighty! What numerous witnesses we shall see on the last day whose boats were on the verge of being lost and dashed to pieces and sunk, but who were saved by the blowing of Thy wind and who arrived at the peace and tranquillity of a safe port! Many, who had lost all hope for their lives, Thy Spirit revived, gave them life and new desires, and gladdened and strengthened them with new hope. And who does all this? The Holy Ghost, who breathed on them and transported them to God without difficulty."

not in the same way as do the theological virtues. The gifts supersede these latter virtues in regard to the divine mode of their operation since they constitute us living organs of the Holy Ghost. Thus they give to the supernatural virtues a new splendor.[78]

Father Froget gives an accurate summary of the interplay between the gifts and the infused and acquired virtues:

> Although inferior in quality to the theological virtues—which unite us to God directly—the Gifts lend them a necessary cooperation: they enliven our faith, hearten our hope, inflame our charity, give us the savor of God and of Divine things. But, above all, they are the precious auxiliaries of the natural and moral virtues, whose action they perfect, supplying, when need be, for their inadequacy. Prudence receives from the Gift of Counsel indispensable lights for its guidance; Justice gains strength to render to each one his due; the soul often is perfected by the Gift of Piety, which inspires us with sentiments of filial tenderness towards God and bowels of mercy towards our brethren. The Gift of Fortitude, as already said, makes us surmount bravely all the obstacles which deter us from good, strengthens us against the dread of difficulties, and inspires us with the necessary courage to undertake the more formidable kind of tasks. Finally, the Gift of Fear strengthens the virtues of temperance against the rude assaults of the rebellious flesh. A more energetic action, more heroic efforts in the practice of virtue—such are the effects of the Gifts of the Holy Ghost. By them the soul easily mounts to much greater heights of perfection, the infused virtues having placed it already in the possession of ordinary holiness, and rendered it capable of accomplishing the ordinary works of the Christian life.[79] The masters of the spiritual life have compared the Gifts to the wings of a bird, and again to the sails of a ship; the bird flies much more swiftly than it walks; and while the boat equipped only with simple oars advances with much labor and slowly, one whose sails are swelled with the wind, is fleet upon the waves.[80]

---

[78] See IIa IIae, q. 9, a. 1, ad 3um: "Rather are all the gifts ordained to the perfection of the theological virtues, as to their end."

[79] St. Thomas, *De carit.*, q. unic., a. 2, ad 17um.

[80] Lallemant, *Spiritual Doctrine*, IV, chap. 3, art. 2: "We who as yet do not partake so abundantly of the gifts of the Holy Spirit must labour and toil in the practice of virtue. We are like those who make way by dint of rowing against wind and tide; a day will come, if it please God, when, having received the gifts of the Holy Spirit, we shall speed full-sail before the wind; for it is the Holy Spirit who by his gifts disposes the soul to yield itself easily to his divine inspirations. With the assistance of the gifts of the Holy Spirit, the saints reach such a height of perfection as to accomplish without labour things of which we should not venture so much as

PARTICIPATION IN THE DIVINE ACTIVITY

It appears clearly evident that the Gifts of the Holy Ghost are truly necessary, wherever the action of our native reason, though it be helped by the infused virtues, is yet insufficient; and that, therefore, a special Divine impulse becomes imperative. Even with the assistance of the Christian infused virtues, human reason is incapable of *surely* leading us to our last end, and of enabling us to surmount *all* the obstacles encountered upon the way, if it is not roused and aided by a particular inspiration from on high, a kind of superior instinct of the Holy Ghost, namely His Gifts.

We have need of that special Divine impulse, and consequently of the Gifts, not indeed constantly, but from time to time, in the course of our life, more or less frequently according to the difficulties which present themselves, or when lofty acts of virtue must be accomplished, a high degree of perfection achieved, according to the good pleasure of the Master of these Gifts who dispenses them as He pleases. There is no period of life, no state, no human condition that can dispense with the Gifts and their Divine influence.[81]

Ven. Mary of Agreda, *City of God*, I, Bk. 2, chap. 13: "As the movements of a stone, if another impulse besides gravity is added, are much accelerated; so the impulse of the will toward virtue is stronger and more excellent, if it is acted upon by the gifts. The gift of wisdom communicates to the soul a certain kind of taste by which it can distinguish the divine from the human without error, throwing all its influence and weight in all things against those inclinations which arise from human ignorance and folly; this gift is related to charity. The gift of understanding serves to penetrate into the understanding of divine things and it gives a knowledge of them vastly superior to the ignorance and the slowness of the natural intellect; while that of knowledge searches the most obscure mysteries and creates perfect teachers to oppose human ignorance; these two gifts are related to faith. The gift of counsel guides, directs, and restrains man within the rules of prudence in his inconsiderate activity. It is closely related to this, its own virtue. That of fortitude expels disorderly fear and gives strength to human weakness; it is superadded to the cardinal virtue of that name. Piety makes the heart kind, takes away its hardness and softens it against its own impiety and

---

to think; the Holy Spirit smoothing away all their difficulties, and enabling them to surmount every obstacle."

[81] Froget, *op. cit.*, pp. 226 f.

stubbornness; it is related to religion. The fear of God lovingly humiliates the soul in opposition to pride, and is allied to humility."

"By the theological and moral virtues," says St. Thomas, "man is not so perfected in respect of his last end, as not to stand in continual need of being moved by the yet higher promptings of the Holy Ghost." [82] Indeed, without that motion, in greater or less degree, we could never be true sons of God, for we are that to the extent that we are animated, moved, and activated by these divine impulses.[83] "Without them," says St. Gregory, "one could not attain life, and through them the divine Spirit always abides in His chosen ones." [84] But He moves them in this way, as St. Augustine says, not that they may become slothful and inert, but that He may make them work with greater energy.[85]

Existence of the Gifts in All the Just

Scripture shows us that the Savior was not only filled with the Holy Ghost, but that He was moved by Him, acted through Him, and was led by Him.[86] In the Acts of the Apostles are found innumerable examples of similar motions [87] by the Spirit, and they also appear frequently in the lives of the saints and, in general, in the lives of all souls that are filled with God. The divine Guest becomes, when it so pleases Him or when the course of our life requires it, the mover and immediate regulator of our actions. He fills the office of our reason and supplies for its deficiencies and thus establishes a norm of conduct which is far superior to any human norm.

That this action be connatural and vital, rather than violent, there is required a proportion or adaptation between the mover and the one moved. Hence, to receive this divine motion and direction connaturally and to use it with docility and facility, we need the proper

---

[82] See Ia IIae, q.68, a.2, ad 2um.
[83] Rom. 8:24.
[84] *Moralia*, Bk. II, chap. 28.
[85] Cf. *De corrept. et grat.*, chap. 2, no. 4.
[86] Luke 4:1; Matt. 4:1. Lallemant, *Spiritual Doctrine*, IV, chap. 3, art. 2: "We should do well to accustom ourselves to notice in the Gospel the gifts of the Holy Spirit, and the actions which our Lord performed in accordance with these principles. The parables belong to [the gift of] understanding. The discourse which Jesus Christ addressed to his disciples after the Last Supper belongs to the gift of wisdom."
[87] Acts 8:39; 10:19; 13:2; 16:6 f.

PARTICIPATION IN THE DIVINE ACTIVITY

dispositions. These dispositions are certain infused qualities which prepare and fit us to be governed, moved, and instructed by God Himself, as it is written: "And they shall all be taught of God."[88] Such are those precious gifts or "spirits" which comprise the mystic septenary announced by Isaias (11:2) when He says that the sevenfold Spirit will rest on the shoot from the tree of Jesse: "And the spirit of the Lord shall rest upon him: the spirit of wisdom, and of understanding, the spirit of counsel, and of fortitude, the spirit of knowledge, and of godliness. And he shall be filled with the spirit of the fear of the Lord."

1. IMPORTANCE AND NATURE OF THE GIFTS

Engrafted as we are on Jesus Christ, we participate in the gifts that repose fully in Him as the Head, and from Him they redound to us according to the proportionate capability of each one and according to the measure of intensity by which we live in Him and adhere to Him. For Christ is our archetype, to whom we ought to be configured so that we may be as so many other Christs, other anointed ones of the Holy Ghost, or, better still, that very Jesus Christ living within us. Through these gifts we receive a living impression of His image and we are transformed into Him in such a manner that, if we offer no resistance, it is not now we who work, but rather He who works all things through us as through His own true organs.[89]

Hence these gifts are so called not only by reason of the fact that they are gratuitous but also by reason of their loftiness. They are infused in us to make us prompt in following divine inspirations whenever these inspirations come and not whenever we desire them. So we regard them as borrowed, since we cannot use them at will, as we can the infused virtues, but only when it pleases the Spirit to put them into operation.

We can make use of ordinary prayer whenever we wish[90] (although, perhaps, not always in the way we would desire); but to use prayer perfectly, we need the theological virtues and the ordinary helps of grace. So also we are unable to possess true infused

---

[88] John 6:45; Isa. 54:13.
[89] St. Catherine of Siena, *Life*, I, chap. 11: "I never cease to make you like unto Myself, as long as you place no obstacle. I desire to renew in your soul that which happened in My life."
[90] Ps. 41:9; 54:17 f.

contemplation if we have not been raised to it, for this is the work of the gifts, and principally those of wisdom and understanding; and the gifts act only when the Holy Ghost moves them.[91] Whence it follows that that state of prayer and, in general, all the states corresponding to the gifts are called supernatural par excellence.[92]

Although they are not actuated without a very special motion, the gifts are not simply transient acts; they are habits, dispositions, and permanent powers. The divine Spirit reposes and dwells with all His gifts in the soul of the just. This soul must be always habituated and acclimated to receive and follow with docility the divine impulses. Thus the seven gifts make the soul apt for cooperating divinely with the motion and direction of the Holy Ghost, just as the seven principal virtues, theological and cardinal, enable it to follow in a human way the evangelical precepts as known and proposed by Christian reason.[93] Therefore to each of those virtues there corresponds some gift which elevates and perfects it. The same proportion is found to

[91] Ecclus. 39:8-10. John of St. Thomas says that these gifts assist us in the consideration of the mysteries of faith and of divine things. Through a certain hidden impulse the Holy Ghost prompts us and unites us to Himself and enables us to understand and judge rightly concerning those mysteries. So it is that mystical theology is especially based on the exercise of these gifts so far as from the affection or union of man with divine things there proceeds that knowledge which is quasi-experimental. By this interior illumination and the taste of divine things the affections are moved to tend to the objects of the virtues in a higher manner, which exceeds that of the ordinary virtues (cf. In Iam IIae, q.68, dist. 18, a.2, no. 13).

[92] Surin, Catéchisme, III, chap. 3: "The mystical or extraordinary supernatural way is a state in which the soul no longer works of itself, but under the direction of the Holy Ghost and with the special assistance of grace. It is called supernatural to distinguish it from the ordinary way, wherein the operation of grace is not manifest. . . . God calls the soul to this way when and how it pleases Him, and all that the creature can do is to dispose itself by being faithful. . . . There are three progressive stages in this way. The first is that in which the soul, prepared and directed by the operation of the Holy Ghost, works entirely through His grace. The second state is that in which the soul ceases its activity and seems to do nothing at all but give itself over entirely to the working of the Holy Ghost. In the third stage the soul receives a new life and is resurrected with Jesus Christ with more power than ever before."

[93] Gardeil, The Gifts of the Holy Ghost, pp. 32 f.: "It is true that the Gifts of the Holy Ghost are limited in number, for there are but seven. Still this number does not exhaust the infinite resources of the divine bounty. Every time that the perfect number seven is used in theology to designate the works of God, it expresses not so much a limit as a plenitude. There are seven sacraments, seven virtues, theological and moral. There are seven sacred orders. Examples could be multiplied. Every time that the plenitude of the divine treasures are spread before us the number seven appears. It is represented before the Ark of the Most High, of Jehovah, in the seven-branched candlestick. We say, then, that there are seven Gifts of the Holy Ghost,

PARTICIPATION IN THE DIVINE ACTIVITY

exist between the gifts and the norm of the Spirit as between the virtues and the norm of reason.

As a consequence, there follows the excellence which the gifts have of themselves over the virtues, and this excellence is indicated by the name "spirit" by which Scripture designates them. "Spirit" in this sense means an inspiration, whereas "virtue" signifies an interior power whose act proceeds manifestly from ourselves. Hence the gifts, as St. Thomas points out, are higher perfections whereby man is disposed to be moved by God.[94] So noble and so elevated are these perfections that they convert us into organs or instruments of the Holy Ghost Himself.[95] Therefore they perfect or complete the virtues, supplying their deficiencies, giving them an extraordinary activity and vitality, and making them do what of themselves they could in no way accomplish.[96] At the same time that they dispose us for the divine motion, they are in themselves powers and abilities

---

fear, fortitude, piety, counsel, knowledge, understanding and wisdom. Do not painters represent the splendor which escapes from the sun by a finite number of rays and do they not place some in relief of which they form the center and binding of each luminous sheaf? There are seven Gifts of the Holy Ghost, but the means which God has of activating us in regard to our end are infinite."

[94] See Ia IIae, q.68, a.1.

[95] Ven. Mary of Agreda, *City of God*, I, Bk. II, chap. 13: "My daughter, these most noble and excellent gifts of the Holy Ghost, which thou hast come to understand, are the emanations of the Divinity communicating themselves to and transforming holy souls: on their own part they do not admit of any limitation but only on the part of the subject on which they act. If the creatures would empty their hearts of earthly love and affections, although their heart is limited, they would participate without measure in the torrent of the infinite Godhead through the inestimable gifts of the Holy Ghost. The virtues purify the creature from the ugliness and guilt of its vices, and thereby they begin to restore the disconcerted order of its faculties, which was first lost by original sin and afterwards increased by actual sins; they add beauty to the soul, strength and joy in doing good. But the gifts of the Holy Ghost raise these same virtues to a sublime perfection, adornment and beauty, by which they dispose, beautify, and fill the soul with graces and introduce it to the chamber of its Spouse, where it remains united with the Divinity in a spiritual bond of eternal peace. From this most blessed condition it proceeds faithfully and truthfully to the practice of heroic virtues, and laden with them it returns to the same source from which it issued forth, namely God Himself. In His shadow it rests and is satiated, freed from the impetuous fury of the passions and disorderly appetites."

[96] Medina, *In Iam IIae*, q.68, a.8: "Innumerable are the works to which God moves us through the inspiration of the Holy Ghost, and these works do not fall under the scope of the infused virtues.... When a man acts under the impulse of the Holy Ghost he is rather acted upon than acting; ... but once motivated by the Holy Ghost, he freely consents and effectively performs the work of wisdom, understanding, etc."

which enable us to second and cooperate with this divine impulse. Thus they render us at the same time passive and active to the highest degree. We are moved and animated by a truly divine activity, which, appearing to enslave us, actually gives us the most glorious liberty, that liberty of the Spirit who makes us children of God. "Our free will could do nothing better," says St. Augustine, "than to let itself be so constrained that it can never do evil." [97]

2. MODE OF OPERATION OF THE GIFTS

Since by means of the gifts we work as inspired, animated, and directed by God Himself, our work is no longer human but superhuman and truly divine. Therefore St. Thomas adds (*loc. cit.*, a. 8) that to be able to cooperate with that motion of the Holy Ghost, we must be called to a higher grade of perfection. From this comes that divine mode of operation which distinguishes the gifts from the virtues. These latter perfect man in regard to the human mode of operation, but the gifts enable him to work in a manner that is beyond the human mode.[98]

In exercising the virtues, then, we act in a connatural manner as if that infused energy by which we work were entirely proper to us. Thus our connatural mode of knowing spiritual and divine things is to raise ourselves from the visible to the invisible through the use of analogy, contemplating the divine in the mirror of material creatures.[99] Supernatural faith, which proposes to us the divine mysteries to which the natural light of our reason could not attain, presents them to us in such a way that we still know them only in the obscure and enigmatic way that is natural to us. Faith broadens the field of our knowledge but it does not elevate the manner of our knowing.

But with the gift of understanding, the veils begin to part and the enigmas gradually disappear so that, up to a certain point, we are able to see the truth uncovered. Thus this gift elevates us far beyond our connatural mode of perceiving divine things.[100] It is this gift of understanding that often communicates to innocent children and unlettered persons who are docile to the Holy Ghost the remarkable intuition of divine mysteries, the profound sense of faith,

---
[97] *De gestis Pelag.*, chap. 3, no. 5.
[98] See St. Thomas, *In III Sent.*, dist. 34, q. 1, a. 1.
[99] St. Thomas, *loc. cit.*
[100] *Ibid.*, a. 2.

PARTICIPATION IN THE DIVINE ACTIVITY

and the perspicacity by which at first glance they discover the poison of error in expressions which might perhaps appear inoffensive to the eyes of many theologians.[101] Only by that gift could St. Jane Frances de Chantal, at the age of five, disconcert and confound a learned heretic who denied the truth of the Eucharist.[102]

In the practical order, the connatural mode of working which is proper to the virtues, consists, with regard to prudence, for example, in a close examination of things and circumstances according to the light of reason; considering the *pro* and *con* for everything, judging according to what is ordinarily done. But at times grave difficulties arise. Sometimes there is need for a quick decision, and everything seems uncertain. Even after consultation with prudent persons, the perplexity remains. Therefore, seeing that the ordinary lights are not sufficient, we should invoke wholeheartedly the Spirit of counsel. Then, if we feel a sudden impulse to take an unforeseen procedure and we find that that proves feasible which, without that superior impulse would have been foolish, then we shall be working in a superhuman manner. We shall be led by the gift of counsel to a most happy conclusion which we never would have dreamed of.[103]

Then the soul knows by experience that, as long as it is governed by God, it will lack nothing (Ps. 22:1). Therefore the soul need not deliberate about those things that are most fitting, for this is the task of Him who governs. It is sufficient that the soul be assured that it is truly moved by the Holy Ghost and that it is ready to follow Him

---

[101] Ecclus. 37:17.
[102] See also St. Thomas, *Contra Gent.*, I, chap. 6.
[103] St. Thomas, *op. cit.*, q.1, a.2. Alvarez de Paz, *De inquis. pacis*, I, Part III, chap. 2: "This light [of the gifts] does not destroy the knowledge and purity of faith, but it perfects it and marvelously augments the understanding of those things which we ponder. Sometimes spiritual men understand divine things so accurately that they seem to gaze upon the things themselves, and so savory is the knowledge they acquire that it is like honey on the tongue. This is effected by the gift of wisdom. Sometimes the dullness of the mind is completely dissipated, and a mystery is known profoundly and almost completely comprehended; and this is the effect of the gift of understanding. Again, they know what should be done in regard to a certain matter and what omitted, or how to live with such great purity that all worldly things are despised; and this pertains to the gift of knowledge. Also, one understands how to proceed, not only in general but also in particular matters; and this is governed by the gift of counsel. . . . Thus by means of these gifts the Spirit of truth teaches the just, who are accustomed to prayer, a perfect knowledge of the mysteries of faith and raises them to the loftiest wisdom. These gifts so incite and impel the just that they advance in virtue with a vehement force, and they tear themselves away completely from all human things."

with docility. "For those who are moved by Divine instinct, there is no need to take counsel according to human reason, but only to follow their inner promptings, since they are moved by a higher principle than human reason." [104]

Therefore it is true that in the beginning, and even for some time after, the divine impulses are not usually so clear that they dispel prudent doubts. For that reason pious souls are accustomed to seek advice from their directors with great care, in order not to believe too readily in every spirit, but to prove that the spirit is from God.[105] But as time passes, as the eyes of the heart are purified, then the divine impulses become so evident that they are supported by subjective testimony; and often they not only forestall all deliberation but they give no room for reflection. The result is that, when the soul takes an accounting, it finds that what the Holy Ghost has suggested was done and done well.

In cases of this type, when a thing is urgent and there is no one to consult and the glory of God is at stake in the prompt execution of the matter, one should heed the sentence of the Savior: "But when they shall deliver you up, take no thought how or what to speak; for it shall be given you in that hour what to speak. For it is not you that speak, but the Spirit of your Father that speaketh in you." [106] This method of procedure is undoubtedly superhuman.

The virtue of fortitude consists in facing difficulties in the measure in which our powers permit; to go further than that on our own initiative is temerity. But if, raised by a supernatural instinct, we attempt and realize a work that is manifestly beyond ourselves, knowing that we could attain none of it except by divine power, then, says St. Thomas, we shall be working in a superhuman manner.[107] The mean or norm of such activity is a divine power, not a natural one.

Since the gifts exceed the virtues in their mode of operation, they ought also to exceed them in the norm which regulates these operations. Virtue, by which one lives rightly according to the rule of reason, has as its norm human reason illumined by faith. But the gifts are more elevated perfections which God communicates "in

---

[104] Cf. Ia IIae, q.68, a.1.
[105] See I John 4:1–6.
[106] Matt. 10:19 f.
[107] See *In III Sent.*, dist. 34, q.1, a.2.

relation to His motion," [108] and since they do not have human reason as director or guide, they cannot have reason as their norm or measure. The norm of the acts of the gifts is the ineffable wisdom of Him who prompts the acts.[109]

Thus human reason, even when aided by faith and infused prudence, could never justify certain actions of the saints, which, nevertheless, are justifiable. It is evident that they obey some other sublime norm which we cannot help but praise and admire, the more so as we are less able to understand it. Though these works surpass the limits of our prudence, they do not on that account cease to be good, and that with a superior goodness. Such works are not temerarious, for they have God Himself as their counsellor and support. They can be justified because God is not, like ourselves, constrained by the limits of our imperfections. For this reason they surpass the limitations of the virtue of prudence.[110] Though our prudence could never authorize those acts, the prudence of the Holy Ghost commands them. This divine Spirit of truth does not have to ask our counsel or permission to move or inspire us, for He knows what is best for us. Since His norm can never be erroneous, it is sufficient for us to follow it faithfully and thus be led to a happy outcome. "Thy good spirit shall lead me into the right land." [111]

Far from being subject to the regulation of human reason, this motion of the gifts, says Father Froget, "anticipates our deliberations, forestalls our judgments, and leads us in a kind of instinctive way to perform works of which we had not dreamt, and which we are justified in calling superhuman, whether because they exceed our natural powers, or because they are accomplished outside the ordinary modes and procedures of nature and of ordinary grace." [112]

This unique mode, which consists in the command and sovereign efficacy with which the divine Guest moves and directs us as He pleases, working and speaking through us as His own organs, is what most distinguishes the gifts from the virtues. Even in the smallest

---

[108] See Ia IIae, q.68, a.1, ad 3um.
[109] St. Thomas, *In III Sent.*, dist. 34, q.1, a.3: "Since the gifts are ordained to acts that are superhuman, it is necessary that the operations of the gifts be measured by some other rule of human virtue. This rule is the Divinity itself as participated by man so that he acts, not now humanly, but as God through participation."
[110] See *L'Ami du Clergé*, 1892, p. 391.
[111] Ps. 142:10.
[112] *Op. cit.*, p. 221.

THE MYSTICAL EVOLUTION

works the Holy Ghost can sometimes move us, since it is not the excellence or heroism of an action but the superhuman mode of operation which distinguishes in general the acts of the gifts from those of the virtues.[113]

3. RARE DISCRETION OF THE SAINTS

When the saints do things that are wholly extraordinary and that not only militate against the domain of prudence but even seem contrary to health and life, and when, nevertheless, they seem to act well and to please God much, evidently they work under superhuman approval and direction. Says Father Froget:

In the same way when the Blessed Henry Suso, of the Order of St. Dominic, traced in deep characters the name of Jesus on his breast, and macerated his body in a way revolting to our self-indulgence. Again, when St. Apollonia, threatened by the pagans with being burnt alive if she did not renounce Christ Jesus, forestalled their plans and cast herself into the flames; when the Stylites, and so many other saints embraced a state of life, which seemed to be a perpetual challenge to nature, can we say that they acted according to the rules of Christian prudence? Certainly not; yet countless miracles attest their holiness, proving that in acting in this manner they were obeying a Divine impulse. All those heroisms of faith, meekness, fortitude, patience and charity, so plentiful in the lives of the Saints; all those extraordinary works undertaken for the glory of God and the salvation of our neighbor—the highest manifestations of the spiritual life—are nothing else than effects of the Gifts of the Holy Ghost. Emanating as they do from a principle superior to that of even the infused virtues, why should we wonder that they so far surpass the latter in brilliancy and edification?[114]

One should not think that these extraordinary things occurred only in the lives of the early saints. In the same way and with even a more divine delicacy, they figure in the lives of modern saints. They are reproduced among us and will continue to be reproduced until the end of the world in all the great servants of God who are truly filled and possessed of His Spirit. The act referred to in the case of Blessed Henry Suso has been repeated by many holy souls who

---

[113] See Ia IIae, q.68, a.2, ad 1um: "The gifts surpass the ordinary perfection of the virtues, not as regards the kind of works . . . , but as regards the manner of working, in respect of a man being moved by a higher principle."

[114] *Op. cit.*, pp. 216 f.

PARTICIPATION IN THE DIVINE ACTIVITY

were prompted by a superior impulse which they could not resist; for example, St. Jane de Chantal and St. Margaret Mary. More recently, in 1904, the angelic Mother Mary of the Queen of Apostles was compelled to engrave deeply on her breast by means of fire the anagram IHS surmounted by a cross and placed between the letters M and R. The letters were as large as the palm of the hand and she would renew the anagram whenever it began to heal. After her death this anagram was seen to be so deeply imbedded in her flesh that the bones were visible.

When asked by myself just before her death (I had the consolation of hearing from her blessed lips the marvelous secrets of her heart) why she had done this "foolishness," she candidly answered me: "I had to; our Lord demanded this sacrifice of me and I was moved toward Him with such violence that I was overwhelmed. It was impossible to resist. . . If the Mother Superior had delayed longer in granting her permission, I believe I would have died in that oppression." And when next I asked her how she had summoned the courage to trace those letters with a flaming stylus (for she was formerly very sensitive and delicate), she said: "Believe me, Father, I can tell you that I did not feel it. What I did feel was a great relief and ease. That external pain was nothing compared to the internal oppression which left me." She also confided to me that it was only on receiving permission to renew her terrifying penances that she began to recover her health, and she lost it whenever she was prevented from these mortifications. For that reason her superiors, on seeing that she was in danger of death, felt obliged (as one of them told me) to grant permission for the most extreme rigors. What for others would have meant death, for Mother Mary was an only remedy.

So it is seen how the norm of the Holy Ghost is justified in itself; and how, in spite of that, perfect subordination to legitimate authority is not excluded. For the Spirit of God is always submissive and gentle,[115] at the same time that He is efficient and imperious.[116] One sees also how faithful souls, even though they know clearly the divine motion whenever it occurs, always seek advice regarding the performance of the work and, above all, permission when their

---
[115] See I Cor. 14:32-40; I John 4:6.
[116] Wisd. 8:1.

THE MYSTICAL EVOLUTION

profession demands it.[117] In this way they assure themselves that the inspiration comes from God and that it is not prudent to resist it; for, granting that it comes from such a height, there is no reason why the poor human reason should interject itself as if it were desirous of giving advice to the Holy Ghost. This would be to displease Him and to deaden His vivifying impulses.[118]

PNEUMATIC PSYCHOLOGY

In Book VII of his *Nicomachean Ethics*, Aristotle admits the existence of divine inspirations, to which reason ought to submit itself and not try to judge what so far exceeds its capacity. Much less should reason actually seek to assert itself in a norm of action which is so superior to its own. Thus does Aristotle explain artistic inspirations and the inspiration to perform certain heroic deeds which transcend the rules of human prudence. Philosophy itself recognizes the possibility and fittingness by which God, as "the reason of our reason," becomes the immediate rule of our conduct and the inspirer of superhuman actions.

---

[117] Lallemant, *Spiritual Direction*, IV, chap. 1, art. 3: "The second objection is, that it seems as if this interior guidance of the Holy Spirit were destructive of the obedience which is due to superiors.

"We reply: 1. That as the interior inspiration of grace does not set aside the assent which we give to the articles of faith, as they are externally proposed to us, but contrariwise gently disposes the understanding to believe; in like manner, the guidance which we receive from the gifts of the Holy Spirit, far from interfering with obedience, aids and facilitates the practice of it. 2. That all this interior guidance, and even divine revelations, must always be subordinate to obedience; and in speaking of them, this tacit condition is ever implied, that obedience enjoins nothing contrary thereto.

"For in the state of faith in which we live, we ought to make more account of the commandment of our superior than of that which our Lord himself might have given us by an immediate revelation, because we are assured that it is his will we should act in this matter after the pattern of the saints, who by submitting to obedience merited to be raised to a higher reward than they would have been had they paid exclusive regard to the revelations they received.

"The only fear is lest superiors should sometimes follow too much the suggestions of human prudence, and for want of discernment condemn the lights and inspirations of the Holy Spirit, treating them as dreams and illusions, and prescribing for those to whom God communicates himself by favours of this kind, as if they were sick patients.

"In such case we must still obey; but in his own time God will know how to correct the error of these rash persons, and teach them to their cost, not to condemn his graces without understanding them, and without being competent to pronounce upon them."

[118] Eph. 4:30; I Thess. 5:19.

PARTICIPATION IN THE DIVINE ACTIVITY

1. LIFE-GIVING ACTION AND INSPIRATION OF THE HOLY GHOST; DIABOLICAL POSSESSION AND SUGGESTION

For the pagan philosophers that divine intervention had to be transitory, passing, and fortuitous. Therefore there was not required in the soul any habitual disposition that would serve as a permanent basis. These philosophers could in no way suspect that mysterious, intimate, and constant vital communication of God with the just soul. This loving indwelling—which is at the same time a continual life-giving action, could be known to us only through faith and supernatural experience. By these two means the Christian philosopher finds and recognizes a firm and permanent basis for receiving those divine impulses which, in the eyes of pagans, seem to be rare and fortuitous.

Speaking of the necessity of the gifts, Father Gardeil says:

It is here, apparently, that St. Thomas goes definitely beyond Aristotle. The latter had refused to recognize a permanent basis for the special action of the Divinity in the nature of man. For him, the entire foundation of Fortune rested on the particular and unceasing attentions of the Divinity. But St. Thomas found himself confronted with a man already possessed of the Divinity, one in whom the Divinity habitually resides, whose soul, as it were, the Divinity is. It is the property of the soul to cause in the being which it vivifies all the organs of which it has need. Why, then, should not charity give rise to perfections and habits analogous to those which make reason's entrance into the moral world so easy? Can charity in the supernatural order refuse to the just man what nature grants to man in the natural order?

Whence follows the need for those divine habits which are called gifts, spirits, instincts, or supernatural tendencies, which come to us to facilitate the impulse and government by God and to enable us to follow Him with docility.

Undoubtedly God does not need these points of contact in order to activate my life. But for me it is necessary that He establish these contacts if I am to be as perfect in the order of divine motions as in the rational order. It is necessary that the inspirations of the Holy Ghost be in me habitually just as the dictates of reason are in me as a habit. I do not wish to give way violently and as if constrained to God who encompasses my soul. I wish to give Him place as the virtuous man yields to his reason—voluntarily, readily, with that ease habit alone can give. I wish to be able to say with the prophet: "The Lord God opened my ear and I did not resist; I have not gone back." [119] . . .

Truly this doctrine of the Angelic Doctor is admirable. For him, the doctrine of the Gifts is contained in the two words, "spirit," and "gift." As the breathings of the Holy Ghost, the Gifts postulate the autonomy of their principle. As Gifts, the inspirations of the Holy Ghost have an actual contact point in our souls. Actual grace, of course, is needed to stir up the will to make use of the Gifts. Actual graces, however, are the breath of the just and prayerful soul.[120]

So the vivifying Spirit always prevails as the permanent mainstay of the activity and life in the souls of the just. When He, the sevenfold Spirit, and the soul of an order more elevated and really divine informs us, His possession is in no way an intrusion nor is His motion and direction in any sense an external and violent imposition. In reality these influences of the Spirit are intimate, vivifying, and autonomous, so that He who is the reason of our reason and the life of our soul is more intimate to us than we are to ourselves. So it is that under His action we feel more free and active than ever.

From all this we see how far this divine vivification and inspiration is removed from diabolical possession and satanic suggestion. If the demon enters into any unfortunate person, it is always to do that person violence, to seduce him, to prompt him to evil, and to harm him as much as he can. Since the devil is not the cause of the soul, he cannot penetrate it; but he can paralyze it or disturb its activity.[121] In possession, he tyrannizes over the faculties and directs them to his own taste, forcing, from within and without, the bodily organs which these faculties need in order to function. In diabolical suggestion, he bewitches from without, with illusory images, striving often to imitate the divine inspirations which come from within, from the core of the soul where God reigns.

Knowing that the perfidious prevaricator disguises himself as an angel of light, we cannot always and easily distinguish his evil instigations from holy inspirations except by the effects. Such discernment will not be possible until the soul has already had much experience and gradually senses more clearly and recognizes immediately the

---

[119] Isa. 50:5.
[120] *The Gifts of the Holy Ghost*, pp. 17-19.
[121] See St. Thomas, *Contra Gent.*, IV, 18.

voice of its own sweet Shepherd.[122] Therefore it is always necessary to test any spirit as long as doubts prevail, to see whether it comes from God or from the enemy.

But when the soul has arrived at true union, then, as St. Teresa says,[123] it will be able to perceive clearly the most sweet touches of the Beloved, and this will dissipate all doubts. The Spirit Himself who dwells in the soul as in His chosen dwelling place and gives testimony that she is the daughter of God, assures her that it is He who inspires her, directs and moves her, without doing her any violence. Rather, He causes extreme joy, suavity, and sweetness and gives her all vigor and facility.

As the norm of our reason He subordinates it, without enslaving it, through pure love and with infinite attractions. As the life of our souls He reigns in them, giving them the most sweet liberty and autonomy. "Where the Spirit of the Lord is, there is liberty." [124]

2. AWARENESS OF THE DIVINE INDWELLING

The soul follows the motion of God with indescribable pleasure because all its pleasure is in following Him. It is aware of being possessed by Him to whom it has totally abandoned itself, and it knows from experience that under His loving control nothing can be wanting to it, for He also communicates Himself without reserve.[125] And thus the soul comes to possess God Himself with His infinite treasures. It possesses its God and its all, the God of its heart and its eternal portion, in the measure in which it is possessed by Him.[126]

---

[122] John 10:27 f.
[123] *Interior Castle*, fifth mansions, chap. 1.
[124] See II Cor. 3:17.
[125] John of St. Thomas, *In Iam IIae*, q.70, disp. 18, sec. 1, n.9: "Not content with giving us His graces, the Lord, by means of the gifts of the Holy Ghost, takes possession of us to enrich us with even greater graces. And this properly pertains to the gifts of the Holy Ghost, in which God so gives and distributes His gifts to men that He thereby subjects men to Himself and makes them docile to His Spirit. Whereas other gifts are received from God by men, in these gifts God accepts men themselves and in the men thus taken, God again takes to Himself both the men and the gifts and makes them His own, after the fashion of money-lending and usury."
[126] Through the virtues we have the Holy Ghost at our command; "we use the Holy Ghost," as the theologians graphically state. But through the gifts it is He who disposes of us, possessing us at the same time that He is possessed. This reciprocal possession, since it is a work of love, perfectly harmonizes liberty with slavery, and subordination with autonomy.
So it is that Father Gardeil says of the child of God: "Being passive in relation

THE MYSTICAL EVOLUTION

This awareness of the supernatural life and of the ineffable operations of God in the soul characterizes to a certain extent and better permits us to recognize the mystical state which is so much discussed today. It also enables us to realize how much in error are those who speak of "pagan mysticism," "Mohammedan mysticism," and the like. The true mystical state implies, together with the vivifying indwelling of the Holy Ghost, His habitual movement and direction, which supplant or complete the direction of supernaturalized reason enriched with the infused virtues. Without the gifts of the Holy Ghost there is not nor can there be anything but the false appearances of mysticism. Those who do not possess the grace of God and especially those who lack even the light of the true faith cannot possess the Holy Ghost and cannot feel the influence of His gifts. The gifts are a chief factor in the growth of the mystical life and, because of the high degree in which they work when they are felt, they presuppose an intense vivifying action.

The pagans could at times experience certain divine inspirations when they were externally moved or illumined by the Holy Ghost without enjoying His indwelling or without being vivified by Him.[127] But since that type of motion or inspiration does not give the vital awareness which constitutes the sense of Christ (*sensus Christi*), it cannot be felt as it was by the true mystics, who were filled with divine life and who understood the truth that frees. At most, such motion from the Holy Ghost may be regarded as something similar to a mystical act, but never as the mystical state. Yet even then, these sensations of the pagans are of a different type.

The just soul finds itself truly possessed and informed by the sevenfold Spirit, who tends to make that soul like to the heavenly man. He imprints on the soul of the just His own seal. He removes from it the ugliness and stains of the earthly man and leads it from glory to glory to the lofty regions of eternal life. And since, as St. Thomas points out,[128] there belongs to every form a proportionate tendency or inclination, so from the indwelling of the Holy Ghost

---

to the Holy Ghost, he possesses Him and uses the influence of this Guest as both slave and free. . . . Such is the strange antinomy of which the gifts appear to us to be the divine solution" (*op. cit.*, pp. 20 f.).

[127] John 1:5: The divine "light shineth in darkness; and the darkness did not comprehend it."

[128] See Ia, q. 80, a. 1.

there result in us those divine instincts or impulses which we call gifts. These are a sort of superhuman heritage, a divine blood which courses through our veins and which, after the fashion of a noble hereditary form, impels us to noble and heroic actions worthy of the children of God and communicates to us those heavenly instincts proper to a divine race.[129] This is the mystical heritage of the servants of God (Isa. 54:17) wherein Wisdom abides. "In all these I sought rest, and I shall abide in the inheritance of the Lord" (Ecclus. 24:11). Yet how many there are who grossly reject this inheritance!

3. LABORIOUS ACTIVITY OF MEDITATION; FRUITFUL PASSIVITY OF CONTEMPLATION

The gifts begin to be manifested very soon, although obscurely, and this takes place in the form of secret impulses which lead us more and more forcibly to a point where reason is unable to direct us. By purifying our souls so that they will not impede these impulses but will follow them with docility, and by noting the wonderful consequences of these impulses, it becomes more and more clear what these impulses are, whence they come, and where they are leading us.[130]

So those whose eyes of the heart are sufficiently cleansed and illumined begin to see God [131] and are able to recognize the presence and beneficent action of the finger of His right hand, the loving Paraclete and most sweet Guest of the soul. He it is who works in us and through us to remedy our weakness, to give a new splendor to the very virtues He has infused in us. As a result we do with facility and utmost perfection, by means of His inestimable gifts, what we could in no way realize through the virtues alone, or only to a limited extent and with extreme difficulty.

To convince ourselves of this truth we have only to read St. Teresa, who shows how laboriously the soul works when it has only the virtues at its disposal and how, through prolonged meditations,

---

[129] Hugon, *Revue Thomiste*, September, 1906, p. 420: "When one bears in his veins the blood of heroes, he rushes to the performance of great deeds as if by instinct. The gifts of the Holy Ghost do that and much more. They prepare and dispose us for the sublime. They are in us as a seed of which the flower must be heroism."
[130] See *The Living Flame*, stanza 4.
[131] Matt. 5:8; Eph. 1:18.

it invigorates itself by drawing but a few drops of water from the deep well of grace. But when the divine Spirit begins to aid the soul in a hidden manner, the soul notes with surprise that it draws much water with little effort, for then the virtues themselves work with much greater facility and power under the secret motion of the gifts. Later, when the gifts prevail, this mystical water of grace comes directly from the river, although the soul, with the help of the virtues, still preserves the power of directing and distributing it. In the next state the water comes directly from heaven and in great abundance, and the soul needs to do nothing but drink of it and be satiated. Finally, there is an end even to the effort of swallowing this water, for the water itself finds its way alone into the heart and, both within and without, it inundates, engulfs, and satiates it in the torrents of divine delights. Then all proper initiative ceases; and when least thinking of it and least striving for it, the soul becomes totally filled with God, inundated and satiated in the ocean of living water. Hence anything that the soul might seek through its own proper initiative would do nothing but place obstacles in the way of the mysterious action of the divine Spirit.[132]

The soul then should strive to cooperate with all its strength. Though it appears to be in a period of sloth, in that state of passivity it is found to be more engaged, more living, and more active than ever. It abounds in vigor and divine energies.[133]

So also the spiritual director, if he is endowed with the light and discretion which are required for this work, will be able to recognize and test this state through these good effects and will be able to reassure the individual soul when it is necessary to pacify it. But if he judges only from appearances and according to human pru-

---

[132] *The Life*, chaps. 11-20.
Dark Night of the Soul, Bk. I, chap. 9: "For in such a way does God bring the soul into this state, and by so different a path does He lead it, that, if it desires to work with its faculties, it hinders the work which God is doing in it rather than aids it; whereas aforetime it was quite the contrary. The reason is that, in this state of contemplation, which the soul enters when it forsakes meditation for the state of the proficient, it is God Who is now working in the soul."
[133] St. Jane Frances de Chantal, *Opuscula*, III, 278: "In this state it is God who directs and teaches, and the soul does nothing more than receive the spiritual goods that are given it, which are successively, attention and divine love. . . . The soul, then, ought to go to Him with a confident heart, without eliciting acts other than those to which it feels itself moved. . . . If it attempts to work and to depart from this simple loving attention which God demands of it, it will merely impede the benefits which accrue to it by means of this state."

PARTICIPATION IN THE DIVINE ACTIVITY

dence, then instead of aiding the soul and setting it right, he will be an obstacle and will do nothing but impede and misguide it. Anyone who has the requisite knowledge and experience will note that if the soul persists, as often happens, in working by itself in the accustomed manner, it will not be able to advance at all, but will actually impede the beneficent effects of the divine action. On the other hand, the soul will advance most if it preserves a simple intuition or loving gaze, heeding and consenting to the most delicate work which God desires to accomplish in it.[134]

At this period the office of the director is reduced to the observation of the mysterious operations of the Holy Ghost. He should advise the soul to remain in this holy inactivity as long as it feels so

---

[134] *Living Flame of Love*, stanza 3, pp. 94 f.: "For it [the soul] knows not how to work save by means of sense, and thus, when God is pleased to bring it into that emptiness and solitude where it can neither make use of its faculties nor perform any acts, it sees that it is doing nothing, and strives to do something: in this way it becomes distracted and full of aridity and displeasure, whereas formerly it was rejoicing in the rest of the spiritual silence and peace wherein God was secretly giving it joy. And it may come to pass that God persists in keeping the soul in this silent tranquillity, while the soul persists in crying out with its imagination and walking with its understanding; even as children, whom their mothers carry in their arms so that they may not have to walk, keep crying and striking out with their feet because they are anxious to walk, and thus neither make any progress themselves nor allow their mothers to do so. Or it is as when a painter is painting a portrait and his subject will not allow him to do anything because he keeps moving.

"The soul in this state must bear in mind that, although it is not conscious of making any progress, it is making much more than when it was walking on foot; for it is because God is bearing it in His arms that it is not conscious of movement. And although it is doing nothing, it is nevertheless accomplishing much more than if it were working, since God is working within it."

This is what directors should say to souls to reassure them and to encourage them to persevere. But unfortunately this is precisely where many directors fail, through lack of the proper spirit and holy science. They likewise cause others to fail because they augment the fears of the soul or they oblige it to be active and thus impede the fruits of that prayer of quiet.

"As navigation ceases when the port is reached and as the means are unnecessary when the end is attained," says Molina (*Oración*, II, chap. 6), "so when a man, having passed through the labors of meditation, arrives at the rest and enjoyment of contemplation, he ought then to put an end to discursive prayer and considerations. Content with the simple gaze of God and His truths, he should be satisfied with looking at Him, loving, admiring, and enjoying Him and exercising other affective acts. . . . Whenever during prayer a man feels this interior recollection and his will is inspired and moved by some affection, he ought not to reject it out of a desire to pursue other considerations or points which he had prepared. He should remain in that state of recollection as long as it lasts, even if it should be for the whole period of the exercise. But when that light and affection pass and the soul feels distressed or arid, then he should return to his meditation and the ordinary routine of his exercises."

THE MYSTICAL EVOLUTION

inclined, or he should set it right when it really becomes stultified to such an extent that it does not reap any fruit. But as long as he sees that the soul is moved by the good Spirit, he should not try to indicate the road it should follow. For at such a time the soul already has within itself One who will direct it and place it on the right path, and any interruption will only impede or disturb that work which is as prodigious as it is silent.

Such is the gradual and insensible transition from meditation to contemplation, and such is its procedure. Such a transition could never be effected by our own efforts alone, but it is freely granted to all those who truly seek it with purity of heart and persevere in asking for it.[135] It begins in a marvelous manner and is developed with great vigor and fruit under the motion of the Holy Ghost if this motion is accepted and used. In the beginning the soul advances painfully and laboriously to the port of salvation by hard rowing, ever fearful of being enveloped by the furious waves of the tempestuous sea of this world or of being wrecked on the hidden reefs or of falling into the hands of pirates. Now, without effort and, we may say, without danger, it sails rapidly and under full sail. It is driven by the breath of the Holy Ghost, which guides it and preserves it from misfortune at the same time that it pushes it on.

Formerly the soul had to walk on foot, sluggishly, like a flightless, terrestial bird which is in danger of falling into the claws of the hawk. Now it has developed strong wings by which it flies without ever tiring and rises to the heavenly heights. But this transition of the soul is realized only at the expense of great labor and after passing through the two "nights," in which, fearing to find death, the soul discovers renewal and life and thereby abandons human procedure to undertake a manner of working that is entirely heavenly and divine.

APPENDIX

1. Conflicts of the Soul and the Happy Transition

"In poverty, and without protection and support in all the apprehensions of my soul—that is, in the darkness of my understanding

[135] Ecclus. 6:18-37; Prov. 2:3-5; 8:17; Isa. 51:1-9; Matt. 11:25; Jas. 1:5.

and the constraint of my will, in affliction and anguish with respect to memory, remaining in the dark in pure faith, . . I went forth from myself—that is, from my low manner of understanding, from my weak mode of loving and from my poor and limited manner of experiencing God, without being hindered therein by sensuality or the devil. . . I went forth from my own human way and operation to the operation and way of God. That is to say, my understanding went forth from itself, turning from the human and natural to the Divine; for, when it is united with God by means of this purgation, its understanding no longer comes through its natural light and vigour, but through the Divine Wisdom wherewith it has become united. And my will went forth from itself, becoming Divine; for, being united with Divine love, it no longer loves with its natural strength after a lowly manner, but with strength and purity from the Holy Spirit; and thus the will, which is now near to God, acts not after a human manner, and similarly the memory has become transformed into eternal apprehensions of glory. And finally, by means of this night and purgation of the old man, all the energies and affections of the soul are wholly renewed into a Divine temper and Divine delight" (*Dark Night of the Soul*, Bk. II, chap. 4.).

Thus, the life which is then begun to be enjoyed is so different and so superior that the soul does not know itself and is filled with admiration on seeing itself so happily changed. Describing the change that is effected in the soul, St. Teresa says: "From this point onward, I am speaking of another and a new book—I mean, of another and a new life. Until now the life I was describing was my own; but the life I have been living since I began to expound these matters concerning prayer is the life which God has been living in me—or so it has seemed to me. For I believe it to be impossible in so short a time to escape from such wicked deeds and habits. Praised be the Lord, Who has delivered me from myself! Now when I began to avoid the occasions of sin and to devote myself more to prayer, the Lord began to bestow favours upon me and it looked as though He were desirous that I should wish to receive them" (*The Life*, chap. 23).

"God imparts life to the soul in the state of abandonment by means which seem more likely to destroy it. There is a time when

God would be the life of the soul, and Himself accomplish its perfection in secret and unknown ways. Then all its own ideas, lights, industries, examinations, and reasonings become sources of illusion. After many experiences of the sad consequences of self-guidance, the soul recognizing its uselessness, and finding that God has hidden and confused all the issues, is forced to fly to Him to find life. Then, convinced of its nothingness and of the harmfulness of all that it derives from itself, it abandons itself to God to gain all from Him. It is then that God becomes the source of its life, not by means of ideas, lights, or reflexions, for all this is no longer anything to it but a source of illusion; but in reality, and by His grace, which is hidden under the strangest appearances.

"The divine operation, unknown to the soul, communicates its virtue and substance by many circumstances that the soul believes will be its destruction. There is no cure for this ignorance, it must be allowed its course. God gives Himself therein, and with Himself, He gives all things in the obscurity of faith. The soul is but a blind subject, or, in other words, it is like a sick person who knows nothing of the properties of remedies and tastes only their bitterness. He often imagines that what is given him will be his death; the pain and weakness which result seem to justify his fears; nevertheless it is under the semblance of death that his health is restored, and he takes the medicines on the word of the physician. In the same way the submissive soul is in no way pre-occupied about its infirmities, except as regards obvious maladies which by their nature compel it to rest, and to take suitable remedies. The languor and weakness of souls in the state of abandonment are only illusory appearances which they ought to defy with confidence. God sends them, or permits them in order to give opportunities for the exercise of faith and abandonment which are the true remedies. Without paying the least attention to them, these souls should generously pursue their way, following by their actions and sufferings the order of God, making use without hesitation of the body as though it were a horse on hire, which is intended to be driven until it is worn out. This is better than thinking of health so much as to harm the soul.

"A courageous spirit does much to maintain a feeble body, and one year of a life spent in so noble and generous a manner is of more value than would be a century of care-taking and nervous fears. One ought to be able to show outwardly that one is in a state of grace and goodwill. What is there to be afraid of in fulfilling the divine will? The conduct of one who is upheld and sustained by it should show nothing exteriorly but what is heroic. The terrifying experiences that have to be encountered are really nothing. They are only sent that life may be adorned with more glorious victories. The divine will involves the soul in troubles of every kind, where human prudence can neither see nor imagine any outlet. It then feels all its weakness, and, finding out its shortcomings, is confounded. The divine will then asserts itself in all its power to those who give themselves to it without reserve. It succours them more marvellously than the writers of fiction, in the fertility of their imagination, unravel the intrigues and perils of their imaginary heroes, and bring them to a happy end. With a much more admirable skill, and much more happily, does the divine will guide the soul through the deadly perils and monsters, even through the fires of hell with their demons and sufferings. It raises souls to the heights of heaven, and makes them subjects of histories both real and mystical, more beautiful, and more extraordinary than any invented by the vain imagination of man.

"On then, my soul, through perils and monsters, guided and sustained by that mighty invisible hand of divine Providence. On, without fear, to the end, in peace and joy, and make all the incidents of life occasions of fresh victories. We march under His standard, to fight and to conquer; 'exivit vincens ut vinceret,' 'He went forth conquering that he might conquer' (Apoc. 6:2). . . .

"It is not to cause the loss of our souls that we have so much to do, and to suffer; but that we may furnish matter for that holy writing which is added to day by day" (Caussade, *Abandonment to Divine Providence*, Bk. II, chap, 4, sect. 8).

2. The Direction of the Holy Ghost; Method of Procedure in this State and of Preparation for the Attainment of this Direction

"And, as all the operations which the soul can perform on its own account naturally depend upon sense only, it follows that God is the agent in this state and the soul is the recipient; for the soul behaves only as one that receives and as one in whom these things are being wrought; and God as one that gives and acts and as One that works these things in the soul, giving it spiritual blessings in contemplation, which is Divine love and knowledge in one—that is, a loving knowledge, wherein the soul has not to use its natural acts and meditations, for it can no longer enter into them as before.

"It follows that at this time the soul must be led in a way entirely contrary to the way wherein it was led at first. If formerly it was given material for meditation, and practised meditation, this material must now be taken from it and it must not meditate; for, as I say, it will be unable to do so even though it would, and, instead of becoming recollected, it will become distracted. And if formerly it sought sweetness and love and fervour, and found it, now it must neither seek it nor desire it, for not only will it be unable to find it through its own diligence, but it will rather find aridity, for it turns from the quiet and peaceful blessings which were secretly given to its spirit, to the work that it desires to do with sense; and thus it will lose the one and not obtain the other, since no blessings are now given to it by means of sense as they were formerly. Wherefore in this state the soul must never have meditation imposed upon it, nor must it perform any acts, nor strive after sweetness or fervour; for this would be to set an obstacle in the way of the principal agent, who, as I say, is God. For God secretly and quietly infuses into the soul loving knowledge and wisdom without any intervention of specific acts, although sometimes He specifically produces them in the soul for some length of time. . . .

"And thus, if the soul at this time desires to work on its own account, and to do aught else than remain, quite passively and tranquilly, in the passive and loving awareness whereof we have spoken, . . . it would place an effective impediment in the way of the blessings which God is communicating to it supernaturally in loving knowledge. This comes to pass first of all in the exercise of interior purgation wherein, as we have said above, it suffers, and afterwards in sweetness of love. . . Therefore the soul must be attached to nothing—to no exercise of meditation or reasoning; to no kind of sweetness, whether it be of sense or spirit; and to no other kind of apprehension. For the spirit needs to be so free and so completely annihilated that any kind of thought or meditation or pleasure to which the soul in this state may conceive an attachment would impede and disturb it and would introduce noise into the deep silence

PARTICIPATION IN THE DIVINE ACTIVITY

which it is meet that the soul should observe, according both to sense and to spirit, so that it may hear the deep and delicate voice in which God speaks to the heart in this secret place, as He said through Hosea (2:14), in the utmost peace and tranquillity, so that the soul may listen and hear the words of the Lord God to it, as David says (Ps. 84:9), when in this secret place He speaks this peace.

"When, therefore, it comes to pass that the soul is conscious of being led into silence, and hearkens, it must forget even the exercise of that loving awareness of which I have spoken, so that it may remain free for that which is then desired of it; for it must exercise that awareness only when it is not conscious of being brought into solitude or interior rest or forgetfulness or attentiveness of the spirit, which, in order that it may be understood, is always accompanied by a certain peaceful tranquillity and interior absorption.

"Wherefore, whatever be the time or season, when once the soul has begun to enter into this pure and restful state of contemplation, which comes to pass when it can no longer meditate, and strives not to do so, it must not seek to gather to itself meditations, neither must it desire to find help in spiritual sweetness or delight, but it must stand in complete detachment above all this and its spirit must be completely freed from it, as Habakkuk (2:1) said that he must needs do in order to hear what the Lord should say to him. I will stand upon my watch—he says—and I will fix my step upon my munition, and I will watch to see that which will be said unto me. This is as though he had said: I will raise up my mind above all the operations and all the knowledge that can be comprehended by my senses, and above that which they can keep and retain within themselves: all this I will leave below. And I will fix the step of the munition of my faculties, not allowing them to advance a step as to their own operation, so that through contemplation I may receive that which is communicated to me from God. For we have already said that pure contemplation consists in receiving.

"It is not possible that this loftiest wisdom and language of God, such as is contemplation, can be received save in a spirit that is silent and detached from sweetness and discursive knowledge. For this is what is said by Isaiah, in these words: Whom shall He teach knowledge and whom shall He make to hear its voice? Them that are weaned from the milk—that is, from sweetness and pleasures—and them that are detached from the breasts—that is, from particular apprehensions and knowledge.

"Oh, spiritual soul, take away the motes and the hairs and the mists, and cleanse thine eye, and the bright sun shall shine upon thee, and thou shalt see clearly" (*Living Flame of Love*, stanza 3).

"When a soul has given itself up to the leading of the Holy Spirit, he raises it little by little, and directs it. At the first it knows not whither it is going; but gradually the interior light illuminates it, and enables it to behold all its own actions, and the governance of God therein, so that it has scarcely aught else to do than to let God work in it and by it whatever he pleases; thus it makes wonderful progress" (Lallemant, *Spiritual Doctrine*, IV, art. 1).

"The principal means by which we obtain this direction of the Holy Spirit are the following:

"1. To obey faithfully God's will so far as we know it; much of it is hidden from us, for we are full of ignorance; but God will demand an account at our hands only of the knowledge he has given us; let us make good use of it, and he will give us more. . . .

"2. To renew often the good resolution of following in all things the will of God, and strengthen ourselves in this determination as much as possible.

"3. To ask continually of the Holy Spirit this light and this strength to do the will of God, to bind ourselves to him, and remain his prisoners like St. Paul, who said to the priests of Ephesus, *Being bound in the Spirit, I go to Jerusalem* (Acts 20:22); above all, in every important change of circumstances, to pray God to grant us the illumination of the Holy Spirit, and sincerely protest that we desire nothing else, but only to do his will. After which if he impart to us no fresh light, we may act as heretofore we have been accustomed to act, and as shall appear best for the time being. . . .

"4. Let us watch with care the different movements of our soul. By such attention we shall come gradually to perceive what is of God and what is not. That which proceeds from God in a soul which is subjected to grace, is generally peaceable and calm. That which comes from the devil is violent, and brings with it trouble and anxiety" (*ibid.*, art. 2).

To those who maintain that this interior guidance of the Holy Ghost is destructive of obedience and prudence, Father Lallemant

PARTICIPATION IN THE DIVINE ACTIVITY

replies that "the guidance which we receive from the gifts of the Holy Spirit, far from interfering with obedience, aids and facilitates the practice of it" and that "the Holy Spirit teaches us to consult enlightened persons and to follow the opinion of others."

As to those who complain that they are unable to obtain this direction or, even if they should receive it, they could not recognize it, the same author continues:

"To them we reply, first, that the lights and inspirations of the Holy Spirit which are necessary in order to do good and avoid evil, are never wanting to them, particularly if they are in a state of grace. Secondly, that being altogether exterior as they are, and scarcely ever entering into themselves, examining their consciences only very superficially, and looking only to the outward man, and the faults which are manifest in the eyes of the world, without seeking to discover their secret roots and to become acquainted with their own predominant passions and habits, without investigating the state and disposition of their soul and the movements of their heart, it is no wonder that they have nothing of the guidance of the Holy Spirit, which is wholly interior. How should they know anything of it? They do not even know their interior sins, which are their personal acts produced by their own free will. But they will infallibly acquire the knowledge, if only they bring the necessary dispositions.

"First, let them be faithful in following the light which is given them; it will go on always increasing.

"Secondly, let them clear away the sins and imperfections which, like so many clouds, hide the light from their eyes; they will see more distinctly every day.

"Thirdly, let them not suffer their exterior senses to rove at will, and be soiled by indulgence; God will then open to them their interior senses.

"Fourthly, let them never quit their own interior, if it be possible, or let them return as soon as may be; let them give attention to what passes therein, and they will observe the working of the different spirits by which we are actuated.

"Fifthly, let them lay bare the whole ground of their heart sincerely to their superior or to their spiritual Father. A soul which acts with this openness and simplicity can hardly fail of being favoured with the direction of the Holy Spirit" (*ibid.*, art. 3).

"In every place, O Truth, Thou givest audience to such as consult Thee, and at the same time dost Thou answer all their demands, be they never so diverse. Thou givest them clear answers, but everyone doth not clearly understand Thee. For all men consult Thee about what they will, but they do not always hear what they will by way of answer. He is Thy best servant, who endeavoreth not to hear that from Thee which he desireth but rather desireth that which he heareth from Thee" (St. Augustine, *Confessions*, Bk. X, chap. 26).

"The consolation of the Holy Ghost is very delicate, and the least thing impedes it. It is not given to those who seek human consolations. . . . With good reason does the Holy Ghost greatly desire to be desired. . . . You must realize in your heart that if you are disconsolate and if you call upon the Holy Ghost and He does not come, then it is because as yet you do not have the proper kind of desire for the reception of such a guest. It is not that He is unwilling to come; rather He wishes you to persevere in that desire and by persevering to make yourself deserving of Him, to open wide your heart and to make it grow in confidence. I assure you that no one who thus calls upon Him will be sent away empty of His consolation. . . . Your thoughts, words, and works will call upon the Holy Ghost, and He will come upon you without your knowing how, and you will find that He has taken up His abode in your heart. You will discover in your soul a great joy, a pleasure so wonderful and so complete that you will be taken out of yourself. You will hear the whisper of the Holy Ghost in your ear, and He will show you all that you must do. . . He whose office it is to console will also exhort you, and that same One who comforts you will reprove you when necessary. . . The Holy Ghost is given through the merits of Jesus Christ. Do not cease to ask for Him; do not cease to desire Him with a great desire and be assured that He will come to your soul. He will bring you such consolation as no one will be able to take from you" (*Trat. 1 del Espíritu Santo*, B. Jaun de Avila).

3. DIVINE MOTION AND INSPIRATION

"The spiritual man is not only instructed by the Holy Ghost regarding what he should do, but also his heart is moved. . . . They are said to be acted upon who are moved by some higher instinct. . . . The spiritual man is inclined to act, not from any movement of his own will principally, but by an instinct from the Holy Ghost" (St. Thomas Aquinas, *In Rom.* 8:14).

"It is most especially with regard to souls that abandon themselves entirely to God that the words of St. John are applicable: 'You have no need that any man teach you, as His unction teacheth you of all things' (John 2:20). To know what God demands of them they need only probe their own hearts, and listen to the inspirations of this unction, which interpret the will of God according to circumstances.

"The divine action, concealed though it is, reveals its designs, not through ideas, but intuitively. It shows them to the soul either necessarily, by not permitting any other thing to be chosen but what is actually present, or else by a sudden impulse, a sort of supernatural feeling that impels the soul to act without premeditation; or, in fine, by some kind of inclination or aversion which, while leaving it complete liberty, yet none the less leads it to take or refuse what is presented to it. If one were to judge by appearances, it seems as if it would be a great want of virtue to be swayed and influenced in this manner; and if one were to judge by ordinary rules, there appears a want of regulation and method in such conduct; but in reality it is the highest degree of virtue, and only after having practised it for a long time does one succeed. The virtue in this state is pure virtue; it is, in fact, perfection itself. One is like a musician who combines a perfect knowledge of music with technical skill; he would be so full of his art that, without thinking, all that he performed within its compass would be perfect; and if his compositions were examined afterwards, they would be found in perfect conformity with the prescribed rules. One would then become convinced that he would never succeed better than when, free from the rules that keep genius in fetters when too scrupulously followed, he acted without constraint; and that his impromptus would be admired as chef d'oeuvres by all connoisseurs. Thus the soul, trained for a long time in the science and practice of perfection under the influence of reasonings and methods of which it made use to assist grace, forms for itself a habit of acting in all things by the instincts implanted by God. It then knows that it can do nothing better than what first presents itself, without all those arguments of which it had need formerly. The only thing to be done is to act at random when unable to trust

THE MYSTICAL EVOLUTION

in anything but the workings of grace which cannot mislead it. The effects of grace, visible to watchful eyes, and intelligent minds, are nothing short of marvellous.

"Without method, yet most exact; without rule, yet most orderly; without reflexion, yet most profound; without skill, yet thoroughly well constructed; without effort, yet everything accomplished" (Caussade, *Abandonment to Divine Providence*, Bk. II, chap. 4, sect. 3).

4. THE ASCETICAL AND MYSTICAL STATE

"In the ascetical state it can be said that the soul works alone, although in reality God always works with it. Otherwise the soul could do nothing in the supernatural order, not even pronounce the name of Our Lord. In the mystical state, on the contrary, it seems as if God works alone, but actually the soul abandoned to His activity works better and is more powerful than ever. Some particular action of God causes the gifts of the Holy Ghost to irradiate from the spirit and the heart and He even infuses in the soul new ideas which enable it, if it is faithful, to transfigure its life more rapidly and more perfectly. . .

"It can be said that in the ordinary states, God is at the mercy of man; that is, at the mercy of poverty and weakness. Therefore, in spite of His omnipotence, how poor, weak, and imperfect are the acts which are performed! . . . But in the mystical states, through His love, the roles are reversed. And the more perfect these mystical states, so much the more freely does the creature place itself under the will of God and, as a consequence, so much the more perfectly does it act, since in this stage the action is that of God Himself. The soul freely placed under the will of God: this is what constitutes the mystical state. The more the soul disposes itself by recollection, mortification, and fidelity in the practice of the virtues for the reception of the divine activity, the better will God unfold His operation in it. How many errors there are concerning contemplatives! They are the ones who do the most because they are the ones who are freely actuated by God. They are His true sons because they are animated by His Spirit (Rom. 8:14). That means that the more we abandon ourselves to the divine activity, so much the more truly active and free shall we be" (Sauvé, *Le culte du C. de J.*, élév. 26).

PARTICIPATION IN THE DIVINE ACTIVITY

Special Work of Each of the Gifts

The gift of wisdom enables us to feel and to taste with ineffable delight the sublime truths which faith presents to us veiled in enigmas and which usually appear arid and obscure to the sinner. Happy the soul that is filled with this gift, because by it the soul will be divinely wise and will possess the sum total of all goods, enjoying even now an anticipated glory.[136] Through the gift of wisdom the soul acquires an experimental knowledge of the things of God that is so positive and so secure that these things are impressed on it with the evidence of a tangible fact.[137] But what the soul thus knows and feels is so sublime that ordinarily it must remain mute, must adore in silence, and not profane this gift with human language.

The gift of understanding enables us to penetrate with the eyes of an illumined heart into the august secrets of the Divinity.[138] By it is removed to some extent the veil of enigmas; and the divine truth is disclosed in all its adorable enchantments, which cannot be described. Through this gift are heard the secret words which it is not permitted to man to speak and which are known only by those who receive them.[139]

"Through the gift of understanding," says Father Juan de los Angeles, "men acquire a knowledge so exalted, celestial, and divine and they experience sensations so profound that no doctor can ever attain them by research and his own study. The things by which the human mind is thus illuminated are ineffable. And there is yet more in it: many times the human intellect is so enriched by this knowledge that the soul receives as many hidden and profound meanings

---

[136] Wisd. 7:7-14.

[137] John of St. Thomas, *In Iam IIae*, q.68-70, disp. 18, a.4: "Since the gift of wisdom is not any kind of wisdom, but the wisdom of the Spirit; that is, proceeding from the affection, the spirit, and the giving itself which we experience in ourselves, which is the good will of God . . . , the formal reason by which the gift of wisdom attains . . . to the divine cause is that very knowledge which is had experimentally of God, so far as He is united to us, penetrates us, and gives Himself to us. . . . As a result of this union the soul is, as it were, connaturalized with divine things and discerns them by tasting them."

[138] Lallemant, *Spiritual Doctrine*, IV, chap. 4, art. 2: "That which faith makes us simply believe, the gift of understanding enables us to penetrate more clearly, and in such a manner as, although the obscurity of faith still remains, appears to render evident what faith teaches; so that he who possesses it marvels that some refuse to believe the articles of our belief, or that they can doubt of them."

[139] Apoc. 2:17.

in Sacred Scriptures as there are words, and in as many ways. All these the soul directs and ordains to feed the divine love. . . . The gift of understanding . seeks the interior man, the man who is dead to the senses and to all sense images, totally dead to nature and living in the spirit." [140]

The gift of counsel makes us act in a wonderful manner which disavows the narrow views of human prudence. It makes us triumph, without knowing how, over the cleverness of our enemies and, by means which are least deliberated, it leads us easily and swiftly to the port of salvation.[141]

The gift of fortitude moves us to execute valiantly what counsel dictates and not to spurn works and sacrifices that contribute to the glory of God and the good of souls. To that end, souls will attempt to perform difficult and dangerous enterprises which manifestly surpass their ordinary powers and can be realized only by divine power.[142]

The gift of knowledge enables us to see the hand of God and His

[140] *Vida perfecta*, IV, 6. "The gift of understanding," says Alvarez de Paz (*De inquisitione pacis*, V, II, 4), "is added to human understanding so that thereby it subtly apprehends the things of faith and penetrates them thoroughly. . . . By means of this gift the just man knows himself intimately and is led to contempt of self. He knows God and divine things more purely and more profoundly and is aroused to admiration and love. . . . He sees the perfection of the divine commands and with a mind purged of all error, he discloses the most secret meanings of Scripture. Therefore, in accordance with the verse in the psalm, *Cantate Domino canticum novum*, one could repeat the same psalm a thousand times, for new mysteries are always revealed to us and thus it is as if we chanted a new psalm each time."

[141] Lallemant, *op. cit.*, IV, chap. 4, a.4: "What faith, wisdom, and knowledge teach in general, the gift of counsel applies to particular cases. . . . The vice that is opposed to the gift of counsel is precipitation. . . . Slowness is a fault which is also opposed to the gift of counsel. We ought to employ mature deliberation; but when once our resolution is taken in accordance with the light of the Holy Spirit, we ought to proceed promptly to its execution by the movement of the same Spirit, because if we delay, circumstances change, and opportunities are lost."

Alvarez de Paz, *loc. cit.*, chap. 4, a.4: "The gift of counsel perfects the gift of understanding that it may hold itself amenable to the dictates of God. . . . In regard to particular cases, God teaches the just man and gives him great certitude and much satisfaction. . . . Whence Bonaventure says (*De donis Spiritus Sancti*, chap. 2): 'The counsels of God are most perfect; they suffice for overcoming every evil and for the most perfect attainment of every good, and therefore they lead by the most direct paths.' . . Perfect men, strongly moved by the impulses of love, welcome these things so that what is loved and believed and sought may be more perfectly and more speedily attained. Therefore God, who knows all things best, openly and clearly counsels us in all things pertinent to perfection and provides us with the power to fulfill them."

[142] Terrien, *op. cit.*, I, p. 98: "By the gift of fortitude, the soul, aided by the Holy

loving providence even in the most ordinary events. It discovers in all things the hidden divine meaning which they have in the supernatural order. It makes us rise above the merely human viewpoint and earthly evaluations of those who are insensible, unable to recognize the divine mission which God confides to all things. Further, the gift of knowledge enables us to fulfill our own divine mission. He who possesses this gift in a high degree readily rises from the creature to the Creator, seeing the divine stamp on all the works of God.[143] At the same time he is able to manifest in a fitting manner, by means of symbols and analogies, the supernatural truths, adapting them to all intellects and capabilities and vanquishing almost instinctively any objections that enemies raise against him. This gift characterizes the holy doctors and preachers, who must explain and define accurately the things of faith and distinguish them from things that are not of faith.[144] When united to the gift of counsel, it characterizes the true directors of souls.[145]

Of this gift Father Lallemant says:

The gift of knowledge enables us to see readily and clearly everything that regards our own conduct and that of others. . . . By this gift a preacher knows what he ought to say to his hearers, and what he ought to urge upon them. A director knows the state of the souls he has under his guidance, their spiritual needs, the remedies for their faults, the obstacles they put in the way of their perfection, the shortest and the

---

Ghost, faces with invincible confidence labors, punishments, and even death itself when the glory of God so demands."

[143] See Caussade, *Abandonment to Divine Providence*, Bk. II, chap. 1.

[144] See IIa IIae, q.9, a.2, ad 1um: "Hence to know what one ought to believe, belongs to the gift of knowledge, but to know in themselves the very things we believe, by a kind of union with them, belongs to the gift of wisdom."

[145] Alvarez de Paz, *op. cit.*, II, chap. 4: "The gift of knowledge is necessary for understanding: 1. that one may understand the things of faith through creatures by reason of the proportionate likenesses and yet, not adhering to them, may transcend to the contemplation of God; 2. that one may know the greatest perfection of each virtue, may hold all the virtues and their acts in high esteem, and never cease to practice them interiorly and to beg for them. This knowledge does not puff up, but edifies, because it is not different from charity. . . . Whence Rupert, explaining the text, 'Knowledge puffeth up; but charity edifieth' (I Cor. 8:1), says: 'He did not wish his statement to be understood in the sense that he opposes knowledge to charity, but that he adds it to charity. For knowledge (without charity) puffs up; but charity (with knowledge) edifies.' So it is that knowledge . . . of holy things is given to the just that they may the more perfectly know what things are to be done and what avoided and thus day by day they may live more holily and more perfectly."

surest road by which to conduct them safely; how he must console or mortify them, what God is working in them, and what they ought to do on their part in order to cooperate with God and fulfill his designs. A superior knows in what way he ought to govern his inferiors.

They who have the largest share of this gift are the most enlightened in all knowledge of this kind. Wonderful things are disclosed to them with respect to the practice of the virtues. They discover therein degrees of perfection unknown to others. They perceive at a glance whether actions are inspired by God and conformable to his designs; let them deviate ever so little from the ways of God, they discern it at once. They remark imperfections where others cannot see them; they are not liable to be deceived in their opinions, neither are they apt to let themselves be surprised by illusions with which the whole world is filled. If a scrupulous soul applies to them, they know what to say to remove its scruples. If they have to make an exhortation, whether to monks or to nuns, thoughts will occur to them suited both to the spiritual needs of the religious themselves, and to the spirit of their order. If difficulties of conscience are proposed to them, they will give an admirable solution. Ask them for the reason of their reply, they cannot tell you, because they know it without reasoning, by a light superior to all reason.[146]

The gift of piety prompts us to consider the things of God or the things that lead us to God with that same interest and affection with which we look upon things of the family. It teaches us to treat God with the filial and childlike affection, confidence, and simplicity of a most loving child for the sweetest of fathers; or of a bride for her beloved. This is the gift that suggests to enamored souls those sweet liberties and noble audacities which are foreign to the worldly and which please God the more because they are prompted by His Spirit of adoption.[147]

[146] *Op. cit.*, IV, chap. 4, art. 3. This is the gift which was so admirable in St. Teresa as a teacher and director of souls. This is the gift that enabled her to recognize and make known the ways of the spirit and to adapt them to the capacity of all. Other great souls, like St. Catherine of Siena, Blessed Angela of Foligno, and St. John of the Cross, are especially renowned for the gifts of wisdom and understanding, by which they soar to such great heights that they are lost from view. And so it is that, though they are more admirable, they are often less admired.

[147] Gardeil, *The Gifts of the Holy Ghost*, p. 53: "Filial piety toward God is one of the characteristic traits of Christianity. . . . Paganism and philosophy have honored the Creator, the Judge, Providence. We adore the consubstantial Father of our Lord Jesus Christ, who is also, by adoption, our Father; and we call Him in all truth, 'Our Father who art in Heaven.'"

PARTICIPATION IN THE DIVINE ACTIVITY

The gift of fear of the Lord, the beginning of heavenly wisdom, is ignored by the mundane and never found in the slothful and the luxury loving. It leads to the practice of great austerities for the purpose of completely rooting out evil inclinations and of avoiding whatever may be even slightly offensive in the eyes of the heavenly Father.[148] The soul possessing this gift seeks at all cost to destroy immediately the body of sin and to live ever protected by the mortification of Jesus Christ so that even the mortal flesh manifests the life of the Savior.[149] Therefore, with great fervor it seeks to be crucified and transfixed with the nails of holy fear, that it may not be the victim of the divine wrath. "Pierce Thou my flesh with fear: for I am afraid of Thy judgments" (Ps. 118:120).

1. MANIFESTATION OF THE GIFTS

The most precious gifts thus enumerated by Isaias in the order of descending perfection and appropriately attributed to the Savior, are usually manifested in us in the reverse order, according to the greater practical importance or necessity which they have in the Christian life. They begin with fear, which inspires an aversion to evil in order to ensure a better practice of the good. Fear causes a detestation of arrogance, pride, and deceit (Prov. 8:13), in order to establish, on the basis of humility and evangelical simplicity, the sublime science of self-knowledge, which leads directly to God and the faithful practice of all the Christian virtues (*ibid.*, 14). Knowing well our own nothingness, we shall know how to despise it as we ought and to appreciate better the divine Allness. We shall desire to root out of ourselves whatever separates us from God, our highest Good, and to purify ourselves entirely, to practice the divine commandments,

---

[148] This holy fear is not destroyed by perfect charity, but it is increased and perfected by it. The saints trembled and were horrified at the sight of sin, or even at the mere idea or mention of it, for this monster, this destroyer of holiness, is in open conflict with the divine attributes. The more the saints were deified, the more they understood and knew from experience the great aversion which God has for sin. This it is that made them tremble, struck them with horror, and impelled them to seek reparations on seeing in themselves or their neighbor the slightest thing which might drag them down or cause a division between themselves and the highest Good.

"When I hear anyone speaking of sins," said Ven. Olier (*Esprit.*, I, 206), "I feel certain reactions which crush and annihilate me and which it is impossible to express."

[149] Rom. 6:6; 8:13; II Cor. 4:10.

and thus be able to attain a happy union with the God of all holiness and justice.

Then the gift of piety suggests the means most efficacious, the devotions most tender and fruitful to please the heavenly Father, the divine Spouse, and the sweet Guest and Consoler of the soul.

The gift of knowledge teaches the science of the saints, which consists in conforming ourselves entirely to the divine will and wholeheartedly venerating the dispositions of Providence, by which all things are directed for our benefit. It shows us the true path of wisdom and leads us by the path of justice so that when we run we shall not meet a stumbling block.[150]

The gift of fortitude prompts the soul to overcome the greatest difficulties, so that it will not refrain from works or hardships when the charity of Christ urges them.[151] It ignites the flame of zeal for the glory of God and the salvation of souls. It is this gift which prompts missioners to propagate the kingdom of God and His justice in spite of all perils. It likewise prompts devoted souls to persevere in the way of prayer in spite of aridity and difficulties and the counsels of worldly prudence, false humility, and cowardice.[152]

---

[150] Prov. 4:11 f.

[151] See II Cor. 5:14.

[152] Lallemant, *op. cit.*, IV, chap. 4, art. 6: "We must be courageous, then, and fearless in the service of God, that we may advance in perfection and become capable of doing great things. Without the gift of fortitude no notable progress can be made in the spiritual life. Mortification and prayer, which are its principal exercises, demand a generous determination to overcome all the difficulties to be encountered in the way of the spirit, which is so opposed to our natural inclinations. ... As the gift of counsel accompanies that of fortitude and directs it, leading us to undertake great things, so also human prudence and timidity keep each other company, mutually supporting one another, and suggesting reasons in self-justification.

"They who are guided only by human prudence are timid beyond measure. This fault is very common in superiors, and makes them, through fear of committing mistakes, fail in doing half the good they might do.

"A thousand apprehensions hinder us every moment, and prevent our advancing in the way of God, and doing a vast amount of good we should do if we followed the light of the gift of counsel, and possessed the courage which springs from the gift of fortitude; but there is too much in us of human views, and everything alarms us."

To this timidity is joined false humility, which closes one's eyes to the divine benefits and thus leads one to ingratitude, imprudence, and cowardice. True prudence, on the other hand, is generous, discreet, and magnanimous. "We may think it humility," says St. Teresa (*Life*, chap. 10), "not to realize that the Lord is bestowing gifts upon us. Let us understand very, very clearly how this matter stands. God gives us these gifts for no merit of ours. Let us be grateful to His Majesty for them, for unless we recognize that we are receiving them, we shall not be

PARTICIPATION IN THE DIVINE ACTIVITY

The gift of counsel inspires us with the means of realizing great enterprises in a divine manner and teaches us how to proceed with superhuman facility and prudence. Finally, when we have chosen, so far as our state and condition permit, the "better part" or the whole (the contemplative life or the fullness of the apostolic life), and when the eyes of the heart have been purified and the spiritual senses have been refined, then we shall begin to discover the divine secrets and taste the infinite sweetness of God through the two sublime gifts of understanding and wisdom.[153]

2. EXCELLENCE OF THE GIFTS

The gifts of the Holy Ghost exceed the infused virtues both on the part of the principal mover and director and on the part of the mode and norm of activity. They are for man, in his relations with

---

aroused to love Him. And it is a most certain thing that, if we remember all the time that we are poor, the richer we find ourselves, the greater will be the profit that comes to us and the more genuine our humility. Another mistake is for the soul to be afraid, thinking itself incapable of receiving great blessings, with the result that, when the Lord begins to grant them, it grows fearful, thinking that it is sinning through vainglory."

In another place (chap. 13) the saint adds: "His Majesty desires and loves courageous souls if they have no confidence in themselves but walk in humility; and I have never seen any such person hanging back on this road, nor any soul that, under the guise of humility, acted like a coward, go as far in many years as the courageous soul can in a few. I am astounded at how much can be done on this road if one has the courage to attempt great things; . . . He (the devil) tries at once to persuade us that all these habits of devotion will kill us, or ruin our health; he even makes us afraid that if we weep we shall go blind. . . . As my own health is so bad, I was always impeded by my fears, and my devotion was of no value at all until I resolved not to worry any more about my body or my health; and now I trouble about them very little. For it pleased God to reveal to me this device of the devil; . . . and since I have been less self-regarding and indulgent my health has been very much better."

[153] Lallemant, *op. cit.*, IV, chap. 4, art. 1: "The gift of wisdom is such knowledge of God, His attributes, and mysteries, as is full of savour. The understanding only conceives and penetrates. Wisdom judges and compares; it enables us to see causes, reasons, fitnesses; it represents to us God, His greatness, His beauty, His perfections, His mysteries, as infinitely adorable and worthy of love; and from this knowledge there results a delicious taste, which sometimes even extends to the body. . . . Thus it is to the gift of wisdom that spiritual sweetnesses and consolations and sensible graces belong. . . . This taste of wisdom is sometimes so perfect that a person who is possessed of it, on hearing two propositions, the one formed by reasoning, the other inspired by God, will at once distinguish between the two. . . . At first, divine things are insipid, and it is with difficulty that we can relish them, but in course of time they become sweet, and so full of delicious flavour, that we taste them with pleasure, even to the extent of feeling nothing but disgust for everything else. On the other hand, the things of earth, which flatter the senses, are at first pleasant and delicious, but in the end we find only bitterness in them."

THE MYSTICAL EVOLUTION

the divine Paraclete, what the moral virtues are to the will with respect to natural reason, and what the infused virtues are to the same reason illumined by faith.

In regard to the simple virtues, whether acquired or infused, reason itself, guided by its own lights or aided by those of the Gospel, is the regulating norm of all things. It directs and orientates even those lights and energies which the Holy Ghost secretly imparts. But with the gifts the divine Spirit Himself is constituted as the sweet Master of the soul with all its faculties, forces, and virtues. He becomes the supreme Director who subordinates and governs reason itself, illumined now with infused prudence, so that without any human considerations to disconcert it, it rises in its flight to the serene regions of eternal light.

Even when supernaturalized by grace and the virtues, the soul cannot perfectly attain to the life of glory, since it does not yet fully possess the divine status. To arrive at this life, it is necessary, at least from time to time, that the Spirit of God be constituted as director and governor of the soul. He must communicate to us certain instincts or divine impulses with their corresponding energies and powers, to the end that we may be able to cooperate divinely with His activity.

Hence the imponderable excellence of the gifts over the virtues. They far surpass the virtues and perfect them. They even enrich, evaluate, and direct charity itself, which never dies but is always aflame with the brightness of the Holy Ghost, who pours it into our hearts.[154] When holy souls are introduced to the mystical wine cellar and inebriated with the infinite sweetness of eternal Wisdom, then they see how charity is "set in order." [155]

[154] Gardeil, *op. cit.*, p. 21: "We now see what charity is with the Gifts. It is not that gentle warmth, that fervor of the virtues which secretly insinuates itself into our moral organism and which takes the human forms of our reason and love. It is the blazing center, making its envelope glow, radiant as the sun. It is the light of the Face of our God resplendent in the sevenfold ray which is His own. Truly it is beautiful! It is the very brilliance of Thy countenance, O Holy Spirit! This light rests upon us. 'There is signed above us the light of your countenance, O Lord!' Not yet lighting our forehead, nor fascinating our gaze as in the Beatific Vision, it envelops our heart. Like a sun whose rays come from it ceaselessly, our heart is actuated and renewed by the action of the Holy Ghost, who enlightens our whole interior world, our truth, love, hope, justice, passions, all, that God may reign over all, directly and according to His own method. 'That God may be all in all things.'"
[155] Cant. 2:4.

PARTICIPATION IN THE DIVINE ACTIVITY

If the gifts enable us to perform divinely heroic works, they also enable us to do with greater perfection and zeal even the most ordinary and lowly tasks. The gifts empower us to perform other works also, for which, absolutely speaking, the virtues alone would suffice although in that case they would not be done under such circumstances or in such a manner as is proper to the children of God, which consists in being moved by His Spirit. He alone can lead us happily to the port of salvation, to full union and the deifying transformation. Therefore this transformation will not be realized in us unless we enter fully into the mystical state. Then it is that "we all beholding the glory of the Lord with open face, are transformed into the same very image from glory to glory, as by the Spirit of the Lord." [156]

Together with the infused virtues the Holy Ghost secretly gives us the power to work out our salvation by performing acts worthy of eternal life; but even though He moves us to work, yet we work in our own manner and as if through our own initiative, deliberating and pondering the various motives in order to proceed prudently. Through His gifts, He anticipates our deliberation; and with Him directing us, we work with greater perfection and facility and even at times without clearly adverting to what we are doing, but proceeding as if by the intuition of instinct.[157] Through the virtues we connaturally perform salutary actions and we work as good "ordinary" Christians or children; but through the gifts we receive and connaturally follow the divine impulses or movements, and then we work as "spiritual" Christians or adults. "The spiritual man," says St. Thomas, "is inclined to a thing not so much from a movement of his own will principally, but from an impulse of the Holy Ghost." [158]

So we see that with simple Christian prudence man still acts as the principal cause and in a manner almost always predominantly human. Although he has assimilated this virtue and uses it as his own, yet it fails him because of his own defects and it becomes vitiated by the evil inclinations of his nature and his flesh. But in the gift of counsel it is the Holy Ghost who moves and directs without

---

[156] See II Cor. 3:18.
[157] Rom. 8:26 f.
[158] *In Rom. 8:14;* lect. 3.

THE MYSTICAL EVOLUTION

taking account of human considerations. Then it is that a man works divinely, carried on by an inspiration or impulse from God.

To understand and follow to advantage the lofty explanations of a truly learned professor, a greater intellectual preparation is necessary than for understanding an ordinary teacher. In much the same way, if we are to be profitable disciples of this sovereign Spirit of truth, we need a divine preparation that will be adequate to His operations. We must be made truly spiritual, pneumatic, if we are to understand His mysterious language and hear those very delicate whisperings by which, with divine unction, He illumines us and teaches us all truth.[159]

This preparation, which will enable us to say with the Psalmist, "I shall hear what the Lord, my God, says to me," consists in recollection, guarding of the senses, vigilance in procuring perfect purity of heart, and the alienation of every sort of delight and consolation. In this way a person acquires the science of the saints and becomes facile in the use of those mystical gifts by which he becomes truly spiritual and divine in his manner of working, knowing, loving, and appraising all things.[160] Then with this increasing facility and the ability to experience the motions and inspirations of God, the faculties are given to us whereby we can put them into effect.

The carnal man and even the purely rational man will not be able to understand these things. They will appear enigmatic and foolish to such men, as does the most profound explanation of higher mathe-

---

[159] John 14:26; 16:13; I John 2:20, 27. Caussade, *op. cit.*, II, chap. 8: "We are not well instructed save by means of the words which God expressly pronounces to us. The knowledge of God is not learned in books. . . . What He teaches us is that which is taking place within us at each instant. . . . What is known perfectly is that which is learned from experience in suffering and action. This is the school of the Holy Ghost who speaks words of life to the soul and from this fount we must draw whatever we have to give to others. Only by virtue of this experience is what we read and see converted into true divine knowledge. . . . In order to be learned in this theology of the heart, which is entirely practical and empirical, we must carefully attend to what God tells us at each moment. We must not heed what others say, but let us heed what is taking place within ourselves."

[160] Isa. 28:9: "Whom shall he teach knowledge? and whom shall he make to understand the hearing? them that are weaned from the milk, that are drawn away from the breasts."

PARTICIPATION IN THE DIVINE ACTIVITY

matics to a school boy. They understand nothing and can appreciate nothing. They consider these things so much folly because they lack the necessary understanding to perceive them.[161]

But the spiritual man understands and worthily appreciates the things of the Spirit because he has the sense for perceiving and investigating them. So it is that he is severely judged by those who are not also spiritual men.[162] Therefore we find certain superiors who, though prudent according to worldly standards, do not strive to "put on Jesus Christ" so that they may understand and judge things according to Him. Instead of encouraging and guiding their more fervent subjects, they do whatever they can to paralyze and mislead them. They foolishly contradict these fervent souls in order to force them to resist what actually are vital impulses of the divine Consoler. Not otherwise can they do who, ignorant of the science of God's ways, seek to judge everything from the viewpoint of human prudence.[163]

But those who have ears to hear, hear what the Spirit says to the Churches.[164] The faithful sheep of Christ know His voice and follow Him and receive from Him eternal life, even in spite of the mercenary shepherds who abandon them or do not know how to guard and instruct them.[165]

3. PNEUMATIC PSYCHOLOGY AND THE ORGANISM OF THE CHURCH

An understanding of this mysterious supernatural psychology is of the greatest importance to pastors and directors of souls. Therefore, that we may examine the imperceptible transition which takes place between the phase of the beginner (the purely rational man, who acts entirely according to the norms of human reason) and the definitive and perfect state of the totally spiritual man (the pneumatic, who proceeds divinely according to the norms and direction of the Holy Ghost), it is well for us to consider again the symbol wherein the Church is presented as an organism. In this symbol each

---

[161] Ps. 91:7: "The senseless man shall not know: nor will the fool understand these things."
[162] See I Cor. 2:12-16.
[163] Apoc. 3:22.
[164] See Lallemant, *Spiritual Doctrine*, IV, chap. 1, art. 3.
[165] John 10:1-28.

of the faithful is represented as an elementary organ with its own autonomous life, yet subordinated to the higher life of the whole body from which it receives, as it were, a sort of new existence of a superior and divine order.

Each organic cell in a body maintains a certain autonomy in the type of life proper to itself with the functions indispensable to its growth and conservation. Yet it is not thereby prevented from being subordinated to the higher life of the organism as a whole. The whole organic life of the animal is subordinated to the sensitive life, whereas in man, both must be subjected to the rational life under penalty of serious conflicts. The same subjection takes place in regard to the rational life proper to each of the faithful when they are incorporated with Jesus Christ and receive the superior life of His Spirit, who is the soul of the Church in which the faithful are as so many organic cells.

When any of the cells breaks away from its neighbors and attends to its own proper activities, or when it takes to itself too much initiative and refuses to accept the influence of the higher directive organs and the superior life of the whole organism, then a lack of balance ensues and the cell gradually loses that higher life and soon dies of anemia.

On the other hand, if properly subordinated, it shares fully in the integral life. Although it must sacrifice some things for the others, it is by that very fact the gainer, for it will receive benefits in the proportion that it makes those sacrifices. Thus, the more closely it is correlated and the more faithfully it follows the promptings of that higher life, so much the more life does it enjoy and so much the more vigorous does it become.

Something similar takes place in the faithful who live as members of Christ. The more unselfishly they sacrifice themselves for their neighbors and the more they deny themselves and their own inclinations in order to follow the impulses of the Holy Ghost, the more intensely they live the divine life and the more happiness they find in that sweetness and peace which they enjoy in union with the Spirit. However enslaved they may appear, living, as they do, bound by the sweet chains of the love of God, they know that they have recovered their true liberty, which consists in breaking asunder the

PARTICIPATION IN THE DIVINE ACTIVITY

bonds of the vices and passions which dominate and assault them.[166] But when they try to work with false independence, following their own inclinations, or when they are guided by the narrow outlook of human prudence, they cut off the flow of sweet impulses from the Holy Ghost. By afflicting and resisting Him, they gradually extinguish the life they have received from Him.

Together with that life, the Holy Ghost gives them the necessary faculties and powers to preserve and increase it by its corresponding acts. These faculties and powers are the virtues and graces which strengthen and perfect the natural potencies so as to raise them to the supernatural order and to constitute both together as one principle of action. Nevertheless it is still human reason which directs all activity, and the soul has no clear realization that it is producing acts of another order and that it is animated by a higher principle. Such is the "spiritual childhood" in which we live by the Holy Ghost without noting His vivifying presence or without being conscious of the life we are living. This life will remain imperfect as long as it is lived in that human manner. But if the soul makes good use of the faculties and powers it has received, if it observes the commandments faithfully, if it endeavors to practice the virtues with all possible perfection, and is solicitous to preserve the union of the Spirit in the bonds of peace, as faith teaches, then it will begin to grow spiritually. The cognitive potencies of the spiritual life will begin to develop; and, once it has arrived at the "age of reason" and has been renewed in the spirit of its mind, the soul will acquire a consciousness of what it is and the life it is living.

Thus, working in accord with faith and the other infused virtues, one grows in all things according to Jesus Christ. The gradual purification of the heart fosters the good use of the gifts of the Holy Ghost which formerly were imprisoned, as it were, under the imperfections

---

[166] Lallemant, *op. cit.*, IV, chap. 3, art. 2: "It is by the gifts of the Holy Spirit that the saints succeed at last in freeing themselves from the slavery of creatures; the plenteous effusion of these heavenly gifts effacing from the mind the esteem, the remembrance, the thought of earthly things, and banishing from the heart all affection and desire for them, so that they think as it were, only of what they will, and are affected only by what they will, and in such degree as they will. They feel no longer the importunity of distractions, nor that disquietude and excitement which troubled them before; and all their powers being perfectly regulated, they enjoy a sovereign peace and the liberty of the children of God."

of self-initiative, just as the rational life of an infant is restricted, so to speak, by the imperfections of organic and sensitive life. By the time the soul arrives at "spiritual maturity," where the things of the Spirit are tasted, experienced, and recognized,[167] the gifts have already attained a development sufficient to permit the soul to experience within itself what Christ felt [168] and to proceed in all things as one of His worthy members. That is to say, it will then be a "spiritual" man and not carnal; it will no longer be an infant in Christ, requiring the milk of consolation and sensible fervors because as yet it is incapable of higher things.[169]

Accustomed as they are to be guided by their own taste, opinions, or caprices, the "infants" must be drawn to God through the delights which the Spirit of piety and wisdom grants to them and accommodates to their delicate palate. Although these sensible fervors proceed from the gifts, the souls themselves must frequently moderate such consolations because as long as these souls remain "infants" they will follow the defective norm of reason and the direction of simple Christian prudence.

So the gifts first appear after the manner of hidden instincts or blind impulses that must be well regulated and tested. Later, by use and development, they are changed into clear intuitions, and then it is clearly manifest from whom they come and whither they are leading.[170] Then, when the heart has been purified by the fire of charity and cleansed of all vices and attachments that would impede the right use of the gifts, the Holy Ghost begins to take in His own hands the reins of interior self-government. He then constitutes Himself the director, master, and regulator of our spiritual life; and, that the soul may not resist Him, He gives clear testimony to it, as a child of God, that He Himself animates, rules, teaches, moves, and leads it surely to the glory of the Father. "Blessed is the man whom Thou shalt instruct, O Lord: and shalt teach him out of Thy law" (Ps. 93:12).

This it is that properly constitutes the mystical state. On the other hand, that state is spiritual childhood wherein the virtues work

---

[167] Rom. 8:5; I Cor. 2:12-16; Col. 3:2.
[168] Phil. 2:5.
[169] See I Cor. 3:1 f.; 13:11; Heb. 5:12-15.
[170] See IIa IIae, q.171, a.5.

PARTICIPATION IN THE DIVINE ACTIVITY

principally but as yet very imperfectly. The manner of working is entirely connatural or aided only by incipient gifts. These latter begin to work as such under our own guidance. In the ascetical state the Spirit is still held in restraint.[171]

Through our own fault, the majority of us Christians never leave this spiritual childhood, if we ever even enter into it. We have the obligation of growing in all things through Him who is the Head, Christ; but we remain inert. We have buried His precious talents, which are the gifts of the Holy Ghost. These talents have been given to us so that by their use we may be able to produce glorious fruits of life. Therefore, if we do not throttle them with selfish affections, defects, and evil inclinations, they will continue to multiply and secretly prompt us to undertake a better life in which the divine Spirit will be our guide and master.[172]

If they truly seek God alone with fervent prayer and purity of heart, with quieted passions and appetites, all those who, with the aid of ordinary grace, have purified their faculties and senses and have been able to exercise and consolidate the Christian virtues, will experience, if not the voice of God, which speaks to the heart in a mysterious tongue, then at least the hidden impulses of the Spirit, who sweetly calls them to a more perfect interior life. He will make them thirst to drink at the fountain of living water and eager to appear before the face of God (Ps. 41:3). And if they do not resist or displease Him, they will surely be able to enter into the place of the wonderful tabernacle (*ibid.*, 5). "Who shall ascend into the mountain of the Lord: or who shall stand in His holy place? The innocent

---

[171] Juan de los Angeles, *Diálogos*, X, sect. 11: "Beginners in virtue and recollection are like infants to God who dwells in them as the soul within their souls. They are like babies securely held in the arms and wrapped tightly in swaddling-clothes and blankets. Yet as the soul gradually grows and begins to give itself entirely to the divine Spouse, He also is increased, grows, and takes complete control of the soul. He is the soul of the soul, the spirit of the spirit, and the life of the life; and soon there is verified that statement of St. Paul that Christ lived more in him than he himself did."

[172] Isa. 63:14. Lallemant, *op. cit.*, IV, chap. 3, art. 1: "The gifts do not subsist in the soul without charity; and in proportion as grace increases, they increase also. Hence it is that they are so very rare, and that they never attain a high degree of excellence without a fervent and perfect charity; venial sins and the slightest imperfections keeping them, as it were, bound down and preventing them from acting. Thus the way to excel in prayer is to excel in these gifts; and indeed the most sublime contemplation is scarcely anything different, for it is by penetrating deeply into supernatural knowledge that the soul falls into ecstasy and swoons away."

in hands, and clean of heart. . . . He shall receive a blessing from the Lord, and mercy from God his Savior." [173]

That they may more completely abandon themselves to Him and more faithfully follow these divine impulses and not suppress them, even unwittingly, the Holy Spirit deprives more advanced souls of the ordinary lights. Then, in this terrifying obscurity and barrenness in which they find themselves during the painful night of the senses, they see and realize their absolute inability to direct themselves as is necessary. As a result they deliver themselves without reserve to His direction and government.

Those who are thus animated and acted upon by the divine Spirit are the true children of God, the children of the Spirit, as Blessed Angela de Foligno calls them.[174] Those who in no way possess Him are strangers to God, for they are not of Jesus Christ.[175] And those who, though they possess the Spirit of filial adoption, keep Him imprisoned within themselves and use Him according to their own desires without ever letting themselves be guided and governed by Him, live by the Spirit, but they do not walk according to the Spirit.[176] They are still children in virtue, infants in Christ, who must be treated with a certain delicacy. They are as yet carnal and not spiritual for they are still filled with human considerations, passions, and miseries.[177] As yet they do not know or feel or taste the things of the Spirit and they are much exposed to peril, for they mind the things of the flesh.[178] Their delicate stomachs seek sensible consolations which are like the milk of infancy. They cannot tolerate, nor do they even try to digest, the solid food of perfect manhood: total abandonment to the hands of the Father, to be treated by Him as was His Son, who said: "I have meat to eat, which you know not.

---

[173] Ps. 23:2-5. Says St. Mary Magdalen of Pazzi (*op. cit.*, I, chap. 33): "Sin prevents the soul from hearing Thy voice, O Lord, and closes the doors of faith. . . . We receive Thy true knowledge from the Spirit of purity who cleanses souls. . . . As soon as they are purified from their vices, not only do they hear Thy words, but they even anticipate Thy wishes and instinctively know what Thou dost desire them to do in atonement for past offenses. They hear Thy voice say to their hearts: Cleanse thyself; be pure."

[174] See "Angela de Foligno," by Paul Doncœur, *Dictionnaire de spiritualité*, (Paris, 1937).

[175] Rom. 8:9-14.

[176] Gal. 5:25.

[177] See I Cor. 3:1 f.; Heb. 5:12-14. See also St. Catherine of Siena, *Letter 106*.

[178] Rom. 8:5 f.

PARTICIPATION IN THE DIVINE ACTIVITY

... My meat is to do the will of Him that sent Me, that I may perfect His work." [179] Since they do not understand the hidden delights of the Cross of Christ, they cannot fully enjoy that true peace and felicity which spiritual souls enjoy in the shadow of this new tree of life. If we live in the Spirit, we shall strive to proceed entirely according to the Spirit, and we shall enjoy His most precious gifts, living as men freed from the law of sin.[180]

Fruits of the Holy Ghost and the Beatitudes

From grace, as from a divine seed sown in the soil of our souls, proceeds the glorious tree of our sanctification, which gives fruits of eternal life. A just man is like a tree planted near a stream of running waters. He is mystically irrigated by the continual influence, manifest or hidden, of the vivifying Spirit, the true fountain of living water who, springing up in our hearts, invigorates the soul and all its faculties. From Him, as the principle of life, and from His sanctifying grace through which we are renewed, justified, and deified, the virtues and gifts burst forth, according to St. Bonaventure, like so many branches which proceed from the same trunk. These virtues and gifts vivify, transfigure, and deify all our faculties so that they may produce fruits of true justice, works worthy of the children of God. Such are the precious fruits of the Holy Ghost.

Our Lord Jesus Christ has chosen us and placed us in the mystical body of His Church that we may prosper and bear fruit and that our fruit may remain.[181] In these few words is contained the whole of the spiritual life, which should be ever increasing, developing, progressing, and made more copious. Only thus can we produce more abundant and exquisite fruits of life that will be at once a pledge and a prelude of eternal happiness.

"But the path of the just, as a shining light, goeth forward and increaseth even to perfect day." [182] He who does not grow, becomes paralyzed and degenerated. He who never bears fruit is like the barren fig tree which, although it bore leaves before its time, was cursed by the Savior. He whose fruits do not ripen, but always re-

---

[179] John 4:32, 34.
[180] Gal. 5:16-25.
[181] John 15:16.
[182] Prov. 4:18.

main unpalatable, never reaches the point where God finds delight in him; and for that reason he will not enjoy true happiness.

On the other hand, "Blessed is the man who hath not walked in the counsel of the ungodly, nor stood in the way of sinners, nor sat in the chair of pestilence. But his will is in the law of the Lord, and on His law he shall meditate day and night. And he shall be like a tree which is planted near the running waters; which shall bring forth its fruit in due season. And his leaf shall not fall off: and all whatsoever he shall do shall prosper." [183] "Blessed is the man that shall continue in wisdom, and that shall meditate in His justice, and in his mind shall think of the all seeing eye of God. He that considereth her ways in his heart and hath understanding in her secrets." [184] Blessed is the man "that is found without blemish: and that hath not gone after gold, nor put his trust in money nor in treasures. . . . Therefore are his goods established in the Lord." [185] In a word, the man who fears to displease God in the slightest matter and is impelled with a strong eagerness to fulfill the divine will in all things is happily on his way to the fatherland. Since this holy fear is already the beginning of true wisdom, which accomplishes all things, he who possesses it will produce copious fruits of blessing and will live full of glory and spiritual riches.[186]

The fruits of life and pledges of blessing and happiness are innumerable. Therefore we ought to bear the fruit of good works in every way so that we may walk worthily of God and please Him in all things. Thus we shall grow in divine knowledge [187] and become blessed and immaculate, walking according to the law of God and seeking Him with our whole heart.[188] These fruits can all be reduced to the twelve principal ones which the Apostle enumerates: "But the fruit of the Spirit is charity, joy, peace, patience, benignity, goodness, longanimity, mildness, faith, modesty, continency, chastity." [189]

By means of the fruits the salutary influence of the Spirit of God

[183] Ps. 1:1-4.
[184] Ecclus. 14:22-27.
[185] *Ibid.*, 31:8-11.
[186] Ps. 111:1-3; 118:1 f.; Prov. 1:7; Ecclus. 1:16; Wisd. 7:11.
[187] Col. 1:10.
[188] Ps. 118:1 f.
[189] Gal. 5:22 f.

PARTICIPATION IN THE DIVINE ACTIVITY

is discernible in our actions. They also enable us to distinguish true from false spirits, to distinguish the faithful servants sent by Jesus Christ from the hypocritical impostors who come in sheeps' garments but are wolves beneath. "By their fruits you will know them." [190] So it is that St. John firmly admonishes us not to give credence too readily to any spirit, inspiration, or impulse we may feel, but to prove it to see whether it comes from God. These things are proved or tested by the fruits they produce. If they cause turbulence, envy, discord, insubordination, disquiet, death-producing sorrow,[191] dejection, harshness, immodest volubility, and the like, then they are in reality carnal, mundane, or diabolical, and not divine.

The breathing and the moisture of the Holy Ghost make the just man produce all his mystical fruits. "And he showed me a river of water of life, clear as crystal, proceeding from the throne of God and of the Lamb. In the midst of the street thereof and on both sides of the river, was the tree of life, bearing twelve fruits, yielding its fruits every month, and the leaves of the tree [symbol of the vigor and luxuriance which the spirit of prayer communicates] were for the healing of the nations." [192] These fruits, says St. Thomas, are "any virtuous deeds in which one delights." [193]

Just as in the sensible order, the flowers of a tree, however beautiful they may be, would be useless if they were not converted into fruit, so in the spiritual order, the same can be said of the beautiful flowers of the virtues and holy desires that are not ultimately converted into the fruits of good works. It is only then that the mystical bride truly consecrates her whole heart to the divine Spouse.[194] So, although the Apostle seems to enumerate the virtues of charity, peace, meekness, and so on, among the fruits, yet he understands by them their perfect exercise and the works of life which they produce.

If these works are so perfect, abundant, and permanent that one is found to be in the state of producing them with facility and perfection, then they are so joyful and delightful that they constitute, as

[190] Matt. 7:15.
[191] See II Cor. 7:10.
[192] Apoc. 22:1 f.
[193] See Ia IIae, q. 70, a. 2.
[194] Cant. 7:12 f.: "Let us see if the vineyard flourish, if the flowers be ready to bring forth fruits, . . . there will I give thee my breasts. . . . In our gates are all fruits: the new and the old, my beloved, I have kept for thee."

it were, a prelude to eternal happiness. Although they may be performed at the cost of annoyance and tribulation, yet they produce in us an ineffable joy to which nothing in this life can be compared. They are truly comparable to the joys of heaven. "For that which is at present momentary and light of our tribulation, worketh for us above measure exceedingly an eternal weight of glory." [195]

The permanent sweetness of the most exquisite fruits of the virtues and gifts constitutes the various states of true happiness obtainable on earth, and these states are rightly called the beatitudes. The beatitudes are most precious fruits in regard to this life, and incomparable flowers which presage the life of glory.[196]

1. COMPARISON OF THE GIFTS WITH THE FRUITS AND BEATITUDES

The fruits of good works can be bitter, especially when they are not ripe; but in the measure that they develop and mature, they become so delightful that the labor spent in producing them is scarcely noticed. There is then no reckoning of the sweat and tears that they cost, because everything contributes to their greater sweetness. In the beginning, therefore, heavenly wisdom seems difficult (as is usually the case with the worldly), and for that reason the foolish do not persevere. But if it is seriously cultivated, in a short time its tasty fruits are recognized and it is changed into pleasure and enchantment and is the beauty of life.[197]

Says Lallemant:

When we have long exercised ourselves with fervour in the practice of the virtues, we acquire a facility in producing acts of them. We no longer feel the repugnances we experienced at first. We have no longer to combat and do violence to ourselves. We do with pleasure what before we did only with difficulty. The same thing happens to virtues as to trees. As the latter bear fruits which, when they are ripe, lose their sharpness, and are sweet and pleasant to the taste; so when the acts of the virtues have attained a certain maturity, we perform them with pleasure, and find in them a delicious flavour. At this stage, these acts

---

[195] See II Cor. 4:17.
[196] See Ia IIae, q.70, a.1, ad 1um: "And so our works, in so far as they are produced by the Holy Ghost working in us, are fruits; but in so far as they are referred to the end, which is eternal life, they should rather be called flowers: hence it is written (Ecclus. xxiv. 23): *My fruits are the flowers of honour and riches.*"
[197] Ecclus. 6:19-32.

PARTICIPATION IN THE DIVINE ACTIVITY

of virtue inspired by the Holy Spirit are called *fruits of the Holy Spirit*; and certain virtues produce them in such perfection and sweetness, that they are called *beatitudes*, because they cause the soul to be wholly filled with God. Now the more God possesses a soul, the more He sanctifies it; and the more holy it is, the nearer it approaches to that happy state in which nature being healed of its corruption, the virtues become, as it were, natural.[198]

"The world," says Father Froget, "comprehends nothing of these delights. As St. Bernard says, it sees the cross, but not its unction. The anguish of the flesh, the mortification of the senses, the works of penance, these do not attract its attention, except painfully; and looking upon them all in horror, it misses the consolations of the Holy Spirit. Pious souls, on the contrary, gladly cry out with the spouse in the Canticle: 'I sat down in the shade of Him whom I have desired, and His fruit is sweet to my palate' (Cant. 2:3)."[199]

In the blessed shadow of the tree of the Cross, the just souls find that happiness and repose which the world cannot know and which increase daily with their works. In the midst of their labors they superabound in joy and divine consolations, so that they can say with the Apostle: "I am filled with comfort; I exceedingly abound with joy in all our tribulation."[200] Each type of work produces a special kind of consolation, and the principal virtue under whose influence it is undertaken constitutes, as it were, a partial state of happiness; that is, one of the beatitudes. For the beatitudes are those states in which there is a copious and continual production of the exquisite fruits which give one a foretaste of glory.

This happiness is felt by the soul even in the midst of its pains. Indeed, the soul glories in its tribulations, for as soon as the perfect fruits begin to manifest themselves, the soul begins to enjoy this prelude to eternal happiness.[201] But the soul can in no sense be called blessed until, after the manner of the mystical spouse, it enjoys these fruits as it sits in the shadow of the Beloved (Cant. 2:3). Nor can it

---

[198] *Spiritual Doctrine*, V, chap. 5, art. 1.
[199] *The Indwelling of the Holy Spirit*, p. 232.
[200] See II Cor. 7:4.
[201] See Ia IIae, q.69, a.2: "In order to make the matter clear we must take note that hope of future happiness may be in us for two reasons. First, by reason of our having a preparation for, or a disposition to, future happiness; and this is by way of merit; secondly, by a kind of imperfect inchoation of future happiness in holy men, even in this life. For it is one thing to hope that the tree will bear fruit, when the leaves begin to appear, and another, when we see the first signs of the fruit."

be called perfect until it enjoys more or less each and every one of the beatitudes, for all of them pertain to the perfection of the spiritual life [202] and for that reason they can be merited *de condigno*.[203]

Therefore not all the fruits are beatitudes, because the beatitudes presuppose perfection in the fruits and an excellence and certain stability in their possession and enjoyment. Inasmuch as they pertain to the fruits that are perfect, copious, and permanent, the beatitudes correspond to the gifts of the Holy Ghost more aptly than to the virtues.[204] Hence he who is content with the ordinary and methodical practice of the virtues, and does not purify or deny himself so as to become totally governed and led by God through His mystical gifts, cannot share in the delights of true happiness.[205]

Each of the gifts, when well developed, makes us taste and enjoy

---

[202] See IIa IIae, q. 19, a. 12, ad 1um: "Since a beatitude is an act of perfect virtue, all the beatitudes belong to the perfection of the spiritual life."

[203] See Ia IIae, q. 69, a. 2. "The goods which are granted to just men through a special act of God's providence, that they may proceed from virtue to virtue until they see God in Sion, fall under merit *de condigno*" (Medina, *In Iam IIae*, q. 114, a. 10).

[204] See Ia IIae, q. 70, a. 3. "Fruits of the Spirit are called acts of the virtues," says St. Thomas in another place (*In Gal.* V, lect. 6), "so far as they possess a certain suavity and sweetness and also because they are a certain ultimate act produced according to the mode of the gifts. . . . But there is this difference between the gifts, the beatitudes, the virtues, and the fruits: A virtue may be considered as a habit and as an act. The habit of the virtue perfects one for acting well and when it gives this perfection of operation in a human manner, it is called a virtue. But if it perfects one to operate above the human mode, it is called a gift. Whence the Philosopher places above the common virtues other virtues which he calls heroic. . . . But the act of a virtue is either a perfecting act, and then it is called beatitude; or it is an act which gives delight, and then it is called a fruit."

[205] Lallemant, *op. cit.*, IV, chap. 5, art. 1: "They who strive after perfection by the way of systematic practices and acts, without abandoning themselves completely to the guidance of the Holy Spirit, never have this sweetness and, as it were, ripeness of virtue; they always feel difficulty and repugnances, they have always to combat, and are often vanquished, and commit faults; instead of which, they who proceed from the direction of the Holy Spirit, in the way of simple recollection, practice what is good with a fervour and a joy worthy of the Holy Spirit, and win glorious victories without a struggle, or if they do have to combat, they do so with pleasure.

"Whence it follows, that tepid souls have twice as much trouble in the practice of virtue as the fervent, who devote themselves to it in earnest and without reserve; because the latter possess the joy of the Holy Spirit, which renders everything easy to them; whereas the former have their passions to fight against, and experience the weaknesses and infirmities of nature, which counteract the sweetness of virtue, and render its acts difficult and imperfect."

Rightly did Mother Mary of the Queen of the Apostles say: "He who gives only half of himself to God is the one who has the most difficulties."

PARTICIPATION IN THE DIVINE ACTIVITY

a partial aspect of glory. As a person excels in the fruits proper to one gift or another, so will he enjoy pre-eminently the corresponding beatitude which comes to him even in this valley of life. But in heaven, when all these partial aspects, these transitory states of incipient happiness, are united and perfected, they will come to full fruition and will lose every trace of bitterness and flatness and the soul will enjoy a full, inamissible, and eternal beatitude. Then it is that the soul, deified and completely purified, will enter into the complete joy of God and be totally immersed in the torrent of divine delights. "And God shall wipe away all tears from their eyes. And death shall be no more, nor mourning nor crying shall be any more, for the former things are passed away." [206]

For the present, however, the life of the just must be a mixture of pain and joy; not to weaken that life, but to make it meritorious. The tears which the fear of the Lord causes to flow are filled with such consolation that the soul would not exchange them for all the pleasures in the world. The servants of God, even when weeping, are happy because they have within themselves the divine Comforter.

The piety which this most sweet Guest inspires in them and by which they cordially and lovingly treat God as a Father and their neighbors as brothers, produces in them abundant fruits of charity, peace, joy, benignity, goodness, and the patience by which they will possess their souls.[207] Preserving the unity of the Spirit under the bonds of peace, these peacemakers enjoy the liberty of the children of God.[208]

The gift of knowledge teaches souls how to recognize and prepare the way of the Lord and to disdain the world in order to do the divine will in all things. With faith and continence they seek, not their own interests, but those of God: His kingdom and His justice. Thus those who hunger and thirst after justice receive their

---

[206] Apoc. 21:4.
[207] Luke 21:19.
[208] Juan de Jesús María, *Escuela de oración*, IX, 6: "To the gift of piety are attributed many extraordinary things which the saints did for the honor of the divine Majesty, for they could not permit that the honor which belongs to God and our Father should be given to idols, nor could they permit anyone to refuse the homage which was owing to sacred images and other holy things. For that reason they even publicly reprimanded the heretical persecutors."

fill with ineffable joy at the fountain of the Savior who, together with His kingdom, gives them all other things besides.[209]

The Spirit of fortitude enables them to endure not only patiently, but even with joy and magnanimity, every kind of labor for the glory of God. By means of this gift they triumph over all their enemies and especially the greatest of them, which is self-love. Once self-love has been vanquished by continual self-abnegation, modesty, continency, mildness, patience, and longanimity, then the truly meek and humble, imitating the divine Lamb, enjoy the fruit of their hard-won victory: complete mastery of self and all their passions. Thus they conquer the mystical kingdom and possess the earth.[210]

The gift of counsel, together with that of piety, moves us, on the one hand, to do unto our brethren, particularly in time of their misfortune, as we would have them do unto us; and on the other hand, to flee from association with evil and impious men. It teaches us to seek the company of the good and the perfect and to honor in a fitting way the saintly friends of God and to invoke them as our protectors and intercessors. In this way do the merciful and pious receive the consolation of obtaining the divine mercy.

The Spirit of understanding enlightens and purifies the eyes of the heart. Perfect purification, though painful, does away with the obstacles that impede the vision of the radiant Sun of justice and enables us to see in some small measure the light of His glory. Those who are truly clean of heart, then, are illumined to the point of seeing God and penetrating His most august mysteries.[211]

The gift of wisdom, which makes us evaluate things in a fitting manner, lifts us up to true poverty of spirit, to disparagement and forgetfulness of self, to the total surrender of anything that is not of God or does not lead to Him, and to a complete indifference to spiritual consolations. Yet to anyone who abandons himself to God with this wise disinterestedness, God delivers and communicates Himself without reserve.[212] The truly poor in spirit enjoy an antic-

[209] Matt. 6:34; Luke 12:31.

[210] In this way are fulfilled the words of Prov. 16:32: "The patient man is better than the valiant: and he that ruleth his spirit, than he that taketh cities."

[211] See Ia IIae, q.69, a.2, ad 3um: "All these rewards will be fully consummated in the life to come: but meanwhile they are, in a manner, begun, even in this life. . . . Again the (mind's) eye being cleansed by the gift of understanding, we can, so to speak, *see God*."

[212] *Imitation of Christ*, Bk. II, chap. 1: "He who tastes life as it really is, and not

PARTICIPATION IN THE DIVINE ACTIVITY

ipated glory and even now possess the kingdom of heaven.

To suffer persecutions for Jesus Christ, in which beatitude all seven are contained, is the greatest glory and happiness that His faithful followers can have in this life. So far as the beatitudes have the aspect of merit, they are flowers of glory, but covered with thorns; and so far as they have the aspect of a reward, adds St. Thomas,[213] they are glory already begun. The divine Master enunciated the beatitudes at the very beginning of His preaching because in them is contained the end of the New Law and in them are gathered together for all eternity the most precious fruits of the evangelical life. "You have not chosen Me, but I have chosen you, and have appointed you that you should go and should bring forth fruit, and your fruit should remain; that whatsoever you shall ask of the Father in My name, He may give it you" (John 15:16).

Besides being permanent fruits, the beatitudes indicate various states of perfection in which those delicious fruits abound, the possession and enjoyment of which constitute a beginning of the life of glory, in which God is all in all and satisfies all.[214] To these various states of perfection Christ invited His disciples and all His hearers. He desired that each one, following the impulse of His Spirit in accordance with his particular vocation, should imitate Him more exactly in some one phase of His life. In this way all His followers taken together would be able to reproduce vividly His divine image and perpetuate His precious life, so full of the fruits of benediction.

2. THE WORKING OF THE HOLY GHOST IN SOULS

Thus does the Spirit of Jesus Christ bear fruit in the just soul.[215] He enters therein to dwell in union with the Word and with the

---

as men say or think it is, is indeed wise with the wisdom of God rather than of men."
[213] *Loc. cit.*

[214] Juan de Jesús María, *op. cit.*, IX, 12: "The state of those whom Christ calls 'blessed' is such that, with that poverty of spirit which is humility, . . . they perform certain acts of the greatest contempt of self and in this self-contempt they experience the kingdom of heaven. . . . It must not be understood that the fruits and beatitudes are strictly acts, because they also possess certain heavenly qualities characteristic of celestial happiness, which accompany and follow the acts themselves; for example, peace, among the fruits, and purity of heart, among the beatitudes."

[215] *Ibid.*, no. 13: "The understanding and consideration of the beatitudes and of the fruits should serve as a solace for spiritual persons who know the inestimable benefits which the Lord communicates to His friends even in this life. They should,

Father. He, the Gift par excellence, gives Himself entirely to the soul and adorns that living temple of His with the splendor of His grace, virtues, and gifts. In this way does He purify, justify, transform, and renew the soul until it is deified and made an object worthy of His divine pleasure. With the divine life which He communicates, He also bestows divine activities by which the soul can live and work as a child of God. These are the infused virtues and the gifts of that same Holy Ghost. They are the fecund seeds of the fruits which God desires to implant in us and the possession of which makes us happy even during this life.

Heed, then, O Christian souls, the voice of the Holy Ghost. Follow His inspirations and "bud forth like the rose planted by the brooks of waters. Give ye a sweet odor as frankincense. Send forth flowers, as the lily, and yield a smell, and bring forth leaves in grace, and praise with canticles, and bless the Lord in His works." [216]

To arrive with certainty at our heavenly goal, we must follow the impulse of the Spirit, who pours forth His charity on us for the purpose of inflaming us with the love of God and His holy desires. He excites and moves and consoles us with His gifts, that we may fly to the object of our love. Once again we turn to the pages of Father Froget's inspiring work:

Who will count all the holy thoughts He arouses in us, the good impulses He imparts, the salutary inspirations of which He is the source? Why is it that obstacles too frequently come to more or less paralyze His beneficent activity and to hinder His purpose? This is why so many Christians in the possession of habitual grace and of the Divine energies which accompany it, remain, nevertheless, so feeble and so sluggish in God's service, so little zealous for their perfection, so inclined to earth, so forgetful of the things of heaven, so easily fascinated by evil. This is why the Apostle exhorts us to "grieve not the holy Spirit of God: whereby you are sealed unto the day of redemption," [217] and, above all, "to extinguish not the Spirit." [218]

There is another reason which finally explains why a seed so prolific of holiness produces oftentimes so sorry a harvest. It is this: that know-

---

therefore, impel themselves to work and to travel along the road of Christian perfection."

[216] Ecclus. 39:17-19.
[217] Eph. 4:30.
[218] See I Thess. 5:19.

PARTICIPATION IN THE DIVINE ACTIVITY

ing but very imperfectly the treasure of which they are the guardians, a number of Christians form only a faint estimate of it and put themselves to little pains to make it yield fruit. Yet what power, what generosity, what respect for self, what watchfulness and what consolation and joy, would not this thought, if constantly held before the mind and piously meditated upon, inspire: *The Holy Ghost dwells in my heart!* He is there, a powerful Protector, always ready to defend me against my enemies, to sustain me in my combats, to assure me the victory. A Faithful Friend, He is always disposed to give me a hearing, and, far from being a source of sadness and weariness, His conversation brings gladness and joy: it "hath no bitterness nor His company any tediousness, but joy and gladness." [219] He is there the ever present witness of my efforts and sacrifices, counting every one of my steps in order to reward them some day, following my whole course, forgetful of nothing that I do for His love and His glory.

The Holy Spirit dwells in my heart! I am His temple, essentially the temple of holiness; I must, therefore, sanctify myself, since the first characteristic of God's house is holiness: "Holiness becometh Thy house, O Lord, unto length of days." [220] I will, therefore, proclaim again with the Psalmist, more by my conduct than by my words: "I have loved, O Lord, the beauty of Thy house, and the place where Thy glory dwelleth." [221]

What is more efficacious than these reflections, to move us to live according to the word of St. Paul: "That you may walk worthy of God, in all things pleasing; being fruitful in every good work, and increasing in the knowledge of God"? [222]

Let us attend, then, to the sweet voice of the Spirit who is whispering to us all truth and, like a tender mother, says to us: "Let thy heart receive my words, keep my commandments, and thou shalt live. . . I will show thee the way of wisdom, I will lead thee by the paths of equity: which when thou shalt have entered, thy steps shall not be straightened, and when thou runnest thou shalt not meet a stumbling block. Take hold on instruction, leave it not: keep it, because it is thy life." [223]

[219] Wisd. 8:16.
[220] Ps. 92:5.
[221] Ps. 25:8.
[222] Col. 1:10. *The Indwelling of the Holy Spirit*, pp. 238 f.
[223] Prov. 4:4-13.

APPENDIX

1. Why Do Not the Gifts Fructify in Many Souls?

"How can we explain the fact that all those who are in the state of grace possess the gift of wisdom, but nevertheless there are very few who possess the gift of contemplation? I answer that there can be various reasons for this sterility: a low degree of purity of life, the frequent commission of venial sins, excessive activity, too little regard for the divine communication, and other similar things. . . . It must be noted that the gift of wisdom aids all the just whenever this help is necessary for salvation. . . . But there are very few who keep such a watch over their heart that they arrive at true divine contemplation and enjoy that most sweet communication of God our Lord which is the beginning of the happiness of glory. Yet it is true that there are more souls who do arrive at other lower grades of contemplation" (Juan de Jesús María, *Escuela de Oración*, tr. 8, dist. 12).

"If anyone desires the precious gift of contemplation, let him strive to pray as he ought. Let him lead a life of mortification and humility and refrain from those things which impede interior quiet and the divine communication. This doctrine ought greatly to prompt spiritual persons to live with great mortification and not to spurn any work that will lead them to some degree of contemplation. . . . They should desire contemplation, not so much for the interior consolation it gives, but for the perfection of life which is thereby attained and the pleasure which the divine Majesty receives through His intimate communication with men" (*ibid.*, dist. 13).

2. The Training and Doctrine Which the Holy Ghost Gives to Each Soul That Seeks His Instruction Wholeheartedly and Strives Earnestly After That Perfect State Which Our First Parents Lost

"The divine Spirit, who knows perfectly the way God works (since He is truly God, as are the Father and the Word), leads and directs us . . . so that we may act in accordance with the will of God. God always begins to provide a remedy for the radical cause

PARTICIPATION IN THE DIVINE ACTIVITY

of the evils which come to us. Since evil came to the entire human race through disobedience, pride, and intemperance, this most wise Master, by means of the great work of justification and sanctification, begins to rid us of those three great obstacles which remain in us even after our redemption. As long as we have those obstacles, not even God Himself can complete the work of our justification. The work begun by the Father is continued by the Son and will be perfected by the Holy Ghost. One can understand clearly why that privileged intellect [St. Augustine] cried out: 'He who created thee without thyself, will not save thee without thyself.'

"Without our cooperation the Holy Ghost cannot of Himself remove those three great obstacles which impede our sanctification. But how can we prepare, that He may dispose of them? By docility; doing what He advises us to do, believing all that He teaches us, rooting out of our hearts everything that He forbids us to have. What could be more fitting than that God should ask us and demand of us that we place His remedy at the root of our evil, ruin, and death? It is especially fitting, since it results in the subjection of our passions to reason. If this is not done, our passions will be the principal cause of our ruin.

"By fasting and penance, performed in a manner dictated by the divine Spirit, we shall succeed not only in putting our passions under control, but we shall truly die to self. . . . The merit of fasting does not lie in that very act, but in doing it under the conditions necessary to make it pleasing to God and profitable to ourselves. It must be undertaken for the purpose which the Holy Ghost proposes. Not every fast is pleasing to God, nor every act of penance. Because of the deep roots of our passions, we often do not seek God in all things, but we seek self. In this regard we are like little children who do not know how to do anything of profit to themselves.

"To avoid this, the action of the Holy Ghost comes to our aid. He guides and protects us as a tender mother does her child when, taking him by the hand, she leads him along the path lest he make a misstep and fall.

"How can the soul do many of the things that are necessary for it in the spiritual life? The soul in this life is like a traveler who desires to return to the land of his fathers, but since he himself was born in a strange land, he is ignorant of the road he must take. What would happen to him if, unaware of the great danger of being lost on the way, he set out alone on his journey?

"He could avoid all danger of this if he would take with him as an experienced guide a native of that beloved country which he desires to reach. Even in this case, if the traveler heeds his timidity and natural cowardice, he will be unwilling to traverse the narrow paths along which he must travel. He will become frightened and say: 'I will not walk along this path where there are scarcely any fellow travelers. I wish to walk where there are many happy and delightful people. Here everything is painful. There are anxieties, privations, darkness, wild animals, and tempests. I see nothing but dangerous crags and I know not what lies ahead. I wish to walk where the road is level and broad.'

"Then the guide, with all tenderness, will try to encourage him and quiet his apprehensions. He will earnestly assure him that he need not fear the wild beasts or anything else. And the path that now seems so narrow, will become easy, straight, and secure. The wild beasts fear the valiant travelers and attack only those who are careless and slothful; those who, forgetful of their journey, amuse themselves by gathering flowers along the way or listening to the songs of strange birds which seek to enchant the unwary so that they will not proceed on their journey. But if the careless traveler stops to listen, he will be torn to pieces by a wild beast. . . .

"If, in spite of all the efforts of the guide, the traveler is still unwilling to go by the path that leads straight to his father's country, . . . but stays behind to pick the flowers . . . , he will ultimately fall into those very dangers that were pointed out to him. What, then, is the fault, but his own temerity?

"What will the prudent and wise and those who pass by say of him? Will they not say that he is entirely responsible for following his own whims and desires and that he freely placed his life in danger? . . .

"The same thing happens to the members of the mystical body of the Church who disavow or ignore the Holy Ghost. He is the wisest Guide that they could ever have. . . . This terrible fate happens to some because they do not know the Holy Ghost; to others, because they do not call upon Him, although they do know Him. He has

PARTICIPATION IN THE DIVINE ACTIVITY

said that He wishes to give us His graces, but He wishes us to ask for them.

"How is it that, although all the members of the mystical body have been selected by God to be temples of the Holy Ghost, there are so few who succeed in raising this temple with perfection? How is it that the Blessed Trinity dwells in so few souls in the manner that has been promised? It is because this divine Spirit is not known by all. . . . They know that Jesus is the way, but they are ignorant of the fact that man alone cannot travel by this way. They must be led by the Holy Ghost.[1]

"O members of the mystical body whose Head is Christ! If, as we recognize Jesus, we would also recognize and acknowledge His Spirit as the master and guide of our souls! How many living temples would there then be in this Church militant wherein the Blessed Trinity could dwell as it dwells in the Church triumphant!

"Through an act of infinite goodness, the Trinity desires that there should be but one thing which differentiates the Church militant from the Church triumphant: that our activity is through faith and hope. . . . Those who belong to the Church triumphant . . live now without faith and hope and will enjoy forever the God in whom they believed and hoped. And in the measure that they believed and hoped, so much more do they enjoy the eternal possession of God.

"Yet the substantial enjoyment of God which is theirs in heaven . . . can be enjoyed even here on earth. . . . This greatest Good loves the soul with an infinite love and with the fullness with which God alone can love. It seems, indeed, that He loves each soul as if there were no other thing to love (from manuscript cited).

"Divine contemplation in souls changes them wonderfully and above all possible description in human language. . . . One quarter of an hour of contemplation can make more impression on a soul than many years of ordinary prayer. The soul which but once enjoys this favor . . . is so enamored of the divine beauty that it disdains all the lovable things of earth. It resolutely practices mortifications

---

[1] Blessed Juan de Avila, *Trat. 1 del Espiritu Santo:* "Although it is true that heaven was opened at the death of Christ and hell was closed, what will it profit you if you do not receive the Holy Ghost? Without the grace of God, how much will anything else profit you? But if you receive the Holy Ghost in your heart, He will make all things profitable for you and He will give you consolation. . . . Oh, if I could but inflame your hearts with devotion to the Holy Ghost!"

THE MYSTICAL EVOLUTION

of the flesh, it abases itself, and devotes itself to those things that will give greater glory to God. It cares not about life or death, or anything at all, except the divine Majesty" (Juan de Jesús María, *Escuela de Oración*, tr. 8, no. 12).

CHAPTER IV

Spiritual Growth

SINCE we are reborn to God as we were born to the world, that is, in the status of infants, we must "grow in grace and knowledge of our Lord and Savior, Jesus Christ" [1] until we reach the state of perfect manhood. This state is not attained fully until glory. If we do not grow, we shall perish like feeble children. Therefore, as newborn babes, we should crave the spiritual milk, that by it we may grow to salvation [2] until Christ is formed in us.[3] So the Apostle charges us frequently to grow in the knowledge of God, in charity, in the fruit of good works, and in all things according to Jesus Christ, that we may be filled with the plenitude of God.[4]

NECESSITY OF GROWTH IN GOD AS INDIVIDUALS AND AS MEMBERS OF THE CHURCH

"Growth is a law," says Father Terrien, "to which the children of God are subject as long as they have not yet arrived at the perfect state of the fullness of Christ. In the spiritual order we find ourselves in the way of formation. . . . Therefore the Church is always our mother, because in baptism she gave us the life of grace and because she has been commanded by Jesus Christ, her divine Spouse, to watch over our growth, to foster and direct it. The same phenomenon occurs in the supernatural life as happens in the natural life:

---
[1] See II Pet. 3:18.
[2] See I Pet. 2:2.
[3] Gal. 4:19.
[4] Col. 1:9 f.; Eph. 4:12-16.

at the beginning we receive the constitutive principles of our being, but these take time to be developed." [5]

Jesus Christ Himself, says St. Luke, "advanced in wisdom and age and grace with God and men." [6] We ought to grow in worthiness to become the sons of God, for the Savior Himself said to His disciples: "Love your enemies; do good to them that hate you; and pray for them that persecute and calumniate you: that you may be the children of your Father who is in heaven." [7] But the disciples were already sons of God, for they could say "Our Father." Nevertheless, says Father Terrien, "it was necessary that they also become so through love of their enemies. What does this signify, except that a son of God can always progress to a higher degree in the measure that he performs works more worthy of his Father and becomes more and more like the divine goodness? Since sanctifying grace can and should increase always, the indwelling of God in souls is ever becoming more intimate; and by that fact the union between the Father and His adopted sons becomes closer." [8]

Hence there is nothing to excuse or impede continual growth in all things according to Jesus Christ by unceasingly aspiring and progressing to ever greater perfection. Neither grace itself, which is eternal life and the participation in the divine life; nor the subject of grace, which, the more grace it receives, the more apt is it to receive more; neither the physical cause, which is the communication of the Holy Ghost; nor the meritorious cause, which is the passion of Jesus Christ: none of these things is opposed to an indefinite growth which will cease only at the end of our earthly course.

1. GROWTH AND MERIT

The Savior desired that we should all aspire to be perfect as the heavenly Father is perfect and that we should have life and have it more abundantly. Indeed, we shall have it if we do not place obstacles in the way of its development, for each vital act we perform increases this new life, instead of exhausting it. The supernatural knowledge and love which we can attain in this life do not satiate us; rather they increase our capacity and dispose us to receive

[5] *Op. cit.*, II.
[6] Luke 2:52.
[7] Matt. 5:44 f.
[8] *Loc. cit.* See also IIa IIae, q. 14, a. 7.

SPIRITUAL GROWTH

more light and more divine fire. Hence one grace is ever invoking another new grace, and he who is not disposed to receive more is exposed to lose what he has already received.[9] So the Apostle forgets what is behind and presses on to that which yet remains,[10] because not to advance is to regress.[11]

We have been given the divine talents of spiritual powers, that is, the infused virtues and the gifts, that they may increase and not be sterile. Only by making them productive can we enter into the joy of the Lord.[12] The evil servant, slothful and profitless, is despoiled of his talents and cast into exterior darkness.[13] On the other hand, all the vital powers by which we strive to increase the divine treasure produce an increase of life and are meritorious of glory.[14]

---

[9] The divine blessings are pledges of new favors. Says St. Augustine: *Beneficia Dei, beneficia et pignora.* St. Paul exhorts us: "We entreat you not to receive the grace of God in vain" (II Cor. 6:1 f.). See also *The City of God*, II, Bk. I, chap. 20.

[10] Phil. 3:13 f.

[11] *Interior Castle*, seventh mansions, chap. 4: "Unless you strive after the virtues and practice them, you will never grow to be more than dwarfs. God grant that nothing worse than this may happen—for, as you know, anyone who fails to go forward begins to go back, and love, I believe, can never be content to stay for long where it is." See also Rodriguez, *Ejercicio de perfección*, I, Bk. 1, chaps. 6 f.

[12] Matt. 25:21-23.

[13] *Ibid.*, 26-30.

[14] Turinaz, *Vida divina*, chap. 5: "The obligation to strive after perfection binds all Christians. The divine precepts which impose this obligation admit of no exceptions. They are universal, absolute, and without restriction or reservation. Even the Old Law, which was but a preparation for the Gospel, states: *Thou shalt be perfect, and without spot before the Lord thy God* (Deut. 18:13) and *Walk before Me, and be perfect*. St. Paul tells us: *Brethren, rejoice, be perfected* (II Cor. 13:11); *Even as He chose us in Him before the foundation of the world, that we should be holy and without blemish in His sight in love* (Eph. 1:4). This great obligation is also indicated in the following statement: *The path of the just, as a shining light, goeth forwards and increaseth even to perfect day* (Prov. 4:18), and in the general command *to perfect the saints for a work of ministry, for building up the body of Christ, until we all attain to the unity of the faith and of the deep knowledge of the Son of God, to perfect manhood, to the mature measure of the fullness of Christ* (Eph. 4:12-14).

"But how is it that progress and advancement in the Christian life do not correspond to these aspirations to greatness, perfection, and infinity, which God arouses in our hearts? Is not all this a proof of the gratitude we ought to show Him for all the benefits received? Without this sense of gratitude, all the gifts destined for our sanctification would be useless. Are not the friends and children of God obliged to manifest the excellence of their dignity through good works? Does not the divine life itself, which has been communicated to us and which unites us intimately with the God of all sanctity, impose on us the obligation of striving for perfection?"

St. Augustine, *Sermo 47, De divers.*, chap. 7: "It must not be thought that those words of Jesus Christ, *Be perfect as your heavenly Father is perfect*, were directed

THE MYSTICAL EVOLUTION

The Council of Trent teaches [15] that the faithful of Christ, "having been thus justified and made the friends and domestics of God, advancing from virtue to virtue, are renewed day by day . . . by the observance of the commandments of God and the Church. They grow in the justice they have received and they are further justified. For it is written: *He who is justified, let him be justified still;* and, in another place, *Do not fear to progress in justice, even until death.* . . . The Church begs this increase of God when she prays: *Grant us, O Lord, an increase of faith, hope, and charity.*" [16] In the same session, an anathema is proclaimed against those who dare to maintain that "justice is not preserved or increased by good works; but that these latter are only fruits and not causes of the increase" or that "they are not truly meritorious . . . of an increase of grace and glory."

Thus every act of a son of God, as such, is meritorious of eternal life,[17] for there are not in him any voluntary actions which can be

---

to virgins alone and not to the married; to widows, but not to wives; to religious, but not to those who have families; to clerics, but not to the laity. The entire Church must follow Jesus Christ, and all the members of the Church, after the example of the Master, must carry the cross and practice His teachings."

This obligation of striving for perfection is fulfilled by embracing our crosses and following the Savior in the accomplishment of the will of the Father. He desires above all things our sanctification (I Thess. 4:3), which consists in being completely animated and directed by the Holy Ghost. We shall sanctify ourselves in truth, as the Savior requested at the Last Supper, if we faithfully endeavor to fulfill all the precepts, both grave and light, all the duties of our state in life, and if we follow with complete docility those internal inspirations which mark out at each step of the way what it is that God desires of us. Without this, we could hardly fulfill the commandment to love God with our whole heart, our whole soul, our whole mind, and with all our strength, in spite of all the gifts and graces received. To acquire this, we must hold in great esteem the evangelical counsels and all the other means of sanctification and apply them as our state in life permits or requires. "It is a great sin," says St. Francis de Sales (*The Love of God*, Bk. VIII, chap. 8), "to contemn the striving after Christian perfection, and a still greater sin to contemn the invitation by which our Savior calls us to it; and it is insupportable impiety to contemn the counsels and means which our Savior offers us for arriving at that perfection."

[15] Sess. VI, can. 10.

[16] St. Augustine, *De natura et gratia*, chap. 13: "The beginning of charity is the beginning of justification; progress in charity is progress in justification; and perfect charity is perfect justification."

[17] Con. Trid., Sess. VI, can. 16: "Christ continually pours out His grace, as the head to the members and as the vine to the branches. This grace always precedes, accompanies, and follows their good works; and without it they could not in any manner be pleasing and meritorious before God."

SPIRITUAL GROWTH

indifferent. Those acts which do not merit are by that very fact evil, because the just man who does not act in conformity with the "new man," ever meriting an increase, works according to the "old man," and falls and loses merit. For an act to be meritorious it must be informed by grace and charity. The former gives it life and makes it a vital act; that is, proper to a son of God. The latter expressly and directly ordains the work to God as the ultimate end whose rule should characterize all our works that they may be entirely good. Inasmuch as they are separated from or forced out of that order, they are evil and disordered, even though they may be basically good as vital acts.[18]

The greater the life of grace and the directive power and impulsive fervor of charity, the more meritorious our actions become. For grace and charity are the two principal sources of merit. But it is not necessary that an explicit act of charity inform and direct our good works. It suffices for their merit that we have a general orientation by virtue of a previous act of charity which perseveres virtually in all our Christian actions, although an explicit renewal of the act of charity will make those actions more pure and meritorious.

The supernatural life is increased, then, even by the most insignificant act, however natural and however lowly, as long as it is performed in grace and directed by charity or, at least, subordinated to a supernatural end.[19] Since each meritorious act produces an increase of grace, and the greater the grace the more meritorious the

---

[18] IIa IIae, q.23, a.8: "Now it is evident, in accordance with what has been said (a.7), that it is charity which directs the acts of all other virtues to the last end, and which, consequently, also gives the form to all other acts of virtue."

[19] Sauvé, *Le culte*, no. 27: "No one can gain heaven and merit the vision and possession of God without being deified. But from the moment the soul is engrafted on God through sanctifying grace and charity, like branches on that vine of which Christ is the life-giving sap, it naturally produces divine fruits as long as its acts are not evil acts."

St. Francis de Sales, *op. cit.*, Bk. XI, chap. 2: "Since the just man is planted in the house of God, his leaves, his flowers, and his fruit grow therein and are dedicated to the service of the divine Majesty."

St. Thomas, *In II Sent.*, dist. 27, q.1, a.5, ad 3um: "As long as a man lacks sanctifying grace, his works have no proportion to the supernatural good which he should strive to merit, because as yet he does not share in the divine being. But as soon as he receives this divine being through grace, his actions attain a dignity sufficient to merit an increase and the perfection of grace."

work, it can be seen that merit and grace increase alternately.[20] A happy consequence of this truth is that by doing all for the love of God and with an upright conscience (and this in even a most ordinary life, occupied almost entirely with lowly and menial tasks) the faithful soul can arrive at a very high degree of sanctity, solely by offering to God whatever it does and by renewing frequently its purity of intention. This applies to all the necessary duties of human life, even those which may seem to be far removed from evangelical perfection. The lives of the saints bear witness to this fact and no one can be excused from not doing likewise. Thus, exercising the truth in charity, that is, exercising all the virtues proper to our state in life, we can grow in all things in Jesus Christ, our Head, by the ceaseless influx of His grace, until we are assimilated with Him and united to Him as much as possible.

2. SPIRITUAL GROWTH OF THE INDIVIDUAL

Evidently the spiritual life grows in a twofold manner. On the one hand, it receives new vital influxes, new increases of that grace which proceeds from Jesus Christ as Head and is continually circulating through the ordinary channels, to be distributed throughout the entire organism. This grace is communicated to all the members who offer no resistance although they do not advert to the vitality which they are receiving. On the other hand, the spiritual life grows by the positive exercise of the virtues and the gifts so that they may be developed to the point of producing such fruits of life as place us in a state of perfection and incipient blessedness. So it is that we advance and fructify, and our fruit remains, and we attain to a life that is more and more abundant.

The means of developing and augmenting the spiritual life, then, are all those things which in one way or another, directly or indirectly, contribute to the fostering of those divine outpourings or the activation of our use of them. Thus we arouse the powers already received so that they may bear fruit and we facilitate or prepare for the communication of new ones or for the removal of the impediments that oppose one or other of them. Thus we are able

---

[20] Turinaz, *op. cit.*, chap. 4, sect. 2: "When a soul is more holy, it is more capable of loving God. Through this greater and more ardent love, it is rendered capable of greater sanctity; and this sanctity, in turn, leads to a more intense love."

to strengthen more and more the union contracted with Christ, our divine Head, and to grow in all things according to Him. But if we do not purify ourselves by getting rid of the obstacles which impede His action, or if we do not strive to cooperate with Him so far as we are able, then we shall always live, weak and withered up, without producing any fruits of life.[21]

3. GROWTH OF MEMBERS OF THE MYSTICAL BODY

We are able to grow in Christ as His brothers and disciples by imitating Him through the unceasing exercise of His virtues and His gifts. We can grow as living members of His mystical body by participating in the functions necessary for the life of that organism as a whole. If this is done, each member will work in perfect harmony and in the union of charity, and the unity of the Spirit will be preserved through the bond of peace.

The mystical body of the Church has as its vital functions the sacraments, which emanate from the Head and are activated through the power of the Holy Ghost who works through those organs which are signed and consecrated for the performance of those particular functions. These consecrated organs are able to incorporate new members, strengthen them, heal them, feed them, and make them grow by the visible distribution of the sacramental graces. (In addition to the visible distribution of the sacramental graces, there is an invisible distribution of the charisms by which the Holy Ghost consecrates many souls for special functions which are as important as they are hidden.) Finally, those consecrated organs dispose souls for the passage to a better life by destroying the last vestiges of the worldly man.

If no resistance is offered and if each member fully cooperates and responds as best he can to these vital functions, to these channels of life and grace, then each one receives life and grace *ex opere operato*. If he does not already possess them, he receives them; or if he does possess them, they are increased. The reception or increase of life

---

[21] Father Lallemant (*op. cit.*, V, chap. 3, art. 1), points out that dissipation and negligence in regulating our interior life have very serious consequences: "It is this living out of ourselves, and this carelessness in ordering our interior, which is the reason that the gifts of the Holy Spirit are almost without effect in us, and that the sacramental graces which are given us by reason of the sacraments we have received, or are frequenting, remain without profit."

and grace through the sacraments is something over and above the life and grace which each member merits *ex opere operantis* through the good use of his own particular activity.

However, to function in this way, even as individuals, as sons of God and living members of Jesus Christ, and to merit anything in the order of grace, it is necessary that they have not only life, but also the faculties, powers, and divine energies that will enable them to produce supernatural acts and fruits of eternal life. Those energies and faculties by which they can of themselves live and increase in merit (apart from the influx which they receive from the collective or sacramental functions) are the actual and habitual graces, the infused virtues, and the gifts of the Holy Ghost, according to the measure in which they are communicated to each one. So it is that there are functions peculiar to the collective life, and others proper to individual life. The former produce grace *ex opere operato;* the latter, *ex opere operantis.*

St. Thomas points out [22] that the spiritual life bears a certain likeness to the natural life in which there are social functions and individual functions. The latter are directly ordained to the good of the individual, either by way of perfecting him or of freeing him from the obstacles which impede that perfection. The former are ordained to the common good by contributing to the good order of society, its propagation, and conservation. So also in the Christian life, there are found spiritual birth, growth, signs of maturity, nourishment, medicine for the sickness of the soul, and means of convalescence. There is, in addition, a hierarchical social order; and even natural propagation, as ordained to the worship and glory of God, is sanctified by the Church.

For each of these principal functions of the Christian life, both private and collective, there is a sacrament. We are reborn through baptism; we are nourished and we grow through the Eucharist; we are strengthened by the character of virility and become soldiers of Christ through confirmation; our spiritual infirmities are cured, and we even recover life anew through penance; we purge the remnants of evil which penance did not erase, and we dispose ourselves to appear before the Supreme Judge by means of extreme unction. By holy orders spiritual government is provided as well as the continued

[22] IIIa, q.65, a.1.

dispensing of the divine mysteries, and by matrimony there is provided the sanctified propagation of Christian people.[23]

Since these social functions require a certain degree of cooperation, they are always collective and for that reason they require a proper sacrament. But the other functions can be realized by each individual in particular, and in performing these functions he merits *ex opere operantis*. Nevertheless he could perform these same functions better by means of a manifest dependence on the collectivity, so that he could at the same time merit *ex opere operato*, through the power of the sacraments. Any particular individual can be reborn, can grow and be healthy, and can even regain life through charity and grace when, unable to receive the sacraments, he has a firm resolution to receive them as soon as he can. But all these functions would be much better and more fully realized by the actual reception of the sacraments, because then he would fully and visibly communicate in the life of the whole mystical body, and he would receive this life in abundance as long as he placed no obstacle. For this life is received from Jesus Christ as the source, and it passes through those channels which are like the arteries of His mystical body conveying His precious blood to all the organs of that body, to reanimate, renew, and purify them.

Each of the sacraments has a special object, whether to regenerate the soul, to nourish it, to purify it, or to stamp it with the seal of the militia of Jesus Christ, the ministerial character, or the grace of the state of life proper to matrimony, or to impart to it the final remedy against our weaknesses. But of all the sacraments, the Eucharist, the food of the soul, which is ordained directly to spiritual growth and the increase of union with Christ; and penance, which purifies and heals us and even, when necessary, resurrects us, are of the greatest importance in the development of the supernatural life. Since Chris-

---

[23] Council of Florence, *Decret. pro Armen.*: "Through matrimony the Church is corporally increased."

Hettinger, *Apologetica*, conf. 31: "We can say that matrimony is a Church of the flesh and that fathers and mothers have a special priestly mission—to give sons and daughters to the Body of Christ, to propagate the kingdom of redemption in coming generations and to work toward the building of the great city of God on earth. As the fathers are members of Christ, so also ought their sons be. In a certain sense, these sons are already saints because before their birth they were separated from the pagans. So the conjugal union rests on the Head of the Church and is rooted in a supernatural foundation."

tian progress consists in growing in grace and expurgating the old ferment just as ordinary life consists in proper assimilation and elimination, so it is that these two sacraments are the most powerful means for fostering spiritual growth.

In this way we live and grow, united to God in our being and our work, and in our cooperation with His mystical activity. In our being we are united by sanctifying grace; in our work, by the infused virtues and especially the theological virtues; in our cooperation, by the gifts of the Holy Ghost. The moral virtues in general perfect the will and the appetites so that they will obey the norms of Christian reason; the intellectual virtues perfect and direct reason itself; and both together, with the gifts, make us docile to the movements and inspirations of the Holy Ghost.

Now we can understand, or at least faintly perceive, the inestimable dignity of the Christian who is thus deified in his being, his faculties, his actions, his goal, and in all things. He has in his heart the sovereign Trinity. He is a true son of the eternal Father, a brother and member of the incarnate Word, and a living temple of the Holy Ghost, who animates and vivifies him as his soul does his body. In him as a member of Jesus Christ, Christ Himself is perpetuated through that real bond which is the life of grace; and this bond is strengthened through good works and the use of the sacraments, which cause the blood of the Redeemer to circulate in his veins. How sublime is the consideration of this type of life, which comes forth from the bosom of the Father, through the merits of the Son, and the power of His Spirit to vivify, renew, purify, and deify us! And what a consolation to behold the way this life is communicated to us through the sacraments, from baptism, which makes us sons of God, to extreme unction, which prepares us to enter into the glory of God the Father!

Individual Growth and Particular Functions

By the theological virtues we are united directly to God; through their use we share in the operations characteristic of eternal life and grow in grace and sanctity. These virtues are completed and enriched by the respective gifts which also direct us to God and strengthen that mystical union. We have already seen that the exercise of these gifts does not depend on us unless the Holy Ghost makes us feel His impulses, although we must dispose ourselves to hear His voice and not sadden Him by being deaf to His inspirations. This requires great purity of heart and soul and much recollection.

1. RECOLLECTION IN GOD

But the exercise of the virtues is within our power. Hence with ordinary grace we can practice them as much as we wish; and we shall practice them as is fitting if we strive to have our conversations in heaven, to walk always in the presence of God, and to meditate on Him at all times with a lively faith. More particularly, within our own hearts, which are His living temples, we can at all times and in all places, even amid the clamor of creatures and the performance of our duties, converse with Him, give Him thanks, ask His mercy, and direct to Him loving affections and tender supplications. Such a practice, instead of being a waste of time, as many suppose, will give us new strength and facility in all things, for godliness is profitable in all respects.[24]

In this way we renew our purity of intention, which is so essential for us that our good works may reap all their merit. Otherwise, by forgetting the supernatural end to which our works should be subordinated, we might vitiate them with earthly views, to the extent that our Lord will say to us: "You have already received your reward."

These frequent introspections, accompanied by fervent aspirations and ejaculations, are as darts of celestial fire which sweetly wound the divine heart and then reflect back to our own hearts to fill them with graces.[25]

---

[24] See I Tim. 4:8. "It must not be believed," says Father Grou (*Manuel*, p. 70), "that the obligations of our state, whether domestic duties, the dispositions of Providence, or social obligations and amenities, can of themselves be prejudicial to recollection. Recollection can and must be observed in the midst of all things. And after a person has, with some effort, trained himself to preserve it, it becomes so natural to him that he maintains this recollection without even being aware of the effort and this to such a degree that he hardly ever departs from it."

Lallemant, *op. cit.*, II, sect. 2, chap. 4, art. 1: "For then our Lord, in the course of one single meditation, will endow a soul with some particular virtue, and even with many virtues in a far higher degree than would be acquired in several years by these external acts."

[25] The following words of the Canticle of Canticles show how much joy the Lord finds in converse with pure souls and in hearing the expression of their ardent desires, their sighs and prayers: "Arise, my love, my beautiful one, and come: my

The saints recommend these introspections as most efficacious means for arriving swiftly and surely at a high degree of perfection. They supply for the defects of prayer and even for its involuntary brevity. They dispose the soul for an awareness of the touch of the Holy Ghost and the entrance into infused contemplation. They excite the ardor of charity so that it enriches all our works and enables us to contract, little by little, the habit of the presence of God. By this last-mentioned habit, we accomplish what the Apostle enjoins, to pray everywhere [26] and continually, giving thanks to God in all things.[27] The Savior Himself has said that we must pray always and not lose heart.[28]

2. PRAYER

That we may not lose heart in the practice of interior recollection, we must at determined hours also recollect ourselves exteriorly. In this way we can more effectively practice prayer, and rid ourselves of the obstacles which usually distract us.[29] We can also occupy ourselves solely in conversing with God and meditating on His holy law and thus reanimate our fervor and inflame ourselves with the ardor of charity.[30] This type of prayer is made by raising our mind and all its faculties to the Lord, through acts of faith, love, trust, gratitude, praise, adoration, and the like. Thus we render to Him a most fitting interior worship, which ought always to animate the exterior. We give thanks for benefits received and we ask favors, lights, and powers which we need to serve Him faithfully and to

---

dove in the clefts of the rock, in the hollow place of the wall, show me thy face, let thy voice sound in my ears: for thy voice is sweet, and thy face comely" (2:13 f.).

[26] See I Tim. 2:8.

[27] See I Thess. 5:17 f.

[28] Luke 18:1. "Perfect men," says Tauler (*Institutiones*, chap. 26), "never depart from this interior conversation, except when the weakness of human nature or the alterations of time demand, and even then only for the briefest time. For as soon as they advert to it, they disregard these things and are again recollected in this worthy and essential practice. All their powers are spent in this activity, without seeking or desiring anything other than to give place to the loving impulses of the Divinity and to prepare themselves for God so that He may complete in them His most joyful operation. Without any other medium, the heavenly Father can speak and produce the paternal Word engendered by Him *ab aeterno* and can bring His divine will to fruition in every place, time, and manner." See also Blosius, *Institutio Spiritualis*, chaps. 3-5.

[29] Col. 4:2.

[30] Ps. 38:4: "My heart grew hot within me: and in my meditation a fire shall flame out."

carry out the holy resolutions we have made during our exterior recollection.[81]

If our prayer is to be fruitful, it must be humble, trusting, persevering, and fervent. It must come forth from the depths of the heart. It must be made with the whole soul and, as Blessed Angela de Foligno says, "it must come from one's very bowels."[32] But if we pray with vacillation, we can expect nothing,[33] and if we deliberately dispose ourselves to pray with our lips only, then that is not praying, but merely provoking God by our irreverence.

There is no true vocal prayer which is not in some way accompanied by mental prayer; but this latter can be even more fervent and efficacious without the former, when we strive to concentrate fully all our soul's energy in the heart.[34] Mental prayer best disposes the soul for an entrance into that mystical tranquillity to which we are all called. Many do not try to converse with God, but utter all their feelings with the mouth alone, so that, if they close their lips, it seems that all their interior fire is thereby extinguished. Yet, as St. Teresa says, if they faithfully persevere in their vocal prayers, they can be raised suddenly to a high degree of contemplation, should the Lord take them at their word and lift them up to do His divine work.[35]

---

[81] Godínez, *Teología Mística*, Bk. I, chap. 6: "They prosper more in the spiritual life who make more resolutions in their mental prayer and then strive to fulfill them. Such souls can, in a short time, arrive at a high degree of sanctity.... But purely speculative mental prayer neither uproots vices nor plants virtues."

[32] *Op. cit.*, chap. 62. "In these times," says Blessed Henry Suso (*Disc. Espir.*, II), "there are many who, in order that they may be useful to others, are so occupied in external works that they have scarcely a free moment for rest. Such individuals should follow my advice: As soon as they have a free hour in the midst of their labors, they should go immediately to God, entering into Him completely and hiding themselves in His heart. During these times they should, by their zeal and fervor, attempt to atone for all the years spent in the life of the senses and wasted on worldly interests. Let them direct themselves to God, not with studied phrases, but from the very core of their heart and with all the energy of their heart, speaking to Him soul to soul and thus adoring Him, as the Lord commands, in spirit and in truth."

[33] Jas. 1:6 f.

[34] "I will pray with the spirit, I will pray also with the understanding; I will sing with the spirit, I will sing also with the understanding" (I Cor. 14:15).

[35] *Way of Perfection*, chap. 25: "In case you should think there is little gain to be derived from practising vocal prayer perfectly, I must tell you that, while you are repeating the Pater noster or some other vocal prayer, it is quite possible for the Lord to grant you perfect contemplation. In this way His Majesty shows that He is listening to the person who is addressing Him, and that, in His greatness, He is

As long as they are not incapacitated or in a passive state, all can remedy the distractions and even the aridity which they involuntarily suffer if they have recourse to the repetition of short and fervent aspirations and supplications, in which the essence of prayer consists. This is the powerful means by which at all times we dispose ourselves to improve our life and to increase divine grace. Our Lord tells us: "Ask, and it shall be given you; seek, and you shall find; knock, and it shall be opened to you." [36]

The saints compare the Christian without prayer to a soldier without weapons, unable to resist the enemy.[37] It is necessary to watch and pray that we may not enter into temptation.[38] Prayer is the shield and weapons of our militia, by which we repel and confuse the tempter and attain to the eternal crown. No matter how arid our prayer, as long as it is accompanied by a sincere desire to please God, it will be so much the more efficacious and meritorious. Devotion does not consist in sensible fervor, but in promptness and firmness of will.

---

addressing her, by suspending the understanding, putting a stop to all thought, and, as we say, taking the words out of her mouth, so that even if she wishes to speak she cannot do so, or at any rate not without great difficulty.

"Such a person understands that, without any sounds of words, she is being taught by this Divine Master, Who is suspending her faculties, which, if they were to work, would be causing her harm rather than profit. The faculties rejoice without knowing how they rejoice; the soul is enkindled in love without understanding how it loves; it knows that it is rejoicing in the object of its love, yet it does not know how it is rejoicing in it. It is well aware that this is not a joy that can be attained by the understanding; the will embraces it without understanding how; but, in so far as it can understand anything, it perceives that this is a blessing which could not be gained by the merits of all the trials suffered on earth put together. It is a gift of the Lord of earth and Heaven, Who gives it like the God He is. . . . In the contemplation which I have just described we can do nothing. It is His Majesty Who does everything; the work is His alone and far transcends human nature."

Molina, *Excelencia, provecho y necesidad de la oración*, Introd., chap. 2: "By the exercise of prayer a person arrives at perfect contemplation and the union of the soul with God. He is made one in spirit with Him, is totally deified and possessed by Him, is transformed into Him in such a manner that he becomes entirely spiritual and divine. . . . It is the greatest happiness that anyone can attain in this life; it is like a novitiate to the glory of heaven." In another place (II, chap. 6) he adds, "I hold for certain that it [contemplation] will not be denied to anyone who continues to do all in his power to realize it."

[36] Matt. 7:7; Luke 11:8.
[37] See Molina, *op. cit.*, Introd. v; Granada, *Oración y consideración*, I, chap. 1; Rodríguez, *Practice of Christian Perfection*, I, chap. 2.
[38] Matt. 26:41.

3. EXTERIOR WORKS

Merit is also increased, and with it the life of grace, by the faithful practice of the Christian virtues which, informed with charity, direct us in our relationships with our neighbors and aid us in doing what is most conducive to our goal. Thus in all things we observe the correct mean of prudence, the norm of justice, the valor of fortitude, and the moderation of temperance.[39] In this way we are able to fulfill our duties faithfully. By the virtue of religion, which is a part of justice, we give appropriate worship to God and, through love of Him, we practice the works of charity and mercy, besides giving to each what is his due. Meanwhile, by temperance and fortitude we strive to conquer self and to sacrifice self for God and our neighbor. We dominate our passions so that they do not contradict reason, and we moderate reason itself so that it is subject to the spirit. Thus we strengthen ourselves by overcoming the difficulties and conquering the obstacles opposed to our spiritual renewal and interior perfection to which we must ordain all our conduct.

Some pious persons, prompted by an indiscreet zeal and perhaps also by a certain measure of vanity, are absorbed in exterior works. They are convinced that by that means alone they can accumulate merits and rapidly advance in Christian perfection. But perfection resides, as we have said, in the interior being rather than exterior activity. The value and merit of our works correspond to the degree of renewal and sanctification of our souls. If we are very holy and always act under the impulse of divine charity, then all our works will be great, valuable, and efficacious in the eyes of God, although outwardly they may appear humble and contemptible. On the other hand, those works that proceed from a heart lacking in generosity are niggardly, even though they may appear grandiose and full of glory.[40]

Therefore, if our perfection is nullified, owing to our death to

---

[39] Ia IIae, q.62, a.1: "Man is perfected by virtue, for those actions whereby he is directed to happiness."

[40] Huby, *Maximes*, no. 12: "There are some souls that diminish everything because they themselves are small. They diminish the greatest actions because they perform them with a poor heart.... To perform some great work with little will is to perform only a small work, and to do a small work with greatness of will is equivalent to performing a great work. What makes our works little or great in the eyes of God is the will with which they are performed."

the life of grace, then the most excellent works which we perform can avail nothing before God. However ostentatious they may be, they are dead and without avail.[41] The more alive we are in Jesus Christ and the more we are filled with His Spirit, the more properly are we the children of God and the more meritorious and divine will our actions be. As St. Thomas says, "an act is so much the more meritorious when the grace that informs it is greater."[42] And when, in conformity with that grace, our works are more and more informed by actual charity, then they are also more pure and vital, more free from the dust of earth and capable of increasing grace and glory. "It may come to pass," says St. Francis de Sales, "that a very small virtue may be of greater value in a soul where sacred love reigns, than martyrdom itself in a soul where love is languid, feeble, and dull."[43]

Thus the holy soul aflame with charity sweetly wounds the heart of the divine Spouse to whom she delivers herself without reserve. "Thou hast wounded my heart, my sister, my spouse, thou hast wounded my heart with one of thy eyes, and with one hair of thy neck. . . ."[44] My beloved to me, and I to him who feedeth among the lilies."[45] Though such a soul be engaged in lowly tasks, her hands distil a precious myrrh [46] because such works are the fruits of charity and self-abnegation. Even when sleeping, her heart keeps vigil. She is so pleasing to the Spouse that He repeatedly warns the daughters of Jerusalem: "I adjure you, O daughters of Jerusalem, that you stir not up nor awake my love till she please."[47]

Finally, the more lofty and noble the virtue which is more and more informed by charity, the more meritorious and excellent are its acts. Hence the virtue of religion surpasses all the other moral virtues, and those of the interior or contemplative life avail more than external virtues. Yet all are necessary in their own right and all

---

[41] See St. Thomas, *In II Sent.*, dist. 27, q. 1, a. 5, ad 3um.
[42] *Ibid.*, dist. 29, q. 1, a. 4.
[43] *Treatise on the Love of God*, XI, chap. 5.
[44] Cant. 4:9. St. John of the Cross, *Spiritual Canticle*, stanza 30: "This hair of hers is her will and the love which she has for the Beloved. . . . She says 'one hair' of her head, and not many hairs, in order to convey the fact that her will is now alone, detached from all other hairs, which are strange affections for others."
[45] Cant. 2:16.
[46] *Ibid.*, 5:5.
[47] *Ibid.*, 2:7; 3:5; 8:4.

mutually assist one another. Complete perfection lies in knowing how to harmonize them.

But the interior is of value in itself, whereas the exterior without the interior is sterile and dead. Of little value before God are the many external works performed without a right intention and purity of heart, both of which wash away the dust of earth. Of little value are works performed without the spirit of prayer, which irrigates the soul with the rain of grace and the ardor of charity; nor does the world's esteem for such prayers alter the situation. Indeed, such works can become utterly useless and even harmful if they so absorb the soul that they drain the source of its energies and serve only as a pabulum for self-love and an inducement to vanity.[48]

The many persons who are prompted by worthy intentions and devote themselves excessively to external activity, would do better to dedicate half the time thus consumed to the care of their own souls and the renewal of their spirit. Then in the other half of the time, say all the great spiritual masters with John of the Cross,[49] they would produce double the fruit with much less effort.[50]

Nevertheless fervor and devotion are themselves increased, especially in beginners, by outward good works and the pious practices that have been approved by the Church if the faithful soul strives to perform them according to the time at his disposal and the special attraction he feels for a certain practice under the impulse of the Holy Ghost. But in these pious practices he must take care to avoid any sentimental emptiness and Protestant taste, as well as to shun the many routine devotions that are readily introduced but that are

---

[48] Lallemant, *op. cit.*, V, chap. 3, art. 2: "Let us be thoroughly convinced that we shall gain fruit in our ministrations only in proportion to our union with God and detachment from all self-interest.... To labour profitably for the salvation of others, we must have made great progress in our own perfection. Until we have acquired perfect virtue, we ought to practice very little exterior action. But if superiors lay too much upon us, we may trust that Providence will so dispose things that the burden will soon be diminished, and all will turn out to the greater good of inferiors, if they are good men."

[49] *Spiritual Canticle*, annotation for stanza 29.

[50] Lallemant, *op. cit.*, IV, chap. 2, art. 1: "And yet the principal point in the spiritual life so entirely consists in disposing ourselves to grace by purity of life, that if two persons were to consecrate themselves to the service of God at the same time, and one were to devote himslf wholly to good works, and the other to apply himself altogether to the purifying of his heart and to rooting out whatever within him was opposed to grace, the latter would attain to perfection twice as soon as the former."

opposed to the Christian spirit and the mind of the Church. The Church desires that these things serve as a preparation for and not as an obstacle to divine inspiration.[51]

4. MORTIFICATION AND HUMILITY

For true progress in prayer and devotion, these must be aided by an unceasing mortification of the senses and passions.[52] The fastidious and delicate soul is unable to know the way of divine Wisdom. If it does not mortify its senses and hold its passions in check and even reduce them to silence, it will not be able to hear the soft voice of the Spirit, who wishes to speak words of peace to its heart. Nor will it be able to feel the delicate movements and impulses by which the Spirit suggests and teaches all truth and guides the soul along the paths of justice and life. For that reason the saints are unanimous in saying that without a deep appreciation of austerities a true spirit of prayer is impossible because this latter requires a great purity of soul and body and therefore a long series of purifications. The more one progresses in these purifications, so much the more is the work of the divine Spirit facilitated and augmented, and hence so much the more does the soul progress in illumination, union, and renewal.

Exterior purity is acquired by the virtue of temperance, which regulates the senses and bodily passions so that they never deviate from reason. To this end it appeals, when necessary, to great rigors and hardships, chastising the body and bringing it into subjection.[53] Interior purity is achieved by the practice of humility, abnegation and penance, and unremitting vigilance over one's secret desires, movements, and affections. This is done to annihilate all that is displeasing to God.

Humility, by making us recognize the futility of our own nothingness, disposes us to receive divine grace, which is given to the humble and denied to the proud. By means of the grace thus received, the soul remains subject to reason in such a way that it never

---

[51] Lallemant, *ibid.*, "Some exercise themselves in many commendable practices and perform a number of exterior acts of virtue; thus their attention is wholly given to material action. This is well enough for beginners, but it belongs to a far higher perfection to follow the interior attraction of the Holy Spirit and be guided by His direction."
[52] See Rodríguez, *op. cit.*, II, I, chap. 1.
[53] See I Cor. 9:27.

presumes anything of itself, but denies itself and renounces its own good pleasures and desires. It becomes docile to the Holy Ghost and in a brief time is able to arrive at an untrammeled perfection.[54]

5. GENERAL AND PARTICULAR EXAMINATION

Penance makes us bitterly regret our faults and seek the means of obtaining pardon, reparation for evil, satisfaction for the offenses against God and neighbors, and amendment of our lives in the future. Pardon will be obtained immediately through perfect contrition, which places the soul wholly in the hands of God. Reparation and satisfaction are made by means of austerities, prayers, and sacrifices, and by works of piety and mercy. Self-correction is accomplished by frequent examination of conscience, wherein we seek the causes of our defects and internal and external faults, in order to avoid or correct them and thus to rid ourselves of such faults and put away every occasion of evil.

Usually, however, those defects are numerous. If we regard them as a whole, we shall never succeed in rooting them out. Hence the necessity of the particular examination of our dominant fault; this examination ought to accompany our general examination and make it more fruitful. If we particularly stress one fault, we can properly begin to correct it. If it happens to be a dominant fault, then with it many others are rooted out.[55] So it is that in a short time the soul becomes much improved and more perfect if it keeps watch over itself so as not to offer resistance or place obstacles to the mysterious renewing action of the divine Spirit.[56]

6. NEED FOR MODERATION AND DIRECTION

Persistent self-abnegation, or rather the interior mortification of the senses and passions, does not offer any danger; rather the greater

---

[54] Blessed Henry Suso, *Unión*, "The profound submission of a holy humility, the disdain of self, and the awareness of our own baseness do not debase us, but rather they enable us to fly to the height of perfect union with God."

[55] *Imitation of Christ*, Bk. I, chap. 11: "If we were to uproot only one vice a year, we should soon become perfect."

[56] Lallemant, *op. cit.*, V, chap. 3; art. 1: "Without performing extraordinary mortifications, or any of those exterior actions which might be the occasion of vanity to us, by simple attention in watching our own interior, we perform excellent acts of virtue and make prodigious advances in perfection; whereas, on the contrary, by neglecting our interior we incur incalculable losses."

it is, the better. Bodily mortification, on the contrary, which has merit only when subjected to the former, ought always to be moderated so that it will not harm the health nor impede us from exercising the virtues instead of fostering their use. So we see that there are some persons who live with much exterior austerity and place all their attention on great bodily rigors, as if by those things alone they could attain a high degree of perfection and thus win sanctity by force of their own efforts. The fact of the matter is that they spend their time uselessly and are incapacitated for the performance of their duties. They are filled with pride and presumption and dominated by their passions, because actually they are not seeking to conquer self, but to gain worldly acclaim by those vain appearances of sanctity.

In order to guard against such disorders, to overthrow self-love, to deny our own will, and to avoid the snares of self-complacency, it is necessary that we have a good spiritual director to whom we subject ourselves with docility in all things so that he may teach us how to exercise ourselves in prayer and the good practice of all the virtues. Although virtue should observe the just mean of prudence, no one is a worthy judge of his own case. A good director will help us to overcome our difficulties and to conquer obstacles, and will preserve us from the wiles of our enemies.

When a person is so far advanced in virtue that he has begun to feel the impulses of the Spirit, who moves him with His gifts to a new mode of prayer and of life, then human direction is not useless, but is all the more needed. In the beginning of contemplation, when the difficulties which appear are so new and so numerous, they disconcert the soul and leave it perplexed. The soul at this early stage does not yet know how to distinguish the divine motions from those that are not divine. It will find itself tempted to resist the good and grow languid or even follow a false course if it has no one to aid, counsel, and free it from error. Then it is that the soul needs a director who knows how to test its spirit and sustain it in the midst of its abasements, pains, and aridities, and to enlighten it in the midst of so many obscurities and desolations.

7. QUALIFICATIONS OF A SPIRITUAL DIRECTOR

St. John of the Cross [57] points out the great difficulty of finding a spiritual guide, for such a one should be at once wise, zealous, discreet, and experienced, or at least well versed in the science of the ways of the Lord. Otherwise, like one blind man leading another, they both fall into the ditch.[58] Inexperienced and ignorant directors do more damage than good to souls. Judging as unlikely even such things as are very ordinary in certain states of the soul, and being incapable of understanding the light which God finds in His faithful servants, they terrify the soul. They may even attempt to lead all souls along the one path which they themselves know. As a matter of fact, He who leads the soul at this stage is the divine Spirit, who moves each according to His pleasure, and to such an extent that there can scarcely be found two souls who proceed in identically the same way.[59]

Therefore, when the Holy Ghost begins to take the reins, desiring to be the only guide, He renders the soul unable to follow the ordi-

---

[57] *Ascent of Mount Carmel*, Prologue; Bk. II, chap. 18; *Living Flame of Love*, stanza 3.

[58] Matt. 15:14; Luke 6:39.

[59] Gratian, *Itinerario*, chap. 7: "We call those masters or guides of the spirit, even though they be not confessors, who can direct the soul in the best method of procedure.... Some very spiritual and devout but unlettered men have done great harm in the Church of God because they wish to lead all by the same path which they themselves travel. Yet this way is not understood well by learning alone, for learned men lacking in devotion have also caused great damage and havoc by disdaining the great benefits which God usually bestows on humble souls and by branding as a fault, a fraud, or a scruple what is actually very real and helpful."

For that reason Godínez (*op. cit.*, Bk. VIII, chap. 13) says that "the great scholastic doctors, if they are not spiritual or if they have no experience in these things, are not usually good spiritual directors."

St. Teresa, *Life*, chap. 34: "We are wrong if we think that in the course of years we are bound to understand things that cannot possibly be attained without experience, and thus, as I have said, many are mistaken if they think they can learn to discern spirits without being spiritual themselves. I do not mean that, if a man is learned but not spiritual, he may not direct a person of spirituality. But in both outward and inward matters which depend upon the course of nature, his direction will of course be of an intellectual kind, while in supernatural matters he will see that it is in conformity with Holy Scripture. In other matters he must not worry himself to death, or think he understands what he does not, or quench the spirits, for these souls are being directed by another Master, greater than he, so that they are not without anyone over them. He must not be astonished at this or think such things are impossible: everything is possible to the Lord. He must strive to strengthen his faith and humble himself, because the Lord is perhaps making some old woman better versed in this science than himself, even though he be a very learned man."

nary norms of prudence or the special methods which the director persists in proposing. He gives the soul a facility for nothing but to remain with a certain loving attention, heeding as one enraptured, but not stupefied, what He intimately suggests or makes the soul feel. If, in spite of this, the soul endeavors to meditate as formerly, it will attempt the impossible and will effect nothing but the strangling of this interior motion, becoming more and more confused, and thus be rendered incapable of doing anything at all. It is here that bad directors fail, because they are not familiar with the ways of the Holy Ghost, or they cause those souls to fail which are not sufficiently courageous or docile to the interior voice. Thinking that such souls are slothful, when actually they are secretly receiving the inactivity and direction from the Holy Ghost, these bad directors oblige them to resist Him, or they impede what He is so lovingly working in them.

If the soul seeks God resolutely and with disinterestedness, all will work out to its greater advantage, for God will know how to lift it up in spite of the director and its own feeble efforts, and He will do this according to the method of prayer which He infuses in it.[60] But if the soul is not sufficiently generous, it will fall away little by little. It will eventually abandon that interior life in which it finds such obscurities and difficulties and will busy itself with other practices more in conformity with its own taste and that of its imprudent director.

These directors, if they were what they should be, would strive to discern exactly whether or not the soul's quiet or sloth is a work of the good Spirit. Knowing this (which is not so difficult to do by means of the fruits of this state), they would refrain from imposing useless laws or impediments to divine inspiration. It is not for the human director to point out the ways by which God must elevate the soul, but only to watch that the soul does not lose itself, is not carried on by its own private judgment, or is not held back by vain timidity. The director must hold back the soul when he sees that it

---

[60] "When God captivates the faculties," says an anonymous writer quoted by Sauvé (*Etats myst.*, p. 74), "the desire to resist Him is a struggle which ordinarily ends in triumph for God. If, by obedience to the confessor, the soul resists, it is at the cost of greatest sufferings; but God rewards the soul, now by raising it to a state of mystical ravishment, now by laying aside the body, as happens in the case of ecstasy."

SPIRITUAL GROWTH

is impulsive. When he finds the soul is indolent, he should stimulate it. But when the soul is advancing as it should, then he must be content to encourage, pacify, and preserve it in humility. To try to go into detail and to decide precisely which way the soul must follow is to restrict it in such a way that it wantonly resists the Holy Ghost.[61] Once it is manifest that the soul is moved by the Holy Ghost, the director must not repeatedly demand proofs, unless very serious doubts occur, for these serve only to harm and disconcert the soul. For confirmation of this, one might turn to the *Didache* of the first century.

When the soul realizes that its director impedes its progress, it ought to seek a better one or at least consult with one who is more learned and more discreet, if such a one is to be found. Only thus can it do all in its power to proceed with certainty. And if the soul does not find what it seeks, let it not forget what St. Teresa said: that it is better for the soul to be without a director than to be badly directed. In any case the soul should sincerely invoke the Father of lights, who gives wisdom in abundance to all who seek it.[62] It should have confidence in His divine Spirit, who knows how to supply to great advantage for the lack or deficiencies of human direction and to make even imprudent actions redound to greater profit for the faithful soul which wholeheartedly seeks the light and remains steadfast in trials.

But if the soul finds a good director, it should strive to follow him with all docility. The only exceptions are those cases where it might be better to follow the advice of one who is better; but never should a person consult many, only finally to follow his own caprice. By the obedience given to the director the soul sacrifices its judgment and

---

[61] La Figuera, *Suma espirit.*, III, dial. 7: " 'My call is more irresistible than theirs,' said our Lord to a certain soul, speaking of spiritual directors, 'and so, although they call souls by a certain way, it is of no avail if I, meanwhile, call them by another. Rather, such a situation brings them wretchedness and torment. For they desire that these souls follow their doctrine humbly and obediently while the souls themselves are unable to resist My Spirit, which places them on another road. This is the reason why, after such directors have exerted every effort to lead souls through fear, in the end the soul always works through love. Therefore it is useless for the director to call the soul to a consideration of the last things when I am calling that same soul through love, and it is futile for the director to insist on the meditation of My humanity, while I consume and inflame that soul with the fire of My divinity.' "

[62] Jas. 1:5.

will and sanctifies all its actions, which then become as so many other victories which the obedient man wins over himself. The least thing done out of obedience, say the holy doctors, avails more in the eyes of God than the most lofty and glorious enterprise done by self-will, even though it be the evangelization of the whole world.[63]

8. THE RELIGIOUS VOWS

This sacrifice or self-abnegation reaches the point of heroism when it is done for a lifetime and is sanctified by the vow of obedience, which is the most important of the three constituting the religious state. In this state the soul promises solemnly to observe, together with the precepts, the principal evangelical counsels. Hence, not content with any kind of life, it aspires always to ever greater perfection and unceasingly follows in the bloody footprints of the Crucified. By the three vows the soul entirely renounces the three great concupiscences that dominate the world.[64] The soul of the religious is consecrated entirely to God. It lives crucified with Christ and is united to Him in a special manner by these three indissoluble chains. The holy doctors compare the merit of the vows to that of martyrdom, and the souls that experience the things of God well know the worth of this loving union which is thus contracted with Him. Therefore they reap a great profit by renewing their vows, for they know how pleasing to God is the ratification of an act so heroic that it could be suggested only by the Spirit of fortitude.

To each vow there corresponds at least one of the principal beatitudes. The pure of heart shall see God; to those who abandon all things for Christ, is given the privilege of sitting with Him on thrones of glory to judge the world; to the poor in spirit, who renounce all attachment to creatures and even their own judgment and will, be-

---

[63] Tauler, *Institutions*, chap. 12: "By reason of the resignation of obedience, all one's works abound in grace. On the other hand, in those works which a virtuous man performs through self-will, it is difficult to discern whether they come from grace or from nature.... The road to hell is closed to him who has renounced his own will, for, as St. Bernard says, the fuel of hell's fire is self-will.... When a man rids himself of self, then God enters. How many religious are martyrs without fruit or merit! Full of self-will, they are their own guides and in their great works they merit little or no grace. If they would but give themselves to obedient resignation, they could become great saints."

[64] See I John 2:16.

longs the kingdom of heaven where the obedient man celebrates his victories.

Thence the great importance in the Church of those souls that are consecrated to God. Holy virgins have always been looked upon as perfect images of the Church itself and esteemed as its very eyes and a principal part of its heart. From among them are recruited the majority of souls that are truly contemplative and that soar in their flight to the sublime spheres of uncreated light.

9. PIOUS CONVERSATIONS AND SPIRITUAL READING

To converse with these souls, that are fervent and filled with God and that are the salt of the earth and the light of the world; to hear their heavenly conversation and see their example is a powerful means of inflaming hearts with holy and divine love. To participate in the communication of such souls is to share in their lights and even in the ardor of their charity. Their words are words of eternal life, words of God Himself, who deigns to speak through their lips. The good odor of Christ which their virtues exhale preserves many from the corruption of the world.[65]

Since the Savior Himself promised to be in the midst of those who are gathered together in His name, these holy conversations and pious friendships have a fruitful influence in animating and mutually illuminating the servants of God. Today, when the poison of impious propaganda is widespread and the ill effects of worldly or satanic influences have infiltrated from all sides, this is one of the most efficacious means for attracting anew many wandering souls to God. This it is that will inflame the weak with His love and will preserve good and fervent souls from timidity and many dangers.

This can even supply in particular cases for the want or absence of the word of God when there are few who preach it with the true spirit. On the other hand, if the preacher is filled with holy zeal and evangelical unction, his mission will give new richness and vigor to

---

[65] See St. Mary Magdalen of Pazzi, *op. cit.*, III, chap. 5, and Prologue.
Blessed Raymond of Capua writes of St. Catherine of Siena that "her words were like flaming darts, and there was no one who, on hearing her burning speech, would not feel is effects.... All who came to hear her, even those who came with the intention of scoffing at her, would leave with a feeling of compunction and correction."

his words. Therefore the ministry of preaching is a powerful means and is even indispensable in the Church for general improvement.

But souls desirous of perfection can, to a certain extent, supply the lack of this holy word, whether ministerial or charismatic, by pious reading, which breathes forth unction and sanctity. Here they will learn the right road, discover the snares of the tempter, and recognize their own faults and negligences. At the same time they will be filled with holy thoughts which preserve them from such thoughts as are vain and dangerous. They likewise receive the lights and inspirations which complete those obtained in prayer and meditation. Thus prayer and spiritual reading are mutual aids, one to the other, and are as two wings by which the soul can rise to God.

APPENDIX

1. Brief Rules of Perfection

"Attend to these few words in which is contained the rule for a pure and perfect life: Keep yourself separated from all mankind; renounce all knowledge of human and worldly affairs; keep a watch over your heart; subdue your affections; raise yourself above the pains and distractions of the world, the flesh, and nature. Direct your spirit to holy contemplation in which I shall be the constant object of your thoughts; ordain to this end all your spiritual exercises, vigils, fasts, poverty, austerities of life, mortifications of the body and the senses. Use these things only when they will aid you in attaining this end and that they may excite in you an awareness of the presence of God.

"In this way will you arrive at a perfection which not one out of a thousand attains because most Christians believe that all perfection consists in external practices. Year after year they exert their efforts in this way but they ever remain in the same state and never reach true perfection. . . .

"I tell you this so that you at least will be aided in arriving at that continual presence of God, that you may desire it and make it the norm of your conduct, consecrating your heart and mind to it. And when you notice that you have departed from this goal by lack of attention to this contemplation, understand that you thus deprive yourself of happiness. Return as quickly as possible to that goal. . . . But if you cannot remain constantly engaged in the contemplation of My divinity, return to it repeatedly through recollection and prayer. . . .

"My son, place all your cares on your God and take care never to forget your interior life. Keep yourself pure and free from all occupations that are not necessary. Lift your thoughts to heaven, fix them on God, and you will become more and more enlightened and you will know the sovereign Good" (Blessed Henry Suso, *Eternal Wisdom*, chap. 22).

"Perfection consists in doing the will of God, and not in understanding His designs. The designs of God, the good pleasure of God, the will of God, the operation of God and the gift of His grace are all one and the same thing in the spiritual life. It is God working in the soul to make it like unto Himself. Perfection is neither more nor less than the faithful cooperation of the soul with this work of God, and is begun, grows, and is consummated in the soul unperceived and in secret" (Caussade, *Abandonment to Divine Providence*, Bk. I, chap. 4).

"Our whole science consists in recognizing the designs of God for the present moment. All reading not intended for us by God is dangerous. . . . What was best for the moment that has passed is so no longer because it is no longer the will of God which, becoming apparent through other circumstances, brings to light the duty of the present moment. . . . If, by the divine will, it is a present duty to read, then reading will produce the destined effect in the soul. If it is the divine will that reading be relinquished for contemplation, then this will perform the work of God in the soul and reading would become useless and prejudicial. Should the divine will withdraw the soul from contemplation for the hearing of confessions, etc., and that even for some considerable time, this duty becomes the means of uniting the soul with Jesus Christ and all the sweetness of contemplation would only serve to destroy this union. Our moments are made fruitful by our fulfilment of the will of God. This is presented to us in countless different ways by the present duty which forms, increases, and consummates in us the new man until we attain the plenitude destined for us by the divine wisdom. . . . This fruit, as we have already said, is produced, nourished, and increased by the performance of those duties which become successively present, and which are made fruitful by the same divine will. In fulfilling these duties we are always sure of possessing the 'better part' because this holy will is itself the better part, it only requires to be allowed to act and that we should abandon ourselves blindly to it with perfect confidence. . . . It is the will of God which bestows through these things, no matter what they may be, an efficacious grace by which the image of Jesus Christ is renewed in our souls" (*ibid.*, chap. 5).

"When God requires action, sanctity is to be found in activity. Besides the duties imposed on everyone by their state in life God may require certain actions which are not included in these duties, although they may not be in any way opposed to them. An attraction and inspiration are then the signs of the divine approval. Souls conducted by God in this way will find a greater perfection in adding the things inspired to those that are commanded. . . . Duties imposed by the state of life and by divine Providence are common to all the saints and are what God arranges for all in general. . As there are souls whose whole duty is defined by exterior laws, and who should not go beyond them because restricted by the will of God; so also there are others who, besides exterior duties, are obliged to carry out faithfully that interior rule imprinted on their hearts" (*ibid.*, chap. 8).

2. Spiritual Direction and the Freedom of the Sons of God

"Set the soul in peace, and draw it away and free it from the yoke and slavery of the weak operation of its own capacity, which is the captivity of Egypt, . and guide it, oh, spiritual director, to the promised land flowing with milk and honey, remembering that it is to give the soul this freedom and holy rest which belongs to His sons that God calls it into the wilderness. . . . Endeavor, then, when the soul is nearing this state, to detach it from all coveting of spiritual sweetness, pleasure, delight and meditation, and disturb it not with care and solicitude of any kind for higher things, still less for lower things, but bring it into the greatest possible degree of solitude and withdrawal. For the more the soul attains of all this, and the sooner it reaches this restful tranquillity, the more abundantly does it become infused with the spirit of Divine Wisdom, which is the loving, tranquil, lonely, peaceful, sweet inebriator of the spirit.

SPIRITUAL GROWTH

Hereby the soul feels itself to be gently and tenderly wounded and ravished, knowing not by whom, nor whence, nor how. And the reason of this is that the Spirit communicates Himself without any act on the part of the soul.

"These blessings, with the greatest facility, by no more than the slightest act which the soul may desire to make on its own account, are disturbed or hindered in the soul, which is a grave evil and a great shame and pity.

"Although this evil is so great and serious that it cannot be exaggerated, it is so common and frequent that there will hardly be found a single spiritual director who does not inflict it upon souls whom God is beginning to draw nearer to Himself in this kind of contemplation. For, whenever God is anointing the contemplative soul with some most delicate unction of loving knowledge—serene, peaceful, lonely and very far removed from sense and from all that has to do with thought—so that the soul cannot meditate or think of aught soever or find pleasure in aught, . . . there will come some spiritual director who has no knowledge save of hammering souls and pounding them with the faculties like a blacksmith, and, because his only teaching is of that kind, and he knows of naught save meditation, he will say: 'Come now, leave these periods of inactivity, for you are only living in idleness and wasting your time. Get to work, meditate and make interior acts, for it is right that you should do for yourself that which in you lies, for these other things are the practices of Illuminists and fools.'

"And thus, since such persons have no understanding of the degrees of prayer or the ways of the spirit, they cannot see that those acts which they counsel the soul to perform, and those attempts to walk in meditation, have been done already, for such a soul as we have been describing . has reached the way of the spirit, which is contemplation, wherein ceases the operation of sense and of the soul's own discursive reasoning, and God alone is the agent and it is He that now speaks secretly to the solitary soul, while the soul keeps silence. And if, now that the spirit has achieved this in the way that we have described, such directors attempt to make the soul continue to walk in sense, it cannot but go backward and become distracted. For if one that has reached his goal begins to set out again for it, he is doing a ridiculous thing, for he can do nothing but walk away from it. . . . And the worst result is that, through the exercise of its natural operation, the soul loses its interior recollection and solitude and consequently spoils the wondrous work that God was painting in it. It is thus as if the director were merely striking an anvil; and the soul loses in one respect and gains nothing in the other.

"Let such guides of the soul as these take heed and remember that the principal agent and guide and mover of souls in this matter is not the director, but the Holy Spirit, Who never loses His care for them; and that they themselves are only instruments to lead souls in the way of perfection by the faith and the law of God, according to the spirituality that God is giving to each one. Let them not, therefore, merely aim at guiding these souls according to their own way and the manner suitable to themselves, but let them see if they know the way by which God is leading the soul, and, if they know it not, let them leave the soul in peace and not disturb it. And, in conformity with the way and the spirit by which God is leading these souls, let them ever seek to lead them into greater solitude, tranquillity and liberty of spirit and to give them a certain freedom so that the spiritual and bodily senses may not be bound to any particular thing, either interior or exterior, when God leads them by this way of solitude, and let them not worry or grieve, thinking that the soul is doing nothing; for though the soul is not working at that time, God is working in it.

"God, like the sun, is above our souls and ready to communicate Himself to them. Let those who guide them be content with preparing the soul for this according to evangelical perfection, which is detachment and emptiness of sense and of spirit; and let them not seek to go beyond this in the building up of the soul, for that work belongs only to the Father of lights, from Whom comes down every good gift and perfect boon" (*Living Flame of Love*, stanza 3).

Collective Growth and the Sacramental Functions

Apart from the above-mentioned means for acquiring an increase of grace, an increase that is in the measure of the spirit of charity with which they are used and by which we are placed in direct communication with God, the Church possesses other means for diffusing life among the members of Christ and for making that life flow from the divine Head through the hierarchical organs. These means either confer grace or increase it, not only by reason of the spirit with which they are used, but by reason of the very work done, *ex opere operato*, even when, through involuntary causes, devotion is lacking or the intention is not actual. Such are the sacraments, those divine-human vital channels or arteries through which the blood of the Redeemer circulates, under the impulse of the charity of the Holy Ghost, to animate, purify, invigorate, heal, or revivify the members that offer no resistance. The sacramental functions consecrate and sanctify both the individual life and the social life of good Christians.

1. THE ROLE OF EACH SACRAMENT

Of all the sacraments, those most indispensable for each of the faithful in particular are baptism, which begins the spiritual life, and the Eucharist, which perfects and completes it, as the Angelic Doctor teaches.[66] The former has for its direct object the giving of life, not its increase. Its function is to make us be born, rather than to make us grow; to establish the bonds uniting us to Jesus Christ, but not to strengthen them, although, *per accidens*, when conferred on a catechumen who is already in the state of grace, it does increase that grace. The Eucharist has as its proper object the conservation of grace and its increase. Therefore, if we do not receive this spiritual food wherein we eat the flesh and drink the blood of the Son of God, we cannot live spiritually.[67]

Lamentable it is that many Christians wait years and years to receive the Eucharist or receive it rarely, although without it one cannot long conserve spiritual life. Indeed, it is more or less the practice to consider the first Communion of a child as the crowning point of its entire religious education and formation. Actually it ought to be but the beginning and the means best suited to promote that religious formation. The first Communion ceremony is surrounded with great solemnity, but it is given a signification far different from what it actually possesses. Instead of being the introduction to a new life, entirely divine, it has become the presentation of the child to society, its debut into the life of the world where he will soon forget

---
[66] IIIa, q. 79, a. 1.
[67] John 6:54.

THE MYSTICAL EVOLUTION

the few religious practices which he had performed up to that time.[68]

The most indispensable sacrament, after baptism, is the Eucharist. Even penance, although very profitable, is not absolutely necessary to one who has not committed grave faults. Confirmation, which seals us as soldiers of Christ and enables us to confess in the name of the Church, is not of strict necessity as long as extraordinary dangers do not threaten, in spite of the importance of the charisms which accompany this mystical seal. But nourishment for life and growth is certainly necessary. The sacrament of confirmation, once received, impresses us with a military character that will last forever, but spiritual nourishment must be continual and, we might add, more and more abundant. So it is true that both of these sacraments strengthen us, but not in the same way. Thus St. Thomas states that in confirmation "grace is increased and perfected for resisting the outward assaults of Christ's enemies"; but that by the Eucharist "grace receives increase, and the spiritual life is perfected, so that man may stand perfect in himself by union with God." [69]

Each of the other sacraments also confer a special grace. In penance it is reparative, curative, medicinal, or revivifying; in extreme unction, the final and supreme remedy against spiritual sorrows and weaknesses, it soothes and comforts at the same time that it purifies. But in Communion the grace is of itself augmentative and unitive. The other two sacraments are ordained to the social life of the Church: matrimony confers on the contracting parties the graces necessary to make their union faithful, holy, fruitful, in imitation of that between Christ and His Church. Holy orders consecrates the ministers of God as dispensing organs of His sacred mysteries and distributors of His graces,[70] thus ensuring the perpetuity of these functions in the mystical body and conferring a special grace on the ordinands, that they may perform their duties worthily and holily.

The sacrament of holy orders cannot be repeated, because it imprints a character. Nor can matrimony be repeated as long as the bond is not broken by the death of one of the contracting parties.

---

[68] Father Arintero is referring, of course, to the practice prevalent in many Latin countries. (Tr.)
[69] IIIa, q.79, a.1, ad 1um.
[70] See I Cor. 4:1.

SPIRITUAL GROWTH

Extreme unction may not be received again unless a new serious illness occurs or an extraordinary danger develops in the same illness. Only penance and the Eucharist can be repeated at our good pleasure. They are the two sacraments directly ordained to our spiritual progress and the two most efficacious means of furthering it, owing to the special graces which they confer: the one purifying and healing, the other nourishing, fortifying, and increasing charity and the deifying union.[71]

2. IMPORTANCE OF THE EUCHARIST AND PENANCE

"The Eucharist," says Suarez, "has a proper characteristic which is not found in any of the other sacraments: it is directly ordained to the nourishment of charity that it may grow and unite us more closely with God. Each of the other sacraments has a special function in virtue of which it confers particular helps with an increase of grace, but the Eucharist is ordained directly to the perfection of the union of the faithful soul with Christ and His mystical body."[72]

"It is," says St. Bonaventure, "the sacrament of union. Its first effect is to unite; not that it produces the first union, but it fortifies that which is already contracted."[73] The Council of Florence teaches that "the effect of the Eucharist is to unite men to Jesus Christ; and,

---

[71] Lallemant, *op. cit.*, V, chap. 3, art. 1: "By sacramental grace is meant the right which each sacrament gives us before God, of receiving from Him certain succours which preserve within us the effect that sacrament has wrought in our soul. Thus the sacramental grace of baptism is a right which baptism gives us to receive lights and inspirations to lead a supernatural life, as members of Jesus Christ, animated by His Spirit. The sacramental grace of confirmation is a right to receive strength and constancy to combat against our enemies, as soldiers of Jesus Christ, and to win glorious victories over them. The sacramental grace of confession is a right to receive an increase of purity of heart. That of communion is a right to receive more abundant and efficacious succours to unite us to God by the fervour of His love. Each time we confess and communicate in a good state, these sacramental graces and the gifts of the Holy Spirit increase in us; and yet we do not perceive their effects in our daily life. Whence comes this? From our unmortified passions, our attachments and disorderly affections, and our habitual faults. We allow these vicious principles to have more dominion over us than sacramental graces and the gifts of the Holy Spirit, so that the former keep the latter, as it were, bound and captive, without the power of producing their proper effects. And why do we let sin and the vicious principles of corrupt nature usurp this despotic empire over the divine principles of grace and the Spirit of God? It is for want of entering often into ourselves. If we did so, we should discover the state of our interior and correct its disorders."

[72] *De Eucharistia*, D. 63, sect. 1.

[73] *In IV*, dist. 12, a. 1, q. 2.

since it is grace that incorporates us in Him and unites us to His other members, so it is that this sacrament produces in us an increase of grace and the virtues." [74]

So, then, the life of grace is received in baptism, strengthened in confirmation, and preserved by the Eucharist as well as developed and perfected. For that reason St. Thomas says that the Eucharist is the perfection of the spiritual life. And since the Eucharist is the bread of the divine life, all the effects which ordinary bread produces in the natural life—nourishment, growth, restoration, and delight—will be produced by this sacrament in the spiritual life, as the Council of Florence teaches, in conformity with the Angelic Doctor.

Nor is this figure of bread a strange one, for the Savior Himself conclusively affirmed it when He said: "My flesh is meat indeed; and My blood is drink indeed." It is worthy of note that this sacrament alone is expressly designated in the Gospel as the sacrament of life, and this with an insistence that cannot be void of meaning: "I am the living bread which came down from heaven. If any man eat of this bread, he shall live forever; and the bread that I will give is My flesh for the life of the world. . . . Amen, amen, I say unto you: Except you eat the flesh of the Son of man, and drink His blood, you shall not have life in you. He that eateth My flesh and drinketh My blood hath everlasting life; and I will raise him up in the last day. For My flesh is meat indeed, and My blood is drink indeed. . . . As the living Father hath sent Me, and I live by the Father, so he that eateth Me, the same also shall live by Me." [75]

"The whole genesis of the supernatural life," says Bellamy, "is contained in these final words, which are amazingly profound. God the Father, who is life par excellence, *Pater vivens*, is the infinite mainstay of this life. He communicates it in its sovereign plenitude to the Word and, through Him, to the Holy Ghost, both of whom eternally live the same life as the Father. In the Incarnation the divine life pours out, so to speak, from the breast of the adorable Trinity to be diffused in the humanity of Jesus Christ in all possible plenitude: *Et ego vivo propter Patrem*. It is from this august font, who proceeds from the Infinite, that the torrents of supernatural life burst forth in our souls when we receive Communion. *Qui manducat*

---
[74] *Decret. pro Armenis.*
[75] John 6:52-58.

me, et ipse vivet propter me. So it is that the life of grace comes to us in a direct line from the inaccessible heights of the most holy Trinity through the incarnate Word ever present in the Eucharist. Communion is, therefore, the sacrament of life, the life proper to God, mysteriously communicated to the human soul." [76]

The Eucharist, then, has the special power of communicating divine life to us. It is certain that this life is identical in whatever way we receive it, for it always consists in a participation of the divine nature and an assimilation to God. Since through reception of the Eucharist the soul approaches to the divine Model in such an intimate manner, it is correct to conclude that the soul receives in the very depth of its being a clearer impression of the Divinity. The very same life that we received in baptism, by which we were reborn in God, is augmented in the Eucharist because in both of these sacraments God communicates to us something of His own nature. There is this difference however: Baptism is the beginning of that life whereas the Eucharist is its growth. In the first, it is the life of the infant; in the second, that of the mature man. And this life is destined to increase continually because of itself it knows neither decline nor languor. As the eternal font of youth and maturity, the Eucharist is the crowning point of the supernatural life.[77]

The involuntary privation of sacramental Communion or the inability to receive it as often as we might wish to is supplanted to a great extent by spiritual Communion. This can be renewed at all times and, depending upon the love with which it is made and the intensity of desire which it manifests for a real reception of the bread of life, it produces a great increase of grace.

Not only must we grow in the spiritual life, but we are obliged to renew ourselves from day to day by purifying ourselves of our imperfections, washing away whatever stains we have contracted,

---

[76] Bellamy, *op. cit.*, pp. 260 ff. Maldonatus, *In Joan.* 6:58: "That eternal and divine life which God has by nature, Christ had as man, through the hypostatic union with the Divinity, so that whatever was in God was shared by His human nature. But we, through the conjunction which is effected in the reception of the body and blood of Christ, are united to Him in a real sense. As the life of Christ's human nature was made divine and happily immortal through the hypostatic union, so also is ours through our union with His body."

[77] "The first act of the spiritual life is given through baptism . . . but in the Eucharist is given the perfection of the spiritual life" (St. Thomas, *In IV Sent.*, dist. 8, q.1, a.2; q.5, a.2).

curing our spiritual languor, and immediately revivifying ourselves if we have the sad misfortune to lose the life of grace. All this is accomplished by the sacrament of penance. No one, without a singular privilege such as that enjoyed by the Blessed Virgin, can pass through this life without having the earthly dust cling to him and without being stained by many small defects, at least involuntary ones.

Hence the importance of this sacrament which, after Communion, is the principal means that souls can employ to foster their spiritual progress either directly or indirectly. By it we rid ourselves of the obstacles to grace and even increase that grace, at least in its medicinal aspect. This grace, in turn, prevents us in some measure from falling into new faults and makes us more vigorous in rooting out the seeds of sin. When received by a soul in grace, sacramental absolution increases life at the same time that it cures, purifies, and invigorates it.

It is true that this sacrament can be supplanted in great measure by frequent reception of the Eucharist and the virtue of penance, as happened in the early centuries of the Church when the discipline of public confession was in force. Indeed the virtue of penance is always absolutely essential so that we may correct our faults as soon as we are aware of them, without waiting for the reception of sacramental absolution. Yet absolution corrects the deficiencies of the virtue of penance, and thus simple attrition is converted into contrition, and satisfaction itself acquires a much greater value, because of the efficacy of the sacrament.

Therefore devout souls are not content with the general examination of conscience and the particular examination on the dominant fault which they are seeking to correct. Nor do they stop at the voluntary imposition of penances and privations as works of satisfaction by which they endeavor to chastise and correct themselves, although all these things are powerful means for advancement. If a confessor is available, these souls purify themselves at least once a week by sacramental confession. It may be noted here that, since the confessor is frequently also the director and regulator of private penances, it is necessary that he himself be well versed in the science of the ways of God.[78]

When spiritual souls are unable to find a worthy priest who knows

[78] See St. Alphonsus Liguori, *Practica del Conf.*, IV.

how to give them, in addition to absolution, the bread of salutary doctrine, in his capacity as an official minister of the Church, then they will do well to seek it from any person in whom they find it, whatever his state or condition. For in persons of all states, sexes, and ages, great souls and even learned theologians and notable prelates have found an excellent direction which they could not find elsewhere. This truth is evident in the lives of St. Catherine of Siena, St. Brigid, St. Catherine de Ricci, St. Teresa, Blessed Angela de Foligno, Blessed Osanna of Mantua, Venerable Mary of Agreda, Venerable Marina de Escobar, Venerable Micaela Aguirre, and many others.

3. THE SACRAMENTALS

After the sacraments come the sacramentals, which ordain and prepare for the sacraments themselves. The sacramentals are all those things which the Church consecrates to increase Christian piety, to help in the sanctification and purification of the faithful, and to make more intimate the bond of union among the members of the "three Churches." Among these sacramentals we may note the following: the devotional use of holy water, which, when received with the right spirit, is helpful in purifying us and preserving us from diabolical annoyances; the recitation of the Our Father; general confession; the blessing of priests; the listening to the preaching of the divine word; indulgences; the cult of the saints; suffrages for the souls in purgatory, and approved devotions (among which, because of its efficacy and universality, the Rosary deserves special mention). Finally and especially, after the Most Holy Sacrifice, which is offered for the living and the dead, we mention the Office which, because of its excellence, is called divine, for it is proper to the angels and the sons of God to be engaged in the perpetual worship of the heavenly Father, Jesus Christ our Redeemer, and the vivifying Spirit.

The Church, animated as it is by this divine Spirit, desires that day and night there should be consecrated souls blessing and praising the Father of mercies and the Savior of men. Consequently at all times there is someone officially praying for those who are indifferent to their eternal salvation and forgetful of the divine benefits. Woe to them if there were no one to assist them by ceaseless prayer! The proper function and principal obligation of those chosen souls is to be occupied in the divine praises. That they may not be molested by other cares and affairs, they receive from the faithful the alms necessary for their daily sustenance so that they, in turn, may spiritually sustain the faithful by prayer and sacrifice.

To these consecrated souls, who pray in an official capacity and in the name of the Church, are closely associated all the faithful of good spirit who, as often as their occupations permit, take part in the public worship by assisting at the Divine Office. Such pious souls prefer the liturgy to their own private devotions, which easily degenerate into vain sentimentality.

The sacramentals also include devotion to the saints, whom we should honor and venerate as friends of God that are already deified and glorified along with Jesus Christ. We ought to make them our intercessors, especially when we see other avenues closed, because the Savior Himself desires it for their honor and our profit. "Where I am," says Christ, "there also shall My minister be. If any man minister to Me, him will My Father honor." [79] Therefore the saints share in the glory which He receives from the Father.[80]

4. DEVOTION TO THE BLESSED VIRGIN

In this cult of the saints that of the glorious Mother of God and our Mother, the Mother of grace and mercy, surpasses all others and is indispensable for the faithful. As the coredemptrix, associated with the Redeemer from the Incarnation to the Ascension, from the crib to Calvary, she is the channel of all graces and the dispenser of all the divine treasures.[81] As the faithful Spouse of the Holy Ghost, she cooperates with Him in the entire work of our renewal and sanctification. "In her is all grace of the way and of the truth, in her is all hope of life, and of virtue. He that shall find her, shall find life, and he shall have salvation from the Lord. But he that shall sin against her, shall hurt his own soul. All that hate her, love death." [82] She is the

---

[79] John 12:26.
[80] IIIa, q.25, a.6: "Now it is manifest that we should show honor to the saints of God, as being members of Christ, the children and friends of God, and our intercessors. Wherefore, in memory of them we ought to honor any relics of theirs in a fitting manner: principally their bodies, which were temples, and organs of the Holy Ghost dwelling and operating in them, and are destined to be likened to the body of Christ by the glory of the Resurrection."
[81] "Hear me, my sons, and believe me," said St. Philip Neri, "I know that there is no more powerful means for obtaining God's grace than the Blessed Virgin."
[82] Ecclus. 24:25; Prov. 8:35 f.

SPIRITUAL GROWTH

Seat of Wisdom and is full of grace and she can give us a share of her plenitude. Therefore devotion to the Blessed Virgin, which consists in honoring her from the heart and imitating her in truth, is one of the surest signs of predestination.[83] Without her mediation it is most difficult, if not impossible, to be saved, for in the mystical body of the Church, Mary unites the Head with the rest of the members and enables them to receive the divine impulses.[84]

So it is that the greatest saints were renowned for their filial devotion to the most holy Virgin. No soul proceeds securely along the paths of virtue and arrives at the mystical union without being under the protection of Mary Immaculate, behind whom all the virgins walk to be presented to the King of Glory.

In addition to these indispensable helps, the sanctifying power of the Church manifests itself in the numerous other means which she has for fostering the general progress of the mystical body as a whole, and of each organ in particular. The Church is ever renewing and adapting these various channels of power in order to make use of those which are more opportune according to the condition of the times or the needs of souls. Thus the Church is ever singing to God

---

[83] Ecclus. 24:31.

[84] Therefore, in a complete exposition of Christian perfection, observes Father Weiss (*Apologie*, X, 22, 3), it is almost as indispensable to speak of Mary as it is to speak of Christ, because, like Him, she is for us "much more than a perfect model of all the virtues. Since she is the Mother of the Source of all graces, she is truly, as the litanies call her, the Mother of divine grace. As without her we never would have possessed the Giver of all grace, so also we do not receive any grace except through her. We deliberately say *through* her, and not *without* her; for not only does she procure grace for us by her intercession, but it is actually through her hands that we receive all the graces which the Redeemer merited for us. So, as she was the channel through which Jesus Christ came to us in human form to effect the work of our redemption, so is she the way by which the fruits of that work come to us (St. Albert the Great, *De laudibus B. Mariae*, IX, 15; St. Bernard, *Nativitas Mariae*, no. 4; Petrus Cellens, *De panibus*, chap. 12). Mary is the mistress and dispenser of everything that pertains to the divine family. She holds the key to all the treasures of the house of God (St. Bernard, *Annuntiatio*, III, 7; St. Albert, *loc. cit.*, X, 17). Further, those treasures consist of graces, but they were not given to her for her own enjoyment alone. If she is full of grace, it is also for our behalf. Therefore, as a bridegroom takes pleasure in honoring his bride by letting pass through her hands the benefits which he desires to dispense, so also does the Holy Ghost, the distributor of graces and her immaculate Spouse, do in regard to Mary. . . . Jesus Christ is the fountainhead of grace, Mary is the ocean to which the Holy Ghost directs the rivulets which flow from the wounds of the Savior so that all may drink thereof (Agreda, *The City of God*, I, no. 603). Therefore he who seeks graces from God ought to turn to Mary, because it is through her that we obtain whatever we receive from Him (St. Bernard, *Nativ. Mariae*, nos. 7 f.)."

a new canticle. In another work [85] we have treated the development of devotions in the Church. We shall now dwell upon the Eucharist, whose efficacy is always new and whose importance in the spiritual life ever increases instead of diminishing.

Singular Importance of the Eucharist

In the Eucharist, the sacrament of sacraments, we are nourished by Jesus Christ, we grow in Him, we live His very life, and we are united to Him to the point of being identified and transformed in Him.

If we are to grow as sons of God, we need a divine food. Actually, were it not for our innate weakness, this food could very well consist in simply doing the will of the Father in order to perfect His work.[86] But since we are so weak and remiss in doing the Father's will, we must reinforce our weakness and repair our losses by being invigorated with the strength of the Word. This we do by eating His flesh and drinking His blood, without which we are unable to maintain life.[87] This divine food so invigorates us that we are able to climb the holy mountain of God and live eternally. In receiving His body, we receive at the same time His blood, His soul, His divinity; in a word, Jesus Christ entirely, as He is in Himself. Thus we are completely transformed. "We eat and drink true God and true man," says St. Ephrem, "and in Him we are absorbed so that we live in Him."

Since it is the food of the soul, the Eucharist presupposes spiritual life. The dead do not eat, and any food inserted in them, instead of vivifying them, would serve only to hasten corruption. The same thing happens to one who dares to receive the Eucharist in sin. Yet, if such a person is in good faith, thinking himself to be in the state of grace, and if he has sorrow for all his faults, then this sacrament of love, not finding any obstacles by reason of an affection for sin,

---

[85] *Evolución Organica*, chap. 2.
[86] John 4:34.
[87] John 6:54. "The Word," exclaims St. Clement of Alexandria (*Pedagog.*, I, chap. 6), "is all things to the infant which He has engendered: He is father, mother, teacher, and nurse. *Eat My flesh*, He says, *and drink My blood*. The Lord offers us a food that is adapted to our condition, so that nothing is wanting to us for our growth. . . . He alone dispenses to the children the milk of love. A thousand times blessed is he who is suckled at these divine breasts."

will turn his attrition into contrition and will produce a true filial love and with it life. Therefore, although destined to cause an increase of grace, the Eucharist can also produce grace itself, *per accidens*.

That this is a sacrament of life, ordained directly to the conservation and increase of that life, is evident from its very institution, where it is presented as the living bread sent from heaven to give eternal life.[88] With such insistence does the Savior thus represent this sacrament that He never wearies of repeating this basic notion as that which is most proper to this sacrament. If the other sacraments can also maintain and increase grace, they do so in an indirect manner, but this sacrament has as its primary object the increase of life and the fostering of our interior growth. "The blood of Jesus Christ," says St. Cyril, "is not only vital, but vivifying." [89] It is the fountainhead of life; by being physically united to it, we receive the torrents of its plenitude.[90] It is in this sacrament that we shall "draw waters with joy out of the savior's fountains." [91]

1. EUCHARISTIC UNION AND THE MYSTICAL MARRIAGE

An increase in the life of grace causes an increase in charity and union with God. It also binds more tightly the bonds which attach us to our divine Head and the other members of the mystical body in the unity of the Spirit. The sacraments effect what they signify. The sacrament of the Eucharist is offered to us in the form of food and it symbolizes the union of the faithful. Therefore it produces this union, but in an analogous manner and in an inverse order to that of ordinary food, which is converted into our own substance.[92] "He that eateth My flesh and drinketh My blood," says the Savior,

---

[88] John 6:48–58.
[89] *Contra Nestor.*, Bk. IV.
[90] Weiss, *op. cit.*, X, 16: "If all the sacraments are fonts of grace, the most sublime of all is, without any doubt, that one which contains the Author and Giver of grace. Through this sacrament we are changed into one body with Him (Cyril of Jer., *Cat.*, 22; Chrysos., *Herb. hom.*, 6, 2). In this intimate communication He courses through our hearts like a fiery torrent, not to be eventually exhausted and extinguished, but to draw us to Himself and to transform us into Himself (St. Gert., *Leg. div. piet.*, 3, 26). We do not change this food into ourselves, as happens with ordinary food, but He changes us into Himself."
[91] Isa. 12:3.
[92] Father Arintero is here referring to the words of St. Paul in his First Epistle

"abideth in Me, and I in him." [93] "The indication that a man truly eats of the body of the Savior," says St. Augustine, "is whether he abides and dwells in Christ and Christ in Him." [94] Although the corporal union and the indwelling of the Eucharist is transitory, the spiritual indwelling, to which it is ordained, ought to be perpetual. Bossuet says that Jesus comes to our bodies that He may be united to our souls.[95] What He seeks above all is the hearts of men; and when men do not give their hearts completely to Him, they do Him violence,[96] and He is obliged to hold back the impetuous river of graces with which He desires to inundate them.

The sacrament of the Eucharist is the work of that prodigious love with which Jesus loved us till the end and by which He draws all things to Himself in order to divinize them.[97] As St. Dionysius says, love is essentially unitive.[98] Hence, in the discourse at the Last Sup-

---

to the Corinthians, 10:16-18: "The chalice of benediction which we bless, is it not the communion of the blood of Christ? And the bread which we break, is it not the partaking of the body of the Lord? For we, being many, are one bread, one body, all that partake of one bread."

This would not be the case if the Eucharistic bread were any kind of bread, for natural food is changed into the substance of him who partakes of it, and therefore the many who eat of the same natural bread are not made one body. But, by receiving the bread which is the body and blood of Christ, all those who partake of that bread are transformed spiritually into Christ and more intimately united with one another. (Tr.)

[93] John 6:57.
[94] *In Joan.*, XXVII, no. 1.
[95] *Sermo I, Nativ. S.V.*
[96] "They do violence to the body and blood," says St. Cyprian, *Lib. de laps.*
[97] Hettinger, *Apologie des Christenthums*, p. 32: "The Word of God, by becoming man and taking His place in creation, has glorified and deified all creatures. ... In man, matter has been raised to the life of the spirit; in Christ, all creation has been elevated to the life of God, and humanity has been set upon a divine throne. What was effected in the Head through the Incarnation, must be continued, completed, and extended through the sacred banquet, to embrace all the members of the body in an ever-widening circle so that all will turn to God through this Mediator, be united with Him, and share in His glory. Christ was united to human nature in a most intimate manner, which only His wisdom was able to invent, only His love was able to desire, and only His power was able to effect. But now, in the mystery of the Eucharist, He is united with each member of the Church in a manner so perfect that only He could have conceived the idea of such a union. This union, this mutual penetration, this fusion of man with Jesus Christ, is so intimate, so sublime, that it can be compared only to the union of the eternal Father with His only-begotten Son, as is seen from the words of the Lord Himself. ... In the Incarnation, Christ raised the whole human race to God; in the sacred banquet, He takes possession of each man individually in order to transport him to the bosom of God."
[98] *De divin. nomin.*, chap. 4.

SPIRITUAL GROWTH

per the Savior prayed for and demanded with great insistence the perfect union of the faithful among themselves and with Him.[99] St. Paul voices this same thought when he says: "We, being many, are one bread, one body, all that partake of one bread."[100] Therefore the Council of Trent calls the Eucharist "the emblem of the union of the mystical body, the sign of unity, the bond of charity, and the symbol of peace and concord."[101]

The Eucharist is a banquet of most familiar union where only the close friends take part. "Eat, O friends, and drink, and be inebriated, my dearly beloved."[102] Those first invited were the Apostles, for they had merited the name of friends and tasters of the secrets of God.[103] The Savior even deigned to wash their feet, as if to show them what purity of heart this banquet requires. No one, under pain of condemnation, can present himself at this banquet unless he has on the wedding garment of charity.[104] Those who are soiled are excluded from the banquet of the nuptials of the Lamb.[105] But those who, clean in heart and clothed in virtue, frequently partake of this divine feast, grow to a marked extent in the union of charity. As long as the first disciples "were persevering in the doctrine of the apostles and in the communication of the breaking of bread and in prayers," as St. Luke says, they had "but one heart and one soul."[106]

Not content with producing that union of conformity, the Eucharist gradually effects a total transformation of souls in Jesus Christ. For it is precisely to bring about this transformation that He comes to us in the form of food. However, there is this difference, that He, being divine and more powerful than we, transforms us into Himself instead of being changed into our own substance.

---

[99] John 17:10-23.
[100] See I Cor. 10:17.
[101] Session XIII, can. 8. Hettinger, *loc. cit.*: "The Most Blessed Sacrament is the divine-human bond, visible and invisible, which unites all the members of the Church with Jesus Christ and among themselves. It is, in the body of the Church, the heart, which gives the impulse to the supernatural life and makes the currents of salvation circulate through all the members."
[102] Cant. 5:1.
[103] "You are My friends if you do the things that I command you. I will not now call you servants, for the servant knoweth not what his lord doth. But I have called you friends, because all things whatsoever I have heard of My Father, I have made known to you" (John 15:14 f.).
[104] Matt. 22:11-13.
[105] Apoc. 19:9; 22:15.
[106] Acts 2:41-46; 4:32.

This is precisely what He promised to St. Augustine when He said: "I am the food of grown men: grow and you shall eat Me. And you shall not change Me into yourself as bodily food, but into Me you shall be changed." [107]

"Since the power of this heavenly bread incomparably exceeds that of those who receive it," says St. Albert the Great, "it changes them into itself." [108] "The partaking of the body and blood of Christ," St. Leo teaches, "effects nothing other than that we become what we receive." [109] St. Dionysius declares: "If anyone approaches the divine banquet with purity, he is transformed into the Divinity as a result of this participation." [110] St. Thomas states that "the proper effect of this sacrament is the conversion of man into Jesus Christ, in such a way that he can truly say: *I live, now not I, but Christ liveth in me.*" [111] In one of the opuscula attributed to the same holy doctor, we read: "The Lord makes the faithful soul that worthily receives Him a member of His body. He incorporates such a one in the union of charity and assimilates him to the image of His sovereign goodness. . . And so, as a drop of water which falls into a vat of wine is transformed into wine . so the immensity of the sweetness and power of Christ, in taking possession of our poor heart, transforms it so that in thought, word, and deed we manifest ourselves no longer as worldly men, or even as ourselves, but as Jesus Christ." [112] Thus we see that the holy doctors attribute to the

---

[107] *Confessions*, Bk. VII, chap. 10.
[108] *In IV*, dist. 9, a.4, ad 1um.
[109] *Sermo 62 de Pass.*, 12, chap. 7.
[110] *Eccl. hier.*, chap. 3, sect. 1.
[111] *In IV Sent.*, dist. 12, q.2, a.1, ad 1um.
[112] *De Sacramento Altissimo*, chap. 20. "Thou hast left to the soul Thy body and blood," says St. Magdalen of Pazzi (*op. cit.*, I, chap. 11), "so that it might continually abide in Thee and see itself, in a sense, deified and transformed by this continual communication and union. What delightful colloquies the soul has with Thee when it leans on Thy heart and Thou on its heart, however little the love it has! How can it help but be inflamed with the ardent flames of Thy charity and in the furnace of love which Thou dost set afire within it when Thou dost enter its breast in so wonderful and loving a fashion? . . . What dost Thou do there? Thou dost introduce thoughts in us which I cannot call anything but thoughts of love, and those who receive Thee share, up to a certain point, in Thy capacity and Thy divine communications. . . . Thou art that new way of which the Apostle speaks: *We have confidence to enter the Holies in virtue of the blood of Christ, a new and living way which he inaugurated for us through the veil (that is, his flesh)*. . . . As the waters which fall into the sea immediately lose their identity and proper existence, so when we enter into this ocean of the Divinity . . . what happens? *I have said: You are gods and all of you the sons of the most High* (Ps. 81:6). But

SPIRITUAL GROWTH

Eucharist in a singular manner the power of transforming Christians into Christ Himself and of perfectly incorporating them in Himself.

Through this loving union and transformation the mystical marriage of the Word with the soul is culminated in the body. Formerly they were spouses in a certain manner through grace, but through the Eucharist they become "two in one flesh" and sharers in the same goods.[113] They enjoy and possess Him at the same time that they are possessed by Him and are able to say: "My beloved to me, and I to him who feedeth among the lilies." [114] Therefore St. Ephrem could rightly say that "in the divine mystery there is effected a union between souls and the immortal Spouse." [115] The fruits of this sweet union overflow into our very bodies, which also participate in the purity, the holiness, the glory and incorruptibility of the body of Jesus Christ.[116]

---

he who is joined to the Lord is one spirit [with Him] (I Cor. 6:17). Moreover, in this union the Spouse comes to us to take part in this banquet and to regulate charity in us. Then it is that there takes place those pure and chaste embraces which can be likened to those which the divine Persons exchange in the unity of the essence of the Trinity and of which the former are no more than an image or figure. How sweet are the delights we experience in the joy of the union of the three divine Persons!"

St. John Damascene (*De fide orthod.*, IV, chap. 14), compares this sacrament to the burning coal which Isaias saw (Isa. 6:6): "For as that coal was aflame with fire, this vivifying bread brings with itself the Divinity so that in receiving it we are not only inflamed, but deified." For that reason St. Thomas Aquinas says that, in addition to being a pledge, this sacrament is, in a sense, the attainment of glory, *Pignus aeternae gloriae* (Office of the Blessed Sacrament). Again in the *Summa* (IIIa, q.79, q.2) he says: "It belongs to this sacrament to cause the attainment of eternal life."

[113] St. Cyril of Alexandria, *Contra Nestor.*, IV: "For what reason do we receive the sacred banquet save that Jesus Christ may dwell in us bodily? The Apostle, writing to the Ephesians, divinely told them that they had become joint heirs, fellow members of the same body, and partakers of the promise in Jesus Christ. And how do they become members of the same body except through the mystical banquet?"

[114] Cant. 2:16.

[115] *De extr. jud. et compunct.*

[116] St. Mary Magdalen of Pazzi, *op. cit.*, I, chap. 33: "To each of the souls that receive Thee, can be said what the Church says to Mary: *Thou hast received into thy womb Him whom the heavens cannot contain.* As Mary, in St. John's vision, showed herself clothed in the sun, so does the soul which receives Thee become clothed in the Sun of Justice, which is Thyself. I would say even more: the soul is then clothed to a certain point in the sun of Thy vision, although this vision is veiled by a cloud which conceals a great part of Thy divine glory. The soul cannot enjoy that vision to the extent of the blessed in heaven, but only as enjoyed by privileged souls on earth; that is, by means of a partial light which I know not how to define and which cannot be understood except by Him who gives it and from whom it is received."

"If there is any one of the sacraments which merits the name of spiritual espousal," says Bellamy, "it is surely the Eucharist, wherein is consummated here below our union with the Savior. What actually constitutes matrimony is the mutual personal giving of the two spouses, and in the supernatural order it is the Eucharist that effects this same mutual giving, for Jesus Christ communicates Himself to us entirely and without reserve."[117] Christ delivers Himself to souls that they may likewise deliver themselves to Him and thus find in Him all their sustenance, to live only for Him and in Him, with so Christlike a life that they are transformed into Jesus Christ, since it is now He who lives in them. The Eucharist, then, is "the knot of the matrimonial bond which unites us to the incarnate Word and thus gives us vastly more than do the other sacraments since it obtains for us, if not a more abundant participation in the divine nature, at least a special union with the humanity of our Lord."[118]

"His body," says Bossuet, "is not now His, but ours; and our body is no longer our own, but Jesus Christ's. This is the mystery of joy, the mystery of the Spouse and the bride, for it is written: 'The husband also hath not power over his body, but the wife.'[119] O holy Church, chaste bride of the Savior! O Christian soul, which has been selected by the Spouse in baptism, in faith, and in mutual promises! Here you possess the sacred body of your Spouse; here you see it on the holy table where it has just been consecrated. It is not in His power, but in yours. 'Take it,' He says, 'for it is yours.' 'This is My body which is given for you.'[120] So you have a real right over His body. But also your own body is no longer yours. Jesus desires to possess it. In this way will you become united, body to body, and you will be two in one flesh, which is the right of the bride and the perfect culmination of this chaste and divine marriage."[121]

It is not to be wondered at, then, that the saints who had the most exalted idea of this divine union were also distinguished for their ardent love of the Most Blessed Sacrament and for their intense desire to receive it daily, to be fortified with this heavenly bread, to be reanimated and renewed in that fountain of life, and to be in-

---

[117] *Op. cit.*, pp. 268 f.
[118] *Ibid.*
[119] See I Cor. 7:4.
[120] See Luke 22:19.
[121] *Médit. sur l'Evang.*, *La Cène*, 24.

ebriated with the delights of divine love.[122] The most remarkable fact in the histories of the great friends of God is that of their devotion to the Blessed Sacrament.[123] "As if by instinct, or a sort of infallible intuition," says Bellamy, "they understood that the entire supernatural world gravitates around the sun of the Eucharist, which is the universal center of attraction for souls desiring to live in grace. So it is that, without neglecting the other sacraments, they sought in Holy Communion the secret of that likeness and that union which constitute the very essence of the supernatural life. Desirous especially of imitating Jesus Christ and of engraving His image on the very core of their souls, the saints rightly believed that the best means of arriving at the reproduction of this divine Exemplar was to approach Him in the sacrament of His love in order to be more directly formed by the hand and heart of the divine Artist." [124] It is not strange, then, that the saints appear as so many copies of the divine Exemplar, for He Himself came in person to imprint His divine image on them.[125]

2. MORE INTIMATE UNION WITH THE FATHER, HOLY GHOST, AND BLESSED VIRGIN

When, in the sacrament of love, the bonds uniting us to the Son are strengthened, those bonds are also tightened which unite us to

---

[122] IIIa, q.79, a.1, ad 2um: "Hence it is that the soul is spiritually nourished through the power of this sacrament, by being spiritually gladdened, and as it were inebriated with the sweetness of the Divine goodness, according to Cant. v. i.: *Eat, O friends, and drink, and be inebriated, my dearly beloved.*" Therefore those who love much and are much loved are inebriated with divine delights which are merely tasted by those who are only friends.

[123] Father Arnold, the confessor of Blessed Angela of Foligno, says of her: "She never received Communion without receiving some wonderful grace, and each time she received a new grace." So also, Father Hoyos once heard the angels say, immediately after he had received the Eucharist, "This is the happiest moment in the life of a mortal."

[124] *Op. cit.*, p. 272.

[125] Lallemant, *op. cit.*, IV, chap. 5, art. 1: "Frequent communion is an excellent means of perfecting virtues in us, and acquiring the fruits of the Holy Spirit; for our Lord, uniting his Body to our body and his Soul to our soul, burns and consumes within us the seeds of our vices, and communicates to us by degrees his own divine temperament and perfections, according as we are disposed and suffer him to operate in us." Speaking of the fire which she experienced during a two hour rapture after Holy Communion, St. Teresa says: "It seems to consume the old man, with his faults, his lukewarmness and his misery. . . . Even so is the soul transformed into another, with its fresh desires and its great fortitude. It seems not to be the same as before, but begins to walk in the way of the Lord with a new purity" (*The Life*, chap. 39).

the Father and the Holy Ghost. Holy love is at once the daughter of God the Father, the spouse of the Son, and the temple of the Holy Ghost. Therefore in the measure in which one of these relations is strengthened, so also are the others. By a greater participation in the image of the Word and in the fullness of life which resides in Him, there is a greater participation in the nature of the Father, and consequently the more are we His sons. Likewise it follows that there is a greater participation in the love, grace, holiness, and communication of the Spirit, who resides in souls as the immediate principle of life and sanctification.

"Therefore," adds Bellamy, "our divine filiation does not reach its plenitude except through the sacrament that gives the fullness of life. It was indeed fitting that this filiation should receive its most perfect expression from Jesus Christ because, as the Son of God by nature, His is the prerogative of seeing modeled in His own likeness all those who are made children of God through grace." [126] Therefore St. Cyril of Alexandria says: "We could not become adopted sons of God without Him who, being the true Son by nature, serves as the exemplar according to which we are fashioned in His likeness." It is in this sacrament that the incarnate Word directly communicates to the just soul something of His double nature, since He enables it to participate in His divine nature at the same time that it receives His human nature. It is certain that the sacred humanity also operates through the other sacraments; but, as Bellamy continues, "the Eucharist closely joins Christ to the Christian, adjusts the copy to the model, and unites, without any intermediary, the human soul with the body and blood of the Savior. As a result our soul, since it is then more perfectly possessed by the divine Spouse, receives in this mysterious and ineffably intimate union a new manifestation of its divine filiation, for it is thereby more directly marked with the effigy of Christ." [127]

Since every increase of grace is accompanied by a greater effusion of the divine Spirit, evidently with every increase of the life of grace the communication of the vivifying Spirit ought to increase proportionately. This Holy Spirit dwells in all His plenitude in the sacred humanity of Christ as in His select dwelling place wherein He takes

[126] *Op. cit.*, pp. 266–68.
[127] *Ibid.*

His pleasure. But there "He waits, nevertheless, to complete the work of love, which is to unite the Head with the members, Christ with the Christian. Thus, by partaking of the body and blood of the Savior, we doubly strengthen the bonds uniting us to the Holy Ghost, for our participation in the Eucharist is a realization of all His desires at the same time that it is a means of uniting us to His divine Person which is eternally established in the humanity of Jesus." [128]

Yet another notable relation is remarkably strengthened and made more intimate by means of this admirable sacrament: the relation we have with the Holy Virgin, the Mother of fair love and Mother of divine grace. If love is perfected according as grace is increased, so much the more will that take place when grace is communicated to us directly through the sacred flesh which was taken from this Blessed Lady. And this it is which is peculiar to the Eucharist: that it enables us to share in the divine nature by means of the flesh and blood of the Savior. For the direct vehicle of divine life in this sacrament is not the soul of Jesus Christ, but His adorable body and His precious blood, as the liturgy clearly states: "May the body of our Lord Jesus Christ preserve your soul to life everlasting."

The Son of God desires to save lost and corrupt human flesh through the immolation of His own most sacred flesh on the altar, as He did upon the cross.[129] "One of the mysterious characteristics of the Eucharist is precisely this transmission of life through death, for here the divine life is communicated to us through the adorable body of Christ which we receive in the condition of a victim." [130]

Therefore the Holy Virgin cannot be alien to this increase of life which we receive through the Eucharist, since it was she who gave to us, in the double mystery of the crib and the Cross, the body and blood of Christ. "Is it not through her that we obtain the marvelous instruments of divine life? For the Eucharist is her natural possession,

---

[128] Bellamy, *op. cit.*, pp. 270 f.

[129] Monsabré, *Meditations on the Rosary*, p. 258: "Everything that happened on Calvary is continually repeated on the altar. Each day the altar is the mount of sorrows, of blood, of sacrifice, and of redemption." Thus we see with what great reverence and love we ought to assist at the Holy Sacrifice wherein is perpetuated the work of our redemption. We see also with what sincere affection we ought to unite ourselves there with the Savior so that His blood will prove profitable to us and to all. See Catherine Emmerich, *Life of Jesus Christ*, Introd.

[130] Bellamy, *loc. cit.*

and over it this incomparable Mother has all the rights. It can be said, in a certain sense, that it is she who gives this divine food to our souls. Certainly in her position as Mother she is ever ready to communicate the life of grace to her children by adoption. Through the Son of her womb, she feeds her adopted children; certain it is that she was made the Mother of God that she might also become the Mother of men. In the reception of Communion we see more clearly than in any of the other sacraments how closely associated this holy Virgin is with the great work of the supernatural life." [131]

It is not to be wondered at that all those heretics who deny the dogma of the Eucharist should greatly despise this Blessed Lady, whereas all the souls that delight in Communion love her and reverence her as a most tender Mother. Love for the most holy Sacrament runs parallel with love for the most pure Virgin. One who distinguishes himself in either of these loves, excels in the other also. If the most signal favors of the mystical life are usually received during Communion, in almost all of them the Virgin intervenes as a pious Mother to whom true mystics hasten in all their needs, difficulties, and obscurities. Even if she did not bear the honored titles which the Church gives her (Seat of wisdom, Mother of grace, Mother of mercy), there would still remain to her that title which the Evangelists bestow on her: "Mother of the Lord," or Mother par excellence; and hers would still be that title which illumined souls use when they cry: "Mother of fair love and holy hope."

3. FRUITS OF THE EUCHARIST

The principal fruit which the Eucharist, the masterpiece of the Savior's charity, produces in well-disposed souls is a great increase of charity, not only habitual but actual. Actual charity, in turn, produces an intimate union and transformation and the subsequent secondary fruits. These secondary fruits are the remission of venial sin (and sometimes, *per accidens*, of mortal sin), the correction of faults and imperfections, and the remission of temporal punishment. Also listed among these secondary fruits are fervor, joy, sweetness, purity, moderation of concupiscence, promptness for good, and the arousing of holy desires, all of which follow the stimulation of charity. Therefore it is very important that we dispose ourselves for the

[131] *Ibid.*

SPIRITUAL GROWTH

reception of this adorable Sacrament with all possible purity and love, so as not to impede, but rather to encourage, the production of such rich fruits.[132] If these fruits result but rarely, it is a sign that our dispositions are defective.[133]

The fruits which the Eucharist produces in the body can be noted in the lives of the saints who were most visibly configured with Jesus Christ, from whose flesh there emanates and redounds in us a power that heals our infirmities and remedies our weaknesses.[134] If in the saints that power is translated into certain divine splendors and heavenly aromas, the ordinary effect in the rest of us is to restrain our concupiscence. This result is accomplished either by the increase of charity which governs our lives, or by the energies which it gives for conquering concupiscence. For it makes us breathe the atmosphere of heaven, which gradually smothers the fire of concupiscence.[135]

---

[132] Cardinal Bona, *Tractatus asceticus de Missa*, chap. 6: "The effects of the Eucharist are: preservation from sin, increase of grace, hatred of all earthly things, love of all things eternal; illumination of the intellect, inflaming of the affections, purity of soul and body, peace and joy of conscience, and inseparable union with God. . . . The soul must be purged of all delights of the flesh and the senses, of tepidity, of all affection for creatures, so that the divine Sacrament may work its effects in us."

St. Augustine, *Manual*, chap. 11: "The powers of my soul are augmented in the sweetness of Thy presence. . . . O fire which ever illumines and love which ever burns, O sweet and good Jesus! . . . Sanctify me that I may worthily receive Thee; remove all malice from my heart and fill it with Thy grace . . . that I may eat the food of Thy flesh to the salvation of my soul so that, being nourished by Thee, I may live in Thee, walk according to Thee, unite myself to Thee, and find my rest in Thee."

[133] St. Bonaventure, *De preparatione ad Missam:* "If after Holy Communion you do not feel a certain spiritual refreshment, it is no small indication of spiritual sickness or death. What if you apply fire to wood and it does not ignite? What if you have honey on your tongue, and yet you do not taste its sweetness? Then do not doubt that this is a most certain sign of ill health."

[134] Surin, *Catéch. spirit.*, VII, 8: "At times, after the reception of the Eucharist, the soul feels Jesus Christ diffusing Himself in it and communicating His own life so that the soul will be able to work in all things through Him. . . . It is aware of this communication of life in its speech, its work, its prayer, and in all things, and it seems that even the natural acts of the soul are animated and aided by Him."

Blessed Raymond writes of St. Catherine of Siena that she felt the desire for Communion in such an extraordinary manner that she not only desired to unite her soul to her Spouse, but also to unite her body to the divine body which gives nourishment to everyone that receives it.

[135] St. Mary Magdalen of Pazzi, *op. cit.*, I, chap. 9: "The souls that worthily receive Thee see fall before Thee, by reason of Thy presence, all the evil desires and disordered habits of their past life. In place of these idols, before which they worshiped with their sins, they raise up so many other altars to adore Thee with each of their faculties."

"Who is able to resist the monster of concupiscence?" asks St. Bernard. "Be confident, for you have the help of grace. And to give us greater security, God has placed at our disposal the body and blood of the Lord which produces in us two wonderful effects: in the lesser attacks of concupiscence it diminishes feeling; in the stronger attacks it removes consent entirely." [136] "The Sacred Eulogy," says St. Cyril, "which delivers us from death, is also an efficacious remedy against our infirmities. When Jesus Christ is within us, He quiets in our members the law of the flesh. He mortifies the turbulent passions, He vivifies our love of God, and He cures all our evils." [137] Therefore with good reason is the Eucharist called the medicine for our wounds and "wine springing forth virgins." [138]

Since it purifies, rectifies, and heals our flesh, the Eucharist is a preservative from corruption and the seed or living pledge of resurrection.[139] Participation in this admirable sacrament imparts to the human body a divine splendor that will remain eternally and will bestow a singular glory on the just who receive it with the greater frequency.[140]

---

[136] *Sermo de Coena Domini*, no. 3.
[137] *Lib. 4 in Joan.*, 6:57.
[138] Zach. 9:17.
[139] "Nourished with the body and blood of the Lord," says St. Irenaeus, "our flesh is made incorruptible; it shares in His life and obtains the hope of the resurrection."
[140] St. Mary Magdalen of Pazzi, *op. cit.*, I, chap. 21: "One of the admirable operations of Wisdom is the glorification and exaltation of so many souls transformed in God through their intimate union with the Word in the most holy Sacrament of the Altar.... By this union the Savior wished to deify the flesh of man, in a certain sense, in the person of all those Christians who would worthily receive His sacred flesh. He wished also to communicate His grace to souls and to resurrected bodies, a power which would make them share in the brilliance of His own glorious body. But understand well that those who have frequently and worthily received this divine food will enjoy in their resurrected flesh a greater accidental glory than those who were not worthy to receive this sacrament so frequently, even though they be equal in merit in all other respects.... No one could ever have imagined such a work; namely, that God would become a creature, and a creature would become God in this ineffable manner and by this double communication."
Tauler, *Institutions*, chap. 38: "Through this sacrament we are transformed into God and we join with Him in a most happy union so that all His goods are ours and His body and heart are one with ours.... He who frequently receives the Eucharist will be as intimately united with God as is a drop of water thrown in a jug of wine, in such a way that no creature could find any distinction or distance between God and the soul.... If there be found two souls equally holy in their lives, the one who receives this sacrament with more worthy dispositions is by that reception made more perfect and, as a resplendent sun, he will shine forever more brightly than the other and will be united with God in a more wonderful union."

SPIRITUAL GROWTH

Therefore we ought to exert ourselves to receive Communion daily and with the greatest possible fervor and purity, since the increase of health and strength, of charity, graces, and fruits of life is proportionate to the dispositions and frequency with which it is received. In this way we shall succeed in truly living in Christ. We shall realize how profitable it is to be incorporated in Him and we shall be consumed with the desire to arrive as soon as possible at the fullest union and possession.[141]

"The faithful know the body of Christ," says St. Augustine, "as long as they do not disdain to belong to Him. Let them become the body of Christ if they desire to live in the Spirit of Christ, because no one lives in His Spirit if he does not form part of His body." [142] In another place he says: "Whoever wishes to live, has the wherewithal to live. Let him approach; let him believe; let him be incorporated in order to be vivified. Let him not disdain the union of the members; let him not be corrupt or contrary lest he merit to be cut off or serve as a confusion for the others. Let him be beautiful and well proportioned; let him adhere to the body and live in God for God." [143]

---

[141] Massoulié, *Tr. amour de Dieu*, III, chap. 7: "Is it possible that the delights which the soul enjoys in this Sacrament, the precious pledge which it receives, and this hidden and veiled possession will not make the soul yearn for the full and manifest possession? Faith makes the soul look at Christ through the species which conceal Him. Like the spouse in the Canticle (2:9), it sees the divine Spouse *behind a wall*, where He is hidden and does not permit Himself to be seen and whence He looks at the soul *through the lattices*. It is, as one of the Fathers says, an artifice of His love. He makes Himself present so that He can be possessed; and He hides Himself that He may be desired. He is present to assuage the sorrow at His absence; He is as it were absent to cause a desire for His presence."

[142] *Tr. 36 in Joan.*, no. 13. Monsabré, *op. cit.*, pp. 272-79: "Since he who eats of this bread will have eternal life, he who eats of it frequently will advance far in perfection. For spiritual progress is the increase of the divine life, and perfection is the superabundance of this life.... Every intimate union with Christ places us in relation with His Spirit.... The great works of the Christian life, ... to what must they be attributed but to this mysterious breathing of Jesus Christ? Wherever we see this breathing suspended or weakened, we see great works fall away and vanish. The sects that have suppressed the Eucharist, since they lack now the active principle of the spiritual life, have only vulgar works of beneficence which are purely natural, without expansion, and condemned to sterility."

Nor does it suffice to receive this divine food only now and then for the preservation and increase of life. As no one can carry on without corporal food, so ordinarily, no one can carry on for long without spiritual food. Therefore ought we to ask of God this "daily bread." "Can it be called such," asks St. Augustine, "if it is eaten only once a year? Receive it every day, for every day it can profit you."

[143] *Tr. 26 in Joan.*

This sacrament of love, the center of holy hearts and the focus of divine blessings, calls out for all our love, all our gratitude, and our continual adoration and reparation.[144] But the love for the sacramental Jesus ought to be like the love He Himself shows for us in that sacrament: a love not beatific, but suffering, mortified, and crucified, for He is there in the form of a victim and not as the glorious victor. So He demands of us and produces in us a love full of sacrifice by which we are associated with His own love.[145] This love is meritorious to the highest degree since in the Eucharist are united the two richest sources of merit, the two great causes of spiritual growth: divine food and a love which sacrifices itself to accomplish the will of God.

By these means principally, although aided by the others also, the mystical body of Christ grows and its various members are sanctified and perfected by developing the seed of eternal life which they receive on being incorporated in it.

[144] In order to remedy as much as possible the abandonment of the King of heaven by bad Christians and to atone for the continual offenses committed against Him, the holy Baroness de Hoogvorst was inspired to found that admirable order of Mary Reparatrix, charged with performing before the tabernacle the office of Mary at the foot of the cross so that there would always be souls, pure and inflamed with charity, who, like the seraphim, would keep the court of the Lord. "This Order," she said, "intends to repair as much as possible the offenses against the divine Majesty and to remedy the evils caused to man by sin. In this it will strive to follow the footsteps of the most holy Virgin, coredemptrix of the human race through Jesus Christ."

[145] With good reason did the Baroness de Hoogvorst (Mother Mary of Jesus) say that "the good Reparatrix nun must have a heart that belongs entirely to Our Lord; a generosity so great and loving that it refuses no sacrifices or sufferings; most profound humility before God and His representatives; a total abandonment to the divine will; an obedience that makes her die to self in order to enjoy true liberty . . . ; in such a way that the sweetness and charity of Jesus is ever found on her lips and in her heart. She must understand that the Reparatrix nun is a victim; and victims do not restrain or save themselves, but they sacrifice themselves."

Hettinger, *Apologie*, Conf. 32: "The life of the Church is a sacrificial life, whose sacrifice is united to that of the spotless Victim. . . . The immolation of the true body of Christ calls for that of the mystical body also. The real sacrifice of the Head serves as the norm and model for the mystical sacrifice of the members."

IIa, q.73, a.3, ad 3um: "The Eucharist is the sacrament of Christ's Passion according as a man is made perfect in union with Christ Who suffered."

SPIRITUAL GROWTH

APPENDIX

1. Frequent Communion

"Thou shouldst receive Me worthily and with humility, as befits My divinity. Keep Me in thy heart without ever losing sight of My presence. Look upon Me and embrace Me as the Spouse of thy heart. Spiritual hunger for this heavenly food must impel thee to receive it frequently. The soul that wishes to give Me the hospitality of a secluded life and to enjoy the sweet effusions of My intimacy must be pure, free from all useless preoccupation, dead to self and all attachments, adorned with virtue, ornamented with the red roses of charity, the fragrant violets of profound humility, and the white lilies of inviolable purity. . . . Sing to Me the song of Sion to celebrate My goodness in this great sacrament and let thy praises be the pulsations of love.

"For My part, I will give thee love for love; I will make thee enjoy true peace, the clear vision of Myself, happiness without alloy, an ineffable sweetness, a prelude to eternal bliss. But these graces are granted only to those of My friends who, in the midst of this rapture, exclaim: 'Verily Thou art a hidden God' (Isa. 45:15). . . .

"What have I better than Myself? When anyone is united to the object of his love, what else has he to seek? And he who gives himself, what can he refuse? In this sacrament I give Myself to thee and take thee from thyself. Thou findest Me and losest thyself to become absorbed in Me. . . . I am a good which is so much the greater as it is more secret and hidden. Things grow, but you do not note their progress until it is fully accomplished. My virtue is secret, My grace hidden, and My gifts are received without being noted or seen. I am the bread of life to well-disposed souls; a useless bread to those who are negligent; a temporal plague and eternal ruin to those who are unworthy. . . . If thou feelest within thyself the increase of grace and a desire for this divine food, thou oughtest to receive it frequently. If thou sense no advance but feel dryness, coldness, or indifference, be not disturbed. Prepare thyself as well as possible and do not stay away from Communion, for the more thou art united to Me, the sooner wilt thou improve. It is better to communicate through love than to abstain through fear. The salvation of the soul is often accomplished in the simplicity of faith, spiritual dryness, and interior pains rather than in spiritual sweetness and delight" (Blessed Henry Suso, *Eternal Wisdom*, chaps. 26 f.).

One day, at the time of Communion, the Venerable Mariana of Jesus, being unusually aware of her lowliness and unworthiness, said to her Lord: "My Lord, the tabernacle in which Thou art is much more clean and beautiful." Christ answered her: "But it cannot love Me." "From this," said the holy nun, "I understood how much more Christ prefers to reside in our souls than in gold or silver or precious jewels which are inanimate creatures incapable of love."

2. Marvels of This Sacrament

"This is the noblest sacrament in which God is received corporally, not that He may be transformed into men, but that men may be transformed into Him. As by the power of the words of consecration, what was bread is converted into the very substance of Christ, so by virtue of Holy Communion he who was man is, in a marvelous manner, transformed spiritually into God. O wonderful Sacrament!

Thou art the life of our souls, the medicine for our wounds, the consolation for our labors, a memorial of Jesus Christ, a testimony of His love, a legacy of His last will, the companion of our journey, the joy of our exile, the burning coal which ignites the fire of divine love, the medium of grace, pledge of the happiness and treasure of the Christian life. By this food the soul is united with its Spouse, the understanding is enlightened, the memory is enlivened, the will is aroused, the interior taste is delighted, devotion is increased, the heart melts, the fountains of tears are opened, the passions are quieted, good desires are awakened, weakness is fortified, and one receives the vigor to travel to the mountain of God" (Louis of Granada, *Oración y Consideración*, I, chap. 10).

3. The Eucharist, a Fount of Blessings

"The Blessed Sacrament is the complement of the work of redemption, of the work of love. By His birth the Word of God became our companion and our guide; by His death He is the expiatory victim sacrificed for our sins; and by His sacramental presence He is our comfort, our nourishment, our delight, our heaven on earth.

This sacrament is not only a grace, but it is the origin and source of grace; the road to glory and true glory in itself. . . . Near this fount grow the lilies of virginity which are united exclusively and forever to Jesus Christ. There they are infused with the strength to become poor for Jesus Christ; there they learn to love their brethren as He loves them. . . . There all wounds are healed and great resolutions are intensified; thence come all the acts of heroism and the victory over the world. The faithful soul never departs from there without having heard a voice full of mystery, without having been enriched with a supernatural power, without bearing in his heart a devout and profound desire of returning again to visit the place of His repose" (Venerable Mother Sacramento, foundress of the Adoratrices).

4. The Eternal Heritage and the Power of the Precious Blood

These are the words of the eternal Father to St. Magdalen of Pazzi: "The heritage which I bequeath to the soul which possesses My incarnate Word and the Holy Ghost is Myself. Here the soul can find assurance and security in this world and glory and eternity in the next. The glory of this heritage is such that only the Trinity can comprehend it. . . . This heritage is gained through the power of the incarnate Word and the merits of His precious blood which was shed upon the cross. . . . Now that He sits at My right hand, that same precious blood flows to you through the channels of the sacraments . . . which bring you the grace that the Word has merited for you. This infusion of grace produces various effects. It causes a germination, a nourishment, an inebriation, a transformation and glorification. . . . He infuses in His spouses an ardent love and continually pours into their hearts the power of His blood, which makes them die completely to self. They become so submerged in this precious blood that they do not see or know or taste anything but blood. They live only in Me and for Me and in all their works they seek only My glory and the salvation of souls. . . . Like innocent doves, they repeatedly bathe themselves, these pure souls, to purify themselves even more. With the ceaseless use of that bath they acquire a radiant purity, which makes them lovable in the eyes of the Spouse, and an ardent charity, the fire of which inflames other creatures and attracts them to Me. By these two virtues they be-

THE MYSTICAL EVOLUTION

come like unto Me in a special way, for as I contain all things in Myself, so through charity these select souls carry in their hearts all other creatures.

"After germinating the lilies of purity, the blood of the Word nourishes the soul with the substance of His divinity, that is, with the knowledge and love of the divine essence which communicates delightful pleasures to the soul and unites it to Me in so intimate a manner that it can say with St. Paul, 'Who will separate me from the charity of Christ?' . . . Then follows the transformation of the soul into the object loved, and this transformation is effected by Myself. . . . I transformed Myself into you at the Incarnation, when My Word assumed the form of a slave for love of you, and from this there follows the transformation of you into Myself. This is caused principally through the union of the soul with My Word in the sacrament of the Eucharist . . . wherein the soul receives a new quality and a divine being that makes it appear other than it was. The iron which comes forth from the furnace shines, sparkles, and burns like a fire, . . . and the same thing happens to the soul in this oven of love wherein it is united to My Word who is the fire which inflames, and who came to cast fire upon the earth in order to enkindle all hearts. Within this furnace, where the breathing of the Holy Ghost makes the fire burn ever more fiercely, the soul is so consumed by this fire that, instead of being human, it becomes wholly divine, transformed into Me and made one thing with Me through charity. It then becomes more perfect in its works, more lofty in its concepts, more ardent in its love, so that we need only to glance at that soul to see that it belongs to Me and to recognize in it the Author of its transformation. . . . Let a soul change itself into what it wishes, but it will never recover the primitive perfection of its being except by being transformed into Me. Only then will it conform to the idea which I had when I created it" (*Œuvres*, IV, chap. 19).

CHAPTER V

Summary and Conclusions

REVIEWING at this point all the doctrine thus far set forth, we shall state briefly in what the supernatural life consists. We shall restate its elements and conditions, its inner nature, its properties and characteristic functions. Finally, we shall recall the manner in which the supernatural life reaches its final and complete manifestation in souls.

The supernatural life, as Broglie observes, presupposes divine adoption, regeneration, a new birth, and the formation of a new man possessing the dignity and title of a son of God and endowed with the right to eternal inheritance. To this is added the indwelling of God in the heart of man, the intimate presence of the divine Persons, fellowship with the Father and the Son, and a participation in the divine nature. Lastly, as a terminus of this marvelous progressive state, there are the vision and possession of God and a transformation into Him.

"To be born anew is to receive a second nature. To be created in Jesus Christ, when we already exist, is to receive a higher life, a second life superimposed on the natural life. But of whom is the regenerated man a son? From whom does he receive this principle of a new existence?"[1] Not from flesh and blood, nor from human will, but from God, who desires that we should all be called His sons and that we should truly be such.

Concept of the Life of Grace

The term "sons of God" is correlative to the term "regenerated"; and it expresses a reality, as does the latter. Therefore this expression

[1] Broglie, *Surnaturel*, pp. 14-24.

is not simply a metaphor nor does it signify mere adoption. Earthly adoption is nothing more than a moral union. It confers new rights, but it does not change the nature of the one adopted nor does it communicate anything to him from the adopting father. Divine adoption, on the other hand, not only implies the name, but also the reality of filiation: "that we should be called and should be the sons of God."[2]

St. John is not content with this term, nor with saying that we have been born of God, but he uses another term which is even more poignant and expressive: *the divine seed*. "Whosoever is born of God committeth not sin; for His seed abideth in him."[3] St. Peter says the same thing: "being born again not of corruptible seed, but incorruptible, by the word of God who liveth and remaineth forever."[4] "Of His own will," says St. James, "hath He begotten us by the word of truth, that we might be some beginning of His creature."[5] It is a new birth by means of the infusion of divine life, which makes us true sons of God, though always adoptive, because this new life is superadded to our own natural life.

By nature we are only servants, but by grace we are elevated to the dignity of friends of God and sharers of His most intimate secrets.[6] What is more, we are even raised to the dignity of true sons,[7] regenerated in His Spirit and possessing the right to the eternal heritage.[8] As a guaranty of this heritage we receive the unction, seal, and pledge of the Spirit Himself in our hearts.[9]

The idea of generation implies some sort of likeness between father and son, and therefore St. John says that, when our manifestation as sons of God shall be perfect, then we shall be like unto Him.[10] This is an entirely spiritual birth, "a renewal which the Holy Ghost

---

[2] See I John 3:1.
[3] See I John 3:9.
[4] See I Pet. 1:23.
[5] Jas. 1:18.
[6] John 15:15: "I will not now call you servants; for the servant knoweth not what his lord doth. But I have called you friends, because all things whatsoever I have heard of My Father, I have made known to you."
[7] Broglie, *op. cit.*, II, 50: "The gulf between nature and grace is the gulf between the creature who trembles before his absolute Lord, and the son who familiarly approaches his father."
[8] "Those who are creatures by nature," says St. Athanasius, "cannot become sons of God unless they receive the Spirit of Him who is the Son of God by nature."
[9] See II Cor. 1:21 f.; Eph. 1:13 f.
[10] See I John 3:2.

produces within the soul, and yet it is a birth as real as is that from the womb into the world." Since the eternal Father is the exemplar of all paternity,[11] "the new birth of the sons of God is more similar to the eternal generation than is our first or natural birth. For this reason the Holy Ghost speaks of the new birth of the sons of God in language which is so absolute and so pointed. He says always that those who are regenerated are really and truly sons of God." This new life of the sons of God entails "an intimate relation, not only with the one divine Essence, but also with each of the three divine Persons, because the Father, Son, and Holy Ghost enter the just soul." [12]

By nature, a creature can know, and this by analogy, only the essential unity of God as the sovereign Author of the universe, the absolute Lord who transcends all creation and before whom all men are less than the vilest slaves, ever trembling in fear. But through God's grace and infinite liberality we have been raised to no less than the dignity of His sons and therefore, with love and filial confidence, we can converse with Him as our Father of mercies. Having been made like unto Him, through the merits of His only-begotten Son, we penetrate into the secrets of His inner life through the power of His Spirit. Thus are we admitted to the society of the three adorable Persons, who communicate in the unity of the divine essence. We thereby contract those ineffable relations that bind us in particular to each of Them and also to the Trinity as a whole. Only through this admirable grace can we arrive at an understanding of the august mystery of the Trinity.

This is precisely what constitutes the supernatural order, the manifestation of eternal life: entrance into fellowship or familiar and friendly relationship with God by sharing in the communication of His life and His intimate secrets. The supernatural order is not, then, anything that our reason can trace out by analogy with the natural order. Nor is it a superior order which has been "naturalized" so as to fit our mode of being. It is not simply "an order which exceeds all the natural exigencies of creatures, whether existing or purely possible," as others have defined it. Such an order is still in some way a projection of the natural; it could easily be a superadded perfection

---

[11] Eph. 3:15: "Of whom all paternity in heaven and earth is named."
[12] Broglie, *op. cit.*, pp. 21-32.

or gratuitous complement to the natural order, without transubstantiating or deifying it.

The true supernatural order, that unique order which actually exists in union with the natural order, is much more than this. It not only exceeds natural exigencies, but it transcends all suppositions and rational aspirations. It is an order which no one could ever know by analogy, nor suspect, nor even dream of, if God Himself, when He raised us to it, had not deigned to make it known. "Eye hath not seen nor ear heard, neither hath it entered into the heart of man, what things God hath prepared for them that love Him." [18]

It is the great hidden mystery which no one could surmise if the Spirit of God had not made it known. Nor is it something incomprehensible in itself, whose existence is known through natural reason. It is the adorable secret of the goodness, wisdom, and munificence of God. By a free disposition of His holy will, He decided to elevate us to that inconceivable participation in His own life and His infinite happiness. In doing so, He lowered Himself and, as it were, "naturalized" Himself in order to raise us up, to supernaturalize us, and to make us His equals to a certain extent so that we would be able to enter into friendly association with Him.

This familiarity with the divine Persons constitutes the very foundation of the supernatural life and supernatural order. For this was God made man: to make men gods and to take His delight in them. He takes them to Himself so that they share in His happiness and glory, and He treats them, not as servants, because the servant is ignorant of the secrets of his master, but as friends who receive His intimate confidences. He deals with them, not as simple creatures who share only in the works *ad extra*, but as true sons, configured with His Word and signed with His own Spirit. They enter into the joy of their Lord to participate in the mysterious impulses of each of the divine Persons in the secret operations *ad intra*.

This is the marvel of all possible marvels. God so loved the world that He gave His only-begotten Son, so that all those who believe in Him may have eternal life. This life is the intimate life of the sacrosanct Trinity in the ineffable communications of the three Persons because all three, and each of them in His own way, contribute to the work of our deificaiton. Therefore, whenever we speak of adop-

[18] See I Cor. 2:9; Isa. 64:4.

SUMMARY

tion, regeneration, sanctification, indwelling of God in the souls, and so on, express mention is made of the divine Persons. It is the Father who adopts us; the Son who makes us His brother and co-heirs; the Holy Ghost who consecrates and sanctifies us and makes us living temples of God, coming to dwell in us together with the Father and the Son.

From the fact that certain privileged creatures are called by grace to penetrate the divine secrets, "to know the divine mystery, to converse familiarly with the divine Persons, to be associated with the Father and His Son, Jesus Christ, and with the Holy Ghost," says Broglie, "it follows that they already see the splendors of the supernatural order. Hence we can understand why these privileged beings who are called to be sons of God and are initiated in the secrets of the Father, no longer merit the name of servants, but that of friends, for they have entered into fellowship with the divine nature." [14] It will also be understood why St. John promised the faithful that eternal life which was from the beginning with the Father and which was manifested to us so that our fellowship might be with Him and with His Son; that sovereign life whose exercise consists in knowing the one true God and Jesus Christ whom He has sent. Finally, we

---

[14] *Surnaturel*, II, 59. "The only-begotten Son of God, desiring that we should be participants in His divinity, assumed our nature: *ut homines deos faceret, factus homo*" (St. Thomas, *Opusculum* 57). From this beautiful text, which the Church uses in the Office for Corpus Christi, can clearly be deduced that, even if there were no sins for which to atone, the deification of the creature would nevertheless require the incarnation of the Word, to serve as the basis for the supernatural order. For He is the first-born of all the sons of God and in Him and through Him both men and angels are constituted in that divine dignity and receive grace, truth, and glory. All things must be created in Christ, who is before all and on whom all depend as the true Head and principle of the whole Church, that He may have primacy in all things. In Him dwells the fullness of the divinity and only from Him and through Him can it redound to others (Col. 1:15-19; John 1:16 f.). So it is that all spiritual blessings come to us through Him and from Him. In Him we have been elected before the foundation of the world (and therefore before the Fall) to be saints in charity, being predestined to adoption through Jesus Christ and to conformity with the divine image by means of the grace by which we have been favored in Him, so that He might be the first-born among many brethren (Eph. 1:3-6; Rom. 8:29).

This is a verification of the teaching of St. Thomas (*In Joan.* 1:16): that all the graces by which the angels were enriched flow, as do those of men, from the incarnate Word, who is their common Head. "The plenitude of grace which is in Christ, is the cause of all graces which are in all intellectual creatures." For that reason, all creatures have always had to believe in the mystery of the Incarnation as the only way of salvation, but they had to believe in the mystery of the Passion only after the state of sin (IIa IIae, q.2, a.7).

can understand why, "knowing and loving God intimately and thus being closely associated with those two infinite and fruitful acts which the divine Persons produce, the soul is elevated above itself, united to God, and made God through grace, according to the expression of the fathers." [15]

The Christian transition from the finite to the infinite is not, then, as in the Gnostic systems, a fall or degeneration of the infinite. Nor is it, as in modern pantheism, an absurd production of the infinite by the finite. It is a free union of the infinite with the finite: an elevation of the creature who, without the loss of essence or personality, approaches to the Creator and is united to Him so intimately that he becomes deified.

The true interpretation of deification is clearly expounded by Bainvel:

If God teaches us that He comes to our aid with His grace in order to make us capable henceforth of producing supernatural and divine acts, that He places in our nature something that transforms it to His image and divinizes it, we shall understand that this transformation does not change our nature and that this marvelous communication of God to our soul is not the impossible and absurd fusion of divine nature with human nature. . . .

In the ordinary states we do not experience what this participation is, and the mystics who seemed to feel it in some measure, cannot describe it without analogies and comparisons which they consider very imperfect. Such are those employed by the fathers, of the iron converted somehow into fire without ceasing to be iron; of the crystal penetrated by the rays of the sun and made luminous and like to the sun. But there is nothing which could give so high an idea of this marvelous elevation as that which is found in texts of Scripture itself. We are adopted sons of God, but by an adoption that touches the very core of our nature, transforming it in such wise that we have within us a divine seed and are made sons of God not in name only but in very truth. We share in the divine nature to the extent of being capable of performing divine operations which, in turn, perfect our likeness to God until we reach that final transformation in which we shall be entirely like Him and shall see Him as He is; brothers, finally, and co-heirs of our Lord Jesus Christ.

What more can be said, and how better express these divine realities

[15] Broglie, *loc. cit.*

than by the word "deification"? This does not in any way destroy the distinction of natures nor the infinite distance which separates the Creator from the creature.... What deification really means, we shall know when we see God face to face. Meanwhile, we must be content with knowing that it is so. If, in addition to this, we strive to form some concept of deification, using the data of Revelation, clarifying them by the analogies of faith (and in particular with that of the union of the divine nature and the human nature in the person of Jesus Christ) and availing ourselves of the comparisons which the saints offer us, then we shall still have to say that the reality is infinitely more beautiful and more sublime than anything we could possibly conceive.[16]

Patristic tradition, far from diminishing the sublime words of Scripture, accentuates them the more, for in translating the various Scriptural expressions it gives θέωσις for divinization; θεοποίησις for deification; ἔνωσις πρός θεόν for unity with God; and finally, θεός κατὰ χάριν to signify that man is made God through grace.

Nature, Function, and Growth of the Supernatural Life

Our elevation to the supernatural order enables us to know the eternal Father, the one true God, together with the Word sent for our salvation and the sanctifying Spirit. Knowing Them, we enter into their fellowship and thus we pass from the sorrowful status of servants to that of friends and, what is more, of guests, sons, brothers, mothers, spouses, and living members. Thus we share not only in the goods but also in the intimate life, happiness, and operations of God, being like unto Him and knowing Him, loving Him, trusting in Him, as His familiars, by the light, charity, and pious security which He infuses into us.

Hence the essence of the supernatural life consists in deification: being in some way like unto God and, as His true sons, increasing in this likeness as the bonds of divine filiation are more and more tightened. When we receive from the incarnate Word the power to become sons of God, the precious seed of the supernatural life begins to develop within us.

The functions and essential or characteristic operations of this life are a divine love and knowledge caused in us by the Spirit who pene-

[16] Bainvel, *op. cit.*, pp. 80–83.

trates the unfathomable mysteries of the divinity and whose charity floods our hearts that we may love God with that same love with which Jesus loves us and with which the divine Persons love one another. As directed to the Father, this love should be a filial love; as directed to the Son, it should be fraternal, marital, and even organic, vital, for He is the first-born, the Spouse of our souls, and the Head of the mystical body of the Church. Finally, as directed to the Holy Ghost, that love must be a love of affectionate friendship and, so to speak, an experimental and vital love, full of sentiment and life and intimate affections, for the Holy Ghost is our guest, tutor, master, director, mover, governor, consoler, sanctifier, and vivifier.

The knowledge which accompanies this love must not be an abstract knowledge but one that is concrete and ever more experimental, because it treats of an admirable and incomprehensible fact that can be realized only by living and experiencing it. For that, we have the light, the knowledge, and the life of Christ, which reveal to us the secrets of the Father and communicate to us that Spirit of love which searches into everything, even the most hidden mysteries.[17] "Neither doth anyone know the Father but the Son, and he to whom it shall please the Son to reveal Him."[18] "Whosoever denieth the Son, the same hath not the Father. He that confesseth the Son, hath the Father also."[19]

The light of faith is perfected by the gifts of the Holy Ghost. Then, when the supernatural life comes to its full expansion and manifestation, faith will be replaced by the *lumen gloriae* which will clearly reveal what we are. In the brilliancy of this supernatural light we shall be entirely like unto God and therefore we shall be able to see Him as He is. At present, by faith, we see only through clouds, enigmas, and obscurities, and from afar off. That is why we sigh for Him and seek Him with holy hope. Yet, to a certain extent, we see and feel with the mind of Christ [20] these sublime realities by which we live. Therefore they do not cause in us that amazement and seeming contradiction which so terrify the incredulous. Rather they appear full of harmony, and it seems to us most natural and easy to admit them because they are in reality vital facts. But in the be-

[17] See I Cor. 2:10-16.
[18] Matt. 11:27. Cf. John 1:8.
[19] See I John 2:23; 5:12-20; John 14:6-20.
[20] See I John 5:20; I Cor. 2:16.

ginning we live and experience them unconsciously, without taking any account of them and without even noting that we see and feel them supernaturally, for faith works in a connatural or human manner.

But when, by the faithful exercise of the virtues, one arrives at the possession of the gifts of wisdom and understanding in a high degree (gifts by which one works knowingly in a superhuman manner),[21] then the privileged soul tastes and experiences those truths as something wholly divine. It then possesses not only the knowledge, but also at times a vivid awareness that it is experiencing and enjoying that prodigious life which God, as the life of souls, communicates to it, as well as the loving and delicate touches of the Consoler who dwells in it. At this state the Holy Ghost Himself gives vivid testimony to the soul's consciousness that it is a son of God.[22] So it is that this divine experimental knowledge, which constitutes the mystical state, becomes a kind of middle ground between simple faith and the true light of glory through which the hidden glory of the sons of God is manifested. This experimental knowledge is continually increased in the measure that one completes the painful purgation of the soul and advances along the glorious ways of illumination and union.

In the last steps of this marvelous progress which leads to deification, which is the most perfect possible assimilation, union, and transformation in God, the soul seems to enjoy certain preludes to eternal glory which are truly an anticipated glory. As the sacred veils are thrust aside and the august mysteries of the kingdom of God are made manifest, the light by which the soul sees these mysteries is more like that of heaven than that which faith gives.

So it is that the mystics can offer us such sublime, dazzling, and precise ideas of that prodigious life of God in just souls, of those ineffable mysteries of the kingdom which are accomplished within themselves, and especially of that most wonderful process of deification. Such are the ideas which come from many simple and apparently ignorant persons, and yet they leave the most eminent speculative theologians astonished and overwhelmed. Such also are the concepts by which the cold speculations of abstract theology are

[21] See St. Thomas, *In II Sent.*, dist. 34, q.2, a.3.
[22] Rom. 8:16.

clarified, perfected, defined, vitalized, and closely examined through contact with the living reality. It is not strange that those lofty concepts are often possessed by many souls that appear to be rude and uncultured. God hides the august mysteries of the kingdom from the wise who presume on their science and prudence, and reveals them only to the little ones, the humble, the simple, and the pure of heart. It is not to be wondered at that these happy souls, although lacking in human instruction, should speak of God and His most profound mysteries with certitude, precision, and amazing exactness. For, according to the expression of St. Teresa, they speak of those things, not as things known through hearing alone—that is, not as something studied or read about—but as experienced facts, intimately realized in all their sublime reality. Hence their testimony, founded as it is on their own inner experience, is most useful to us in evaluating and making known to others as best we can the ineffable nature of the supernatural life and the mysterious process of its evolution and expansion.[23]

Therefore we can say with Broglie: "The supernatural is a gratuitous elevation of the creature far beyond his proper nature, in virtue of which he shares in the intimate life of God. He is made like to God and he enters into fellowship with the three divine Persons of the most holy Trinity and is called to enjoy the intuitive vision of God and His own happiness." [24]

We grow in the divine life by fulfilling the will of the heavenly Father, by exercising faithfully the infused virtues and the gifts and

[23] Bainvel, op. cit., p. 77: "The unity of the supernatural life and especially the identity of the mystical life with the life of grace has greatly influenced the concept of the supernatural. The mystics have a certain experience of the supernatural realities which we possess through grace, of the ineffable love of the three divine Persons and of their special indwelling in the soul of the just. It is precisely in this experience of the supernatural that the mystical states seem to consist. So it happens that, in order to describe these things, the mystics use expressions which, if they are less exact, at least they are more vital and more concrete than the theological formulas. They discover analogies and images which, although imperfect, are most apt and are the closest substitute for the experience itself. This is of great help to theology, for in this way the theologian comes in contact with reality. So a word from St. Bernard or an unknown monk on the silence of the soul in the presence of God, on the divine touch in the very depth of the soul, on God's mysterious passage like a lightning flash in the dead of night, make us glimpse these things better than abstract formulas would do and in a singular manner they serve to vivify these same formulas."

[24] Op. cit., II, 62.

charisms of the Holy Ghost, and by receiving the vital influxes of the Savior through His sacraments.

Such is the essence and such are the functions of the supernatural life, the divine life, the eternal life, and the kingdom of God in souls. The way it is developed to full expansion and glorious manifestation is something somber, sad, and extremely painful, until the soul is stripped of the old man and clothed in the new; created, according to God, in true sanctity and justice. But after the soul has tasted the living water, then the more it drinks, the more thirsty it becomes. It discovers that with this water come all blessings and an indescribable purity. He who finds the living water, finds life and drinks the salvation of the Lord; those who hate it, love death and hate themselves. The soul then sees that it has within itself the fount of eternal life and it begins to live a life hidden from those who are worldly. Then are disclosed horizons undreamed of, where all is light and fragrance and where the delights of the glory of God are already enjoyed.

The process of deification is admirably summarized in the beautiful words of Monsignor Meric:

We know with what art the Holy Ghost prepares and molds and transfigures those who are predestined. The first hour is sad and bloody. Whether they live in the cloister like St. Teresa, or in the world like St. Rose of Lima, they must invariably pass through the same desperate but glorious crises of the purgative way. Even today, across the centuries, we can hear the echoes of their infinite groanings. They will be oppressed; they will be tormented by temptations, fears, despair, and terrible abandonments by Him who denies them even the slightest manifestation of His divine tenderness. They will experience afflictions which crucify the body and torments which oppress the soul. From the heights of the cross reddened by their blood, they will implore pity; they will ask a drop of water to appease their devouring thirst in that cruel hour in which they believe themselves to be abandoned by God and men. *Sitio!* But it is in this martyrdom that the new man bursts forth.

And indeed it is a new creature which has just been born. Master over self, unswerving in its resolutions, dead to the concupiscences of the world, it has passed through the terrible ordeal of the purgative way. Henceforth it is prepared to taste the joys of the illuminative and the unitive ways which are the crown. But these joys will be interrupted again by the sufferings which preserve and perfect the likeness of the soul to Jesus Christ. The new creature will never lose the love of voluntary mortification and bloody immolation. Yet, in the midst of these sufferings so ardently desired, the soul now sees clearly where God wishes to lead it and it experiences joys so profound that they are indescribable. Its vision embraces the boundless horizon of the realities which do not pass away and this horizon is strengthened and enlarged with heavenly splendors. The soul, thus united to God by grace, hears His voice, perceives His living and moving image, participates in a certain way in His life with a marvelous familiarity: *familiaritas stupenda nimis*. This familiarity disconcerts the mystics themselves who try to explain in human words this divine fellowship. It also elevates humanity to incomparable heights. . . . Thus we see how, over and above the known laws which govern earthly things, there are other laws as yet unknown which govern the harmony of divine things. These laws are the singular expression of the wisdom and tenderness of God.[25]

Since the process of spiritual renewal is so admirable in itself and so deserving of being known by all the faithful, and in particular by directors of souls, it is now necessary for us to examine it closely and in detail. To do this, we must attend to what we are taught by experienced souls who have themselves attained the great heights of the mystical life. These souls, as Father Monsabré says, can in some measure "tell us what they see, what they feel, and what they enjoy. Let us ask them; let us read their writings; and they will tell us how the veil of nature was rent to disclose to them the mysterious perfections of the divinity . . . ; how they arrived at the science of holy truth; how their hearts were inflamed with divine love; how, after they cut themselves off from servitude to the life of the senses, God has taken them in His arms to let them taste the sweetness of a union which has no name in human language." [26]

[25] *Manuel de théol. myst.*, pp. 6–8.
[26] *Op. cit.*, V, 3.

www.ingramcontent.com/pod-product-compliance
Lightning Source LLC
LaVergne TN
LVHW020358250825
819359LV00048B/950